مفاهيم يجب أن تصحح

NOTIONS THAT MUST BE CORRECTED

Shaykh Muḥammad b. ʿAlawī al-Mālikī al-Ḥasanī

Foreword by Shaykh Ḥasanayn Muḥammad Makhlūf

Translated by Suraqah Abdul Aziz

SUNNI PUBLICATIONS

Sunni Publications ©
First Edition August 2008
Second Edition December 2010

ISBN 978-90-79294-15-2

Notions That Must Be Corrected

Shaykh Muḥammad b. ʻAlawī al-Mālikī al-Ḥasanī

Translated by Suraqah Abdul Aziz

Design by: Abu Nibras
Printed by: HooibergHaasbeek, The Netherlands

Published by Sunni Publications
Rotterdam, The Netherlands
www.sunnipubs.com
info@sunnipubs.com

Translator's Introduction

My first exposure to the book *Notions That Must Be Corrected* was many years ago: a time in which I had many of the same incorrect notions mentioned by our esteemed author. Years later, Allah enabled me to return to this book, *not* as an opponent, but as a lowly student taking benefit from the author's written words and spiritual state. Most who possess the incorrect notions that Shaykh Muḥammad b. 'Alawī al-Mālikī attempted to correct are people with good intentions and zealousness for Allah's religion. In their pursuit of religious purity and simplicity they have lent their ears to those who speak with the loudest voices and label others with epithets of misguidance, disbelief, and innovation. With Allah's mercy and by means of books like this, it is hoped that such individuals may realize the error of imputing others with misguidance and disbelief due to matters of independent scholarly judgement (*ijtihād*) over which scholars have differed.

We hope and pray that this long overdue translation will have the same effect in correcting the many mistaken notions that have appeared in our communities in the West. May Allah bless the author, his family, his students, and all who played a role in making this prolific work available in the English language.

All praise belongs to Allah, the Lord of the worlds.

Though not from them, the righteous I love
that I might earn their intercession
Those who trade in disobedience I abhor
even if I am equally tried with rebellion

Suraqah Abdul Aziz
August 23, 2008

Publisher's Introduction

Praise be to Allah, the Lord of the worlds, and prayers and peace be upon our Master Muḥammad the Messenger of Allah, and upon his family, his companions, and those who follow in their footsteps.

It is a great honour to finally present the long awaited English translation of the illustrious work *Notions That Must Be Corrected*, written by the Sword of Ahl al-Sunna in the Ḥijāz, the late Gnostic, Sayyid Shaykh Muḥammad b. 'Alawī al-Mālikī al-Ḥasanī ﵀. Perhaps the most renowned book of the Sayyid, better known as *Mafāhīm Yajib An Tuṣaḥḥaḥ*, it rightly earned a reputation as being one of the most important contemporary Islamic books of our time.

We thank Allah for aiding us in the publishing of this book, and we would like to thank all those who worked tirelessly to help bring this book into fruition. We request those who benefit from it to pray for all those who supported us.

We pray Allah showers His blessings upon the soul of the Sayyid, Shaykh Muḥammad al-Mālikī ﵀, and upon his father, Sayyid 'Alawī al-Mālikī ﵀, and upon his grandfather, Sayyid 'Abbās al-Mālikī ﵀. May Allah preserve their children and grandchildren.

8/1429
8/2008

About the Author

The Sayyid, Shaykh Muḥammad b. ʿAlawī al-Mālikī al-Ḥasanī was born in Mecca in the year 1367 H. A descendant of the Prophet's ﷺ grandson, our Master Ḥasan b. ʿAlī b. Abī Ṭālib, Shaykh Muḥammad was born into a long line of pious scholars originally hailing from Morocco. His grandfather, al-Sayyid ʿAbbās al-Mālikī was the Muftī of Mecca and the Imām of the Ḥarām during the Ottoman, then Hashemite times, and continued to hold that position after the Saudi Kingdom was established. His father, Sayyid ʿAlawī, was the leading Mālikī scholar of Mecca and a teacher in the Ḥarām for over forty years.

Shaykh Muḥammad's most important teacher was his noble father but he also studied with various other leading scholars throughout the world such as: Shaykh Muḥammad Nūr Ṣayf, Shaykh Muḥammad al-Mashāt, Shaykh Muḥammad Amīn al-Kutbī, Shaykh Ḥasan Fadʿaq, Shaykh Muḥammad al-Ḥāfiẓ al-Tijānī, Shaykh Aḥmad Riḍwān, Shaykh ʿAbd al-Ḥalīm Maḥmūd, Shaykh Ṣāliḥ al-Jaʿfarī, Shaykh Saʿīd Yamanī and Shaykh Muḥammad Zākī Ibrāhīm. The Shaykh also obtained a PhD in the science of Ḥadīth from al-Azhar University.

Shaykh Muḥammad was, like his father, particularly close with the Bā ʿAlawī scholars of Yemen, and remained in their proximity throughout his life. Following his father's death, the scholars of Mecca nominated Shaykh Muḥammad to take his place as a teacher in the Ḥarām. He also taught at Umm al-Qurā' University in Mecca and started his own school at his home. The Shaykh wrote numerous books in various fields. He attended meetings, gatherings and celebrations worldwide and became one of the world's most respected and beloved scholars. The noble Sayyid returned to his Lord on the 15th of Ramaḍān 1422 H. Hundreds of thousands of his admirers attended his funeral, and many millions mourned his loss. May Allah bless and pardon him.

Transliteration Table

ا/آ/ى	ā	ظ	ẓ
ب	b	ع	ʿ
ت	t	غ	gh
ث	th	ف	f
ج	j	ق	q
ح	ḥ	ك	k
خ	kh	ل	l
د	d	م	m
ذ	dh	ن	n
ر	r	ه	h
ز	z	و	w/ū
س	s	ي	y/ī
ش	sh	ة	a/t
ص	ṣ	ء	ʾ
ض	ḍ	أ	a
ط	ṭ	إ	i

Formulaic Expressions

عَزَّ وَجَلَّ	Mighty and Majestic is He
سُبْحَانَهُ وَتَعَالَى	Exalted and Sublime is He
صَلَّى اللهُ عَلَيْهِ وَسَلَّمَ	May Allah bless him and give him peace
عَلَيْهِ السَّلَامُ	May peace be upon him
رَضِيَ اللهُ عَنْهُ	May Allah be pleased with him
رَضِيَ اللهُ عَنْهُمْ	May Allah be pleased with them

Contents

Part II: Prophetic Areas of Research

Clarifying the Unique and Special Qualities of the Prophet ﷺ, the Reality of Prophethood, the Reality of Humanity, and the Reality of the Isthmus Life

Part III: Miscellaneous Areas of Research

The Legality of Visiting the Prophet ﷺ and other Related Matters such as Seeking Blessings through Relics, Visiting Sanctuaries and Observing Special Occasions

Scholarly Commendations

بسم الله الرحمن الرحيم

Foreword
by Shaykh Ḥasanayn Muḥammad Makhlūf ﷺ

All praise belongs to Allah, the Lord of the worlds. May prayers and peace be upon our Master Muḥammad, and upon his family, companions, and followers. To proceed: This tremendous book of the noble scholar and researcher, the teacher and Sayyid, Muḥammad 'Alawī al-Mālikī, contains important and beneficial areas of research, as well as other noteworthy subjects; it will prove useful to the Muslims in this day and age. In order to serve Islam in this day and age and support Islamic beliefs and summon others to hold fast to what the Messenger stressed to his Umma, the Muslims are in need of taking a solid stand with important facts and general rulings and calling to them with goodly preaching. This is a time in which Islam is being attacked by many enemies who seek to aid and assist misguided principles and false claims against the religion and its adherents. Allah shall complete His light for His Muslim servants by giving success to the noble scholar (and author of this book), aiding him in spreading his call and verifying its subject matter, and guiding others to the splendid knowledge, valuable benefits, and important topics that embody true guidance and sound knowledge. This will certainly open the way for a goodly invitation that arrests disputes, conflicts, arrogance, and vying.

From perusing the areas of research within this book, it is obvious that it is a sound proof, a strong evidence, a truthful statement, and a clarification. It contains honour and nobility for the Muslims and it is an investigation which fulfils the sacred trust. Disseminating this book is counted as an honour to Islam and a means of foiling the enemies' plots.

The author—may Allah protect him—went to great lengths in order to explain things with clarity. In this book, he spoke with resplendent knowledge and carried out clear investigation concerning important issues. He made (others) aware of the correct and sound notions and responded to every incorrect notion and understanding: all in order to foil the plots of the enemies and establish the plain truth in the lands of Islam and the Muslims. The areas of research found within his book, his true call, and his unshakable style focus on the following:

Warning Against Carelessly Accusing Muslims with Disbelief: in this chapter, he cited the consensus that it is forbidden to impute with disbelief anyone from the people of the *qibla* (direction of prayer).

Differentiating Between the Station of the Creator and the Station of Creation: this is the decisive criterion between disbelief and Islam.

Logical Metaphor: and that it must be taken into consideration in the matters of disbelief and faith and must be balanced between worship and etiquette.

The Intermediary between the Creator and Creation: in this chapter he clarified the intermediary of idolatry.

Innovation and the Scholars' Division of it: in this chapter, he explained the correct understanding of innovation and how the scholars divided it, clarifying the facts to the people of mistaken notions and constricted chests—those who fight every new thing and censure every beneficial and novel matter.

The Ash'arīs: in this chapter, he clarified their school of thought and mentioned some of those who were ascribed to it, encouraging all who point the arrow of misguidance and apostasy at them to fear Allah.

The Reality of *Tawassul*: in this chapter, he clarified the *tawassul* that is agreed upon as well as the Ḥadīth of Ādam's *tawassul* through the Prophet ﷺ. The author quoted valuable words and a good opinion from Shaykh Ibn Taymiyya, Muḥammad b. 'Abd al-Wahhāb, and al-Shawkānī concerning the permissibility of *tawassul* through the Prophet ﷺ.

At the end of the research in this chapter, he mentioned the famous notables among the major Imāms and Ḥadīth masters who approved of *tawassul*.

Intercession: in this chapter, he mentioned its reality, how the companions sought the Prophet's intercession, and Ibn Taymiyya's explanation of the verses that pertain to it.

The Correct Understanding of Seeking Aid: in this second section of the book, he clarified the correct understanding of this and seeking aid from the Prophet ﷺ, and also responded to some false claims that are raised about this topic. He mentioned therein many valuable areas of research pertaining to the unique Prophetic qualities, the reality of prophecy and humanity, and the understanding of the Isthmus (*barzakh*) life.

In a separate chapter, the author spoke about seeking blessings and the mistaken notions many people have concerning it and its reality. In the third section of the book, he spoke about miscellaneous issues for which a researcher would thirst. He spoke about the legality of undertaking visitation to the Prophet and other related matters. He also spoke about the correct understanding of the Ḥadīth: "Do not undertake a journey..." and the words of the Imāms of the Salaf (predecessors) who spoke of the legality of visiting him ﷺ, and other related matters. In this section, the author presented delightful areas of research connected with the Prophetic relics, the concern shown toward them, how the Qur'ān itself has shown concern with the relics of the past Prophets, and how the companions took care of some of the Prophetic relics. He also spoke about the correct understanding of (religious) gatherings and the Prophet's birthday and mentioned the story of Thuwayba's manumission and how it was understood by the scholars.

This is but a brief outline of the book's contents. The author is considered one of the scholars of the two Sacred Sanctuaries (Mecca and Medina) who is well versed in the Divine seas and the Prophetic Sunna. He holds scholarly gatherings and delivers Prophetic lessons which are attended by a sizable number of those who seek benefit.

He has participated in numerous scholarly ventures and juridical councils through his work with the Islamic World League and has attended many Qur'ānic memorization competitions and conferences dedicated to the Prophetic Sunna. He is the author of over thirty written works in various topics such as the Qur'ān and its ancillary disciplines, Ḥadīth and its sciences, the Prophetic biography, religious counsel, and social reform. All of this calls for assigning great value to this book and encouraging the Muslims to read it and invite with its call. This book should be required reading for the Islamic world, and should be studied and taught to children because of the explicit truth, correct views, and defence of Islam's sanctities that it contains. This book clarifies the misguidance, lies, and false claims of the enemy, and certainly, Allah shall aid His righteous servants by aiding His religion. In conclusion, we ask Allah, the Exalted, to enable all of the Muslims to read this work and assist its call. We ask Allah, the Exalted, to reward its author and to protect him from plots—as the Qur'ān stated regarding the victory of he who aids the truth and religion, and the abject loss of the callers to falsehood among the enemies of the religion. Allah is the One who grants success and He is the guide to the plain truth.

—Ḥasanayn Muḥammad Makhlūf

Former chief Muftī of Egypt
Member of the Council of Senior Scholars, al-Azhar University
Member of the Council of Senior Scholars, al-Azhar
Member of the founding Council of the Islamic World League
Winner of the King Fayṣal Prize for Service to the Islamic Call

Confirmed by:
—Shaykh Muḥammad b. Aḥmad b. Ḥasan al-Khazrajī, U.A.E.
—Dr. Muḥammad al-Ṭayyib al-Najjār, Egypt
—Shaykh Abū al-Wafā' al-Taftazānī, Egypt
—Shaykh Muḥammad b. 'Abd al-Raḥmān Āl al-Shaykh b. Sālim, Islamic Republic of the Comoros Islands
—Sayyid 'Alī b. 'Abd al-Raḥmān al-Hāshimī al-Ḥasanī, U.A.E.
—Imām Mūsā Ḍayfullāh, Chad

بسم الله الرحمن الرحيم

Preface

All Praise belongs to Allah, the Lord of the worlds, and may prayers and peace be upon the noblest of Messengers, our Master Muḥammad, and upon his family, and companions.

Certainly, Allah has bestowed upon us numerous bounties, the greatest and most esteemed bounty being that of the religion of Islam—and what a noble bounty it is indeed! Other bounties include the security that we take delight in, the tranquillity, and contentment in these lands, the bounty of implementing the Sacred Law of Islam by carrying out the prescribed punishments, and seeking Judgement in the Book of Allah and the Sunna of the Messenger of Allah, Muḥammad b. 'Abdullāh ﷺ. That is by the grace of Allah first and foremost, and then by the grace of the rulers whom Allah has placed as guardians over the two Holy Sanctuaries, those to whom Allah has given success in serving these two cities and who were honoured with the trust of safeguarding, protecting, and looking after them, and enabled to expand their utmost efforts in that path.

All praise belongs to Allah, they have found help among the sons of the sincere and loyal people who pledged their fealty with truth, guarded the contract with sincerity, and looked after the agreement in their presence and absence. We are firmly upon that pledge and loyal to the agreement on account of our pure faith and creed taken from the Salaf (predecessors) and Prophetic methodology. By the grace of Allah, these lands are free of all filth and free of all acts of idolatry, as the Messenger of Allah ﷺ informed us when he said: "No two religions shall coexist in the Arabian peninsula." He also ﷺ said: "Satan has despaired from ever being worshipped in your peninsula," meaning the Arabian Peninsula.

He ﷺ also said: "O Allah! Do not make my grave an idol that is worshipped." And certainly, his prayers are answered. He ﷺ said: "That which I fear the most for my Umma (nation) is associating partners with Allah. I do not say that they shall worship the sun, the moon, or an idol, however (this association) shall be doing actions for other than Allah and (having a) hidden desire for being well-known."[1] He informed us that these lands shall be the stronghold of faith, the place of retreat for its people, and the place of refuge for those who carry it. He ﷺ said: "Indeed, faith returns to Medina just as a snake returns to its hole." And in another narration, he ﷺ stated: "Indeed, faith returns to the Ḥijāz."

The Imāms and leaders of this land have been, from the very beginning, working to inculcate and establish these notions in the hearts of the citizenry—starting from King 'Abd al-'Azīz, who united the Kingdom, brought the people together, removed their bigoted divisions, and tore down the racial barriers. After him, the citizenry lived with each other in mutual love and unity upon one foundation, and their affairs were straightened out under one banner: *There is no god but Allah, Muḥammad is the Messenger of Allah*. They lived with each other on this basis, even if they had different opinions and ways of understanding, for their foundation and allegiance was one, their fealty true, and loyalty a duty.

There have been, however, some foreign miscreants and puppets who loved to fish in murky waters, alter reality, spread dissention, and don loyal people who knew not hypocrisy with the garment of evil and desire for wrong. In this way, they opened a door that need not be open and they directed the people's attention to things which they were previously unaware of. With this we say, no matter the case, reliance is upon Allah, and we have good thoughts about our rulers who are people of intelligence and vision and who inspire the people's confidence, that they will not take the words of the slanderers and callers to dissention serious; those who have no other concern than splitting the ranks of the Muslims.

---

[1] Narrated by Ibn Mājah in the "Book of Asceticism."

We are in the shade of this Sunni country that safeguards the correct and pure doctrine, and expands its efforts in spreading and inviting to it. We are in the shade of the nation of *tawḥīd* that aids knowledge and its carriers and callers. It encourages scholastic and objective research in all fields of knowledge and in every direction, and it honours researchers with generous prizes and large endowments—be the researchers Muslims or non-Muslims, Saudi citizens or non-Saudis. Support is given to researchers in the field of Islamic invitation and practical research (for certainly, the measure of knowledge is not knowledge for its own sake, but rather action). They work to polish the mirrors of the intellect, enlighten the inner eyes, and share the thoughts expressed and felt by scholars and researchers alike, giving them the opportunity to express their views and understandings. Undoubtedly, this is one of the most powerful methods of ascertaining the truth, because clarity and openness is one of the basis for building a sound society and cohesive citizenry. Such a society is not built unless people are allowed to express their views and understandings on any topic, be it Islamic or otherwise. This principle serves as an important basis that must be adhered to in invitation to Islam.

Islam has given its enemies the opportunity to investigate and analyze. Allah said: ﴾If any of the idol worshippers comes to you seeking protection, protect him until he is able to hear the speech of Allah.﴿ (al-Tawba: 6)

Islam has also given the opportunity for the opponent and denier to express any concern, opposition, understanding, or evidence he has. Allah said: ﴾Say: "Bring your proof if you are truthful."﴿ (al-Baqara: 111)

Allah has sought from the idol worshippers that they investigate and think deeply about the religion—sometimes addressing individuals, and other times, addressing groups. Such activity can be carried out with gatherings and conferences for the sake of dialogue regarding the reality of the religion and the reality of the inviter: Muḥammad ﷺ.

Allah said: ﴾Say: "I warn you only one thing: that you stand for Allah (seeking truth), in pairs and as individuals and then give thought."﴿ (Sabā': 46)

Nay, greater than both of these, He (Allah ﷻ) has given confidence to the opponent to come forward to speak and express himself and his feelings so he may sense that in his stance he is a living entity with his own mind that should be understood, and that he has his own unique understanding that should be comprehended. Having said this, when it comes to understanding and comprehending such a person, it is a must that his understanding produces a fruit. The Exalted said: ﴾Indeed, either you or we are upon guidance or in manifest error.﴿ (Sabā': 24) This is what Allah, the Exalted, ordered His Prophet ﷺ to say to the idol worshippers—those wrongdoers and misguided ones who had no correct religion or solid doctrine—when arguing and debating with them. So he would say to them: ﴾It is either you or I who is upon guidance and it is either you or I who is upon manifest error!﴿

In light of all this, I present to you O reader, these notions regarding certain Islamic issues that are differed over among the scholars—issues in which no one is entitled to say that the scholars have a unanimous opinion. It is a duty that these notions are presented to the scholars and thinkers for investigation and research. If what is contained here is correct, then all praise belongs to Allah for His granting me success. If there is to be found any mistake here, it is from me and my own effort (*ijtihād*). The purpose of this book is to explain certain realities and correct certain mistaken notions. We have no other intention behind this work other than bringing about reform and rectification and aiming for what is correct; for we are only human—one who is correct at times and incorrect at other times. Any of us may have his views accepted or rejected, save the Divinely protected and infallible liege lord who speaks not of his own desires, speaking only revelation that is revealed unto him.

Every book can do with additional information or the removal of some parts from it, just as it can do with replacing some words with others or editing—every book that is, save the Book of Allah, which cannot be approached with falsehood in any direction, and whoever claims otherwise is a fraudulent inventor of lies. We seek refuge with Allah lest we be among those who learn knowledge with the intent of arguing or debating, as the Messenger of Allah ﷺ said: "Whoever seeks knowledge in order to debate the ignorant, behave arrogantly toward the scholars, or turn the faces of people to his attention, then Allah will place him in the fire."[2]

This book of ours is like any other book: it can be corrected or revised. All praise belongs to Allah, I admit to this in every book I write. At the end of every work I write, I say in closing: I ask Allah to grant me success and uprightness in what I write. If what I have written is correct, then it is from Allah. If what I have written is incorrect, then it is from myself and personal *ijtihād*. It is my hope that whoever discovers any errors will please inform me and show me my error. The scholars have never ceased correcting each other in their writings. When a work gains wide pleasure and acceptance, none hesitate from taking from it save an arrogant one. Unless of course, such a person had an interpretation, view, evidence, or something resembling evidence. In that case, for such a person, if he is unable to make excuses (for what he is opposed to) then the least he can do is to remain silent. Dialogues between scholars are distinguished in that they stick to the subject matter in question, possess the spirit of seeking mutual understanding, as well as scrupulousness and fear of Allah, the Exalted and Sublime. Their intention is to comprehend, guide, and defend the sanctities of Allah, and take the people by their hands and lead them to every good. They are the inheritors of the Prophets. I ask Allah, the Exalted and Sublime, that He turn us away from the sources of error and that He guide us to the straight path; indeed, He is All Hearing and the One who responds to the supplicants. My success is with none save Allah.

—Muḥammad b. ʿAlawī al-Mālikī al-Ḥasanī

---

[2] Narrated by al-Tirmidhī.

Important Notice

Regarding the Ḥadīth Narrations Cited in this Work

In this book we have cited a large number of Ḥadīth and other reports. We have also quoted the views of the Imāms among the major early scholars of Ḥadīth and their judgements on those narrations and their strength. Among them are those who authenticated some of them, others among them declared them good (*ḥasan*), and others were undecided, and others declared them weak.

Regarding the grading of the Ḥadīth reports as authentic, good, or weak, if it is established from one of the scholars of Ḥadīth among the early Imāms such as al-Tirmidhī, al-Bayhaqī, al-Mundhirī, and al-Haythamī, then that suffices us from doing any further research and checking the books of biographical reports and the books on Ḥadīth criticism.

If none of the early scholars of Ḥadīth spoke on a particular Ḥadīth then the door is wide open for whoever wishes to investigate and research. This is a wide open arena and spacious field. Hundreds of such Ḥadīth await those who will investigate and classify them.

Part I

Various Matters of Doctrine

Explaining the Corruption Found in the Scales of Modern-Day Charges of Disbelief and Misguidance

بسم الله الرحمن الرحيم

Warning from Careless Accusations of Disbelief

Many people err, may Allah rectify them, in their understanding of the real reasons that expel one from the fold of Islam and necessitate the ruling of disbelief. You see them rushing headlong in judging a Muslim to be a disbeliever due to a mere contravention of Sacred Law, to the point where (in their view) there no longer remains a Muslim on the face of the earth—save a few. Out of good thoughts for them we search for an excuse and say: perhaps their intention is good in that their motive is to fulfil the obligation of enjoining the good and forbidding the evil; however, what has escaped them is that the obligation of commanding the good and forbidding the evil must be carried out with wisdom and good exhortation.

If enjoining the good requires argumentation, it must be done in a way that is best as Allah the Exalted said: ﴾Invite to the way of your Lord with wisdom and good exhortation and argue with them in a way that is better.﴿ (Sūra al-Naḥl: 125) That is more likely to be accepted and closer to obtaining what is hoped for. Opposing this is a mistake and foolishness.

So if you invite a Muslim—one who prays, carries out the obligations of Allah, abstains from what He has forbidden, invites to His religion, builds His houses of worship and schools—to accept something that you believe to be the truth while he views it differently—and the opinion (of Islamic scholars) affirming and denying it has been divided since time immemorial—then if he doesn't heed your opinion and you accuse him of disbelief due to this mere disagreement in opinion, you have committed an ugly enormity and brought a grievous matter that Allah forbade you from, having rather called you to criticize with wisdom and goodness.

The 'Allāma and Imām, Sayyid Aḥmad Mashhūr al-Ḥaddād said:

> Scholarly consensus has established that it is unlawful to charge with disbelief anyone from the people of the *qibla*, except in that (matter) which contains denial of the All Powerful Creator (the Mighty and Majestic), or clear idolatry (*shirk*) that does not carry the possibility of interpretation (*ta'wīl*), or denial of Prophethood, or denial of that which is known to be from the religion by necessity, or denial of that which is reported (of narrations) from multiple chains of transmission, or what has been unanimously agreed to be from the religion by necessity. Anyone who denies that which is known to be from the religion by necessity, such as the Divine oneness (*tawḥīd*) Prophethood, the finality of the Message of Muḥammad ﷺ, the Resurrection on the Last Day, the Account, the Recompense, the Paradise, and the Hellfire, is a disbeliever, and none of the Muslims are excused for ignorance therein, save the one who is a recent convert to Islam, for he is excused until he learns those matters, after which he is not excused for his ignorance.
>
> *Tawātur* is the transmission of information that is narrated by a large group whose mass narration precludes the possibility of their likes gathering upon a lie, who have, in turn, handed it down to a group similar to themselves. This (*tawātur*) is either by way of the chain of narration, such as the Ḥadīth: "Whoever intentionally lies about me, then let him take his seat in the Hellfire." Or, alternatively, it is by way of an entire generation, such as the transmission of the Qur'ān, which was passed on by entire generations who learned, memorized, recited, and taught it all over the earth from East to West, so that everyone received it from everyone else; it therefore stood in no need of a chain of transmission.

There is also the possibility of mass transmission through action, such as the mass transmission of an action in a certain way in the time of the Prophetic message up till now. It could also be mass transmission of a given knowledge, such as the mass transmission of the Prophetic miracles. Individually, some of these reports are transmitted by single chains (*āhād*), however, the general portion of all of them taken together reaches the level of mass transmission, constituting decisive knowledge for every Muslim.

Judging a Muslim with disbelief in other than these matters that we have detailed is certainly a dangerous matter. In the Ḥadīth it states: "If a man says to his brother: 'O disbeliever', it [the statement] falls upon one of them."[3]

It is not correct for this judgement to be made, save by one who knows with the light of the Sacred Law, the ins and outs of disbelief, and the distinct boundaries between disbelief and faith set forth in the rules of the noble Sacred Law.

It is not permissible for any person to rush into the field and charge another with disbelief based on mere speculation and conjecture without verification, certainty, and strong knowledge. Otherwise, the torrent would flood the valley floor and no Muslim would remain on the earth save a small few. It is likewise not allowed to accuse others of disbelief based on the committal of disobedience while there is faith and conviction in the two testimonies of faith. In the Ḥadīth reported from Anas ﵁, he ﷺ said: "There are three things that are from the foundation of faith: [One] refraining from harming the one who says *Lā Ilāha Illā Allāh*. We do not accuse others of disbelief due to a sin or expel them from Islam due to an action. [Two] *jihād* (sacred struggle) shall remain from the time that Allah has sent me until the last of my nation fights the Dajjāl (Anti-Christ). It will not be invalidated due to the crime of the criminal or the justice of the just one. And [three] faith in the Divine decree."[4]

---

[3] Transmitted by al-Bukhārī from Abū Hurayra ﵁.

[4] Transmitted by Abū Dāwūd.

If we were asked to distinguish the expressions that deserve to be considered disbelief from those that do not, we would reply that this is a wish for something pointless to wish for, being too distant a reach and too stony a path to tread, involving the very bases of the science of *tawḥīd*; someone who does not attain to the furthest reaches of the facts cannot arrive at anything reliable to justify his criteria for disbelief.

It is for this reason that we severely warn from carelessness in accusing others of disbelief in other than the previously mentioned places which have been clarified. This is because it is extremely dangerous, and Allah is the Guide to the straight path and to Him is the return.

THE STANCE OF SHAYKH MUḤAMMAD B. ʿABD AL-WAHHĀB

In this field, Shaykh Muḥammad b. ʿAbd al-Wahhāb took a strong position that many who claim to ascribe to him would deny: those who recklessly weigh the ruling of disbelief against all who oppose his (Muḥammad b. ʿAbd al-Wahhāb's) method and throw out his ideology. But here is Shaykh Muḥammad b. ʿAbd al-Wahhāb denying all that is ascribed to him of these foolish and silly slanders. He said while mentioning his creed in his letter addressed to the people of Qaṣīm:

> Then it is not hidden from you, that it has reached me that the letter of Sulaymān Suhaym has arrived to you and that some of the people ascribed with knowledge among you have accepted it and confirmed it. Allah knows that this man has invented things against me that I have not said, most of which have not even crossed my mind. If this is made clear, then these (are) issues that he censured me for; From them is that which is pure slander, such as his claim that I invalidate the four juristic schools of thought, and that I say that for over six hundred years, the people are not upon anything, and that I claim *ijtihād* for myself, and that I am out of the realm of *taqlīd* (following qualified scholarship), and that I say that the

differences among the scholars are a punishment, and that I impute disbelief upon those who perform *tawassul* through the righteous, and that I impute disbelief upon al-Buṣayrī due to his statement: *O noblest of creation*, and that I say if I was able to demolish the dome (over the grave) of the Messenger of Allah ﷺ, I would demolish it, and that if I was in authority over the Ka'ba, I would take the (golden) fount and (put in its place) a wooden fount, and that I forbid visitation of the grave of the Messenger of Allah ﷺ and that I deny visitation of the graves of (one's) parents and others, and that I impute disbelief upon those who swear by other than Allah.

So, these are twelve issues, and my response to all of them is to say: ﴾Glorified are You, this is a manifest slander!﴿ (Sūra al-Nūr: 16) And before him, there was the one who slandered Muḥammad ﷺ, saying that he insulted 'Īsā b. Maryam and insulted the righteous. So their hearts resembled each other in inventing lies, and bearing false witness. The Most Exalted said: ﴾Only those who do not believe in the signs of Allah invent lies.﴿ (Sūra al-Naḥl: 105) They slandered him ﷺ, by saying that he says: "The Angels, 'Isā, and 'Uzayr are in the fire." So in response to that, Allah revealed: ﴾Verily those for whom the good has preceded from Us, they will be removed far there from (Hell).﴿ (Sūra al-Anbiyā': 101)

See the first letter from the personal letters contained in *Majmū'a al-Mu'allafāt al-Shaykh al-Imām Muḥammad b. 'Abd al-Wahhāb* that has been distributed by the efforts of al-Imām Muḥammad b. Sa'ūd Islamic University.

ANOTHER IMPORTANT LETTER FROM THE SHAYKH ON THIS SUBJECT

This letter was sent by Shaykh Muḥammad b. 'Abd al-Wahhāb to al-Suwaydī, a scholar from the people of Iraq, who had sent a book to him, asking him about what the people say about him. He answered with this letter, saying:

> Indeed, spreading slanderous rumours is something that the intelligent person is ashamed of narrating, much less inventing.
>
> And from what you have said, that I impute disbelief upon all of the people except those who follow me—how amazing; how can this enter the intellect of an intelligent person? Does a Muslim say this?
>
> And from what you have said, that if I were able to demolish the dome [over the grave] of the Prophet I would demolish it, and (what you said) concerning *Dalā'il al-Khayrāt* and my forbidding of it, and that I forbid sending prayers upon the Prophet ﷺ no matter what form it takes—then this is from slander. The Muslim does not think in his heart that there is anything nobler than the Book of Allah.

And on p.64 from the same book, he said—may Allah have mercy upon him:

> And from what you have said, that I impute disbelief upon those who perform *tawassul* through the righteous, and that I impute disbelief upon al-Buṣayrī due to his saying: *O noblest of creation*, and that I deny [the permissibility of] visiting the grave of the Prophet ﷺ, and that I deny [the permissibility of] visiting the grave of (one's) parents or others, and that I impute disbelief upon those who swear by other than Allah—my response to all of that is to say: Glorified are You my Lord, this is a tremendous slander!

INSULTING A MUSLIM IS CORRUPTION AND FIGHTING HIM IS DISBELIEF

You should know that hating Muslims, boycotting them, and fighting them are forbidden. Insulting a Muslim is corruption (*fusūq*) and fighting him is disbelief if it is declared to be permissible.

The Ḥadīth of Khālid b. al-Walīd ﷺ is sufficient as a deterrent from this. In one expedition, he went out to Banū Judhayma and invited them to Islam. When he reached them he said: "Embrace

Islam." They responded: "We *are* Muslims." He said: "In that case, place your weapons down and disembark from your steeds."

"No," they replied, "By Allah, after placing our weapons down there is nothing left except being killed. We do not feel safe from you and those with you."

Khālid said: "I will not give you security until you disembark." A group of them disembarked, while the rest of them departed. In another narration it states that Khālid reached the people and said: "Who are you all (meaning, are you Muslims or disbelievers)?" They responded: "We are Muslims who pray and believe in Muḥammad ﷺ. We have built mosques in our area and call the *ādhān* (call to prayer) in them." In their way of speaking, they were not able to correctly say: "We have embraced Islam (*aslamnā*)," so they said: "*Saba'na, Saba'na.*" He (Khālid) said: "If that is so, then why are you armed?" They replied: "There is animosity between us and some of the Arab (Bedouins) and we were afraid that you are from them so we took our weapons." He (Khālid) said: "Lower your weapons," and so they did. He said: "Surrender," and afterwards, he ordered some of them and tied up some and then distributed them to his companions. When the night time approached, a caller of Khālid's called out: "Whoever has a prisoner, then let him kill him," so Banū Sulaym killed those with them, while the Muhājirūn (immigrants) and Anṣār (helpers) withheld from that and set their prisoners free. When news of this and Khālid's action reached the Prophet ﷺ, he said twice: "O Allah, I declare myself free unto you from what Khālid did."

It could be stated that Khālid understood their words to be a form of rejection, pride, and refusal to submit to Islam, and that the Prophet ﷺ only censured him due to his hastiness and lack of verification concerning their affair before knowing the intent of their statement: "*Saba'na.*" He ﷺ said (concerning Khālid): "What a good slave and brother to his family Khālid b. al-Walīd is! He is the sword of Allah that Allah has unsheathed against the disbelievers and hypocrites."

Similarly, there is the narration found in al-Bukhārī regarding Usāma b. Zayd, the beloved of the Messenger of Allah and the son of his beloved.

Ibn Dhabyān said: "I heard Usāma b. Zayd say: 'The Messenger of Allah ﷺ dispatched us to al-Ḥirqa and we descended upon them in the morning and defeated them. One man from the Anṣār and I came upon a man from them. When we surrounded him, he said *Lā Ilāha Illā Allāh*. The Anṣārī kept back from him, while I stabbed him with my spear and killed him. When we returned, this (news) reached the Messenger of Allah ﷺ and he said: "O Usāma, did you kill him after he said *Lā Ilāha Illā Allāh*?" I replied: "He was saying it as a shield (from being killed)." He (the Messenger of Allah ﷺ) did not cease repeating his words until I had wished that I had not embraced Islam that day.' " In another narration it states that the Messenger of Allah ﷺ said to him: "Did you split open his heart so as to know if he was truthful or lying?" Usāma said: "I shall not kill anyone who says *Lā Ilāha Illā Allāh*."

'Alī ﷺ was once asked about some of his opponents from one of the sects: "Are they disbelievers?" "No," he replied, "It was from disbelief that they were fleeing." He was then asked: "Are they hypocrites?" "No," he replied, "The hypocrites do not remember Allah but a little, whereas these people remember Allah in abundance." He was then asked: "So what are they?" He replied: "They are a people who were afflicted with a trial, so they were blinded and made deaf."

THE STATION OF THE CREATOR AND THE STATION OF CREATION

The difference between the station of the Creator and that of the creation is the dividing line between disbelief and faith. We believe that those who mix up the two stations have fallen into disbelief, and Allah's refuge is sought.

For every station there are special rights. There are some matters, however, that might lead to confusion for some—especially those matters which relate to the unique qualities that pertain to the Prophet ﷺ.

These qualities distinguish him from the rest of mankind and elevate his rank above them. Confusion might arise for some people because of the limitations of their intellects, the weakness of their thinking abilities, and their shallow views and bad understanding, thereby causing them to fall in to haste in imputing disbelief upon those who affirm such unique qualities and expelling them from the fold of Islam. They think that these matters mix between the stations of the Creator and creation and raise the Prophet ﷺ to the level of Lordship. From that, we declare our disavowal in front of Allah ﷻ.

By the bounty of Allah, the Exalted, we know what is necessary (*wājib)* for Allah, and what is necessary for His Messenger ﷺ. We know what is the sole right of Allah the Exalted and what is the sole right of His Messenger ﷺ—without extremism and exaggeration that reaches the point of describing him ﷺ with the special attributes of Lordship (*Rubūbiyya*) and Divinity (*'Ulūhiyya*) in (matters such as) giving and withholding, bringing benefit and harm (in such a way that is independent of Allah), complete dominion and comprehensive caretaking, creation, disposing of the affairs, singularity of perfection, exaltedness, holiness, and singularity of worship in its various types, situations, and ranks.

As for the "extremism" that means intensity in loving him, obeying him, and attaching oneself to him, then this is loved and sought after, as appears in the Ḥadīth: "Do not exaggerate about me as the Christians have exaggerated with Ibn Maryam." This means exaggerating and lauding him in blameworthy ways. If the meaning of (the Ḥadīth) was somehow other than that, then the intended meaning of it would be a prohibition of lauding him and praising him completely. It is known that not even the most ignorant of the Muslims would say such a thing, for Allah the Exalted, has praised the Prophet ﷺ in the Qur'ān in the highest forms of praise. It is obligatory upon us to praise the one whom Allah has ordered us to praise... Yes, it is necessary that we do not describe him with the qualities of Divine Lordship. May Allah have mercy upon the one who said:

Leave aside what the Christians have claimed for their Prophet
Then praise him as you like, but do so well

There is no disbelief or idolatry to be found in praising him with that which doesn't include qualities of Divine Lordship; nay, that is from the greatest acts of obedience and of the greatest means of achieving closeness.

This is also the case with all whom Allah has glorified, such as the Prophets and Messengers, may the prayers of Allah and His peace be upon them all, as well as the Angels, the truthful ones, the martyrs and the righteous. Allah the Exalted, said: ﴾And whosoever honours the Symbols of Allah, then it is truly from the piety of the heart.﴿ (al-Ḥajj: 32) And the Exalted said: ﴾And whoever honours the sacred things of Allah, then that is better for him with his Lord.﴿ (al-Ḥajj: 30)

This also includes the sanctified Ka'ba, the Black Stone, and the prayer place of Ibrāhīm a. These are stones that Allah has ordered us to glorify by performing circumambulation of the house, touching the Yemeni corner, kissing the black stone, and praying behind the prayer place of Ibrāhīm ﷺ, standing for supplication at the right side of the Ka'ba's door, and at the *multazim*. When we do all of these things we have not worshipped anyone but Allah, the Exalted; we have not believed in any independent causation besides He who brings benefit or harm. None of that is established for anything save Allah.

THE STATION OF CREATION

Regarding the Prophet ﷺ, indeed we believe that he ﷺ is a human and that it possible for him—as it is possible for other humans—to have incidental qualities and sicknesses that do not necessitate deficiency and turning (the people) away with aversion, as the author in creed stated:

It is permissible for them to have incidental qualities
Without necessitating a deficiency—such as a light illness

We also believe that he is a slave; he does not possess any harm, benefit, power over death, life, or resurrection, except as Allah wills. The Exalted said: ﴾Say (O Muḥammad): "I possess no power of benefit or hurt to myself except as Allah wills. If I had the knowledge of the *ghayb* (unseen), I should have secured for myself an abundance of wealth, and no evil should have touched me. I am but a warner, and a bringer of glad tidings unto people who believe."﴿ (al-A'rāf: 188)

We believe that he conveyed the message, fulfilled the trust, advised the Umma, removed distress, and waged *jihād* in the path of Allah until Allah brought certainty (death) to him, thereby moving to the company of his Lord, being pleased and well-pleased with as the Exalted said: ﴾Indeed you and they shall die.﴿ (al-Zumar: 30) And He said: ﴾And We granted not to any human being immortality before you (O Muḥammad), then if you die, would they live forever?﴿ (al-Anbiyā': 34)

Slavehood is his noblest quality ﷺ. This is why he took honour in it and said: "I am only a slave." Allah described him with slavehood in the highest station (when He said): ﴾Glorified is He (Allah) who took His slave on a journey.﴿ (al-Isrā': 1) And He said: ﴾When the slave of Allah stood up invoking (his Lord Allah) in prayer to Him, they (the *jinns*) just about made round him a dense crowd as if sticking one over the other.﴿ (al-Jinn: 19)

His humanity was the essence of his wondrous nature for he was a human from the human family, yet he was distinguished from them by qualities with which no one else can equal him or compare, as he ﷺ said concerning himself in the authentic Ḥadīth: "I am not like you, for verily I spend the night with my Lord and He feeds me and gives me drink."

Having said all this, it is now clear that describing him with human qualities must also be juxtaposed with describing him with the qualities that distinguish him from the rest of humanity—such as the aforementioned qualities. This is not restricted to him ﷺ alone, rather it is general for all of the Messengers of Allah ﷺ. Our view of the Prophets is commensurate with their stations.

Looking only at their normal humanity, stripped of these other qualities is a view of the time of ignorance (*jāhiliyya*) and idolatry. There are numerous testimonies in the Qur'ān for this. From them, is the statement of the people of Nūḥ concerning him that Allah mentioned: ﴾The chiefs of the disbelievers among his people said: "We see you but a man like ourselves..."﴿ (Hūd: 27)

From that also is the statement of the people of Mūsā and Hārūn that they said about them: ﴾They said: "Shall we believe in two men like ourselves, and their people are obedient to us with humility (and we use them to serve us as we like)."﴿
(al-Mu'minūn: 47)

From that also is the statement of the people of Thamūd, to their Prophet Ṣāliḥ: ❮You are but a human being like us. Then bring us a sign if you are of the truthful.❯ (al-Shu'arā': 154)

From that also is the statement of the people of Ayka to their Prophet Shu'ayb: ❮They said: "You are only one of those bewitched! You are but a human being like us and verily, we think that you are one of the liars!"❯ (al-Shu'arā': 185-186)

From that also is the statement of the polytheists to our Master Muḥammad ﷺ—those who saw him in the light of mere humanity free (from his special qualities): ❮And they say: "Why does this Messenger eat food, and walk about in the markets (like ourselves)?"❯ (al-Furqān: 7)

Indeed, the Messenger of Allah ﷺ spoke the truth about himself concerning Allah's honouring him with mighty attributes and miracles that he was distinguished with apart from the rest of mankind.

From that is what appears in an authentic Ḥadīth that he said: "My eyes sleep, but my heart does not sleep." In the authentic collection (of al-Bukhārī) he said: "Indeed I see you from behind just as I see you from the front." And in (another) authentic report (of al-Bukhārī) he said: "I was granted the keys of the treasure houses of the earth."

Even though he ﷺ died, he is still alive in a perfect sense in the Isthmus (*barzakh*) life; he hears speech, responds to salutations, and the prayers of those who send prayers upon him reach him. The actions of the Umma are presented to him, and he becomes delighted with the deeds of the good-doers and seeks forgiveness for those who commit sins. Allah has forbidden the earth to consume his body, so he is protected from blemishes and the (changes brought about by being in) the earth.

It is reported from Aws b. Aws ﷺ: "The Messenger of Allah ﷺ said: 'From the best of your days is Friday. On that day, Ādam was created and on that day his soul was taken. On that day shall be the blowing (of the trumpet), and on that day will be the thunderclap, so frequently perform prayer upon me on that day, for your prayers are presented to me.' They said: 'O Messenger of Allah! How can our prayers be presented to you when you will have (turned to) dust?' He said: 'Indeed, Allah has forbidden the earth to consume the bodies of the Prophets.' "

Concerning this, there is an essay by Ḥāfiẓ Jalāl al-Dīn al-Suyūṭī titled: *Tanwīr al-Ḥalak*.

Ibn Mas'ūd ﷺ narrated that the Messenger of Allah ﷺ said: "My life is a great good for you, you will relate about me and it will be related to you, and my death is a great good for you, your actions will be presented to me (in my grave). If I see goodness I will praise Allah, and if see other than that I will ask forgiveness of Him for you." Al-Haythamī said: "This is narrated by al-Bazzār and its men in the chain are the men in the *Ṣaḥīḥ* (collection of al-Bukhārī)."

Abū Hurayra ﷺ narrated that the Messenger of Allah ﷺ said: "No one greets me except Allah returns my soul to me so that I can return his greeting."

This has been narrated from Aḥmad and Abū Dāwūd. Some of the scholars have said: "returns my soul to me" means: "returns my faculty of speech."

'Ammār b. Yassār ﷺ narrated that the Messenger of Allah ﷺ said: "Indeed Allah has entrusted an Angel at my grave to whom Allah has given the names of the creation. No one sends prayers upon me until the Day of Judgement except that he (the Angel) conveys to me his name and the name of his father (saying): 'So-and-so, the son of so-and-so has sent prayers upon you.' "

This has been narrated by al-Bazzār, Abū al-Shaykh, and Ibn Ḥibbān (whose narration contains the wording): "The Messenger of Allah ﷺ said: 'Indeed Allah, the Blessed and Exalted, has an Angel to whom He has given the names of the creation and he is standing by my grave when I die. So no one sends prayers upon me except that he says: "O Muḥammad! So-and-so, the son of so-and-so has sent prayers upon you.' Then he said: 'Then the Lord, the Blessed and Exalted, will send prayers upon that man ten times for every time (he sends one prayer).' " This is (also) narrated by al-Ṭabarānī in his *al-Kabīr* with the likes of it.

Despite the fact that he ﷺ passed, his virtue, station, and rank with his Lord all remain. There is no doubt or reservation concerning that with the people of faith. It is for this reason, that *tawassul* by means of him unto Allah ﷻ in reality, goes back to the belief in these realities and belief in his love and nobility with his Lord and (this also goes back to) faith in him and his message.

This is not worship of him ﷺ, for no matter how exalted his level and no matter how high his station, he is (still) a created being that can neither harm nor benefit besides Allah, save with His (Allah's) permission. The Exalted said: ﴾Say: "Indeed, I am only a man like yourselves; it is revealed to me that your God is one God."﴿ (al-Kahf: 110)

MATTERS THAT ARE SHARED BETWEEN THE TWO STATIONS AND DO NOT CONTRADICT DIVINE TRANSCENDENCE

Many people have erred in their understanding of some of the matters that are shared between the two stations (the station of the Creator and the station of the creation). Some have thought that ascribing it to the station of the creation is *shirk* with Allah, the Exalted. From that are some of the special Prophetic qualities that some err in their understanding of. They weigh them with the scales of humanity and for that reason, the find it extreme and exaggerated to attribute them to the Messenger of Allah ﷺ. They believe that describing him with such qualities (is on par with) describing him with some of the unique Divine qualities. This is complete ignorance, because He ﷻ gives to whomever He wills, as He wills, and without any necessary binding cause; nay, (it is) purely from His bounty and largesse for whom He wishes to honour and whose station He wishes to raise and in order to manifest his (the receivers) bounty over others among mankind. In this, there is no conflict with the rights of (His) Divinity and transcendence (*'Ulūhiyya*), for that is guarded with what is appropriate to the station of al-Ḥaqq (the Real, Allah) ﷻ.

If a created being is described with any of these (qualities), then it is in accordance with and befitting his humanity. It is limited and acquired by the permission of Allah and His Bounty and Will—not by the power, decision or command of the created one, for he is incapable and weak, not possessing any ability of (bringing) harm, benefit, death, life, or quickening. Indeed, how many matters have appeared (in the texts) showing something to be the right of Allah ﷻ, however He ﷻ (at the same time) bestowed it upon His Prophet ﷺ and upon others?

So in this case, for him to be described with (these qualities) does not elevate him to the station of divinity or make him a co-sharer or partner with Allah ﷻ. These qualities (include):

Intercession. Intercession belongs to Allah, as He said: ﴾Say: "To Allah belongs the intercession."﴿ (al-Zumar: 44) And (at the same time) it is affirmed for the Messenger ﷺ and others besides him that they are intercessors (who do so) with the permission of Allah, as appears in the Ḥadīth: "I was given the intercession." And the Ḥadīth: "I am the first intercessor and one to have his intercession accepted."

Knowledge of the Unseen. Knowledge of the unseen belongs to Allah ﷻ: ﴾Say: "None in the heavens and the earth know the unseen save Allah."﴿ (al-Naml: 65) However, it has been established that Allah, the Exalted, has taught the Messenger ﷺ some of the unseen: ﴾The knower of the unseen, He does not reveal what is unseen with Him to anyone save one whom He is pleased with of a Messenger.﴿ (al-Jinn: 26-27)

Guidance. Guidance is unique to Allah, the Exalted. Allah the Exalted said: ﴾Indeed you do not guide the one you love, however Allah guides whom He wills.﴿ (al-Qaṣaṣ: 56) It has also come (in the text) that he (the Prophet) ﷺ has a portion of that. The Exalted said: ﴾Indeed, you certainly guide to the straight path.﴿ (al-Shūrā: 52) The first (type) of guidance is not like the second. This is only understood by those of intellect from among the believers who are aware of the difference between the Creator and the creation. If it were not for that, it would have been necessary to say: "Indeed you guide (others) with the guidance of direction," or to say: "Indeed, you guide (others) in a way that is different from our guidance." However, none of that occurred. Rather, He (Allah) affirmed guidance for him that is general and without any restrictions or conditions, because the believer in Divine oneness from the people of Islam (the *muwaḥḥid*) among us who is addressed (with this verse) understands the meanings of the expressions and the differences indicated with respect to its ascription to Allah and its ascription to the Messenger of Allah ﷺ.

Similar to this is the description found in the Qur'ān describing the Messenger of Allah ﷺ with pity and mercy when He (Allah) said: ﴾With the believers he (the Prophet) is full of pity and mercy.﴿ (al-Tawba: 128) And Allah ﷻ also described Himself with that in more than one place (in the Qur'ān), for He ﷻ is: ﴾Full of pity and mercy.﴿

It is well known that the second type of pity and mercy is not like the first (type). When Allah described His Prophet ﷺ with that description, he described him with it in a general fashion without any restriction or condition. This is because the one that is addressed is a believer in Divine oneness and a believer in Allah who knows the difference between the Creator and the creation. If it were not for that, He would have needed to say in His description of him: "Full of pity and merciful—of the type that is different from Our pity and mercy," or to say: "Full of pity that is a special and distinct form of pity, and full of mercy that is a special distinct form of mercy," or to say: "Full of pity that is a pity fit for humans and merciful that is a mercy fit for humans." However, none of that occurred; He affirmed for him pity that is unrestricted, and mercy that is unrestricted, without any limit or condition. He said: ﴾Full of pity and mercy for the believers.﴿

LOGICAL METAPHOR AND ITS USE

There is no doubt that figurative speech is used in the Book and the Sunna. From that, are the words of the Exalted: ﴾And when our verses are recited to them, they increase them in faith.﴿ (al-Anfāl: 2) Linking the increase to the verses is figurative because (in reality) they are a cause for the increase. It is Allah alone who actually increases it (the faith).

Also, the statement of the Exalted: ﴾A day which shall turn young children grey haired.﴿ (al-Muzammil: 17) Linking (the word) "turn" to the day is figurative because the day is the place in which they will be made grey haired. So the "turning" mentioned here shall occur *on* that day, whereas the one who 'turns' in reality is Allah, the Exalted.

Also, the statement of the Exalted: ﴾Nor Yaghūth, Ya'ūq, or Nasr; they have certainly misguided many.﴿ (Nūḥ: 23–24) Linking misguidance to the idols is figurative because they were a means for misguidance, whereas the one who guides and misguides (in reality) is Allah alone.

Also the statement of the Exalted, narrating the (story) of Pharaoh: ﴾"O Hamām! Build a tower for me."﴿ (Ghāfir: 36) Linking the act of building to Hamām is figurative because he was a cause (for it) in that he was the one commanding (for it to be built) and not that he was building it himself. The builder was the one doing the action: in this case, it was the workers.

As for the Ḥadīth reports (containing figurative speech), they are many. They are known to those who have come across them and who know the difference between the linkage (of an act) to that which is literal and that which is figurative. There is no need to spend a long time quoting them.

The scholars have said: "The utterance of this linkage from a believer in the Divine oneness is sufficient in making it a figurative linkage because the correct belief is that the Creator of the servants and their actions is Allah alone. He is the Creator of the servants and their actions. There is no independent effect for anyone besides Him—be they dead or alive."

This belief is the pure *tawḥīd*, as opposed to one who believes other than this, which constitutes *shirk*.

THE NECESSITY OF PERCEIVING THE FIGURATIVE PORTION IN THE SCALES OF FAITH AND DISBELIEF

Certain factions of misguidance have held to the tail of a doubt based upon the outwardly apparent and literal expressions, without looking to the circumstantial elements (*qarā'in*) and intentions, and without seeking to reconcile and join (between the texts) in a way that does not lead to mutual contradiction, such as those who believe in the creation of the Qur'ān, holding firm to the likes of Allah's statement: ﴾Indeed We have made it an Arabic Qur'ān.﴿ (al-Zukhruf: 3) Similarly, those who believe in absolute free will, holding firm to Allah's statement: ﴾With what your hands have earned.﴿ (al-Shūrā: 30) and: ﴾And due to what you have done.﴿ (al-Mā'ida: 105) And like those who believed in absolute fatalism (*jabr*) holding firm to Allah's statement: "And Allah created you and that which you do.﴿ (al-Ṣāffāt: 96) and:

﴾You did not throw when you threw but it was Allah who threw.﴿ (al-Anfāl: 17)

Uncovering the facts surrounding all of this, it is said: all of the Umma, with the exception of the Qadariyya (sect), believe that the actions of the slaves are created by Allah, the Exalted: ﴾Allah created you and that which you do.﴿ And He said: ﴾You did not throw when you threw but it was Allah who threw.﴿ This is the case, even if it is allowed for the servant to be described with such actions in another type of linkage, expressed as "acquisition" (*kasb*), as is found in the statement of the Exalted: ﴾He gets reward for that (good) which he has earned, and he is punished for that (evil) which he has earned.﴿ (al-Baqara: 287) The Exalted also said: ﴾Due to what their hands have earned.﴿ There are many other verses which are explicit in attributing acquisition to the slave. It is not necessary that the linkage of power to the one enabled (with the act) be through independent creation (*ikhtirā'*) only, for the power of Allah is pre-eternally linked to the world (all things but Him) before it was created by Him. When He created the world, it was linked to Him with another type of linkage.

THE REALITY OF ASCRIBING ACTIONS TO THE SERVANTS

From this it becomes clear that the linkage of power (*qudra*) is not restricted to the obtainment of that which is decreed. The actions of the servants are ascribed to them by way of acquisition and *not* independent creation. Allah is the One who creates them, decrees them, and wills them. It is impossible for someone to object and say: "How can He desire that which He prohibits?" This is because the command is distinct from the will, as is proven by the fact that He commanded all people to have faith while (at the same time) He did not will it from the majority of them, as He said: ﴾Most of the people will not believe even if you were covetous of that.﴿ (Yūsuf: 103)

Ascribing the actions to the servants is ascribing the thing "caused" to the cause or the intermediary, and there is no contradiction in that. The One who brings about the causes is the One who created the intermediary and created within it, the meaning of 'intermediary'. If it were not for that which Allah has placed in it, it would not be fitting to be an intermediary, whether it is something that has not been given intellect, such as solid objects, constellations, rain, and fire, or something that does have intellect such as an Angel, human, or Jinn.

THE DIFFERENCES OF MEANING BASED ON THE DIFFERENT ASCRIPTIONS

Perhaps you will retort: "But ascribing one single action to two different doers does not make sense, because it is impossible to join between two actors upon one action." We say (in response): Yes. It is as you have said, however, that is only the case if the meaning of the word "doer" has only one meaning that is used. If, on the other hand, it has two meanings, then the word is general, being used to express both ascriptions.

If this is the case, then it is possible that it may be expressed in a general context, as is well known in the usage of homonyms, or in literal and figurative speech. This is just as it is said: "The emir (leader) killed so-and-so" and "The executioner killed him." So, the meaning of the word "kill" with respect to the emir means something entirely different than its meaning with respect to the executioner. When we say: "Allah, the Exalted, is the Doer," it means that He is the One who creates and brings into being, and when we say: "The created being is the doer," it means that he is the locus in which Allah, the Exalted, created the ability after having created the will and knowledge (in that being). Linking ability with will, and linking movement with will, is (called) the linking of the caused with the cause, and linking the created thing with the created thing.

This is if the locus is one that is living, otherwise, if it is not, then it is from the category of arrangement of causes upon their means. So, it is correct to call everything which has a link with ability "a doer" however the link may be. Similarly, it is correct to call the executioner a killer in one respect, and the emir in another respect. This is because killing has been linked to the both of them. Even if this linkage is in two different respects, it is still allowed to call both of them "doers." This is like considering the decreed matters with two abilities.

The evidence for the permissibility of this ascription and its appropriateness is when Allah, the Exalted, ascribed actions to the Angels on some occasions, while on other occasions, ascribed them to others among His servants, while on other occasions, He ascribed them to Himself.

The Exalted said: ﴾Say, "The Angel of death that has been entrusted to you will cause you to perish."﴿ (al-Sajda: 11) And the Exalted said: ﴾Allah causes the souls to perish when they die.﴿ (al-Zumar: 42) The Exalted said: ﴾Tell Me! The seed that you sow in the ground...﴿ (al-Wāqi'a: 63) He ascribed this to us, then He said (in another chapter): ﴾Indeed, We pour forth water in abundance, and We split the earth in clefts, and We cause therein the grain to grow.﴿ ('Abasa: 25–27)

And the Exalted said: ﴾Then We sent to her Our *Rūḥ* (the Angel Jibrīl) and he appeared before her in the form of a man in all respects.﴿ (Maryam: 17)

Then the Exalted said (in another chapter): ﴾Then We breathed into her from our *Rūḥ* (spirit).﴿ (al-Anbiyā': 91). Although the one who breathed (into her) was Jibrīl ﵇. The Exalted said: ﴾And when We (Allah) have recited it to you, then you follow its (the Qur'ān's) recital﴿ (al-Qiyāma: 18) even though the reciter whose recitation the Prophet ﷺ heard was Jibrīl. The Exalted said: ﴾You did not kill them but it was Allah who killed them﴿ (al-Anfāl: 17) and: ﴾You did not throw when you threw but it was Allah who threw.﴿ (al-Anfāl: 17)

Allah negated that they killed and He then affirmed it for Himself. He also negated his (the Prophet's ﷺ) throwing and affirmed it for Himself. What is intended here is not negating their killing of the disbelievers and his throwing dust at them from a sensory perspective, rather, what this means is that they did not kill them or throw at them according to the meaning of killing and throwing that Allah affirmed for Himself—which is in the sense of creating and decreeing. These are two different meanings. Sometimes the action is linked to both of them together as it appears in the statement of Allah, the Exalted: ﴾If only they were pleased with that which Allah and His Messenger gave them and said: "Allah is sufficient for us. Allah will give us of His bounty as well as His Messenger."﴿ (al-Tawba: 59)

It has been narrated from 'Ā'isha—may Allah be pleased with her—that she said "When Allah, the Blessed and Exalted, wishes to create a child in the womb, He dispatches an Angel that enters the womb and takes the clot with its hand and fashions it into a body and says: 'O Lord, shall it be a male or a female? Shall it be straight or crooked?' The Exalted says what He wills and the Angel creates."

In another narration it states: "So the Angel fashions (the baby) and breaths into it the spirit decreed with either felicity or wretchedness."

If you have understood this, it will become clear to you that an action can be expressed in different ways and there is no contradiction between any of them. It is for this reason that an action can be ascribed to a solid inanimate object sometimes, as is in the statement of the Exalted: ﴾Giving its fruit at all times, by the leave of its Lord.﴿ (Ibrāhīm: 25)

The tree does not (literally) come and give its fruits. Another example of this is found in the statement of the Prophet ﷺ who said to the man to whom who he gave a date: "Take it. If you do not come to it, it will come to you." This is found in (the collection of) al-Ṭabarānī and Ibn Ḥibbān. Here, the ascription of "coming" when applied to a man differs from its ascription to a date. The coming of a date is different than the coming of a man. Coming (from both a man and a date) is figurative and different in their ascriptions. The figurative expression for coming with respect to a man means that Allah created within him the ability and will to come. The coming of the fruit means that Allah places someone as a means to brings it, whereas in reality, for both cases, "coming" is ascribed to Allah.

Due in part to the different ways of considering the intermediaries, sometimes looking to intermediaries in actions is disbelief. This is mentioned in the response of Hārūn to Mūsā ﷺ when the former said: ﴾I was only given this due to knowledge that I have.﴿ (al-Qaṣaṣ: 78)

In addition to this, there is a Ḥadīth that states: "Some of my servants have awoken as believers in Me, and (some as) disbelievers in Me. As for the one who says: 'We have received rain from the Bounty of Allah and His Mercy,' they are believers in Me and disbelievers in the stars. Those who say: 'We have received rain from the movements of such-and-such a star,' are disbelievers in Me and believers in the stars."

This is disbelief if one considers that the intermediary (the stars) possess independent causation and ability to create.

Al-Nawawī said:

> The scholars have differed regarding the disbelief of one who says: "We were sent rain due to such-and-such stars." There are two different views: [One] It is disbelief in Allah, the Exalted, which removes the root of faith and expels one from the religion of Islam. They said: "This is regarding the one who says that while believing that the star is in itself a doer that manages and spreads the rain—as was claimed by some of the people from the time of ignorance (*jāhiliyya*). Whoever believes this, then there is no doubt concerning his disbelief." This view is the one upheld by the majority of the scholars, al-Shāfi'ī being among them, and it is the apparent (meaning) of the Ḥadīth. They (the scholars) said: "Based upon this, if someone said: 'We were given rain by such-and-such a star,' while believing that it is from Allah and His mercy, and that the star is a sign and time post for it customarily (indicating the onset of rain), then it is as if he said: 'Rain came to us at such-and-such a time.' This one has not disbelieved." They (the scholars) differed concerning it being reprehensible (or not), however, it is preferably disliked (*makrūh tanzīhī*) without there being a sin in that. The reason for it being disliked is that it is a word that teeters between disbelief and other than that, so perhaps it is so that (one) might think badly about this person because it is a saying of pre-Islamic times and those who traverse their way.
>
> [Two] Regarding the basic interpretation of the Ḥadīth, the second opinion states: "What is intended is denial of the blessings of Allah, the Exalted, due to ascribing the rain to the star only. This is with respect to the one who does not believe in the independent control of the star." This interpretation is supported by the last narration in (this) section (stating): "Some of the people have awoken as grateful and some as rejecters (*kāfir*)."

> And in another narration (it states): "Allah has not sent down anything of blessings from the heavens except that a group of people wake up as ungrateful (*kāfirūn*) for them." His statement: "for them" proves that it is rejection of blessings (*kufr al-ni'ma*), and Allah knows best.

You see here that he mentioned the agreement of the scholars that whoever ascribes the action to an intermediary then he has not disbelieved unless he believes that it is the doer, manager, and originator. If the attention to the intermediary is not in this manner, in such a way that the intermediary is seen as a sign or a locus in which the created thing is decreed, then it is not disbelief. On the contrary, sometimes, the Law Giver (Allah) encourages one to take notice of it (the intermediary), such as in the Prophet's ﷺ statement: "Whoever does good to you, then reciprocate. If you are unable, then supplicate for him until you know that you have reciprocated." And his ﷺ statement: "Whoever is not thankful to the people is not thankful to Allah."

Taking notice of the intermediary in this manner does not negate seeing the bounty of Allah ﷻ. Allah has praised—nay, rewarded—His servants in some places (in the Qur'ān) due to their actions and He is the cause for them to possess the will to do them and the One who creates their ability as well.

He said: ﴾How excellent a slave! Verily, he was ever oft-returning in repentance.﴿ (Ṣād: 30) He said: ﴾For those who do good there will be goodness and more.﴿ (Yūnus: 10) He said: ﴾Successful indeed is he who purifies it (i.e. his heart).﴿ (al-Shams: 9) When it becomes clear to you that a verb may be used in various ways (you will see) these meanings are not contradictory. This is (of course) if you understand with a correct and sound understanding.

Meanings are more expansive that outward expressions and the chests (of men) are more expansive than the books and (other) written materials. If we were to deal with just the literal expressions without the figurative (meanings), we would not find it permissible to join or separate between the (primary) texts.

Have you not read what Allah informed us of regarding Ibrāhīm when He said: ﴾My Lord, indeed they have led astray many among mankind﴿ (Ibrāhīm: 36)?

Do you hold the view that Ibrāhīm associated partners with Allah, the Exalted, by way of solid inanimate objects, while he is the one who also said: ﴾Do you all worship that which you carve while Allah created you and that which you do?﴿ (al-Ṣāffāt: 95–96)

The comprehensive statement regarding this is that whoever associates partners with Allah, the Exalted, in (independent) creation and effect, then he is a polytheist, regardless (if the thing) associated was a solid inanimate object, a human Prophet, or other than that. On the other hand, whoever believes that any of these things are a means—be it demonstrated or not—while believing that Allah, the Exalted, made it a means for obtaining other things (*musababāt*) and that the doer is Allah Alone, with no partner, then he is a believer, even if he was mistaken in what he thought to be a means that was (in fact) not a means. This is because his mistake was in the means, not in the One who facilitates the means; the Creator and Manager, the Glorified and Exalted of Lofty Stature.

GLORIFICATION: BETWEEN WORSHIP AND ETIQUETTE

Many people err in understanding the reality of glorification and the reality of worship, thereby mixing between the two. They consider that any type of glorification is in fact worship of the one who is glorified. Standing, kissing hands, glorifying the Prophet ﷺ with (the terms) our "Sayyid" (master) or "Mawlānā" (liege lord), standing in front of him during visitation (of his grave) with etiquette, respect, and humility—according to them, all of this is extremism that leads to worshipping other than Allah, the Exalted. In reality, this is sheer ignorance and going beyond the bounds that Allah and His Messenger are not pleased with. It is going too far and is rejected by the spirit of the Islamic Sacred Law.

Take Ādam, who is the first of mankind and the first of Allah's righteous servants from this species. Allah, the Exalted, ordered the Angels to prostrate to him out of glorification and honour toward him due to what He gave him of His knowledge, and in order to inform them that he is the Chosen One from among His creation.

The Exalted said: ﴾And remember when We said to the Angels: "Prostrate to Ādam," so all of them prostrated except Iblīs. He said: "Shall I prostrate to one whom You created from mud? Have you seen that this one has been given honour over me?"﴿ (al-Isrā': 61–62) In another verse He said: ﴾I am better than him, You have created me from fire, whereas You have created him from mud.﴿ (al-A'rāf: 12) And in another verse: ﴾So all of the Angels prostrated in entirety, save Iblīs. He refused to be among those who prostrate.﴿ (al-Ḥijr: 30–31)

The Angels glorified the one who was glorified by Allah. Iblīs on the other hand, was too arrogant to prostrate to one who was created from mud. He was the first one to use false analogy in the religion. He said: "I am better than he." His reasoning for this statement was that he was created from fire, whereas Ādam was created from mud. He was too proud to admit that he (Ādam) was given honour over him, and was too arrogant to prostrate to him. He was the first of the arrogant ones who did not honour the one honoured by Allah, and was thus expelled from the mercy of Allah due to his arrogance against this righteous servant (Ādam). This is the peak of arrogance against Allah because the prostration was only for Allah, as it was by His command. He only ordered them to prostrate to Ādam for the sake of ennobling and honouring him above them. So (although) he (Iblīs) was a monotheist, his monotheism did not benefit him.

With regards to honouring the righteous, Allah, the Exalted, said concerning Yūsuf ﷺ: ﴾He raised his parents upon the throne and they fell in prostration to him.﴿ (Yūsuf: 100) This was done out to salute, ennoble, honour, and glorify him above them. This prostration to the ground performed by his brothers is proven in the words of the Exalted: ﴾...fell...﴿ Perhaps it was permissible in their law, or it was similar to the prostration of the Angels towards Ādam ﷺ that his parents did for the sake of honouring, glorifying, and complying with the command of Allah, and as a fulfilment of Yūsuf's dream—as the dreams of the Prophets are revelation.

As for our Prophet Muḥammad ﷺ, Allah, the Exalted, said concerning him: ﴾Indeed we have sent you as a witness, a bringer of glad tidings and a warner, in order that you all may believe in Allah and His Messenger and glorify him and exalt him.﴿

(al-Fatḥ: 8–9) And He said: ❮O you who believe do not put yourselves forward above Allah and His Messenger.❯ (al-Ḥujurāt: 1) And: ❮O you who believe, do not raise your voices above the voice of the Prophet.❯ (al-Ḥujurāt: 2) And: ❮Do not make your calling out to the Messenger like your calling out to each other.❯ (al-Nūr: 23)

He (Allah) forbade putting oneself forward in front of him ﷺ with words and bad etiquette by preceding him in speech. Sahl b. 'Abdullāh said: "Do not speak before he speaks." This means that one should not speak before him, and when he speaks, one should listen attentively. They (the companions) were forbidden from being forward and rushing into a matter before he initiated it, or to deliver legal verdicts concerning fighting or other affairs of their religion save by his command, or to precede him in it. Then Allah admonished them and warned them against opposing this: ❮And fear Allah. Indeed Allah is All Hearer and All Seer.❯ (al-Ḥujurāt: 1) Al-Sulamī said: "Fear Allah lest you neglect his rights and abandon the proper observance of the sanctity due to him. Indeed, he hears your words and knows your actions."

Then He forbade them from raising their voices above him and being overly loud with speech as they speak with one another raising their voices. It has been said: "As some of them call out to one another using the first name." Abū Muḥammad al-Makkī said: "This means: do not precede him with speech or address him rashly and in an uncouth manner. Do not call out to him using his first name in the manner that you call out to each other, rather, glorify him, honour him, and call out to him using the noblest of titles that he loves to be called with such as: 'O Messenger of Allah' and 'O Prophet of Allah.' "

This is similar to the words of the Exalted: ❮Do not make your calling out to the Messenger like your calling out to each other.❯ (al-Nūr: 23) Others said: "Do not address him except as one who is seeking understanding." Then Allah, the Exalted, caused them to fear lest their deeds be invalidated by calling out to him like they did to each other, and then He warned them from Himself.

This verse was revealed concerning a group that came to the Prophet ﷺ and called out to him saying: "O Muḥammad, come out to us."

Allah, the Exalted, reproached them for (their ignorance) and described them by saying that most of them do not understand.

'Amr b. al-'Āṣ said: "There was no one who was more beloved to me than the Messenger of Allah and no one nobler in my eye than him. I was not able to fill my eyes with him out of esteem for him. If I were asked to describe him I would not be able to do so as I never filled my eyes with him."[5]

Al-Tirmidhī narrated from Anas that the Messenger of Allah used to go out to his companions among the Muhājirūn and the Anṣār while they were sitting down, and among them were Abū Bakr and 'Umar. No one among them would raise their eyes to look at him save Abū Bakr and 'Umar. They would both look at him and he would look at them, and they would smile at him and he would smile at them." Usāma b. Shurayk said: "I came to the Prophet while his companions were around him and it was as if birds were sitting on their heads." (And in his description he said): "...And if he would speak, they would lean their heads forward as if there were birds on their heads."

'Urwa b. Mas'ūd was directed by the Quraysh to go to the Messenger of Allah in the year of the conflict and he saw how the companions used to glorify and honour him, and how, when he would perform the ablutions, they would race to him and fight for the traces of the water used, and how he would not spit or expel phlegm except that they would take it with the palms of their hands and wipe their faces and bodies with it.

He saw that when a hair of his would fall, that they would rush to take it, and that when he commanded them with something, they would immediately comply, and that if he spoke they would lower their voices in front of him, and they would not look directly at him out of glorification of him. So when he saw all of that and returned to the Quraysh, he said: "O assembly of the Quraysh! Indeed I have visited the kingdom of Chosroes, the kingdom of Caesar, and the kingdom of the Negus, and by Allah, I have not seen a king among his people like Muḥammad and his companions."

---

[5] Narrated by Muslim in *Kitāb al-Īmān*.

In another narration it states: "I have never seen a king who has been glorified in the manner that the companions of Muḥammad glorify him. I have seen a people that will never surrender."

Both al-Ṭabarānī and Ibn Ḥibbān narrated from Usāma b. Shurayk ﷺ that he said: "We were once sitting with the Messenger of Allah ﷺ as if birds were upon our heads. No one from among us would speak. When the people would come to him and ask: 'Who are the most beloved of the servants of Allah to Allah?' He replied: 'The best of them in character.' "[6]

Abū Ya'lā narrated in his *Ṣaḥīḥ* from al-Barā' b. al-'Āzib ﷺ who said: "I used to desire to ask the Messenger of Allah ﷺ a question about a matter, but would delay asking him for two years out of *hayba* (awe) toward him."

Al-Bayhaqī narrated from al-Zuhrī who said: "I have been informed by one whom I do not accuse among the Anṣār, that when the Messenger of Allah ﷺ would perform ablution or expel phlegm, they would rush to take his phlegm and wipe their faces and skins with it, so the Messenger of Allah ﷺ would ask: 'Why are you all doing this?' They would reply: 'Seeking blessings from it.' So the Messenger of Allah ﷺ would say: 'Whoever loves that Allah and His Messenger should love him, then let him speak the truth, fulfil the trusts, and not harm his neighbour.' "[7]

Having presented all of this, there are two mighty matters here that must be noticed. The first of them is the obligation of glorifying the Prophet ﷺ and elevating his rank above that of the rest of creation. The second matter is singling out Allah's lordship and believing that He, the Blessed and Exalted, is unique in His Essence, attributes, and actions from all of His creation. Whoever believes that something of the creation shares with the Creator ﷻ in anything of this, then he has associated a partner (with Allah), like the idolaters who believed in the lordship of the idols and that they deserved worship. Whoever depreciates the Messenger's rank ﷺ, then he has either disobeyed or disbelieved.

---

[6] Also narrated in *al-Targhīb* (4:187) and he said: "Narrated by al-Ṭabarānī with men who are used in the *Ṣaḥīḥ* collection."
[7] *Kanz al-'Ummāl*, 8:228.

As for the one who intensely glorifies him ﷺ with various types of glorification, yet does not describe him with anything from the attributes of the Creator ﷻ, then he has arrived at the truth and safeguarded the rights of both lordship and the message together. This is the view that contains neither extremism nor negligence.

If there is found in the speech of any of the believers, that which indicates the ascription of anything to other than Allah, the Exalted, it is obligatory to carry it upon a figurative meaning and there is no way to impute disbelief upon them, for this type of figurative speech is used in the Book and the Sunna.

THE INTERMEDIARY OF *SHIRK*

Many people err in their understanding of the reality of intermediaries, and recklessly rush to the judgement that any intermediary is *shirk*, and that he who takes an intermediary, whatever the fashion, has associated partners with Allah, and that his state in this affair is that of the pagans, who said ﴾We do not worship them except that they might bring us near to Allah﴿ (al-Zumar: 3)

This statement is rejected, and the attempt to use this verse as evidence here is misplaced. This is because the noble verse is explicit in its censure of the pagans for their worship of idols and taking them as gods besides Allah, the Exalted, and their association of them with Him in His Godhood, claiming that their worship of these idols is nothing more than a means of drawing nearer to Allah. The disbelief and paganism of their action stems from both their worship of these idols, and their belief that they are lords besides Allah. Something of great importance which must be explained here is that this verse confirms that the pagans were not sincere in their justification for their worship of idols by claiming that they used them to draw closer to Allah. For had they been truthful in this, Allah would have been greater to them than their idols, and they would not have worshipped other than Him.

Allah forbade the Muslims from insulting the idols of the pagans. He said: ﴾Do not curse those upon whom they call beside Allah, lest they wrongfully curse and revile Allah through ignorance. Thus to every nation have we made their deeds seem fair. Then to their Lord is their return, when He will inform them of that which they used to do.❳ (al-An'am: 108)

It is narrated from 'Abd al-Razzāq, 'Abd b. Ḥamīd, Ibn Jarīr, Ibn al-Mundhir, Ibn Abī Ḥātim, and Abū al-Shaykh, from Qatāda ﷺ, who said: "The Muslims used to curse and revile the idols of the disbelievers, and so the disbelievers reviled and cursed Allah, the Mighty, the Magnificent. So Allah revealed ❲Do not curse those upon whom they call beside Allah, lest they wrongfully curse and revile Allah through ignorance.❳"

This is the reason for the revelation of this verse, which strongly forbids the believers from insulting the idols that the pagans used to worship in Mecca, because such insults would enrage those who believed in their hearts that those statues and idols were gods, with the ability to grant benefit and harm. This rage would drive them to meet the believers with similar insults against the One whom they worshipped, the Lord of the worlds, and so they would ascribe to Him defects, though He is far removed from all defects.

Again, if they were truly sincere in their claim that their idol worship was only a means of drawing nearer to Allah, they would not have dared insult Him to avenge their idols when they were insulted. It is explicitly clear from this that the pagans held Allah in far less esteem than they held their own idols. Similar can be said with regards to Allah's words: ❲And if you were to ask them who created the heavens and the earth, they would surely say "Allah!"❳ (al-'Ankabūt: 61)

If the pagans truly believed that Allah, the Exalted, is the only Creator, and that their idols had not created anything, they would have worshipped Allah instead of their idols, or at the very least, their reverence toward Allah would have been greater than their reverence toward their stones and statues. Is this consistent with their insults toward Allah, the Mighty, the Magnificent, out of jealousy for their own idols against Him? It is abundantly clear that it is not consistent in the least. Furthermore, the verse that we are considering is not the only proof that Allah was lower in the esteem of the pagans; rather, there are many similar examples. Among them is the statement of Allah the Exalted:

❮They assign to Allah a portion of the crops and cattle which He created, and they say "This is for Allah," in their imagination, "And this for (His) partners in regards to us." Thus, that which they apportion for His partners in them does not reach Allah, and that which they apportion to Allah goes to their partners. Evil is how they judge.❯ (al-An'am: 137)

If they did not hold Allah in lesser esteem than their idols they would not have judged in such a manner, which is mentioned in this verse, and which made them deserving the Judgement of Allah upon them: ❮Evil is how they judge.❯

Similar to this is the call of Abū Sufyān ﷺ, before he embraced Islam: "Exalted be Hubal!" as was related by al-Bukhārī. He was calling upon the idol named Hubal in order that he might, in that moment of difficulty, overwhelm the Lord of the heavens and the earth and His army of believers, who desired to overwhelm their idols. This is a clear measure of the state of the pagans, and how they viewed their idols in relation to Allah, the Lord of the worlds.

It is essential that this be understood with true comprehension, for many people build their arguments upon false premises related to this without any understanding.

Do you not see that when Allah ordered the Muslims to face the Ka'ba in their prayers, they turned toward it when they worshipped, and took it as a direction of prayer (*qibla*)? The worship was not directed to the Ka'ba, and neither was the kissing of the Black Stone anything other than the worship of Allah, the Exalted, and imitation of the Prophet ﷺ. Were any of the Muslims to intend to worship either of them, he would be a pagan, like those who worship idols.

Intermediaries are inescapable, and cannot be deemed as idolatry. It cannot be said that everyone who takes an intermediary between him and his Lord is a pagan; if it were otherwise, then every single human being would be a pagan, for all of our affairs require intermediaries. The Prophet ﷺ received the Qur'ān through the intermediation of Jibrīl, and so Jibrīl is the intermediary of the Prophet ﷺ, and he was the greatest intermediary to the companions—may Allah be pleased with all of them—for they would rush to him in times of crisis, complain of their needs to him, and seek his intercession and supplication.

In those times, the Prophet ﷺ, never said to them: "You have committed idolatry and disbelief! It is not permissible to complain to me, or to seek anything from me; rather, you must go and supplicate and ask Allah yourselves, for verily Allah is closer to you than I am!" On the contrary, he ﷺ would stand and supplicate for them, although they knew full well that the Bestower in reality is Allah, and that the Preventer, and the Expander, and the Provider is Allah alone, and they knew also that the Prophet ﷺ would not avail them anything save with the permission of Allah, and through His Bounty. The Prophet himself ﷺ said "I am nothing but an apportioner; Allah is the One who bestows."

Therefore, it becomes clear that it is permissible and correct to describe any ordinary person as one who "delivers from distress," and "satisfies needs," that is, he is an intermediary for them, so what of the noble Master and esteemed Prophet, the most illustrious of mankind and jinn, the undisputed Best of creation?

Did the Prophet ﷺ not say—as reported in the *Ṣaḥīḥ* collection of al-Bukhārī: "He who delivers a Muslim from distress, Allah delivers him from the distress on the Day of Resurrection"? So the Believer is a deliverer from distress and crisis. Did he not say ﷺ "He who fulfils the need of his brother, I will stand at his balance (on the Day of Judgement), and if (his good deeds) do not outweigh (his bad), I will intercede for him."? So the believer is a fulfiller of needs. Did he ﷺ not say in the *Ṣaḥīḥ* collection: "He who shelters a Muslim, Allah will shelter him on the Day of Resurrection"? Did he ﷺ not say "Verily, Allah has among His creation those who are sought for in times of need"? Did he not say in the *Ṣaḥīḥ* collection: "Allah shall aid His servant as long as the servant is in the aid of his brother"? And did he ﷺ not say: "He who comes to the aid of someone in need, Allah writes for him ninety-three good deeds"?[8]

So the believer relieves hardships, aids, protects, fulfils needs, and is sought out in times of trial - although in reality, it is Allah, Exalted and Magnificent, who aids, fulfils, and protects. However,

---

[8] Narrated by Abū Ya'lā, al-Bazzār, and al-Bayhaqī.

as the believer is the intermediary in all of this and it is valid and correct to ascribe actions to him.

Many Prophetic Ḥadīth have been related from the Messenger of Allah ﷺ which illustrate that Allah ﷻ repels punishment from the people on earth by means of those who seek His forgiveness and those who maintain His mosques, and that by their means, He provides the people of earth with sustenance and support and protects them from afflictions and drowning.

Al-Ṭabarānī related in *al-Mu'jam al-Kabīr*, and al-Bayhaqī in *al-Sunan* from Māni' al-Daylamī ؓ that the Messenger of Allah ﷺ said: "Were it not for the sake of the servants of Allah whom He makes bow to Him, infants whom He makes suckle, and cattle that He makes graze, He would unleash His punishment upon you all, and would destroy you utterly and completely."

Al-Bukhārī related from Sa'd b. Abī Waqqās ؓ that the Messenger of Allah ﷺ said: "Are you given victory and provision except by means of the weak ones among you?" Al-Tirmidhī related from Anas ؓ that the Messenger of Allah ﷺ said: "It may be that you are provided with sustenance by means of him." Al-Ḥākim declared this Ḥadīth to be rigorously authentic.

'Abdullāh b. 'Umar ؓ narrated that the Messenger of Allah ﷺ said: "Verily, Allah has men whom He created for the needs of the people, who rush to them in times of crisis. They are those who are safe from the punishment of Allah the Exalted."

Jābir b. 'Abdullāh ؓ narrated that the Messenger of Allah ﷺ said: "Truly, Allah confers righteousness upon a Muslim's child, his grandchild, and his family, and the families of his neighbours, by means of that Muslim's piety and righteousness, and they are in the protection of Allah as long as he is among them."

Ibn 'Umar ؓ said: "Verily Allah, by the means of a pious Muslim, protects one hundred of his neighbours from hardship and strife." Ibn 'Umar then recited the verse: ﴾And had Allah not repelled some people by means of others, the earth would have been corrupted.﴿ (al-Baqara: 251) Al-Ṭabarānī narrated from Thawbān ؓ a version of the aforementioned narration and ascribed it to the Prophet ﷺ with the addition: "There will remain among you seven men by whom you will be given victory, rain, and sustenance, until the Affair of Allah arrives (the Day of Judgement)."

'Ubāda b. al-Ṣāmit narrated that the Messenger of Allah ﷺ said "The *Abdāl* (chosen saints) of my community are thirty: by means of them you are all provided with sustenance, rain and victory." 'Ubāda said "I hope Ḥasan is one of them."

These four Ḥadīth cited above were mentioned by Ḥāfiẓ Ibn Kathīr in his explanation of the aforementioned Qur'ānic verse: ﴾And had Allah not repelled some people...﴿ and they are fitting to be used as evidence, and when taken all together, they all reach the level of being rigorously authentic.

Anas b. Mālik ﷺ narrated that the Messenger of Allah ﷺ said: "The earth will never be deprived of forty men of the like of the Intimate friend (Khalīl) of Allah; by means of them you are given water and succour. Each time one of them dies, Allah substitutes another in his place."

THE GREATEST INTERMEDIARY

On the Day of Resurrection, the Day of Divine oneness, the Day of faith, the Day in which the Throne will appear manifest, the benefit of the greatest intermediary will come to light: that of the possessor of the lofty station (*al-maqām al-maḥmūd*), he whose intercession is never rejected, and whose surety is never dispelled by He who promised never to disappoint him, debase him, dismay him, or grieve him on account of his community—when all of creation seek him out and plead for his intercession, and he stands before his Lord and does not return except with the height of nobility and honour revealed to us by the words of Allah to him: "O Muḥammad! Raise your head, and intercede, your intercession will be met; and ask, you shall be given!" May the prayers and peace of Allah be upon him, and upon his family, companions, and all those who follow them until the Day of Judgement.

A Garment of Falsehood

There are many false claimants to reality and many childish ones, while reality is free from them. The poet said:

All claim love for Laylā
but Laylā does not confirm them in that

In addition to this, they also give a bad image and reputation to Islam. The precise Prophetic description applies to them when he said: "The one who gains satiety by that which he has not been given, is like the one who wears a garment of falsehood."

We, the congregation of Muslims, have been afflicted with many of these types. They sully the purity of the Umma, cause splits between groups, and cause enmity to spread between brothers and between children and parents.

They enter the realm of correcting notions regarding Islam through the door of disrespect (*'uqūq*), and while attempting to hold fast to the reports of the Salaf, they traverse the path of denial. They replace wisdom, good exhortation, softness, and mercy with coarseness, harshness, bad manners, and lack of taste. From among these pretentious claimers are those who ascribe themselves to Sufism, even though they are the furthest of people from its essence and reality.

They have given a bad image to Sufism and sullied its honour, corrupted its track record, and brought harsh criticism to it and its Imāms among the noble Gnostics and spiritual trainers.

We do not know Sufism to be superstitions, falsehoods, trickery, and sleight of hand techniques. We do not know of Sufism to be philosophical theories, foreign ideas, and beliefs of idolatry, indwelling, or (Divine) union. We declare ourselves free in front of Allah from all of this, and consider everything that opposes the Book and the Sunna without an acceptable interpretation as false, foreign and held onto only by those of sinful hands and weak souls.

We believe Sufism to be a collection of knowledge-based schools, all of them, with their various methods, programs, and paths, representing the highest peak of Islamic thought and the most beautiful side of its manners and examples. It represents perfection in faith and perfection in every matter of life. It represents the pure summary of every Lordly invitation.

It is truthfulness, fulfilment of trusts, loyalty, preference to others over oneself, generosity, assistance of the weak, rescue of the distressed, assistance of one another in piety and righteousness, encouragement for one another upon truth and patience, and racing to perform acts of good that represent correct and upright character.

It is with this fragrant history and pure character that the bravery of the first generations, its Imāms and heroes manifested. It is by this that the Islamic personality became manifest in its most exalted condition, complete manner, and highest example. History has narrated to us the glory, pride, leadership, honour, struggle, resistance, and lessons of the Islamic civilization.

It is from all of this that we comprehend with certainty that the larger resistance is only built upon the messages of the soul and the inspirations of faith. It is not founded upon anything save high moral character that takes its source from pure beliefs. The moral, psychological, and spiritual character traits are the capital wealth of peoples and the biggest treasure stores that build nations and lead humankind to their highest potential. When one looks at the biographies of the righteous Salaf and the noble Gnostics among them, he sees how these examples and foundations were the direct cause and impetus for the clear acts of resistance that were witnessed and well known in the history of Islam. They did not have influence and power save through faith—the highest example of faith, in fact—a faith that is free, living, and focused on longing and love. It is the faith of the heart that releases the bright spark that seeks Allah, and shows how a man from them can constantly live in the station of *iḥsān* (spiritual perfection), seeing Allah in everything, watching Him and being vigilant with every movement and even in his breaths—all without there being any Divine indwelling, mixing with the creation, or atheism. It is faith that brings about constant awareness in life and adds deep awareness of the Lordly management of the universe - and awareness that dwells in the soul and knows the whisperings of the heart, the deception of the eye, and that which the breasts conceal.

Between a Good Innovation and a Bad Innovation

Among those pretentious claimants are those who ascribe themselves to the righteous Salaf. They call to the way of Salafiyya with rudeness, blind partisanship, withered intellects, sickly understandings, and constricted chests. They wage battle against every new thing and reject every beneficial thing that is invented, claiming that it is a blameworthy innovation and that every innovation is misguidance, without differentiating between the types of innovation, even though the Sacred Law of Islam obliges us to distinguish between them and say: from among them are blameworthy innovations as well as good innovations. This is what is necessitated by sound intellect and penetrating insight.

This is what has been thoroughly investigated by the scholars of the theoretical basis of jurisprudence among the Salaf of this Umma—may Allah be pleased with all of them—such as Imām al-'Izz b. 'Abd al-Salām, al-Nawawī, al-Suyūṭī, al-Maḥallī, and Ibn Ḥajar.

The Prophetic narrations (when taken all together) explain themselves and complete each other. It is a must that one looks at all of them at one time and sees to it that they are explained in light of the spirit of the Sacred Law and its understanding that is agreed upon among the people of investigation.

It is for this reason that we find that in order for many of the noble Ḥadīth to be explained, there is a need for the intellect of a capable person who possesses penetrating insight, appropriate understanding, and a heart with taste that is able to take from the sea of the noble Sacred Law and take the states and needs of the Umma into consideration and lead it, while remaining within the boundaries of the principles of Sacred Law and the Qur'ānic and Prophetic texts that must not be neglected.

An example of this is in the Ḥadīth: "Every innovation is misguidance." It must be said that the innovation here is the blameworthy one that does not have a basis in the Sacred Law. This particular restriction is to be found in another Ḥadīth that states: "There is no prayer for the one who lives next to the mosque except in the mosque." So even though this Ḥadīth seems to indicate generality in negating the prayer of the one who lives next to the mosque, the generalities of (all of) the Ḥadīth (on this topic) restrict this, and the conclusion is that it is not a complete prayer.

Another example is the Ḥadīth: "There is no prayer when food is presented." They (the scholars) said: "This means that the prayer is not complete." Also the Ḥadīth: "None of you truly believe until he loves for his brother what he loves for himself." They said: "This means complete *īmān* (faith)." And the Ḥadīth: "By Allah, he does not believe, By Allah, he does not believe, By Allah, he does not believe. It was said: 'Who, O Messenger of Allah?' He ﷺ said: 'The one whose neighbour does not feel safe from his evil.' " And the Ḥadīth: "The slanderer will not enter paradise," and: "The one who severs the ties of kinship will not enter Paradise," and: "The one who disrespects his parents." The scholars said: "This person will not enter among the foremost, or, he will not enter Paradise if he declares (such actions) to be permissible."

Thus, they did not take (these narrations) upon their apparent meaning; rather, they employed a type of interpretation. The Ḥadīth that concerns innovation is in this realm, for the generalities of the (other) Ḥadīth and conditions of the companions indicate that what is intended is in fact, the blameworthy innovation that does not fall under the jurisdiction of a comprehensive (legal) foundation. There is also the Ḥadīth: "Whoever initiates a good *sunna* will have the reward for it and the reward of those who act upon it until the Day of Judgement." And: "Stick to my Sunna, and the Sunna of my rightly guided Caliphs." 'Umar used to say concerning the *tarāwīḥ* prayers: "What a good innovation this is!" And to Allah belongs all success.

THE NECESSARY DISTINCTION BETWEEN INNOVATION FROM THE STANDPOINT OF SACRED LAW AND INNOVATION FROM THE STANDPOINT OF LANGUAGE

Some people censure the distinction between good innovation and blameworthy innovation and censure those who espouse it in the most severe manner. Nay, some of them accuse others (holding to this view) of corruption and misguidance because, according to them, this is in opposition to the explicit statement of the Messenger ﷺ who said: "Every innovation is misguidance." So this statement is explicit in its generality and explicit in describing every innovation as misguidance. From this starting point, you will hear such a person say: "So is it correct, after hearing the statement of the legislator and carrier of the message, that every innovation is misguidance—is it correct, for a *mujtahid* or jurist, no matter how high his rank, to come and say: 'No. Not every innovation is misguidance. Rather, some are misguidance, some are praiseworthy, and some are blameworthy?"

This is the entry point that deceives many people; they end up shouting among the shouters and censuring among the censurers and swelling the ranks of those who have not understood the goals of the Sacred Law or tasted the spirit of the Islamic religion. Only a short time will remain, before such a person is forced to come up with a way out to solve the problems that confront him and show him the reality that he is living in. He is forced to come up with another method, and if not for that, he would be unable to eat, drink, live, or even dress, breath, get married or interact with his self, family, brothers, or society. This method is for him to say in clear words: "Innovation is divided into religious innovation, and worldly innovation." How exalted Allah is from imperfections! This careless person has allowed for himself to invent this (new) categorization, or at the bare minimum, invent this term.

Even if we were to admit for arguments sake that this meaning was present since the time of prophecy, still, the term 'worldly' and 'religious' was clearly not present during the time of Prophetic legislation, so from where did he get this categorization and from where did this innovated term come? Whoever says: "The division of innovation into praiseworthy and blameworthy innovation was not brought by the Law Giver," we say in response: "Likewise, the division of innovation into that which is religious and unacceptable, and that which is worldly and acceptable is itself the peak of innovation and inventing!" The Lawgiver said: "Every innovation is misguidance" in a general way, whereas this person says: "No. Not every innovation is misguidance without restriction. Rather, innovation is divided into two categories: the religious innovation that is misguidance, and the worldly innovation that is harmless."

For this reason, we must clarify an important issue here, so that hopefully, it may remove some of the confusion, Allah willing. The speaker here is the Wise Legislator, therefore, His word is the law. Hence, it is a must that His words be understood according to the legal scales with which He came. So, if you know that innovation is everything that is invented and innovated without there being a precedent for it, it will not be hidden from you that the blameworthy inventions or additions are the additions to the religion that are added in order that they become a part of the religion and become part of the fabric of the Sacred Law that is followed and ascribed to the possessor of the Sacred Law. This is what our Master, the Messenger of Allah ﷺ warned us from when he said: "Whoever innovates in this affair of ours that which is not from it, it is rejected." Having said this, the clear dividing line in this matter is his saying ﷺ: "...in this affair of ours..." Based upon this, our division of innovation into that which is praiseworthy and that which is blameworthy—in our understanding, is nothing more than the linguistic innovation that is merely inventing and bringing something about. None of us doubt that the innovation defined in Sacred Law is anything other than misguidance and tribulation that is blameworthy, rejected, and hated. If only those who censure (others) would understand this meaning, it would become clear to them that in reality, the area of agreement is close and the area of dispute is far.

In order to make this more discernable to the minds, let me state that it is my view that those who censure this division only censure the division of innovation as defined in the Sacred Law; the proof for this being that they divide innovation into religious and worldly innovation and consider that a necessity. Those who hold to the view (that innovation) is divided into that which is praiseworthy and blameworthy see that this is only with regard to the linguistic innovation because they say: "Adding and increasing upon the religion and the Sacred Law is misguidance and an enormous sin." There is no doubt with them concerning this, therefore, the difference is only semantical.

Having said this, I would like to say, however, that those among our brothers who deny the division of innovation into that which is praiseworthy and blameworthy, and rather say it is divided into that which is religious and worldly—they were not fortunate in being precise in their expression. This is because once they ruled that the religious innovation is misguidance—which is true—and then ruled that the worldly innovation is neutral, they were wrong in their ruling because by this, they judged that every worldly innovation is permissible. This is a very dangerous matter that can bring about tribulations and problems. Hence, it is necessary and obligatory that there be some detail to this issue. They should instead say: "From the worldly innovation, there are matters that are good, and matters that are bad." This is something that is witnessed by all currently and none deny it save a blind ignorant person. This addition must be mentioned.

A sufficient actualization of this meaning is found in the precise statement of the one who says; "Innovation is divided into that which is praiseworthy and blameworthy." It is known that this is referring to the linguistic innovation, which those who deny this refer to as worldly (innovation). This statement is at the peak of precision and scrupulousness and calls for every new matter to be categorized according to proper guidelines and submission to the rule of Sacred Law and the maxims of the religion. This forces the Muslims to present every new and invented matter in both their public and private worldly lives in front of the Sacred Law of Islam in order to see the ruling of Islam in it no matter what that innovation is. This cannot be properly actualized without this great division that is given proper consideration among the scholars of the theoretical basis of jurisprudence (*uṣūl al-fiqh*). So, may Allah be pleased with the Imāms of *uṣūl* and their delineation of the correct expressions that lead to correct meanings without deficiency, alteration, or false interpretation.

The Call of the Imāms of Sufism to Acting in Accordance with the Sacred Law

Sufism is wronged and unjustly accused. How few are those who are fair with it. Nay, the audaciousness and coarseness of some have reached the point where they have made it an insulting and blameworthy term that can invalidate someone's testimony and undermine his uprightness. So he says: "So and so is unreliable and his reports are not accepted." Why? Well he is a Sufi.

What is strange and amazing is that we see some of those who condemn Sufism, wage war against its people, and behave with animosity towards them, say what they say, and do what they do, all the while having no shame in quoting in their speeches and talks on the pulpits of the Friday prayer and teaching chairs, the words of the Imāms of the Sufis. So one of them says with all audacity: "Al-Fuḍayl b. 'Iyāḍ said..., Junayd said..., Ḥasan al-Baṣrī said..., Sahl al-Tustarī said..., al-Muḥāsibī said..., and Bishr al-Ḥāfī said..." These are the Imāms of Sufism, their poles, pillars, foundations and structures. The books of Sufism are crammed pack with their statements, spiritual states, and traits. So, I do not know, is it mere ignorance (on their part) or is it feigning ignorance? Is it blindness or pretending to be blind?

It is my wish to quote the words of the Imāms of the religion who are the pillars of Sufism and its men. It is my desire to quote their words regarding the Islamic Sacred Law in order for us to know their real stance, because it is a must that we know a person from his own words, as he is the best one suited to speak about his own view and more trustworthy in making manifest what he possesses inside. Imām al-Junayd said: "The path is cut off from the creation, save the one who carefully follows the reports of the Messenger of Allah, follows his Sunna, and sticks to his path. This is because the paths of goodness are all open to him and those who follow him and his reports."

It was reported that Abū Yazīd al-Bisṭāmī (may Allah sanctify his secret) said one day to his companions: "Let us go to look for the one who is well known for his sainthood." The narrator said: "So we went and we saw a man who was entering the mosque and spit in the direction of the *qibla*, so Abū Yazīd left and did not greet him. He said: 'This one is not truthful enough with one piece of etiquette from the etiquette of the Messenger of Allah ﷺ, so how can he be truthful with what he claims regarding the stations of the saints and the righteous?' "

Dhū al-Nūn al-Miṣrī once said: "Speech revolves around four things: loving that which is great, hating that which is paltry, following the revelation, and fearing a change of heart. From the signs of love for Allah is following the beloved (the Prophet ﷺ) in his manners, actions, commands, and Sunna."

Al-Sarī al-Saqaṭī said: "Sufism is a word that has three meanings: the one whose light of gnosis does not extinguish his light of scrupulousness, the one who does not speak of the inner secrets of a knowledge that is contradicted by the apparent texts of the Book and the Sunna, and the one whose miracles do not cause him to uncover the veils of what Allah has forbidden."

Abū Naṣr Bishr b. al-Ḥārith al-Ḥāfī said: "I saw the Prophet ﷺ in a dream and he said to me: 'O Bishr, do you know why Allah elevated you among your peers? I said: 'No, O Messenger of Allah.' He said: 'It is because of you following my Sunna and your service to the righteous, your good advice to your brothers, and your love for my companions and my household. That is what caused you to attain the rank of the pious.' "

Abū Yazīd b. Ṭayfūr b. 'Īsā al-Bistāmī said: "I once wished to ask Allah to suffice me from the need to eat and the need for women, but I then said: 'How can it be allowed for me to ask Allah for this, while the Messenger of Allah ﷺ never asked Him for it', so I did not ask Him. Then, Allah sufficed me from needing women to the point where I did not care if it was a women or a wall facing me." He also said: "If you see a man given such miracles that he can even fly in the air, do not be fooled by him until you see how he is with regard to the commands and prohibitions, guarding the boundaries (of Allah), and in compliance with the Sacred Law."

Sulaymān b. 'Abd al-Raḥmān b. 'Aṭiyya al-Dārānī said: "Perhaps a part of the knowledge of the folk (the Sufis) enters my heart for some days, but I do not accept it save with the two upright witnesses: the Book and the Sunna"

Abū al-Ḥasan Aḥmad b. Abū al-Ḥawārī said: "Whoever does an action without following the Sunna of the Messenger of Allah ﷺ, then it is false."

Abū Ḥafṣ 'Umar b. Salama al-Ḥaddād said: "Whoever does not weigh his actions at every moment with the Book and the Sunna, and does not accuse his innermost thoughts, then he is not counted in the register of real men."

Abū al-Qāsim Junayd b. Muḥammad said: "Whoever has neither memorized the Qur'ān nor written Ḥadīth, he is not to be followed in this affair, because our knowledge is confined by the Book and the Sunna." He also said: "Our way is confined to the foundations of the Book and the Sunna and this knowledge of ours is guided by the Ḥadīth of the Messenger of Allah."

When Abū 'Uthmān Sa'īd b. Ismā'īl al-Ḥīrī was near death, his son Abū Bakr tore his own garment and Abū 'Uthmān opened his eyes and said: "O my son! The Sunna in the outward is a sign of perfection in the inward." He also said: "Taking company with Allah is with good manners and constant aspirations; taking company with the Messenger of Allah ﷺ is with following his Sunna and sticking to the outward knowledge; taking company with the friends of Allah, the Exalted, is by respect and service; taking company with one's family is by good manners; taking company with the brethren is by constant smiling as long as there is no sin; and taking company with the ignorant is by supplication and mercy."

He also said: "Whoever orders the Sunna upon himself in both statement and action will speak with wisdom, and whoever orders vain desire upon himself in both statement and action will speak with innovation. The Exalted said: ﴾If you obey him you will be guided.﴿ (al-Nūr: 54)

Abū al-Ḥasan Aḥmad b. Muḥammad al-Nūrī said: "Whomever you see claiming to have a spiritual state with Allah that removes him from the limits of legal knowledge, do not come close to him."

Abū al-Fawāris Shāh b. Shujā' al-Kirmānī said: "Whoever lowers his gaze from that which is forbidden, holds himself back from vain desires, fills his inner self with constant vigilance and his outer self with following the Sunna, and accustoms himself to consuming the permissible, he will never have his inner insight fail him."

Abū al-'Abbās Aḥmad b. Muḥammad b. Sahl b. 'Aṭā' al-Ādamī said: "Whoever forces himself to hold fast to the manners of the

Sacred Law, Allah will enlighten his heart with the light of gnosis and by it, he will be given the station of following the beloved one (the Prophet ﷺ) in his commands, actions and manners." He also said: "Whatever you ask about, seek it out in the realm of knowledge. Then, if you do not find it there, look in the field of wisdom. If you still do not find it, weigh it with the scale of Divine oneness. If you do not find it in these three places, throw it back in the face of Satan."

Abū Ḥamza al-Baghdādī al-Bazzāz said: "Whoever knows the path of the Real (Allah), the Exalted, traversing it will be easy. There is no guide upon the path to Allah, the Exalted, except by following the Sunna of the Messenger ﷺ in his states, actions, and statements."

Abū Isḥāq Ibrāhīm b. Dāwūd al-Raqī said: "From the signs of loving Allah are: preferring His obedience and following His Prophet ﷺ." Mimshād al-Daynūrī said: "The manners of the disciple consist in looking after the sanctity of the Shaykhs, serving to the brethren, leaving off (relying on) the means, and guarding the manners of the Sacred Law in himself."[9]

Abū Muḥammad 'Abdullāh b. Manāzil said: "No one leaves off an obligation from the obligations except that Allah afflicts him with abandonment of the *sunnas*. No one is careless in abandoning the *sunnas* except that it is soon to be that he is tried with innovation."

The Ash'arīs

Many sons of the Muslims are ignorant of the Ash'arī school, whom it represents, and its positions on doctrinal matters. Some of them are not God-fearing enough to refrain from accusing it of deviance, departure from the fold of Islam, and heresy regarding

---

[9] Having said this, the virtuous 'Allāma, Shaykh 'Abd al-Ḥafīẓ al-Makkī, wrote a beneficial essay called: "The Stance of the Imāms of the Salafī Movement Regarding Sufism and Sufis." He gathered the statements and opinions of Imām Aḥmad b. Ḥanbal, Shaykh Ibn Taymiyya, Ibn al-Qayyim, al-Dhahabī, Ibn Kathīr, Ibn Rajab, and Muḥammad b. 'Abd al-Wahhāb and their positions in support of Sufism and their compliments and praise of the noble Shaykhs of the Sufis.

the attributes of Allah. This ignorance of the Ash'arī school is a cause of shredding the unity of the Ahl al-Sunna and dispersing its ranks. Some have gone as far as to consider the Ash'arīs among the misguided and heretical sects, although I know not how the people of faith be linked with the people of misguidance, or how Ahl al-Sunna can be considered equal with the most extreme factions of the Mu'tazila and Jahmiyya (sects). ﴾Shall We deal with Muslims as We do criminals? How is it that you judge?﴿ (al-Qalam: 35–36)

The Ash'arīs are the Imāms of the notable figures of guidance among the scholars of the Muslims, whose knowledge has filled the world from both east to west, and whom people have unanimously agreed regarding their excellence, scholarship, and piety. They include the first rank of scholars from Ahl al-Sunna and the most brilliant of their luminaries, who confronted the excesses committed by the Mu'tazila. Shaykh al-Islam Ibn Taymiyya said regarding them: "The scholars are the helpers of the religious sciences, and the Ash'arīs are the helpers of the fundamentals of the religion."[10] They include whole sections of the foremost Imāms of Ḥadīth, Sacred Law, and Qur'ānic exegesis. Shaykh al-Islam Aḥmad b. Ḥajar al-'Asqalānī, the mentor of the scholars of Ḥadīth and author of the book *Fatḥ al-Bārī fī Sharḥ Ṣaḥīḥ al-Bukhārī*, which not a single scholar can dispense with, was an Ash'arī. The Shaykh of the scholars of Ahl al-Sunna, Imām al-Nawawī, author of *Sharḥ Ṣaḥīḥ Muslim* and many other famous works, was an Ash'arī. The master of Qur'ānic exegetes, Imām al-Qurṭubī, author of *al-Jāmi' li-Ahkām al-Qur'ān* was an Ash'arī. Shaykh al-Islam Ibn Ḥajar al-Haytamī, who wrote *al-Zawājir 'an Iqtirāf al-Kabā'ir* was an Ash'arī. The Shaykh of Sacred Law and Ḥadīth, the reliable proof, Zakariyyā al-Anṣārī, was an Ash'arī. Imām Abū Bakr al-Bāqillānī, Imām al-'Asqalānī, Imām Nasafī, Imām al-Shirbīnī, Abū Ḥayyān al-Tawḥīdī, author of the Qur'ānic commentary: *al-Bahr al-Muhīt*, Imām Ibn Juzayy, author of *al-Tashīl fī 'Ulūm al-Tanzīl* and others—all of these were Imāms of the Ash'arīs.

---

[10] *Al-Fatāwā*, vol.4.

If we wanted to name all of the top scholars of Ḥadīth, Qur'ānic exegesis, and Sacred Law who were Imāms of the Ash'arīs, we would be hard pressed to do so and it would require volumes to merely list these virtuous figures whose knowledge has filled the earth from east to west. It is obligatory upon us to give credit where credit is due and recognize the merit of those of knowledge and virtue who have served the Sacred Law of the greatest Messenger ﷺ. What good is to be hoped for us if we level our foremost scholars and righteous predecessors with charges of deviance and misguidance?

How should Allah give us the benefit of their scholarship if we believe it is deviance and departure from the way of Islam? I ask you, is there a single Islamic scholar of the present day, among all the PhDs and geniuses, who has done what Ibn Ḥajar al-'Asqalānī or Imām al-Nawawī have done in service to the pure Prophetic Sunna? How can we dare charge them and all Ash'arīs with deviance when it is we who are in need of their scholarship? How can we take knowledge from them if they were in error? For as Imām al-Zuhrī said, "This knowledge is religion, so look well to see from whom you are taking your religion."

Is it not sufficient for someone opposed to the Ash'arīs to say, "May Allah have mercy upon them, they used their best efforts (*ijtihād*) in figuratively interpreting the Divine attributes, which it would have been fitter for them not to do," instead of accusing them of deviance and misguidance, or showing anger towards whoever considers them to be from Ahl al-Sunna? If Imāms al-Nawawī, al-'Asqalānī, al-Qurṭubī, al-Bāqillānī, Fakhr al-Dīn al-Rāzī, al-Haytamī, Zakariyyā al-Anṣārī, and many others were not among the most brilliant scholars and illustrious geniuses, or from Ahl al-Sunna, then who are Ahl al-Sunna?

I sincerely invite all who call others to this religion or who work in the field of invitation Islam to fear Allah regarding the honour of the community of Muḥammad ﷺ—especially with respect to its noble scholars and most choice jurists. The Umma of Muḥammad ﷺ is possessed of goodness until the Final Hour, and we shall be bereft of any good if we fail to acknowledge the worth and excellence of our learned.

There are many matters that are subjects of research among the scholars in the area of doctrine—things that Allah, the Exalted, has not ordered us with. I am of the opinion that research into these matters removes the grandeur and splendour of these realities. Examples of this include the difference of opinion over the issue of the Prophet ﷺ seeing Allah, the Exalted, and how this was. The differences between the scholars in this issue are long and wide. Some among them say that he saw Him with his heart, and some say that he saw Him with his eyes. Every scholar brings his evidence and gives strength to it to no end. I am of the opinion that all of this is a waste that contains no benefit. Rather, its harm is greater than its benefit, especially if the common folk hear of this, for without doubt, it will enter doubt into their hearts. If only we were to have left off research in these matters and been sufficed with relating these facts as they appear (in the texts), they would have remained honoured, and glorified in the souls, and we would have merely said: He saw his Lord; stopping at that and leaving off the remaining (discussions).

Allah Spoke Directly to Mūsā ﷺ

An example (of this kind of research) is that which takes place among the scholars in their research concerning the reality of Allah's speech and the major difference that revolves around this. Some say that the speech of Allah is inner speech (*kalām nafsī*), and some say that His speech is with both letter and sound. I am of the belief that both of these opposing groups seek the reality of Divine transcendence for Allah and that both are far from idolatry in all of its forms. The issue of speech is real and affirmed and there is no room to deny it, for denial of it contradicts Divine perfection—this is from one angle. From another angle, belief in His attributes and affirmation of that which appears in the Qur'ān is obligatory, for no one knows Allah, but Allah. The view that I hold and call to is that of affirming (the speech of Allah) without going into the details of the "howness" and quiddity. So, we affirm speech for Allah and say that this is the speech of Allah and that He speaks. Beyond that, we give no glance to the falsehood of it being inner speech or not, or whether it is with sounds and letters or not. All of this is extremism that was not articulated by the Chosen One who brought *tawḥīd* ﷺ, so why should we make this addition to what he came with? Is this not the ugliest of innovations. Glory be to You (Allah), this is but a manifest slander! Indeed, the Prophet ﷺ shall speak to us on the day that we shall gather with him in front of Allah. We are calling for our discussions to always be about this reality and its likes, being far removed from delving into its quiddity, image, and appearance.

I See You from Behind Me

Another example of this kind of research that takes place among the scholars is the research concerning the reality of his ﷺ statement: "Indeed I see you from behind me just as I see you from the front of me." Some scholars say: "Allah, the Exalted, gave two eyes to the Prophet ﷺ in the back of his head." Some say: "Allah gave the two eyes in the front of his head the power to see from behind." Some say: "Allah reversed that which is behind him and placed its image in front of him." All of this is extremism that removes the beauty and splendidness of (this Ḥadīth) and diminishes esteem for it from the hearts. As far as him seeing from behind just as he sees from in front, this is an established reality that he himself ﷺ informed us of in authentic reports, so there is no room for denial of it. What we call to and believe in is that this report is to be reported as it has come without entering into its quiddity and appearance. It is obligatory to believe that it is possible. The fruit of this is that we witness a miracle from his miracles that defy the (understanding) of the common means and as such, it manifests the power of the Unique One, the Overpowering (Allah) and it demonstrates the virtue of the chosen Prophet ﷺ.

Jibrīl ﷺ Takes the Form of a Man

Another example of this is the difference among the scholars regarding the manner that Jibrīl ﷺ took when he came in the form of a man when bringing the Divine revelation. Some have said that Allah caused the remaining parts of him to disappear. Some said that he folded some of himself into the rest of himself until he became small. I am of the view that all of this is a waste of time and that research into this is tiresome and without benefit. We believe that Allah is able to do that and that this occurs and is witnessed. Many people have seen the companions in that manner and image, and the method by which the Angel's image is changed into a man does not concern us. We entreat our brothers among the students of knowledge to mention this fact without delving into the other differences beyond it. This must be done in order for this report to remain glorified and noble in the souls.

THE UNDERSTANDING OF *TAWASSUL*

Many people err in their understanding of the reality of *tawassul*.[11] For this reason, we shall clarify the correct understanding of *tawassul* in our view. Before that however, we must explain some realities:

One: *Tawassul* is one of the methods of supplication and it is a door among the doors of turning to Allah. The real and primary intent behind such supplication is Allah. The one through whom *tawassul* is performed is only an intermediary and means of drawing closer to Allah. Whoever believes otherwise has fallen into idolatry.

Two: The one who performs *tawassul* does not perform it with a certain intermediary except due to his love for him and his belief that Allah loves him. If the opposite was shown to be true, then this person would be from the furthest of people from it and have the most disdain for it.

Three: If the one performing *tawassul* believes that the one through whom he makes *tawassul* unto Allah actually brings harm and benefit by himself, independently as Allah does or even less than Allah, then he has fallen into idolatry.

Four: *Tawassul* is not an obligation or a necessary matter, neither is the response to the supplication conditional upon it. Rather, the basis for supplication is to call upon Allah the Exalted, as Allah said:

---

[11] *Tawassul*: to supplicate to Allah through an intermediary, such as saying: "O Allah! I ask you by the rank of Your Prophet..."

﴾And if my servants ask you concerning me, then say that I am close.﴿ (al-Baqara: 186) and: ﴾Say, "Call upon Allah or call upon al-Raḥmān. Whatever you call him by—to Him belong the best names."﴿

WHAT IS AGREED UPON CONCERNING *TAWASSUL*

No one among the Muslims differs regarding the legality of *tawassul* unto Allah with righteous actions. So, whoever fasts, prays, reads the Qur'ān, or gives charity, he can perform *tawassul* with his fasting, praying, Qur'ānic recitation, and charity. Indeed it is more apt to be accepted and it is greater in obtaining what is sought. No two differ regarding this. The proof for this is the Ḥadīth of the three who were trapped in the cave. One of them performed *tawassul* to Allah through his kindness to his parents. The second one performed *tawassul* to Allah based on him having removing himself from illegal sexual intercourse even though he had been given the ability to do it. The third one performed *tawassul* to Allah based on his fulfilling the trust and guarding someone else's wealth and giving it back. Allah removed them from their predicament. This type of *tawassul* has been clarified with its evidence and issues by Shaykh Ibn Taymiyya—may Allah have mercy upon him—in his books, especially his work 'A Noble Principle Concerning *Tawassul* and Means.'

The Point of Difference

The area where people differ in the issue of *tawassul* is *tawassul* with other than the deed of the one performing it, such as *tawassul* through things and people by saying: "O Allah! I seek a means to you by way of Your Prophet Muḥammad ﷺ", or "I seek a means to you by way of Abū Bakr al-Ṣiddīq, 'Umar b. al-Khattāb, 'Uthmān, or 'Alī." This type of *tawassul* is forbidden according to some people.

We are of the view that the difference here is one of form and not one of substance. This is because, in reality, *tawassul* through a person goes back to performing *tawassul* based on his actions, the permissibility of which is agreed upon. If the one who prohibits it was only to look into the issue with insight, the matter would become clear to him and the tribulation that has befallen some, leading them to judge the Muslims with idolatry and misguidance, would cease.

I shall clarify how the one who performs *tawassul* by someone else is really performing *tawassul* through his actions that are ascribed to him and are from his own acquisition.

I say: Know, that the one performs *tawassul* through a particular person, does so because he loves him and believes that he is pious and possesses closeness (to Allah) and virtue and has a good opinion of him—or because he believes that Allah loves him as Allah said: ﴾He loves them and they love Him.﴿, or he believed all of these things with regards to the one by whom *tawassul* is performed.

If you contemplate this matter, you will find that this love and this belief are from the actions of the one performing *tawassul* because it is his belief that is firm in his heart. It is ascribed to him and he is the one asked about it and rewarded for it. It is as if he is saying: "O Lord! Indeed I love so and so and I believe that he loves you, that he is sincere to You and that he strives in your path. I believe that You love him and are pleased with him; so I use him as a means to you by my love for him and my belief in him that he does such-and-such." This is the case, although most of those who perform *tawassul* do not explicitly express it as such, sufficing themselves with the knowledge of the One from whom nothing is concealed in this world or in the heavens; He knows the deception of the eyes and that which the breasts conceal.

He who says: "O Allah, I seeks a means to You by Your Prophet ﷺ," and the one who says: "O Allah, I seeks a means to you by my love for Your Prophet ﷺ" are both the same. This is because the first one only said what he did due to his love and faith in his Prophet ﷺ and if not for this faith and love, he would not have performed *tawassul* through him. This is also said regarding the other friends (of Allah) in the Umma.

With this, it becomes clear that in reality, the difference is in form and does not necessitate all of this division, enmity, and charges of disbelief on those who perform *tawassul*; removing them from the fold of Islam. ﴾Glory be to you O Lord, this is a manifest slander!﴿

THE EVIDENCE FOR THE *TAWASSUL* PERFORMED BY THE MUSLIMS

Allah, the Exalted, said: ﴾O you who believe, fear Allah and seek a means of approach to Him.﴿ (al-Mā'ida: 35). The means are everything that Allah made as a means to draw one closer to Him and bring him to that which will fulfil his needs. This revolves around the fact that the "means" possess rank and sanctity with the one to whom *tawassul* is performed. The expression "means," used in this verse, is general as you see and it includes *tawassul* through virtuous people from the Prophets and righteous in both life and death and bringing actions that are commanded with, and performing *tawassul* by means of them after they are done.

You shall now see some Ḥadīth and narrations that clarify this generality. So listen attentively while witnessing so you may see that *tawassul* through him ﷺ is established before his existence, after his existence in the world and after his death in the Isthmus life and after the resurrection on the plains of the Day of Judgement.

TAWASSUL THROUGH THE PROPHET ﷺ BEFORE HIS EXISTENCE

There is a Ḥadīth stating that Ādam ﷺ performed *tawassul* through the Prophet ﷺ. Al-Ḥākim said in his *al-Mustadrak* on the authority of 'Umar: "When Ādam committed his mistake he said: 'O my Lord! I am asking you to forgive me by the right of Muḥammad.' Allah said: 'O Ādam! How do you know about Muḥammad whom I have not yet created?' Ādam replied, 'O my Lord! After You created me with Your Hand and breathed into me of Your Spirit, I raised my head and saw written on the heights of the Throne: *Lā Ilāha Illā Allāh Muḥammad Rasūl Allāh*. I understood that You would not place next to Your Name any but the Most Beloved one of Your creation.' Allah said: 'O Ādam! I have forgiven you, and were it not for Muḥammad, I would not have created you.' "

This was reported by al-Ḥākim in his *al-Mustadrak* who authenticated it,[12] Ḥāfiẓ al-Suyūṭī in his *Khaṣā'iṣ* who authenticated it, and al-Bayhaqī in *Dalā'il al-Nubuwwa*—who did not narrate fabricated reports as he mentioned in his introduction. It was also authenticated by al-Qasṭalānī, and al-Zurqānī in his *al-Mawāhib al-Laduniyya*, and al-Subkī in *Shifā' al-Siqām*. Ḥāfiẓ al-Haythamī said: "It was narrated by al-Ṭabarānī in *al-Awsaṭ* and it contains one whom I do not know."[13]

There is another route of transmission from Ibn 'Abbās with the expression: "If it were not for Muḥammad, I would not have created Ādam or the Paradise or the Fire." This was narrated by al-Ḥākim in *al-Mustadrak* and he said: "Its chain is rigorously authentic. It was also authenticated by Shaykh al-Islam al-Bulqīnī in his *Fatāwā* and was also narrated by Ibn al-Jawzī in *al-Wafā'* in the beginning of his book, and was quoted by Ibn Kathīr in *al-Bidāya*.[14]

Some of the scholars have opposed this, and spoke negatively about the strength of the Ḥadīth. It was rejected and declared a fabrication by the likes of Imām al-Dhahabī and others. Some (scholars) declared it weak, while others declared it rejected (*munkar*). With this, we see that they did not concur upon one ruling concerning it. So based on this the issue revolves around research between acceptance, rejection, affirmation, negation, and taking no position based on their difference regarding the strength of the Ḥadīth. This is with respect to the chain of narration and establishment of the authenticity of the Ḥadīth. With respect to the meaning, then we shall leave it to Shaykh al-Islam Ibn Taymiyya to speak on it.

OTHER SUPPORTING ḤADĪTH FOR THE ḤADĪTH OF THE *TAWASSUL* OF ĀDAM ﷺ

Ibn Taymiyya narrated two Ḥadīth on this subject and brought them in order to use as examples. He said: Abū al-Faraj b. al-Jawzī

---

[12] 2:615.

[13] *Majma' al-Zawa'id*, 8:253.

[14] 1:180.

narrated with his chain up to Maysara who said: "I said: 'O Messenger of Allah! When were you (first) a Prophet?' He replied: 'When Allah created the earth: ﴾Then He turned to the heaven, and fashioned it as seven heavens﴿ (al-Baqara: 29), and created the Throne. He wrote on the leg of the Throne: "Muḥammad the Messenger of Allah is the Seal of Prophets," then Allah created the Garden in which He made Ādam and Ḥawwā dwell, and He wrote my name on its gates, its tree-leaves, its domes and its tents, at a time when Ādam was still between spirit and body. When Allah, the Exalted, breathed life into him he looked at the Throne and saw my name, whereupon Allah informed him that "He is the Master of all your descendants." When Satan deceived them both, they repented and sought intercession to Allah with my name.' "

Abū Nu'aym narrated in the book *Dalā'il al-Nubuwwa* by way of Shaykh Abū al-Faraj to 'Umar b. al-Khaṭṭāb who said: "The Messenger of Allah ﷺ said: 'When Ādam committed his mistake he said: "O my Lord! I am asking you to forgive me for the sake of Muḥammad." Allah said: "O Ādam! How do you know about Muḥammad whom I have not yet created?" Ādam replied: "O my Lord! after You created me with Your Hand and breathed into me of Your Spirit, I raised my head and saw written on the heights of the Throne: '*Lā Ilāha Illā Allāh Muḥammad Rasūl Allāh.*' I understood that You would not place next to Your Name any but the Most Beloved one of Your creation." Allah said: "O Ādam! I have forgiven you, and were it not for Muḥammad I would not have created you." ' " This Ḥadīth supports the one before it and both of them explain the authentic Ḥadīth.[15]

I say: This proves that according to Ibn Taymiyya, the Ḥadīth is suitable for use as evidence and is given consideration. That which is fabricated or false cannot be used as an example according to the scholars of Ḥadīth, yet here you see Ibn Taymiyya using it here as an explanation.

---

[15] *Al-Fatāwā*, 2:150.

Ibn Taymiyya's Correction of the Meaning of this Uniqueness

Shaykh Ibn Taymiyya spoke very well and beautifully about this issue in such a manner that shows great intellect, insight, and balance. Even though he denied the existence of a Ḥadīth from the Prophet ﷺ speaking of this meaning (according to his knowledge at that time), he still, however, gave strength to that meaning and explained it in an understandable way and affirmed the correctness of this statement. By this, he clearly refutes those who claim that it is disbelief and idolatry, and he refutes those who say that the meaning is corrupt and false—claiming that it is an affront to the station of Divine transcendence and *tawḥīd*. This is nothing but vain desires, blindness, shallow understanding and narrow mindedness. May Allah enlighten our insights and guide us to what is correct and true. He is the One who guides to the correct path. Shaykh Ibn Taymiyya said in *al-Fatāwā*:

> Muḥammad is the Master of the children of Ādam, the best of creation, and the most noble of them in Allah's sight. This is why it has been said that: "Allah created the universe because of him," or "Were it not for him, He would not have created the Throne, the Pedestal, the heaven, earth, sun or moon." This is not a Ḥadīth of the Prophet ﷺ, either authentic or weak. It was not related by any of those versed in the Ḥadīth sciences on the authority of the Prophet ﷺ. Nor is it known to have come from any of the companions. In fact, it is not known who actually uttered it.
>
> It is possible, though, to explain it from a correct perspective, such as Allah's saying: ﴾He has subjected to you whatever is in the heavens and the earth.﴿ And by His words ﴾He subjected the ships to you that they may run upon the sea at His command, and He subjected the rivers to you. He subjected to you the sun and the moon, constant in their courses, and subjected to you night and the day. And gave you of all you ask Him; and if you count the bounties of Allah, you shall never number them.﴿

There are other passages similar to these, all of which clarify that Allah created the creation for humanity's sake: even though it is known that Allah, in doing so, had in mind an immense wisdom besides this and far greater than this. Here, though, He explains to humanity the benefits creation contains for them and how they are immersed in Divine favours. So if it is said: 'He did such and such for this or that reason', it does not exclude the possibility of there being other wisdoms for the act. Similarly, the statement: 'Were it not for so and so, such and such would not have been created', does not negate the possibility of there being another higher wisdom behind the act. Instead, it implies that since the most pious of humanity is Muḥammad ﷺ, creating him was a desirable end of deep-seated wisdom more so than for creating anyone else, and that the completion of creation and the crown of its very perfection only occurred with Muḥammad.

AN IMPORTANT ANALYSIS CONCERNING THE OPINION OF IBN TAYMIYYA THAT HAS BEEN ABSENT FROM THE MINDS OF HIS FOLLOWERS

May Allah have mercy upon you. Look at the words of Ibn Taymiyya and his deep insight, and wide understanding in explaining this uniqueness that is well known and spread wide.

Concerning it, there is the Ḥadīth of Ādam's *tawassul* that was narrated by al-Ḥākim and authenticated, declared *ḥasan*, and accepted by those among the Imāms of Ḥadīth who were mentioned. Here is Shaykh Ibn Taymiyya saying that these words have a correct understanding. How does this compare to one who goes into an uproar and expels those who agree with it from the fold of Islam and describes them with misguidance, idolatry, or innovation and superstition—afterwards falsely claiming that he is a Salafī follower of Ibn Taymiyya? He is extremely far removed from Ibn Taymiyya and Salafiyya. His manner and behaviour is not restricted to this issue alone. Rather, it is noticed that he is with Ibn Taymiyya in every issue except those issues in which there is glorification of the Prophet ﷺ or support for his miracles, greatness and rank. In this subject, he is hesitant and he thinks and investigates, whereas here, he pretends to defend the station of *tawḥīd*. Glorified are You O Lord, this is a manifest slander!

The Third Supporting Evidence for the Ḥadīth of Ādam's *Tawassul*: The third supporting evidence for the Ḥadīth of Ādam's *tawassul* was narrated by Ibn al-Mundhir in his Qur'ānic exegesis from Muḥammad b. 'Alī b. Ḥusayn b. 'Alī who said: "When Ādam made his mistake, his distress became tremendous, and his regret became severe. Jibrīl a came to him and said: 'O Ādam, shall I not guide you to the door of your repentance that through it, Allah will turn to you in repentance?' He said: 'Of course O Jibrīl!' He said: 'Stand in your station wherein you entreat your Lord and glorify Him and praise Him; there is nothing more beloved to Allah than praise.' Ādam asked: 'So what should I say O Jibrīl?' Jibrīl replied: 'Say: 'There is nothing that deserves worship in truth but Allah, He is One without any partner, to Him belongs the dominion and the praise, He brings life and causes death. All good is in His Hand, and He is over all things powerful,' then, admit to your mistake and say: 'Glorified are you O Allah and to You is all praise, there is nothing that deserves to be worshipped in truth but You, my Lord, indeed I have wronged myself and done bad, so forgive me. Indeed, no one forgives sins but You. O Allah, I ask You by the rank of Muḥammad: Your slave, and (I ask You) by his nobility with You, that you forgive me of my mistake.'

"So Ādam did so, and Allah said to him: 'O Ādam, who taught you this?' He replied: 'O my Lord! when you breathed the spirit into me and made me an upright man where I see, hear, think and understand, I saw written upon the heights of the Throne: 'There is nothing worthy of worship in truth but Allah, He is alone and without any partner, Muḥammad is the Messenger of Allah. So I saw that You have not placed the name of any Angel or Prophet along with Your name but his, I knew that he is the most noble of Your creation.' He (Allah) said: 'You have spoken truthfully, and I have turned to you in repentance and forgiven you.' "[16]

---

[16] *Al-Durr al-Manthūr* of al-Suyūṭī, 1:146.

Muḥammad b. ʻAlī b. Ḥusayn is Abū Jaʻfar al-Bāqir and he is from the reliable followers of the second generation and from its noble ones. He is a narrator in all of the six Ḥadīth collections and has narrated from Jābir, Abū Saʻīd, Ibn ʻUmar and others.

The Fourth Supporting Evidence for the Ḥadīth of Ādam's *Tawassul*: The fourth supporting evidence for the Ḥadīth of Ādam's *tawassul* is narrated by Abū Bakr al-Ājurī in his book *al-Sharīʻa*. He narrated up to ʻAbd al-Raḥmān b. Abī Zinād from his father who said: "From the words that caused Allah to turn to Ādam in repentance were: 'O Allah, I ask You by the right of Muḥammad upon You.' Allah the Exalted said: 'And what would make you understand who Muḥammad is?' He (Ādam) said: 'O my Lord! I raised my head and saw written on Your Throne: 'There is nothing worthy of worship in truth but Allah and Muḥammad is the Messenger of Allah', and then I came to know that he is the most noble of Your creation.' "

So adding this report to the Ḥadīth of ʻAbd al-Raḥmān b. Zayd increases its strength as is not hidden.

PARADISE IS FORBIDDEN UNTIL MUḤAMMAD ﷺ ENTERS IT

Another example of this Divine favour upon the person of the Prophet ﷺ is the Ḥadīth stating that the Paradise is forbidden to the Prophets until our Prophet ﷺ enters it. ʻUmar b. al-Khaṭṭāb ؓ narrated that the Messenger of Allah ﷺ said: "Paradise has been forbidden for the Prophets until I enter it, and it has been forbidden for the other nations until my nation enters it."[17]

---

[17] Narrated by al-Ṭabarānī in *al-Awsaṭ*. Al-Haythamī said: "Its chain is good." (*Majmaʻ al-Zawāʼid*, 1:69)

More examples of this Divine favour include the reports stating that the name Muḥammad is spread through the higher gathering. Ka'b al-Ahbār said: "Allah sent down staffs to Ādam that equal the number of the Prophets and Messenger. Ādam then turned to his son Sheth and said: 'O my son! You are my successor after me so take these with the strong structure of piety and the firm hand hold. Every time you remember Allah, remember the name of Muḥammad as well, for I saw his name written upon the heights of the Throne when I was between the state of mud and spirit. Afterwards, I travelled through the heavens and did not see any place except that I also saw the name Muḥammad written upon it. I saw the name Muḥammad written upon the necks of the heavenly maidens (*al-ḥūr al-'īn*), upon the leaves of the trees of paradise, upon the leaves of the tree of Ṭūbā, the leaves of the *sidra al-muntahā* (great Lote tree), on the edges of the veils, and between the eyes of the Angels.

You should frequently remember him for indeed the Angels remember him in all of their hours.'[18] Al-Zurqānī said in his commentary: "It was narrated by Ibn 'Asākir." I say: A report similar to this one was mentioned by Shaykh Ibn Taymiyya. He said: "It has been narrated that Allah wrote his (the Prophet Muḥammad's ﷺ) name upon the Throne and the doors, domes, and leaves of Paradise. Many reports have been narrated that agree with these established Ḥadīth showing the elevation of his name and his high mention therein."

In a narration from Ibn al-Jawzī from Maysara: "I said: 'O Messenger of Allah! When where you (first) a Prophet?' He replied: 'When Allah created the earth ﴾Then He turned to the heaven, and fashioned it as seven heavens﴿ (al-Baqara: 29), and created the Throne, He wrote on the leg of the Throne: "Muḥammad the Messenger of Allah is the Seal of Prophets," then Allah created the Garden in which He made Ādam and Ḥawwā dwell, and He wrote my name on the gates, its tree-leaves, its domes and its tents, at a time when Ādam was still between the spirit and the body.

---

[18] *Al-Mawāhib al-Ladūniyya*, 1:186.

" 'When Allah, the Exalted breathed life into him he looked at the Throne and saw my name, whereupon Allah informed him that "He is the Master of all your descendants." When Satan deceived them both, they repented and sought intercession to Allah with my name.' "[19]

Important Benefits taken from the Ḥadīth of Ādam's *Tawassul*: From them: *Tawassul* through the Messenger of Allah ﷺ before the world was honoured with his presence in it and that the validity of *tawassul* revolves around he on whose behalf *tawassul* is made and his possession of a high rank with his Lord and that it is not a condition that he is living in the life of this world.

From them: Those who say that *tawassul* is not allowed except with one who is alive in the abode of this world is following his desires without any guidance from Allah.

Conclusion: The conclusion is that this Ḥadīth is authentic with all of its supporting narrations and it has been reported by a group of the most erudite of scholars, Imāms of Ḥadīth, and its Ḥuffāẓ of well known status and high rank. They are the trustworthy guardians of the Prophetic Sunna, among them: al-Ḥākim, al-Suyūṭī, al-Subkī, and al-Bulqīnī.

It has also been reported by al-Bayhaqī in his book that his collection was conditional in that he would not narrate fabricated reports. It is the same book, concerning which al-Dhahabī said: "Stick to this (book) for indeed all of it is guidance and light."

Ibn Kathīr mentioned it in *al-Bidāya* and Ibn Taymiyya inferred from it in his *Fatāwā* collection. The fact that the scholars have differed concerning it—with some rejecting it and others accepting it—is not strange at all because many of the Prophetic Ḥadīth have been differed over and critiqued much more than this one.

For this reason, these tremendous works were authored, containing proofs, critical comments, review and critique. None of that ever led to some accusing others of idolatry, disbelief,

---

[19] *Al-Fatāwā*, 2:150.

misguidance, and leaving the fold of the faith due to differences concerning the strength of a certain Ḥadīth. This Ḥadīth under discussion is one such example of this.

THE *TAWASSUL* OF THE JEWS THROUGH HIM ﷺ

The Exalted said: ﴾And when there came to them a scripture from Allah, confirming that in their possession—though before that they were asking for a signal triumph over those who disbelieved—and when there came to them that which they know (to be the truth) they disbelieved therein. The curse of Allah is on disbelievers.﴿ (al-Baqara: 89) Al-Qurṭubī said: His ﷻ statement ﴾And when there came to them﴿—meaning the Jews—﴾a scripture﴿—meaning the Qur'ān—﴾from Allah, confirming...﴿—this is a description for a book and it is possible that it is for other than the Qur'ān. It is in the accusative form (*manṣūb*) based on it being for *ḥāl* (state or condition in which the agent occurs at the time of the action), and it is in the accusative form within the *muṣḥaf* (copy) of Ubay' as has been narrated—﴾confirming that in their possession﴿—meaning the Torah and the Gospel informing them of what they contain—﴾though before that they were asking (*yastaftiḥūn*) for a signal triumph﴿—meaning: they were seeking help. *Al-Istiftāḥ* is to seek help. In the Ḥadīth it says: "The Prophet ﷺ used to seek victory (*yastaftiḥ*) through the impoverished among the Muhājirūn."—meaning that he would seek help through their supplication and prayers. Another example of this (is the verse of the Qur'ān): ﴾So perhaps Allah will bring a victory (*fatḥ*) or matter from Him.﴿ Help (*naṣr*) is to open up something that is closed, hence the word goes back to their statement (in the Arabic language): "I opened (*fataḥtu*) the door."

Al-Nasā'ī narrated from Abū Sa'īd al-Khudrī from the Prophet ﷺ that he said: "Allah only gives victory to this Umma by virtue of its weak ones—through their supplications, ritual prayers, and sincerity." Al-Nasā'ī also narrated from Abū al-Dardā' that he said: "I heard the Messenger of Allah ﷺ say: 'Seek me out with the weak ones for you are only given victory and provision by virtue of your weak ones.' "

Ibn 'Abbās said: "The Jews of Khaybar were fighting the tribe of Ghatfān. When they met in battle, the Jews were defeated so the Jews supplicated with this supplication: "Indeed we ask You by the right of the unlettered Prophet who You promised to send to us at the end of time, that you give us victory against them." When they met (the tribe) of Ghatfān in battle again, they called out with this supplication and defeated them. When the Prophet ﷺ was sent, they disbelieved in him, so Allah revealed: ﴿Though before that they were asking for a signal triumph over those who disbelieved—and when there came to them that which they know (to be the truth) they disbelieved therein. The curse of Allah is on disbelievers.﴾ (al-Baqara: 89)[20]

TAWASSUL THROUGH THE PROPHET ﷺ IN HIS LIFE AND AFTER HIS DEATH

From 'Uthmān b. Ḥunayf ﷺ who said: "When a blind man came to the Messenger of Allah ﷺ complaining from his loss of sight, he said: 'O Messenger of Allah! I have no one to lead me and things are difficult for me. The Messenger of Allah ﷺ said: 'Go perform *wuḍū'*, pray two units of ritual Prayer, then supplicate: "O Allah, I ask you and turn to you through Your Prophet, the Prophet of Mercy. O Muḥammad, I turn to your Lord through you so that He returns to me my sight. O Allah, grant him intercession for me, and grant me intercession for myself." ' 'Uthmān said: "By Allah, we did not part company or speak for very long, before the man came to us as if there was nothing wrong with him."

Al-Ḥākim said: "This Ḥadīth is rigorously authentic and was not narrated by (the two Shaykhs [al-Bukhārī and Muslim])." Al-Dhahabī said concerning this Ḥadīth: "It is rigorously authentic."[21] Al-Tirmidhī said in the section of supplications at the end of the *Sunan*: "This Ḥadīth is *ḥasan ṣaḥīḥ gharīb*, we do not know of it from other than this route from the Ḥadīth of Abū Ja'far and he is not al-Khatmī." I say: What is correct is that Abū Ja'far is in fact al-Khatmī al-Madanī, as is explicitly stated in the

[20] *Tafsīr al-Qurtubī*, 2:26-27.
[21] *Siyar 'Alām al-Nubalā'*, 1:519.

narrations of al-Ṭabarānī, al-Ḥākim and al-Bayhāqī. Al-Ṭabarānī added in *al-Muʿjam al-Ṣaghīr* that his name was ʿUmayr b. Yazīd and that he is reliable. The ʿAllāma and scholar of Ḥadīth, al-Ghumārī said in his essay ʿA Gift to the Clever':

> It would not make any sense for the Ḥuffāẓ to concur in declaring a Ḥadīth to be authentic while there is an unknown person it its chain—especially al-Dhahabī, al-Mundhirī and al-Ḥāfiẓ (Ibn Ḥajar)."

Al-Mundhirī said: "It was also narrated by al-Nasāʾī, Ibn Mājah, and Ibn Khuzayma in his *Ṣaḥīḥ*."[22]

This is not restricted to his ﷺ life, rather, some of the companions used this form of *tawassul* after his ﷺ death. Al-Ṭabarānī narrated this Ḥadīth and in the beginning of it mentioned the story of a man who repeatedly approached ʿUthmān b. ʿAffān but ʿUthmān did not pay attention to him or his need. The man then met Ibn Ḥunayf and complained to him about the matter, so ʿUthmān b. Ḥunayf said: "Go to the place of ablution and perform *wuḍū'*, then come to the Mosque, perform two units of ritual prayer, and say: ʿO Allah, I ask You and turn to You through our Prophet Muḥammad, the Prophet of Mercy: O Muḥammad, I turn through you to my Lord, that He may fulfil my need,'—and mention your need."

The man left and did as he had been told, then went to the door of ʿUthmān b. ʿAffān ؓ. The doorman came, took him by the hand, brought him to ʿUthmān b. ʿAffān, and seated him next to him on a cushion. ʿUthmān asked; "What do you need?" The man mentioned what he wanted, and ʿUthmān fulfilled it for him, and said, "I did not remember your need until just now, so whenever you need something, just mention it." The man departed, met ʿUthmān b. Ḥunayf, and said to him, "May Allah reward you! He didn't see to my need or pay any attention to me until you spoke with him." ʿUthmān b. Ḥunayf replied; "By Allah, I didn't speak to him, but I have seen a blind man come to the Messenger of Allah ﷺ and complain to him of the loss of his eyesight. The Prophet ﷺ

---

[22] As found in *al-Targhīb wa al-Tarhīb* in the book on extra prayers in the section on the prayer of need, 1:438.

asked: 'Can you not bear it?' The man replied: 'O Messenger of Allah, I do not have anyone to lead me around, and it is a great hardship for me.' The Prophet ﷺ told him, 'Go to the place of ablution and perform, *wuḍū'*, then pray two units of ritual prayer and make the supplications.' " Ibn Ḥunayf went on, "By Allah, we did not part company or speak long before the man returned to us as if nothing had ever been wrong with him."

Al-Mundhirī said: "It was narrated by al-Ṭabarānī, and he said after mentioning it: 'It is *ḥasan ṣaḥīḥ*.' "[23] Shaykh Ibn Taymiyya said: "Al-Ṭabarānī said: 'This was narrated by Shu'ba from Abū Ja'far. His name is 'Umar b. Yazīd, who is reliable. 'Uthmān b. 'Umar was alone in this report from Sh'uba.' " Abū 'Abdullāh al-Maqdisī said: 'The Ḥadīth is authentic.' " I say: Ibn Taymiyya mentioned his lone narration (*tafarrud*) according to the extent of his knowledge, and the narration of Rūḥ b. 'Ubāda from Shu'ba did not reach him, and its chain is authentic and clarifies that it was not only from 'Uthmān b. 'Umar.[24]

So the upshot of this story is that the narrator of the Ḥadīth, 'Uthmān b. Ḥunayf, who witnessed this story, taught this supplication to the one who complained of the Caliph's delay in fulfilling his need. This supplication contains *tawassul* through the Prophet ﷺ and entreating him and seeking aid through him after his ﷺ death. When the man thought that his needs were fulfilled because of 'Uthmān speaking with the Caliph, 'Uthmān immediately denied that and told him of the event that he heard and witnessed (of the blind man) in order to assure him that his need was fulfilled because of his *tawassul* through the Prophet ﷺ and his entreating him and seeking aid through him. He made sure to emphasize this with an oath that he did not speak to the Caliph regarding his need.

ANOTHER EXAMPLE AND IBN TAYMIYYA'S SUPPORT OF IT

Ibn Abī al-Dunyā said in his book *Mujābī al-Du'ā*: "Abū Hāshim narrated to us that he heard Kathīr b. Muḥammad b. Kathīr b. Rafā'a say: 'A man came to 'Abd al-Malik b. Sa'īd b. Abjar and 'Abd

[23] *Al-Targhīb*, 1:440 and *Majma' al-Zawā'id*, 2:279.
[24] *Al-Tawassul wa al-Wasīla*, p.101.

al-Malik grasped the man's stomach. He ('Abd al-Malik) said to him: "You have an illness that in incurable." The man asked him: "What is it?" He replied: "It is called *al-dubayla* (and it is an aggressive parasite that settles in the digestive tract and usually kills the carrier)." The man then turned to the side and said: "O Allah, O Allah! Allah is my Lord I associate none with my Lord. O Allah, I turn to you through Your Prophet Muḥammad, the Prophet of Mercy ﷺ. O Muḥammad! I turn to your Lord and my Lord through you that He has mercy upon me in this affliction of mine." He ('Abd al-Malik) then grasped his stomach once more and said: "You have been healed and have no problem." '

Ibn Taymiyya said: "I say: This supplication and its likes have been narrated to be from the supplications of the Salaf."[25] It is known that Ibn Taymiyya mentioned this narration in order to explain it according to his intent and interpret it the way he wanted, however, what concerns us here is that he has confirmed that the Salaf used this kind of supplication and that healing is obtained through it. This amount (of confirmation) of the issue is what concerns us. As far as his own comments on the narration are concerned, that is his own opinion, and the only thing that concerns us here is the affirmation of the text so we can use it as evidence for what we want. He is entitled to use it as evidence as he likes.

FUTILE ATTEMPTS

Some people have obsessed and harped on the Ḥadīth on the *tawassul* of Ādam and 'Uthmān b. Ḥunayf and others, expanding all of their efforts in rejecting them with all their strength. They have debated, argued, fluttered up and down, and fumed with rage in this subject. There is no benefit to any of this, because no matter how much they attempt to reject the Ḥadīth that have been narrated on this subject, the luminaries among the major scholars have spoken and they are greater than them in intellect, more expansive in knowledge and expertise, of deeper understanding, and greater in light, piety and sincerity. An example of one such (scholar) is Imām Aḥmad b. Ḥanbal who

[25] *Al-Tawassul wa al-Wasīla*, p.93.

upheld the view of *tawassul*—as Ibn Taymiyya quoted from him, not to mention al-'Izz b. 'Abd al-Salām. Ibn Taymiyya himself has one view specifically in support of *tawassul* through the Prophet ﷺ. The conclusion of Shaykh Muḥammad b. 'Abd al-Wahhāb is that he censured those who ascribed to him the view that he imputes disbelief upon those who perform *tawassul*. Nay, he explicitly stated in his legal verdicts that *tawassul* is from the subsidiary matters and not from the fundamentals—as shall be discussed in detail, Allah willing. Having said this, the 'Allāma, the scholar of Ḥadīth, 'Abdullāh al-Ghumārī authored a special essay concerning this Ḥadīth that he called: 'The Glass Lantern Concerning the Prayer of Need.' He excelled and benefited therein and brought that which heals, suffices and enriches.

TAWASSUL THROUGH HIM ﷺ AT THE PLAINS ON THE DAY OF JUDGEMENT

As for *tawassul* through him at the plains on the Day of Judgement, there is no need to go into much detail, because the Ḥadīth about the intercession have reached the level of mass transmission. All of the narrations contain explicit texts showing that when the people are left standing (at the plain on the Day of Judgement) for a long time, and the difficulties increase, they will seek aid with the Prophets to remove their hardships. They will first approach and seek aid with Ādam, then Nūḥ, then Ibrāhīm, then Mūsā, then 'Isā. Then, all of the people will go to the Master of the Messengers and seek aid with him, who will then hasten to give them aid and fulfil their request. He will say: "I am for that, I am for that." Then, he will fall down in prostration and will remain in such state until it is called out: "Raise your head and intercede for your intercession shall be accepted."

So (this Ḥadīth contains) a consensus from the Prophets and Messengers as well as the rest of the believers, and the tacit approval from the Lord of the worlds that seeking aid with the elite of those who are drawn close (to Allah) during times of immense difficulty is indeed from the greatest of keys in removing difficulties and something that brings about the pleasure of the Lord of the worlds.

THE LEGALITY OF *TAWASSUL* ACCORDING TO THE METHODOLOGY OF IBN TAYMIYYA

Shaykh Ibn Taymiyya says in his book 'A Noble Principle Concerning *Tawassul* and Means', when speaking about the words of the Exalted: ﴾O you who believe, fear Allah and seek a means of approach unto Him.﴿ (al-Mā'ida: 35):

> Seeking a means of approach to Allah ﷻ is only achieved by the one who performs *tawassul* to Allah through his own faith in Muḥammad and following him. This *tawassul* through faith in him and obedience to him is obligatory upon every single person and at every time, both internally and externally, both during his ﷺ life and after his death, and in his presence and absence. *Tawassul* through faith in him and obedience to him is not lifted from anyone of the creation under any circumstance after the proof has been established upon him. This is not lifted with any excuse. There is no way to achieve the grace of Allah, His mercy, and salvation from His chastisement and punishment save by *tawassul* through him and obedience to him. He ﷺ is the one who shall intercede for the creation, he is the possessor of the lofty station (*al-maqām al-maḥmūd*) whom the first and last envy him over. He is the greatest of the intercessors in stature, and the highest of them in rank with Allah. Allah said about Mūsā a: ﴾And he was a possessor of rank with Allah﴿ (al-Aḥzāb: 69).
>
> He said about 'Īsā a: ﴾A possessor of rank in this world and the next﴿ (Āl 'Imrān: 45). Muḥammad ﷺ is greater in rank than all of the Prophets and Messengers, however, his intercession and supplication will only benefit the one who he intercedes and supplicates for. So, whoever the Messenger supplicates and intercedes for, he may perform *tawassul* to Allah through his intercession and supplication just as his companions performed *tawassul* to Allah through his supplication and intercession, and just as the people shall perform *tawassul* to Allah on the Day of Judgement through his ﷺ supplication and intercession.

In the *Fatāwā al-Kubrā* it states: Shaykh al-Islam—may Allah have mercy upon him—was asked: "Is it permissible to perform *tawassul* through the Prophet ﷺ or not?" He replied:

> All praise belongs to Allah. As for *tawassul* through faith in him, love for him, obedience to him, (sending) prayers and peace upon him, and (through) his supplications and intercession and its likes from his own actions and the actions of the servants that are ordered with respect to (behaviour/dealings) with him, then this is (Islamically) legal according to the agreement of all of the Muslims.[26]

I say: Two things are understood from the words of Shaykh Ibn Taymiyya. **One:** That it is allowed for the Muslim who is obedient, loves the Messenger of Allah ﷺ, follows him, and believes in his intercession, to perform *tawassul* through his obedience to him, his love for him and his belief in that. Indeed, if we perform *tawassul* through the Prophet ﷺ, then Allah is our witness that we only perform *tawassul* by our faith in him, our love for him, his virtue, and his nobility. This is the primary intent of *tawassul*. It is unimaginable that anyone can perform *tawassul* through the Prophet ﷺ for other reason. It is not possible that it could be otherwise from the rest of the Muslim that perform *tawassul*. The only thing here, is that the one who performs *tawassul* might explicitly state this, or he might not explicitly state this—all the while relying on the primary intent behind the *tawassul* which is (through) his faith in the Prophet ﷺ, and love for him and nothing more. **Two**: Another thing understood from the words of Shaykh Ibn Taymiyya is that whoever the Messenger ﷺ supplicates for, it is then allowed for that individual to perform *tawassul* to Allah through his ﷺ supplication. It has been established that he ﷺ supplicated for his Umma in numerous Ḥadīth such as:

'Ā'isha—may Allah be pleased with her—said: "Once, I saw the Prophet ﷺ in a very joyous mood, so I asked him: 'O Messenger of Allah, supplicate to Allah on my behalf.' He then said: 'O Allah, forgive 'Ā'isha's past and future sins: that which she did openly

---

[26] *Al-Fatāwā al-Kubrā*, 1:140.

and that which she concealed.' " 'Ā'isha then laughed until her head fell in her lap out of heavy laughter. The Messenger of Allah then asked her: "Does my supplication make you happy?" She replied: "And how could it not make me happy?" He then said: "Indeed, it is my supplication for my Umma in every prayer." This is narrated from al-Bazzār and its narrators are those found in the authentic collection (of al-Bukhārī and Muslim) save Aḥmad b. Manṣūr al-Ramādī who is reliable (as noted in *Majma' al-Zawā'id*). For this reason, it is allowed for every Muslim to perform *tawassul* to Allah ﷻ with that by saying (for example): 'O Allah, Your Prophet Muḥammad ﷺ supplicated for his Umma and I am a member of that Umma. So I perform *tawassul* to You through this supplication: that You forgive me and have mercy upon me'—and so on and so forth. If he says that, he has not left the command that is agreed upon by all of the scholars among the Muslims. If he says: 'O Allah, I perform *tawassul* unto You through Your Prophet Muḥammad ﷺ', he did not explicitly declare his intention and clarify what his heart is settled upon, which is the intent of all of the Muslims and does not go beyond this because the one who performs *tawassul* through the Prophet ﷺ does not intend anything, save these meanings that relate to his ﷺ self of: love, closeness, rank, status, virtue, supplication, and intercession—especially when, in his Isthmus (*barzakh*) life, he ﷺ hears the prayers and peace (being conveyed to him) and responds to that in a manner that is fitting and appropriate: such as greetings of peace and asking for forgiveness, as was reported in the Ḥadīth from the Prophet ﷺ:

"My life is better for you and my death is better for you: you bring up new matters and new matters are brought up for you. Your actions will be shown to me; if I see goodness I shall praise Allah and if I see evil I shall ask forgiveness of Him for you."

This was narrated by Ḥāfiẓ Ismā'īl al-Qāḍī in the single volume work on prayers upon the Prophet ﷺ. Al-Haytamī mentioned it in *Majma' al-Zawā'id* and authenticated it by saying: "It was narrated by al-Bazzār and its men are found in the authentic collections (of al-Bukhārī and Muslim)."

This (narration) is explicitly clear in stating that he ﷺ seeks forgiveness for his Umma while in the Isthmus (*barzakh*) life. Seeking forgiveness is a supplication that the Umma benefits from. In another Ḥadīth, it states that the Prophet ﷺ said: "There is no one who sends salutations upon me, except that Allah returns my soul to me so I can respond to his greetings."

This was narrated by Abū Dāwūd from Abū Hurayra ؓ. Al-Nawawī said: "Its chain is authentic." This (Ḥadīth) explicitly states that the Prophet returns the greetings to the Muslim. The greeting of peace is a greeting that denotes security. So the greeting of peace is in fact, a supplication for security for the Muslim—and the Muslim benefits from that.

The Legality of *Tawassul* through the Prophet ﷺ Specifically according to Imām Aḥmad b. Ḥanbal and Ibn Taymiyya

This is based upon the fact that Shaykh Ibn Taymiyya affirmed the permissibility of *tawassul* in some places in his books without differentiating or making a distinction between his life and death, or his presence and absence. In his *al-Fatāwā al-Kubrā* he quoted Imām Aḥmad and al-'Izz b. 'Abd al-Salām stating its permissibility.

The Shaykh said:

> Similarly, what is allowed as well is *tawassul* through him ﷺ in supplication, as appears in the Ḥadīth narrated by al-Tirmidhī and authenticated by him: "The Prophet ﷺ taught someone to say: 'O Allah, I ask you and perform *tawassul* to You through Your Prophet Muḥammad, the Prophet of Mercy. O Muḥammad! I turn through you unto your Lord so that He may fulfil my need and relieve it so He may allow you to intercede on my behalf.' " This form of *tawassul* is good.[27]

He also said:

[27] *Al-Fatāwā al-Kubrā*, 1:105.

> *Tawassul* to Allah through other than our Prophet ﷺ, whether it be called *istighātha* (seeking aid) or not called as such, we do not know any of the Salaf that performed it nor is there any report concerning it. We do not know about it, save the legal verdict of the Shaykh forbidding it. As for *tawassul* through the Prophet ﷺ, there is a Ḥadīth concerning it in the *Sunan*, narrated by al-Nasā'ī, al-Tirmidhī and others (stating that) a Bedouin Arab came to the Prophet ﷺ and said: "O Messenger of Allah! I have an affliction in my eyes, so please supplicate to Allah for me." The Prophet ﷺ said to him: "Perform ablution and pray two units of ritual prayer, then say: 'O Allah, I ask You, and turn to You through Your Prophet Muḥammad. O Muḥammad! indeed I seek intercession through you in getting my sight returned. O Allah, allow Your Prophet to intercede for me.' " He (the Prophet ﷺ also) said: "If you have any other need then do the same." Allah then returned his sight to him.

So based upon this Ḥadīth, the Shaykh excluded *tawassul* through him (from that which he forbade).[28]

Shaykh Ibn Taymiyya said elsewhere:

> It is for this reason that Aḥmad said in (his book) of *Manāsik* (the rites of Ḥajj) that he wrote to his companion al-Marrūdhī, that one should "perform *tawassul* through the Prophet ﷺ in his supplication." However, others besides Aḥmad said: "This is swearing an oath of sorts by him unto Allah, and Allah is not to be sworn by through the creation." In one narration, Aḥmad is reported to have allowed that and for that reason he permitted *tawassul* through him."[29]

---

[28] Ibid.

[29] Ibid. 1:140.

The Permissibility of *Tawassul* according to Imām Shawkānī

The Salafī Imām and scholar of Ḥadīth, Shaykh Muḥammad b. ʿAlī al-Shawkānī said in his essay called: *al-Durr al-Naḍīd fī Ikhlāṣ Kalima al-Tawḥīd*:

> As for *tawassul* unto Allah ﷻ through any of His creation in something that the servant seeks from his Lord, then the Shaykh, al-ʿIzz b. ʿAbd al-Salām said: "It is not allowed to perform *tawassul* unto Allah through anyone besides the Prophet ﷺ if the Ḥadīth about it is authentic." Perhaps, he is pointing to the Ḥadīth that was narrated by al-Nasāʾī in his *Sunan*, al-Tirmidhī, and authenticated by Ibn Mājah and others, that a blind man came to the Prophet ﷺ (the Ḥadīth). He (al-ʿIzz) then said: "The people have two opinions regarding the meaning of this. The first opinion states that *tawassul* is that which was mentioned by ʿUmar b. al-Khaṭṭāb رضي الله عنه when he said: 'If we experienced drought, we would perform *tawassul* through our Prophet ﷺ to You (O Allah) and You would send us rain. Now, we perform *tawassul* to You by the uncle of the Prophet ﷺ.'
>
> "This narration is in the authentic collection of al-Bukhārī and others. ʿUmar رضي الله عنه mentioned that they used to perform *tawassul* through the Prophet ﷺ during his life for seeking rain, then he (ʿUmar) would perform *tawassul* with his uncle al-ʿAbbās after his death. This *tawassul* was their way of seeking rain, for he would supplicate, and they would in turn supplicate along with him—thereby, he was their means (*wasīla*) unto Allah and in this sense, the Prophet ﷺ was an intercessor for them and would pray for them."
>
> "The second view is that *tawassul* through him ﷺ may be performed in his life, and after his death, as well as in his presence and absence. It is not hidden to you that *tawassul* through him during his life ﷺ is established, and *tawassul* through other than him after his death is also established by the consensus of the companions—a consensus of silent tacit approval (*ijmāʿ sukūtī*) because none of them censured ʿUmar رضي الله عنه for his *tawassul* through al-ʿAbbās رضي الله عنه."

In my (al-Shawkānī) view, there is no justification for restricting the permissibility of *tawassul* to only the Prophet ﷺ as was claimed by Shaykh 'Izz al-Dīn b. 'Abd al-Salām. This is for two reasons. **One:** due to what we informed you of regarding the consensus of the companions, may Allah be pleased with them all. **Two:** *tawassul* unto Allah through the people of virtue and knowledge in actuality, is *tawassul* through their righteous actions and virtuous distinctions, as there is no one who is virtuous save with his actions. So if someone says: "O Allah, I perform *tawassul* unto You through the scholar such and such," this is considering the knowledge that is present with that scholar. It has been established in the two authentic collections (of al-Bukhārī and Muslim) and others, that the Prophet ﷺ spoke of the three who were trapped in a cave that was sealed with a large rock. Each of the three performed *tawassul* unto Allah through the greatest action they each performed until the stone was removed.

If *tawassul* through righteous actions was impermissible or idolatry as claimed by some overly severe ones like Ibn 'Abd al-Salām and those who share his view among his followers, then their (the people of the cave) supplication would not have been answered and the Prophet ﷺ would not have remained silent without rebuking them after he narrated the story about them. By this, you know that the evidence cited by the opponents of *tawassul* through the Prophets and righteous is irrelevant, such as the words of the Exalted: ﴾We only worship them in order that they may bring us nearer to Allah﴿ (al-Zumar: 3) And: ﴾Do not call on any other god with Allah, or you will be among those who will be punished﴿ (al-Shu'arā': 213) And: ﴾Say: Call on those besides Him whom ye fancy; they have no power to remove your trouble from you or to change them. Those unto whom they cry seek for themselves the means of approach to their Lord, which of them shall be the nearest; they hope for His mercy and fear His wrath: for the wrath of your Lord is something to take heed of﴿ (al-Isrā': 57)

These verses are irrelevant to this issue, and they are used as evidence for something that is unrelated to the point of contention. The verse ﴾We only worship them in order that they may bring us nearer...﴿ explicitly states that they worship them for that purpose, whereas the one who performs *tawassul* through a scholar, for example, doesn't worship him, but knows that he has a special distinction with Allah for being a carrier of knowledge, and that is why he uses him as a means. Similarly irrelevant to the issue is Allah's saying: ﴾Do not call on any other god with Allah.﴿ This verse forbids that one should call upon another along with Allah, as if saying: "O Allah and O so-and-so." The one who performs *tawassul* through a scholar, for example, doesn't call upon other than Allah. He only seeks a means to Him through the excellent works that one of His servants achieved, just as the three men in the cave who were blocked by the rock used their righteous actions as means to have their supplication answered.

Similarly irrelevant to the issue is Allah's saying: "Those unto whom they call..." for it refers to people who call upon those who cannot fulfil their request, while at the same time not calling upon Allah who can; whereas one who performs *tawassul* through a scholar, for example, calls not except upon Allah, and none other besides Him.

The above cited examples show the reader that those who object to *tawassul* bring forth evidence that is irrelevant to the point of dispute at hand. Even more irrelevant is their citing of the verse: ﴾The Day when no soul shall have power to do anything for another: for the Command, that Day, will be all with Allah.﴿ (al-Infitār: 19) This noble verse contains nothing more than the fact that Allah alone decides everything on the Day of Judgement, and that none other will have any say at that time. The one who performs *tawassul* through one of the Prophets or one of the scholars does not believe that the one through whom he performs *tawassul* is in partnership with Allah on the Day of Judgement! Whoever believes such a thing in relation to a Prophet or non-Prophet is in manifest error.

Equally irrelevant is their objection to *tawassul* by citing the verses: ﴾Not for you is the decision in the least.﴿ (Āl 'Imrān: 128) And: ﴾Say: I have no power over good or harm to myself except as Allah wills.﴿ (al-An'ām: 188) These two verses are explicit in that the Prophet ﷺ has no say in Allah's decision and that he has no power to benefit or harm himself in the least, let alone someone else. There is nothing in those two verses to prevent *tawassul* through him or any other of the Prophets, friends of Allah, or scholars.

Allah has given His Prophet the lofty station (*al-maqām al-maḥmūd*)—the station of the Great Intercession (*al-shafā'a al-'uẓmā*), and He has instructed the creation to ask that station for him and to request his intercession, and He said to him ﷺ: "Ask and you shall be granted what you asked! Intercede and your intercession shall be accepted!" In His Book, He has made this dependent on the fact that there is no intercession except by His leave, and that none shall possess it except those with whom He is pleased.

Equally irrelevant is their adducing as proof against *tawassul*: ﴾And admonish your nearest kinsmen﴿ (al-Shu'arā': 214) Whereupon the Prophet ﷺ said: "O So-and-so son of So-and-so, I cannot benefit you unto Allah in the least, and: O So-and-so, daughter of So-and-so, I cannot benefit you unto Allah in the least." In this narration, there is nothing other than the plain declaration that he cannot benefit anyone for whom Allah has decreed harm, nor harm anyone for whom Allah has decreed benefit, and that he does not have any guarantee from Allah for any of his close relatives, let alone others. This is known to every Muslim. There is nothing in it, however, that prohibits performing *tawassul* to Allah through the Prophet, for *tawassul* is a request to the One Who holds power to grant and deny all requests. The petitioner who performs *tawassul* only desires to place, at the front of his petition, what may be a cause for the granting of his supplication by the One Who alone gives and withholds, the Owner of the Day of Judgement.

Muḥammad b. ʿAbd al-Wahhāb Permits *Tawassul*

Shaykh Muḥammad b. ʿAbd al-Wahhāb was asked about the statement of the jurists regarding *istisqā'* (seeking rain): "There is no problem with performing *tawassul* through the righteous," and the statement of Aḥmad: "*Tawassul* is to be performed through the Prophet ﷺ only" (and how this is joined with) the jurists' statement: "Help is not to be sought from the creation."

He responded:

> The distinction (between the two) is very clear and has nothing to do with what we are speaking about. So, some give a dispensation for performing *tawassul* through the righteous and some give dispensation for performing *tawassul* through the Prophet ﷺ. Most scholars (however), prohibit it and see it as detestable. This issue is from the issues of jurisprudence. Even though what is correct according to us is the view of the majority; that it is detested, we do not censure the one who performs it for there is no censure in issues of *ijtihād*.
>
> Our censure is only against the one who supplicates to the creation more than he supplicates to Allah, and the one who goes out to the grave humbling himself in front of the shrine of ʿAbd al-Qādir or other than him, seeking removal of difficulties, rescue from distress, and having his wishes granted. So where is this in comparison to the one who supplicates to Allah, being sincere to Him in the religion and not calling upon any other along with Allah while at the same time saying: "I ask You by Your Prophet" or: "By the Messengers" or: "Your righteous servants," or the one who goes out to a well known grave or other than that, while supplicating at it however not calling upon any other than Allah: in sincerity to Him in the religion. So how does that compare to what we are discussing?[30]

[30] *Fatāwā* of the Shaykh, Imām Muḥammad b. ʿAbd al-Wahhāb in *Majmūʿa al-Mu'allafāt*, 3:68, distributed by Imām Muḥammad b. Saʿūd Islamic University during Muḥammad b. ʿAbd al-Wahhāb week.

This proves that *tawassul* was permissible according to him. The most that can be said regarding his view is that it is detested (*makrūh*) according to the majority. That which is detested is not forbidden, much less being something that is idolatry or innovation.

MUḤAMMAD B. ʿABD AL-WAHHĀB DECLARES HIS DISAVOWAL OF THOSE WHO IMPUTE DISBELIEF UPON THOSE WHO PERFORM *TAWASSUL*

In Shaykh Muḥammad b. ʿAbd al-Wahhāb's letter addressed to the people of Qaṣīm, he strongly rebuked those who linked him to imputing disbelief upon those who perform *tawassul* through the righteous. He said: "Sulaymān b. Suhaym invented things against me that I have not said, most of which have never even crossed my mind. From them: That I impute disbelief upon the one who performs *tawassul* through the righteous, that I impute disbelief upon al-Buṣayrī due to his statement: *O noblest of creation*, and that I burn the (book) *Dalā'il al-Khayrāt*. My response to all of this is to say: Glorified are you my Lord, this is a manifest slander." Another statement of his in support of this is found in another essay that he sent to the people of al-Majmaʿa wherein he said: "If this is clear, then these issues for which he rebuked us, some of it is clear slander, such as when he said that I impute disbelief upon those who perform *tawassul* through the righteous, that I impute disbelief upon al-Buṣayrī..." He then said: "My response to this is to say: Glorified are you my Lord, this is manifest slander."[31]

TAWASSUL THROUGH HIS PERSONAL RELICS ﷺ

It is established that the companions used to seek blessings through his personal relics ﷺ. This seeking of blessings only has one meaning and it is performing *tawassul* unto Allah through his

[31] See essay 1 and essay 11 in the *Rasā'il al-Shaykh Muḥammad b. ʿAbd al-Wahhāb*, 5:12 & 64.

personal relics.

This is because *tawassul* occurs in many different ways and not just one. Do you see it feasible that they perform *tawassul* through his personal relics and not through him? Is it correct to perform *tawassul* through the branch (his personal relics) and not through the root (himself)? Is it correct to perform *tawassul* through a relic that has no nobility, grandeur, or honour except due to its owner: Muḥammad ﷺ, only to have someone come along and say: "It is not allowed to perform *tawassul* through him?" Glorified are you my Lord, this is manifest slander!

The primary text proofs that have been cited in support of this are abundant. We shall point to the most famous of them. We have the leader of the believers, 'Umar b. al-Khaṭṭāb رضي الله عنه, when death was approaching him, being extremely eager to be buried close to the Messenger of Allah ﷺ. He sent his son 'Abdullāh to go seek the permission of Lady 'Ā'isha for that. Upon hearing this, Lady 'Ā'isha announced that it was she who wanted that space for herself. She said: "I wanted it for myself and I shall prefer him over myself in this."'Abdullāh went to his father to bring him the glad tidings, whereupon his father said: "All praise belongs to Allah. There was nothing more important to me than that." See the details of this story in (the collection of) al-Bukhārī.

What is the meaning of this eagerness from 'Umar and 'Ā'isha? Why was being buried close to the Messenger of Allah ﷺ the most beloved and important thing to 'Umar? There is no explanation for that except to say that it was *tawassul* through the Prophet ﷺ after his passing by seeking blessings through proximity to him. Take Umm Sulaym, who cut the spout of the water jug that the Messenger of Allah ﷺ drank from. Anas رضي الله عنه said: "It is now with us." The companions used to contend with each other in taking one strand of hair from his head when he cut it. Take Asmā' b. Abī Bakr who preserved the cloak of the Messenger of Allah ﷺ and said: "We wash it for the benefit of our sick and seek healing through it." Take the ring of the Messenger of Allah ﷺ. It was guarded after him by Abū Bakr, 'Umar, and 'Uthmān, then it fell away from him into the well.

All of these Ḥadīth are established and authentic as we shall mention in the section dedicated to seeking blessings. Here we wish to ask: Why did they—may Allah be pleased with them—take care to guard the personal relics of the Prophet ﷺ: the water spout, the strands of hair, the sweat, the cloak, the ring and the place of prayer—what was their intent behind all that? Was it for mere sentimental remembrance or was it to guard these personal relics so they could be placed in a museum? If the answer is the former, then why did they take great care with them when they were supplicating or turning to Allah when affliction or illness struck them? If the answer is the later, then where was that museum and where did this innovated idea come from? Glorified are You O Lord, this is manifest slander! No other answer remains except to say that it was for seeking blessings with his personal effects in order to perform *tawassul* through them unto Allah in supplication, because Allah is the Giver and He is the one who is asked. All are His servants and under His command. No one possesses anything of themselves much less that of others except with the permission of Allah ﷻ.

TAWASSUL THROUGH THE PERSONAL RELICS OF THE PROPHETS

Allah the Exalted said: ﴾And their Prophet said to them: "Indeed, the sign of his dominion is that he comes to you with the box containing tranquillity from your Lord and the remains of that left from the people of Mūsā and the people of Hārūn. It is carried by the Angels. Indeed, in this is a sign for you if you are indeed believers."﴿ (al-Baqara: 248)

Ḥāfiẓ Ibn Kathīr said in his book of history:

> Ibn Jarīr said about this box: "If they ever fought one of the enemy they would have the ark of the covenant that was in the *qubba al-zamān* ('the dome of time') as was previously mentioned.
>
> They would gain victory by virtue of its blessing and the tranquillity that Allah placed therein and the remains of the people of Mūsā and the people of Hārūn. Once, while in battle with the people of Gaza and Ashkalon, they were defeated and overpowered and their enemies took it from their possession."

Ibn Kathīr further said: "They used to gain victory over their enemies because of it. It used to contain a golden bowl that was used to wash the breasts of the Prophets."[32]

Ibn Kathīr said in his exegesis:

> It used to contain the staff of Mūsā, the staff of Hārūn, two tablets from the Torah, and the garments of Hārūn. Some said that it contained a staff and sandals.[33]

Al-Qurṭubī said:

> According to what has been mentioned, the ark was sent down to Ādam ﷺ and was with him until it reached Ya'qūb ﷺ, thus reaching the Children of Israel. By it, they would defeat those they met in battle. This was until they disobeyed (Allah), and as a consequence, were defeated (in battle), thus losing the ark (to their enemies) among the Amelkites who took it from them.[34]

In reality, this is nothing but *tawassul* through the personal relics of those Prophets. There is no logical reason for them to bring it with them in the battles except for that. Allah, the Blessed and Exalted, was pleased with that, and this is proven by the fact that He returned it to them and made it a sign and indication of the validity of the dominion and kingship of Ṭālūt and he did not censure them for this action.

The *Tawassul* of the Prophet ﷺ through His Right and the Right of the Prophets and Righteous

In the collection on the merits of Fāṭima b. Asad Umm 'Alī b. Abī Ṭālib, it is mentioned that when she died, the Prophet ﷺ dug the niche in the ground for her with his own hands and removed the dirt. When the Messenger of Allah ﷺ completed this, he entered

---

[32] *Al-Bidāya wa al-Nihāya*, 2:8.
[33] *Tafsīr al-Qur'ān al-'Aẓīm*, 1:313.
[34] *Tafsīr al-Qurtubī*, 3:247.

into it, reclined, and said: "O Allah, the One who brings life and causes death. The Ever Living One who does not die, forgive my mother Fāṭima b. Asad. Deliver her evidence to her (the testimony of faith), expand her entry point for her by the right of Your Prophet and the Prophets before me. Indeed, You are the Most Merciful of those who show mercy." Then he prayed the funeral prayer over her, and he ﷺ, al-'Abbās, and Abū Bakr placed her in the grave.

This was narrated by al-Ṭabarānī in (*al-Mu'jam*) *al-Kabīr* and the *Awsaṭ*. It contains Rawḥ b. Ṣalāh. Ibn Ḥibbān and al-Ḥākim declared him reliable although he contains weakness, and the remaining people in the chain are narrators found in the authentic collections (of al-Bukhārī and Muslim).[35]

Some scholars differed regarding the status of Rawḥ b. Ṣāliḥ, however, Ibn Ḥibbān mentioned him among the reliable ones. Al-Ḥākim said that he was: "Reliable and trustworthy." Both of these two Ḥadīth masters authenticated it as well as al-Haytamī in *Majma' al-Zawā'id*, and the men (in the rest of the chain) are men from the authentic collections.

It was also narrated by Ibn 'Abd al-Barr from Ibn 'Abbās, and Ibn Abī Shayba from Jābir. It was also narrated by al-Daylamī and Abū Nu'aym. All of the routes of transmissions strengthen each other with force.

The Shaykh and Ḥāfiẓ, al-Ghumārī, said in 'A Gift to the Clever':

> The weakness of this Rawḥ in the chain is a light weakness according to those who weakened him—as is understood from their expressions. It is for this reason that the Ḥāfiẓ, al-Haytamī expressed it in such a way that it indicates the minor nature of this weakness, as is not hidden to those who are adept in the books of this science. This Ḥadīth is no less than *ḥasan* (fair), nay, upon the conditions of Ibn Ḥibbān, it is authentic."[36]

---

[35] As found in *Majma' al-Zawā'id*, 9:257.

[36] *Ithāf al-Adhkiyā'*, p.20.

We also notice here in this Ḥadīth and others, that the Prophet ﷺ performed *tawassul* by the rights of the Prophets who had already died, thus, this establishes the permissibility of performing *tawassul* unto Allah through the right or through the people of the truth be they dead or alive.

THE *TAWASSUL* OF THE PROPHET ﷺ THROUGH THE RIGHT OF THOSE WHO ASK

From Abū Sa'īd al-Khudrī who said that the Messenger of Allah ﷺ said: "Whoever departs from his house to go to the prayer and says: 'O Allah, I ask You by the right upon You of those who ask, and by the right of this walking of mine—for I have not gone out for the sake of arrogance, insolence, showing off, or seeking to be heard. I have gone out seeking to avoid Your wrath and to seek Your Good pleasure. I ask You to protect me from the fire, and to forgive my sins. Indeed, no one forgives sins except You.' Whoever says this, Allah will turn to him with His countenance and seventy thousand Angels will seek forgiveness for him."

Al-Mundhirī said in *al-Targhīb wa al-Tarhīb*: "It was narrated by Ibn Mājah with a chain that has some controversy, and it was declared *ḥasan* by our Shaykh, Ḥāfiẓ Abū al-Ḥasan."[37] The Ḥāfiẓ, Ibn Ḥajar said in *Natā'ij al-Afkār*: "This Ḥadīth is fair (*ḥasan*). It was narrated by Aḥmad, Ibn Khuzayma in *Kitāb al-Tawḥīd*, and Abū Nu'aym and Ibn al-Sunnī."[38] Al-'Irāqī said in his grading of the Ḥadīth reports found in the *Iḥyā'* (of al-Ghazālī) regarding this Ḥadīth: "It is *ḥasan*."[39] Al-Būṣīrī said in the *Zawā'id* of Ibn Mājah titled *Miṣbāh al-Zujāja*: "Narrated by Ibn Khuzayma in his *Ṣaḥīḥ*."[40] Ḥāfiẓ Sharaf al-Dīn al-Dimyāṭī said in *al-Muttajir al-Rābiḥ*: "Its chain is *ḥasan*, Allah willing."[41]

The investigating scholar of Ḥadīth, 'Allāma al-Sayyid 'Alī b. Yaḥyā al-'Alawī said in his exquisite essay, *Hidāyat al-Mutakhabbiṭīn*:

---

[37] *Al-Targhīb wa al-Tarhīb*, 3:119.
[38] *Natā'ij al-Afkār*, 1:272.
[39] *Al-Mughnī 'an Ḥaml al-Aṣfār fil Asfār*, 1:323.
[40] *Miṣbāh al-Zujāja*, 1:98.
[41] *Al-Muttajir al-Rābiḥ*, p.471.

> Ḥāfiẓ 'Abd al-Ghanī al-Maqdisī declared this Ḥadīth to be fair, as did Ibn Abī Ḥātim before him. From this, it becomes clear to you that over eight of the major Ḥuffāẓ of Ḥadīth and its Imāms have declared this Ḥadīth to be either *ṣaḥīḥ* or *ḥasan*, and they are: Ibn Khuzayma, al-Mundhirī, his Shaykh: Abū al-Ḥasan, al-'Irāqī, al-Būṣīrī, Ibn Ḥajar, Sharaf al-Dīn al-Dimyāṭī, 'Abd al-Ghanī al-Maqdisī, and Ibn Abī Ḥātim among them.

So is there any room for someone to speak after they have spoken? Is it correct for someone of intellect to abandon the judgement of these erudite sires from the Ḥuffāẓ of mastery for the view of the childish ramblers at the table spreads of Ḥadīth? ﴾Do you seek to replace that which is better for that which is worse?﴿ (al-Baqara: 61) ﴾It is not the eyes that are blinded, rather it is the hearts that are in the chests.﴿ (al-Ḥajj: 46)

TAWASSUL THROUGH THE GRAVE OF THE PROPHET ﷺ BY THE INSTRUCTION OF LADY 'Ā'ISHA

The Imām, Ḥāfiẓ al-Dārimī said in his *Sunan*, 'Chapter: Allah's Honouring of His Prophet ﷺ after his Death:' "It was narrated to us by Abū al-Jawzā' Aws b. 'Abdullāh who said: 'The inhabitants of Medina suffered a severe drought, so they went and complained to 'Ā'isha who said: 'Go to the Prophet's grave and open a window towards the sky so that there will be no roof between him and the sky.' They did so, after which they were watered with such an abundance of rain that vegetation grew and the camels became fat. That year was named the Year of Plenty."[42]

This is *tawassul* through his ﷺ grave. It is not (*tawassul* through it) just because it is a grave, rather, because it contains the body of the most noble of creation and the beloved of the Lord of the worlds. It is by this great closeness that it (the grave) deserved such a noble merit.

---

[42] *Sunan al-Dārimī*, 1:43.

The Status of the Ḥadīth: As for (one of the narrators known as) Abū al-Nuʻmān, he is Muḥammad b. Faḍl who is nicknamed al-ʻĀrim. He is a Shaykh of al-Bukhārī. Al-Ḥāfiẓ (Ibn Ḥajar) said about him in *al-Taqrīb*: "He is reliable yet he changed in his latter years." I say: This does not harm him or malign his narration because al-Bukhārī narrated over one hundred Ḥadīth from him in his *Ṣaḥīḥ*, and after he mixed narrations up later in his life, he (al-Bukhārī) did not narrate from him. This has been stated by al-Dāraquṭnī, and no one can inform you like one who is well informed. Al-Dhahabī refuted Ibn Ḥibbān's statement when the later said: "He has Ḥadīth that are rejected" Al-Dhahabī countered: "Ibn Ḥibbān was unable to bring even one rejected Ḥadīth from him, so where is that which he claimed?"[43]

As for Saʻīd b. Zayd (another narrator in the chain), he is acceptable although having some errors (*ṣadūq lahu awhām*), which is also the condition of ʻAmr b. Mālik al-Nakrī as Ḥāfiẓ Ibn Ḥajar stated about the two in *al-Taqrīb*.

The scholars have affirmed that this expression: 'acceptable with some errors' (*ṣadūq yahim*), is from the expressions denoting reliability and not from the expressions denoting weakness.[44]

As for Abū al-Jawzā', he is Aws b. ʻAbdullāh al-Rubʻī. He is reliable and from the narrators of the two *Ṣaḥīḥ* collections, so this chain has no problem (*lā ba's bihi*), rather he is fine according to me, for the scholars have accepted and used as evidence many like him and even those who were less than him in status.

LADY ʻĀ'ISHA AND HER STANCE REGARDING THE GRAVE OF THE PROPHET ﷺ

As for what some say, that this report is attributed up to ʻĀ'isha, and she is a companion, and the actions of the companions are not a proof, our response to this is: Even though this is the opinion of ʻĀ'isha, she is known for her profundity of knowledge. She did what she did while in Medina in the midst of the scholars of the companions. This story is enough for us as proof that

[43] *Mīzān al-ʻItidāl*, 4:8.

[44] See *Tadrīb al-Rāwī*.

'Ā'isha—the mother of the believers—knew that the Messenger of Allah ﷺ did not cease being merciful and interceding for his Umma after his death, and that whoever visits him and seeks intercession through him, he will intercede for him. It is not idolatry or a means that lead to idolatry as is mistakenly asserted by those who impute disbelief and misguidance upon others. 'Ā'isha and those who witnessed her were not ignorant of idolatry or that which leads to it.

This story demolishes these types of people and establishes that the Prophet ﷺ has concern for his Umma while in his grave after his death. It is also established that the Mother of the believers, 'Ā'isha said: "I used to enter my apartment that contained the Messenger of Allah ﷺ and I would remove my outer garments and say: 'It is only my husband and father here.' However, when 'Umar was buried there, by Allah, I did not enter unless I was fully covered, out of shyness in front of 'Umar."[45] Ḥāfiẓ al-Haythamī said: "Its narrators are narrators of the *Ṣaḥīḥ*[46] It was also narrated by al-Ḥākim in *al-Mustadrak* and he said: "It is authentic according to the conditions of the two Shaykhs (al-Bukhārī and Muslim) and al-Dhahabī did not oppose it with anything.[47] 'Ā'isha did not know this to be false, rather, she knew that the Prophet ﷺ and his two close companions knew those who were at their graves.

The Prophet ﷺ said to Mu'ādh when he dispatched him to Yemen: "Perhaps you shall pass by my grave and Mosque."[48] When the Messenger of Allah ﷺ died, Mu'ādh went to the grave of the Prophet ﷺ and was crying. 'Umar b. al-Khaṭṭāb witnessed him in this state. The following conversation took place between him and Mu'ādh, as narrated from Zayd b. Aslam from his father who said: "'Umar went out to the Mosque, and found Mu'ādh b. Jabal crying at the grave of the Prophet ﷺ, so he said: 'What causes you to cry?'

[45] Narrated by Aḥmad.

[46] *Majma' al-Zawā'id*, 8:26.

[47] *Al-Mustadrak*, 4:7.

[48] Narrated by Aḥmad and al-Ṭabarānī. Its narrators are reliable except Yazīd who did not hear from Mu'ādh—as stated in *Majma' al-Zawā'id*, 10:55.

" 'Mu'ādh replied: 'A Ḥadīth that I heard from the Messenger of Allah ﷺ: A small portion of ostentation is polytheism.' " Al-Ḥākim said: "It is authentic and has no known defect (in the chain)."

Al-Dhahabī agreed with him saying: "It is authentic containing no defect."[49] Al-Mundhirī said in *al-Targhīb wa al-Tarhīb*: "It was narrated by Ibn Mājah, al-Bayhaqī, and al-Ḥākim who said that it was authentic without any defect." Al-Mundhirī agreed with him.[50]

TAWASSUL WITH THE GRAVE OF THE PROPHET ﷺ DURING THE CALIPHATE OF 'UMAR ؓ

Ḥāfiẓ Abū Bakr al-Bayhaqī said: "From Mālik who said: 'The people suffered a drought during the caliphate of 'Umar, whereupon a man came to the grave of the Prophet ﷺ and said: 'O Messenger of Allah, ask for rain for your Umma, for verily they have all but perished!' Afterwards, the Prophet appeared to him in a dream and told him: 'Go to 'Umar and give him my greetings, and tell him that they will be watered. Tell him: 'You must be clever, you must be clever!' The man went and told 'Umar, who said: 'O my Lord, I spare no effort except in what escapes my power!' " This chain is authentic.[51]

It was (also) narrated by Ibn Abī Shayba with an authentic chain from the narration of Ṣāliḥ al-Simān from Mālik al-Dār, who was the treasurer of 'Umar, who said: "The people suffered a drought during the caliphate of `Umar, whereupon a man came to the grave of the Prophet ﷺ and said: 'O Messenger of Allah, ask for rain for your Umma, for verily they have all but perished,' after which the Prophet appeared to him in a dream and told him: 'Go to 'Umar...' " It was narrated by Ṣayf in al-Futtūḥ that the one who saw the dream was Bilāl b. al-Ḥārith al-Muzanī, one of the companions. Ibn Ḥajar said: "Its chain is authentic."[52]

Not even one of the Imāms who narrated this Ḥadīth, or those

---

[49] *Al-Mustadrak*, 1:4.

[50] *Al-Targhīb wa al-Tarhīb*, 1:32.

[51] As narrated by Ḥāfiẓ Ibn Kathīr in *al-Bidāya* (1:91) concerning the events of year 18 H.

[52] *Ṣaḥīḥ al-Bukhārī*, 'The Book of *Istisqā*". *Fatḥ al-Bārī* (2:415).

Imāms after them who perused their works said that this is disbelief or misguidance. None of them criticized the text of the Ḥadīth. This Ḥadīth was cited by Ibn Ḥajar al-ʿAsqalānī and he authenticated its chains as has proceeded—and he is who he is (being known) for his knowledge, virtue, and weight among the Imāms of Ḥadīth, and that needs no detail.

THE *TAWASSUL* OF THE MUSLIMS THROUGH HIM ﷺ ON THE DAY OF YAMĀMA

Ḥāfiẓ Ibn Kathīr mentioned that the rallying cry of the Muslims at the battle of Yamāma was: 'O Muḥammad' (*Yā Muḥammadā*). He said: "Khālid b. Walīd battled them until he passed through their ranks and went to the mountain of Musaylama. He was watching closely, waiting to find him and kill him. He then returned to where he was previously and stood between the two opposing armies and called for individual one-on-one combat saying: 'I am Ibn al-Walīd the one who returns, I am Ibn 'Āmir and Zayd.' He then called out with the battle cry of the Muslims, and their battle cry on that day was: O Muḥammad!"[53]

TAWASSUL THROUGH HIM ﷺ IN ILLNESS AND SEVERE DIFFICULTIES

From al-Haytham b. Khanās who said: "We were with 'Abdullāh b. 'Umar ﷺ when his leg was feeling severe numbness. A man came to him and said: 'Bring to mind the most beloved person to you.' He (Ibn 'Umar) said: 'O Muḥammad.' Afterwards, it was as if it was freed from its tether."

Mujāhid said: "A man's whose foot was numb was in the presence of Ibn 'Abbās ﷺ. Ibn 'Abbās said to him: 'Bring to mind the most beloved person to you.' The man said: 'Muḥammad ﷺ' and his numbness went away completely."[54]

So this is *tawassul* through calling out.

---

[53] *Al-Bidāya wa al-Nihāya*, 6:324.

[54] Mentioned by Shaykh Ibn Taymiyya in *al-Kalim al-Ṭayyib*, 47:165.

From 'Utba b. Ghazwān, who said that the Prophet of Allah ﷺ said: "If one of you loses something, or needs assistance while he is in a far off land where he doesn't have a companion, let call out: 'O servants of Allah, assist me.' For certainly, Allah has servants we do not see.' " This has been tried. This was narrated by al-Ṭabarānī and its narrators have been declared reliable with some weakness among them, except for Yazīd b. 'Alī who did not meet 'Utba.

Ibn 'Abbās said that the Messenger of Allah ﷺ said: "Indeed, Allah has Angels other than the *Ḥafaẓa* (the guardian Angels) that write down the leaves that fall from the trees. So if one of you is afflicted by a injury in a strange land, let him call out: 'Assist me O servants of Allah.' " This was narrated by al-Ṭabarānī and its narrators are reliable.

'Abdullāh b. Mas'ūd said that the Messenger of Allah ﷺ said: "If one of you loses his mount in a strange land, let him call out: 'O servants of Allah, restrain (the mount). O servants of Allah restrain (the mount).' Allah has (Angels) present in the earth that will restrain it." This was narrated by Abū Ya'lā and al-Ṭabarānī who added: "They will restrain them for you." It contains (in the chain) Ma'rūf b. Ḥassān who is weak.[55] This is also *tawassul* in the form of calling.

In another Ḥadīth it states that the Prophet ﷺ said after praying the two units of the *fajr* prayer: "O Allah, the Lord of Jibrīl, Isrāfīl, Mikā'īl, and Muḥammad the Prophet ﷺ: I seek refuge with You from the fire." Al-Nawawī said in *al-Adhkār*: "It was narrated by Ibn al-Sunnī." Al-Ḥāfiẓ (Ibn Ḥajar) said after citing the source (of the Ḥadīth): "It is a fair (*ḥasan*) Ḥadīth."[56]

Singling these out with mention is an indication of *tawassul* through them, as if he was saying: 'O Allah, I ask You and perform *tawassul* unto You through Jibrīl...' Ibn 'Allān pointed this out in his explanation (of *al-Adhkār*) when he said: "*Tawassul* unto Allah through (His) Lordship over these mighty souls..."

---

[55] *Majma' al-Zawā'id*, 10:132.

[56] *Sharḥ al-Adhkār* of Ibn 'Allān, 2:139.

Ibn 'Allān also explicitly supported the permissibility of *tawassul* when he said in commentary upon the Ḥadīth, 'O Allah, I ask You by the right of the supplicants.': "This contains *tawassul* by the right of the possessors of good among the supplicants in general, and similar to them, nay *a fortiori,* are the Prophets and Messengers."[57]

THE MEANING OF 'UMAR'S *TAWASSUL* THROUGH AL-'ABBĀS

Al-Bukhārī narrated in his *Ṣaḥīḥ* from Anas ﷺ, who said that if there was a drought, 'Umar b. al-Khaṭṭāb ﷺ would seek rain through al-'Abbās b. 'Abd al-Muṭṭalib: "O Allah, we used to perform *tawassul* through our Prophet, and now we perform *tawassul* through the uncle of our Prophet, so send us rain."

Al-Zubayr b. Bakkār narrated in *al-Ansāb* this same story in a shorter form from another route. Its summary states: "From 'Abdullāh b. 'Umar who said: "Umar sought rain through al-'Abbās b. 'Abd al-Muṭṭalib in the year of cinders (called such because of the abundant sandstorms due to the lack of rain). He addressed the people and said: "O people, the Messenger of Allah ﷺ used to look to al-'Abbās as a son looks to his father. So, follow the Messenger of Allah ﷺ with respect to his uncle al-'Abbās, and take him as a means unto Allah." He said: "Supplicate, O 'Abbās!" His ﷺ supplication was: "O Allah, truly no tribulation descends except due to sins, and never was one removed except through repentance.

"The people have turned to you by means of me because of my position in relation to Your Prophet, and here are our hands (raised up) for You despite our sins, and our forelocks in repentance, so send down the water for us and preserve Your Prophet in the person of his uncle." Immediately afterwards, the sky let down water like mountains and the earth was soaked and the people lived and came over to al-'Abbās passing their hands over him saying: "Congratulations to you, irrigator of the two Sanctuaries!"

---

[57] Ibid. 2:129.

'Umar said: "He is, by Allah, the means to Allah and the place of nearness to Him!" '

Concerning this, 'Abbās b. 'Utba, his nephew, sung some lines of poetry. From them:

By my uncle, Allah irrigated the Ḥijāz and its people
In the night time and 'Umar sought water by his elder

Ibn 'Abd al-Barr said: "And in some narrations it states that the skies let down water that came down like mountains until the holes in the ground were equal to the hills and the earth was soaked and the people lived. 'Umar said: 'By Allah this is the means unto Allah and the place of nearness to Him!'

Ḥassān b. Thābit said:

The Imām who was acquainted with our suffering
through the drought asked
And heavy rain clouds irrigated the land
for the sake of al-'Abbās
The uncle of our Prophet who is the spitting image of his father
He who inherited that from the Prophet
and no one else among the people
By him, Allah brought life to the lands
And after despair the rolling hills became green

Al-Faḍl b. 'Abbās b. 'Utba said:

By my uncle, Allah irrigated the Ḥijāz
and its inhabitants in the darkness of night
And 'Umar sought rain through his elder
He directed himself towards al-'Abbās in hopeful desire
And (al-'Abbās) did not even repeat his supplication
before the rain fell upon Medina

In one narration it states: 'The people came over to al-'Abbās and touched him passed their hands over him and said:

" 'Congratulations O irrigator of the two sanctuaries!' "[58]

It would have been 'Umar's right to lead the people in (the prayer) for rain, however, he withdrew from his right and put al-'Abbās forward for the prayer for rain out of exaltation of the Messenger of Allah ﷺ, esteem for his family, and giving preference to his uncle ﷺ over himself and as an emphasized form of *tawassul* to the Messenger of Allah ﷺ in what extent he was capable. He encouraged the people to take al-'Abbās as a means unto Allah, the Exalted, just as he himself took him as a means by putting him forward to supplicate so that he stood in the position for the Messenger of Allah ﷺ when he was alive. He sought rain for them in the prayer place in order that it may be greater in exaltation and greater in manifesting the virtue of his progeny and family.

'Umar clarified this in his supplication when he said: "O Allah, we used to perform *tawassul* through our Prophet, and now we perform *tawassul* through the uncle of our Prophet, so send us rain."—meaning; 'we used to perform *tawassul* unto you by him ﷺ going out with the people to the prayer place, supplicating for them and leading them in prayer, and since this is impossible for us now as he has passed on ﷺ, I bring forward one from his family so the supplication is more likely to be accepted and responded to.'

When al-'Abbās supplicated, he performed *tawassul* through the Messenger of Allah ﷺ when he said: "The people have turned to you by means of me because of my position in relation to Your Prophet"—meaning, my closeness to him—"so preserve Your Prophet in the person of his uncle"—meaning, accept my supplication by virtue of Your Prophet ﷺ.

So this issue is with respect to seeking rain, and it has no connection to the *tawassul* we are speaking about which is differed over. This is known to every possessor of eyes because the story clearly proves this. They were afflicted with a drought and were in need of seeking aid through the prayer for seeking rain. This calls for an Imām to lead the people in prayer, supplicate for them and establish this Islamic rite that the Prophet ﷺ used to establish when he resided in this world among

[58] *Al-Isti'āb* of Ibn 'Abd al-Barr under the biography of al-'Abbās.

the other rites such as leading the prayer, *jumu'a*, and the sermon. These are all duties that are enjoined upon those of legal responsibility and cannot be performed by the people of the Isthmus (*barzakh*) life because they are removed from legal responsibilities and are busy with what is much greater that it.

Whoever understands from the words of the leader of the believers ('Umar), that he only performed *tawassul* through al-'Abbās and not the Messenger of Allah ﷺ because al-'Abbās was alive and the Prophet was dead, then his understanding is what is dead and his false notions have overcome him. He has demonstrated his deplorable condition or his overpowering bigotry. This is because 'Umar only performed *tawassul* through al-'Abbās because of his close relation to the Messenger of Allah ﷺ, which is implied in his words: "...and now we perform *tawassul* through the uncle of our Prophet, so send us rain." So, in this way, he performed *tawassul* through the Prophet in the most beautiful of ways.

The one who accused the Muslims of idolatry because of this—while at the same time saying that it is allowed to perform *tawassul* with the living—is far removed from what is correct. Surely, if *tawassul* was idolatry, it would not be allowed for either the living or the dead. Do you not believe that it is idolatry and disbelief and impermissible to believe in either this life and the next—for the one who believes in the Lordship of other than Allah, such as a Prophet, Angel, or saint, or believes that they deserve worship? Have you ever heard someone say: "Believing in the Lordship of other than Allah is permissible (if that 'other') is alive, however, after his death, it is idolatry"?

So you have come to know that taking a means unto Allah, the Exalted, is not worship of that means unless one believes that (this means) is a lord, as was the condition of the idol worshippers with their idols. If one believes that Allah has commanded us to take means, then this taking of means (unto Him) is an act of worship towards the One the commanded it.

THE STORY OF AL-'UTBĪ AND *TAWASSUL*

The Imām, the Ḥāfiẓ, Shaykh 'Imād b. Kathīr said:

> A group among them, such as Shaykh Abū Manṣūr al-Ṣabbāgh in his book *al-Shāmil*, have mentioned the famous story from al-'Utbī: "As I was sitting by the grave of the Prophet, a Bedouin Arab came and said: 'Peace be upon you, O Messenger of Allah! I have heard Allah saying: ﴾If they had only, when they were unjust to themselves, come unto thee and asked Allah's forgiveness, and the Messenger had asked forgiveness for them, they would have found Allah indeed Oft-returning, Most Merciful﴿ (al-Nisā': 64), so I have come to you asking forgiveness for my sin, seeking your intercession with my Lord.' Then he began to recite poetry:
>
> *O best of those whose bones are buried in the deep earth,*
> *And from whose fragrance the depth*
> *and the height have become sweet,*
> *May I be the ransom for a grave which thou inhabit,*
> *And in which are found purity, bounty and munificence!*
>
> Then the Bedouin left, and sleep overcame me, and I saw the Prophet ﷺ in my sleep. He said to me: 'O 'Utbī, run after the Bedouin and give him glad tidings that Allah has forgiven him.' "

This story was narrated by Imām al-Nawawī in his well known book *al-Īḍāḥ*, in chapter six, p.498. It was also narrated by the Ḥāfiẓ 'Imād al-Dīn Ibn Kathīr in his well known exegesis in commentary upon the verse: ﴾If they had only, when they were unjust to themselves...﴿ It was also narrated by Abū Muḥammad Ibn Qudāma in *al-Mughnī*,[59] Shaykh Abū al-Faraj Ibn Qudāma in *al-Sharḥ al-Kabīr*,[60] and Shaykh Manṣūr Ibn Yūnus al-Bahūtī in his well known book *Kashhāf al-'Qinā'*—one of the most famous books of the Ḥanbalīs.[61]

---

[59] *Al-Mughnī*, 3:556.

[60] *Al-Sharḥ al-Kabīr*, 3:495.

[61] *Kashhāf al-Qinā'*, 5:30.

The reliance of the Qur'ānic exegete, Imām al-Qurṭubī mentioned another story that resembles this (story of al-'Utbī) in his exegesis known as *al-Jāmi'*. He said:

> Abū Ṣādiq narrated that 'Alī said: "A Bedouin came three days after we had buried the Messenger of Allah ﷺ. He threw himself upon the grave of the Messenger ﷺ, scattered its dust upon his head and said: 'O Messenger of Allah, you have spoken and we listened to your words. You gained understanding from Allah and we gained understanding from you. From what Allah revealed to you is: ﴾If they had only, when they were unjust to themselves...﴿ I have wronged myself and come to you in order that you seek forgiveness for me.' The Bedouin was called out from the grave: 'You have been forgiven.' "[62]

So, this is the story of al-'Utbī, and these are the (scholars) who quoted it. It is irrelevant if this report is authentic or weak. We inquire: Did these (scholars) quote something that is idolatry and misguidance? Did they quote from something that invites to idol worship and grave worship? If that is indeed the case, then what reliability is there to be found in them or their books? Glorified are You my Lord this is a manifest slander!

THE LINES OF AL-'UTBĪ'S POETRY UPON THE METAL GRILL OUTSIDE THE GRAVE OF THE PROPHET ﷺ

The lines of poetry that the Bedouin sung during his visit to the Prophet ﷺ have been mentioned and narrated by al-'Utbī. They are:

O best of those whose bones are buried in the deep earth,
And from whose fragrance the depth
and the height have become sweet,
May I be the ransom for a grave which thou inhabit,
And in which are found purity, bounty and munificence!

[62] *Tafsīr al-Qurtubī*, 5:265.

By the grace of Allah, these lines of poetry are written upon the noble structure on the Pillar that is between the metal grill outside of the grave in the Prophet's apartment. It has been seen by all sort and sundry for hundreds of years—even during the time King 'Abd al-'Azīz, Kind Sa'ūd, King Fayṣal, and King Khālid thereafter—may Allah have mercy upon them—and continuing today with King Fahd, the custodian of the two Sacred Sanctuaries. It shall remain by the permission of Allah, based upon the instructions of the custodian of the two Sacred Sanctuaries to guard everything contained in the noble Prophetic Mosque, and not remove anything therein of its ancient relics.

Summary: In summary, there is no doubt that the Prophet ﷺ possesses high rank, lofty position, and tremendous stature with Allah. So with that, what legal or rational prohibition is there to prevent *tawassul* through him—not to mention the evidence that affirms it in this life and the next? In that, we are not asking others besides Allah, the Exalted, nor are we supplicating to anyone but Him. So, we supplicate to Him by that which He loves no matter what it may be. On occasion, we ask Him by virtue of our own righteous actions because He loves them, and on occasion, we ask Him by virtue of the one whom He loves among His creation, such as what is found in the Ḥadīth regarding the *tawassul* of Ādam that was mentioned earlier, or the Ḥadīth of Fāṭima b. Asad that we mentioned, or the Ḥadīth of 'Uthmān b. Ḥunayf mentioned earlier as well. Sometimes, we ask Him through His beautiful names, as he ﷺ said: "I ask You by the fact that You are Allah," or (we ask Him through) His attribute or action, as is in the other Ḥadīth: "I seek refuge with Your pleasure from Your wrath, and from Your pardon from Your punishment." It is not confined to that constricted circle as is imagined by some extremists.

The secret behind this is that everything Allah loves may be used in *tawassul* as well as everyone who loves Him among the Prophets and saints. This is obvious to everyone who has a sound inner disposition (*fiṭra*). There is nothing that rationally or legally prohibits it, rather, the legal (texts) and the rational (arguments) stand in support of its permissibility. The One asked in all of this is Allah who is Alone and without any partners—not a Prophet, not a saint, not a living person, and not a dead person. ﴾Say, all of it is from Allah. So how is it that these people are almost incapable of understanding speech?﴿ (al-Nisā': 78)

If it is allowed to ask by virtue of (one's) actions, then it is allowed (to ask by virtue) of the Prophet ﷺ *a fortiori* because he is the best of creation—and his actions being among them. Allah has more love for him ﷺ than our actions or anything else. Would that I know what prohibits that, when the expression used does not indicate anything more than saying that the Prophet has a rank with Allah? The one performing *tawassul* does not intend any other meaning, and whoever denies his rank with Allah, then he is a disbeliever as we stated previously.

So in conclusion, the issue of *tawassul* indicates the greatness and the love of the one on whose behalf (Allah) is asked. Asking by the Prophet is only due to his greatness with Allah or due to His (Allah's) love for him—and there is no doubt about this, for *tawassul* through actions is agreed upon. So, why is it that we do not say: The one performing *tawassul* through the Prophets and righteous is in fact performing *tawassul* through their actions that Allah loves? The Ḥadīth about the men in the cave was already mentioned which is the point of agreement.

There is no doubt that the one performing *tawassul* through the righteous only does so because of their righteousness, so this issue goes back to the righteous actions, and *tawassul* through actions is agreed upon as we mentioned in the beginning of this research.

A Rejected Doubt

All of these Ḥadīth and reports affirm and support *tawassul*, so if one objects by saying: "This is particular to his lifetime"—the reply is: This restriction has no evidence, especially when (it is affirmed) that the soul remains and that by it, there occurs feelings, comprehension, and sensation. The way of Ahl al-Sunna is that the dead can hear, sense, feel, benefit from good and become delighted, and become annoyed and saddened with evil. This is with regards to every person. It is for this reason that he ﷺ called out to the tribe of Qulayb from the disbelievers of

Quraysh on the day of Badr and said: "O 'Utba, O Shayba, O Rabī'a!" It was said to him: "How can you call out to them and they have already died?" He replied: "You do not hear as well as they do, however they are not able to respond."

If this is general for all people, then how about the most noble, exalted and best of human beings? There is no doubt that he is more complete and perfect in sensing, more complete in comprehension, and stronger in feeling. It has been explicitly stated in numerous Ḥadīth that he hears speech, returns the salutations, and that the deeds of this Umma are presented to him and he seeks forgiveness for their evil deeds and praises Allah for their good deeds. The true value of the human being is only in accordance with his senses, feelings, and comprehension—not in his mere physical life. It is for this reason that we see many of the living who have been prevented by Allah, the Exalted, from human feelings and emotions—along with a foolish nature and lack of good-taste, so they are not benefited and they are among the ranks of the dead, and refuge is sought with Allah.

THE CLAIM OF SOME OF THE IGNORANT FOLK THAT THE PROPHET ﷺ DOES NOT HEAR, SEE OR KNOW US

And from among the dead people mentioned above is the one who claims that the Prophet ﷺ does not hear, see, or know about us, nor supplicates to Allah, the Exalted, on our behalf. So what insolence is greater, and what ignorance is uglier than this—along with such foul manners and diminishment from the status of the Prophet ﷺ? Indeed, there are copious amounts of Ḥadīth and narrations that have affirmed that the dead can hear, sense, and know, whether that deceased was a believer or a disbeliever. Ibn al-Qayyim said in *Kitāb al-Rūḥ*: "And the Salaf concurred upon this, and on this basis, multiple mass transmissions have been reported from them." Shaykh Ibn Taymiyya was also asked about this issue and he delivered a legal verdict in support of it. Refer to *al-Fatāwā*, 24/331-362.

So if this is the case regarding the generality of humans, what are your thoughts concerning the generality of the believers, nay, the elite of the servants of Allah among the righteous, nay, the leader of the first (of mankind) and the last of them: our Master Muḥammad ﷺ. We have delved into this issue in detail in a special area of research is this book of ours called: 'The Isthmus Life is a Real Life' and: 'A Life Unique to the Prophet ﷺ'.

SUPPORT FOR *TAWASSUL* AMONG THE IMĀMS OF THE MUSLIMS

Here, we shall mention the names of those who are well known among the major Imāms and guardians of the Sunna who have affirmed *tawassul*, or quoted the evidence for it.

1. Imām al-Ḥāfiẓ Abū 'Abdullāh al-Ḥākim in his book *al-Mustadrak 'alā al-Ṣaḥīḥayn*. He mentioned the Ḥadīth of Ādam's *tawassul* through the Prophet ﷺ and authenticated it.
2. Ḥāfiẓ Abū Bakr al-Bayhaqī in his book *Dalā'il al-Nubuwwa*. He mentioned the Ḥadīth of Ādam and others. He took it upon himself (in his book) that he would not narrate any fabricated reports.
3. Imām al-Ḥāfiẓ Jalāl al-Dīn al-Suyūṭī in his book *al-Khaṣā'iṣ al-Kubrā*. He mentioned the Ḥadīth of Ādam's *tawassul*.
4. Imām al-Ḥāfiẓ Abū al-Faraj Ibn al-Jawzī in his book *al-Wafā'*. He mentioned this Ḥadīth (of Ādam) and others.
5. Imām al-Ḥāfiẓ Qāḍī 'Iyāḍ in his book *al-Shifā' bi-Ta'rīf Ḥuqūq al-Muṣṭafā*. He mentioned many of these (narrations) in the chapter on visitation and the virtue of the Prophet ﷺ.
6. Imām Shaykh Nūr al-Dīn al-Qārī', known as Mullā 'Alī Qārī', in his explanation of *al-Shifā'* in the same places mentioned above.
7. 'Allāma Aḥmad Shihāb al-Dīn al-Khafājī in his explanation of *al-Shifā'* called *Nasīm al-Riyāḍ* in the same places mentioned above.

8. Imām al-Ḥāfiẓ al-Qasṭalānī in his book *al-Mawāhib al-Laduniyya* in the first part of the book.
9. 'Allāma Shaykh Muḥammad 'Abd al-Bāqī al-Zurqānī in his explanation of *al-Mawāhib* (1/44).
10. Imām Shaykh al-Islam Abū Zakariyyā Yaḥyā al-Nawawī in his book *al-Īḍāḥ* (6/498).
11. 'Allāma Ibn Ḥajar al-Haytamī in his marginalia upon *al-Īḍāḥ*, p.499. He also has a separate work concerning this called *al-Jawhar al-Munaẓẓam.*
12. Ḥāfiẓ Shihāb al-Dīn Muḥammad b. Muḥammad b. al-Jawzī al-Dimashqī in his book *al-Ḥiṣn al-Ḥaṣīn*, in the section on the manners of supplication.
13. 'Allāma Imām Muḥammad b. 'Alī al-Shawkānī in his book *Tuhfa al-Dhākirīn*, p.161.
14. 'Allāma Imām and scholar of Ḥadīth, 'Alī b. 'Abd al-Kāfī al-Subkī in his book *Shifā' al-Siqām fī Ziyāra Khayr al-Anām.*
15. Ḥāfiẓ 'Imād al-Dīn Ibn Kathīr in his exegesis of Allah's words: ﴾If only they had, after having wronged themselves...﴿ (al-Nisā': 64). He mentioned the story of al-'Utbī with the Bedouin who came to visit with the intent of seeking intercession through the Prophet ﷺ, and he did not oppose it with anything. He also mentioned the story of Ādam's *tawassul* through the Prophet ﷺ in *al-Bidāya wa al-Nihāya* and he did not rule that it was fabricated (1/180). He also mentioned the story of the man who went to the grave of the Prophet ﷺ and performed *tawassul* through him. He (Ibn Kathīr) said: "Its chain is authentic." (1/91). He also mentioned that the battle cry of the Muslims was: 'O Muḥammad!' (6/324).
16. Imām al-Ḥāfiẓ Ibn Ḥajar, who mentioned the story of the man who went to the grave of the Prophet ﷺ and performed *tawassul* through him. He authenticated its chain of narration in *Fatḥ al-Bārī* (2/495).
17. The Imām and scholar of Qur'ānic exegesis: Abū 'Abdullāh al-Qurṭubī, in his exegesis of the words of the Exalted: ﴾If only they had, after having wronged themselves...﴿ (5/265).

The Companions Seek Intercession through the Prophet ﷺ

Some have claimed that it is impermissible to seek intercession from the Prophet ﷺ in the life of this world. Nay, others among the extremists have gone so far as to say that this is idolatry and misguidance. They seek to prove this through the words of the Exalted: ﴾Say: to Allah belongs the intercession in its entirety.﴿ (al-Zumar: 44) This inference from the verse is false and this (verse) does not support their corrupt understanding for two reasons:

1. There is no text in the Book or the Sunna that prohibits seeking intercession from the Prophet ﷺ in this life.

2. This verse does not prove that at all. Rather, its nature is like other verses that explain Allah's sole ownership of that which is His and no other. This means that it is He who has total control over it. This does not negate that He may give it to whoever He wills if He wills that. He is the King of kings, He gives dominion to whomever He wills, and removes dominion from whomever He wills. This is similar to His words: ﴾To Him belongs the dominion and to Him belongs all praise.﴿ (al-Taghābun: 1)

He described Himself saying that He is the King of kings, while at the same time saying: ﴾He gives dominion to whom He wills, and removes dominion from whoever He wills.﴿ (Āl 'Imrān: 26) And the words of the Exalted: ﴾Whoever desires honour, then to Allah belongs all honour.﴿ (al-Fāṭir: 10) Along with His words: ﴾And to Allah belongs all honour, and His Messenger, and the believers.﴿ (al-Munāfiqūn: 7)

Likewise with regard to intercession, He said: ﴾Say: to Allah belongs the intercession in its entirety.﴿ (al-Zumar: 44) along with His words: ﴾They do not possess the (power of) intercession, save he who takes a covenant with Allah.﴿ (Maryam: 87) and His words: ﴾Those who they call upon besides Allah do not possess intercession—save the one who witnesses to the truth while knowing.﴿ (al-Zukhruf: 86)

So, just as He ﷻ gives to whomever He wills, whatever He wills, He also gives honour as He wills to His Messengers and the believers—and this is the case with intercession. It all belongs to Him yet He has given it to the Prophets and His righteous servants, nay, even the common folk among the believers as mentioned in authentic Ḥadīth reports that are mass transmitted by their meaning (*mutawātir maʿnawī*).

What harm is there for someone to seek from the King some of what He owns—especially since the one asked is Generous and the supplicant is in severe need for what he is requesting. Is intercession anything other than supplication, and supplication is permitted, possible, and accepted—especially from the Prophets, and the righteous in this life and after death; in the grave and on the Day of Judgement? Intercession is given to the he who takes a covenant with Allah, and is accepted with Him, the Exalted, for everyone who dies upon *tawḥīd*.

It has been established that some of the companions asked the Prophet for intercession, and he ﷺ did not say "Your request of intercession from me is idolatry, so seek it from Allah! Do no associate any partners with your Lord!" Take Anas b. Mālik ؓ who said: "O Prophet of Allah, intercede for me on the Day of Judgement." He ﷺ responded to him: "I shall do it with Allah's will." This was narrated by al-Tirmidhī in his *Sunan* in the chapter describing the traverse (*ṣirāṭ*). Others besides Anas also asked him ﷺ for intercession.

Take Sawād b. Qārib who said in front of the Messenger of Allah ﷺ: "I bear witness that there is no lord besides Allah and that you are the one entrusted (by Him) upon all of the unseen things and that you are indeed the closest of the Prophets in being a means unto Allah, O son of the two generous and good ones...*So be one to intercede for me on the day when there will be no intercessor besides you that will suffice Sawād b. Qārib*."

This was narrated by al-Bayhaqī in *Dalā'il al-Nubuwwa*, Ibn ʿAbd al-Barr in *al-Istiʿāb*, Ḥāfiẓ Ibn Ḥajar in *Fatḥ al-Bārī* (5/180) in the chapter on the Islam of ʿUmar ؓ. The Messenger of Allah ﷺ assented to his request for intercession and did not censure him for that. Māzin b. ʿAḍūb also sought intercession from him when he came to him as a Muslim. He sung in some lines of poetry:

To you O Messenger of Allah I rode out with my riding beast
Upon the slender hills from Oman to 'Araj
In order that you—the best one to walk over ground—
may intercede for me—
So my Lord may forgive me and I return with my need [63]

'Ukāsha b. Mihṣan also sought intercession from him ﷺ when he ﷺ mentioned the seventy thousand that shall enter paradise without any account. 'Ukāsha said: "Ask Allah to make me from them." He ﷺ said immediately after that without any hesitation: "You are from them."

It is known that no one—no matter who they are—can obtain this favour until after his greater intercession ﷺ for the people of the plains (on the Day of Judgement), as is established in the mass transmitted Ḥadīth. This is concerning the meaning of seeking intercession.

There are many other examples of this in the noble books of the Sunna. They all prove the permissibility of seeking intercession from him ﷺ in this life. Some of them explicitly sought it with their words: "Intercede for me," or they sought to enter paradise, or sought to be from the foremost, or sought to be from the people of the pond (*ḥawḍ*), or sought his companionship in paradise—so he ﷺ showed them the way by saying: "Assist me against yourself with abundant prostration." He did not say to him or any other who sought paradise, companionship, or hoped to be from the people of paradise, or hoped to be from the people of the pond, or to be of those who are forgiven—he did not say to any of them this is forbidden and that it is not allowed to seek it now (in this life) for its time has not yet come. He did not say: "Wait until Allah permits the intercession or until He allows (them) to enter paradise or drink from the pond"—even though all of these things that are sought after will not take place until after the greater intercession. This is the meaning of seeking intercession and the Prophet ﷺ gave them glad tidings of that and promised them so as to put their worries at ease and provide a coolness to their eyes. Allah forbid that this could be forbidden yet he ﷺ did not clarify that out of false civility and flattery—

[63] Narrated by Abū Nu'aym in *Dalā'il al-Nubuwwa*, p.77.

while he is the one who does not fear the blame of the blamer when it is for the sake of the truth. Indeed, he would only put their worries at ease and please their souls with that which revolves around the truth and derives from the root of the religion and is far from every falsehood and hypocrisy.

If it is correct to seek intercession from him in the life of this world before the hereafter, this means that he shall obtain it in reality in its proper time on the Day of Judgement and after Allah, the Exalted, allows the intercession of the intercessors—not that he shall obtain it before its time.

In reality, this is similar to his tidings that he gave to many of the believers. This means that they shall enter paradise on the Day of Judgement after Allah gives permission (for them) to enter on the appointed time. It does not mean that they shall enter it in this life or in the Isthmus (*barzakh*) life. I do not believe that a single intelligent person from the commonality of the Muslims believes differently.

If it is correct to seek intercession from him in the life of this world, we say: There is no harm in seeking it from him after his death as well, based upon what is attested to among Ahl al-Sunna that the Prophets are alive in the Isthmus life. Our Prophet ﷺ is the most complete of them and the greatest of them in that, for he hears speech and the deeds of the Umma are presented to him, where he then either seeks Allah's forgiveness for them, or praises Allah. The prayer of those who send prayers upon him reaches him even if they are in the furthest reaches of the world, as is reported in the Ḥadīth that was authenticated by a group of Ḥuffāẓ: "My life is an immense good for you: you bring up new matters and new matters are brought up for you. My death, also, is an immense good for you: your actions will be shown to me; if I see goodness I shall praise Allah and if I see evil I shall ask forgiveness of Him for you." This Ḥadīth was authenticated by the Ḥuffāẓ: al-'Irāqī, al-Haytamī, al-Qasṭalānī, al-Suyūṭī, and Ismā'īl al-Qāḍī. We detailed its source elsewhere.

So if you sought intercession from him ﷺ, he is able to supplicate to Allah and ask Him just as he did in this life. The servant shall then obtain it in its proper place after Allah, the Exalted, permits it, just as someone shall obtain paradise if he was given the glad tidings of it in this life.

He shall obtain it in its appropriate time after Allah permits him to enter paradise—both are equal. This is what we believe and to which our hearts firmly cling.

IBN TAYMIYYA'S EXPLANATION OF THE VERSES PERTAINING TO INTERCESSION IMPLIES THAT IT IS PERMISSIBLE TO SEEK INTERCESSION FROM THE PROPHET ﷺ IN THE LIFE OF THIS WORLD

Shaykh Ibn Taymiyya mentioned a very beautiful point in his *Fatāwā* concerning the verses that are cited in (proving) the prohibition of intercession, that it does not benefit, and the prohibition of seeking it—verses that are used as proof for those who believe that it is prohibited to seek intercession from the Prophet ﷺ in the life of this world. It seems apparent from the words of Shaykh Ibn Taymiyya concerning the meaning of these verses, that those who use them as proof for what they claim are using them in the wrong place and that they are altering the words from their proper places.

The Shaykh said:

> Those who denied intercession used as evidence, the words of the Exalted: ﴾Fear the day that one soul shall not avail another soul one bit, nor shall intercession be accepted from them, nor shall justice be taken from them.﴿ (al-Baqara: 48) And His words: ﴾No justice shall be accepted from them, nor shall intercession be of any benefit for it (the soul).﴿ And His words: ﴾The wrong doers shall have no close companion or intercessor that is obeyed.﴿ (Ghāfir: 18) And His words: ﴾The intercession of the intercessors shall not benefit them.﴿ (al-Muddathir: 48)
>
> The response of Ahl al-Sunna is that these (verses cited) indicate two things:
>
> **One:** It will not benefit the idol worshippers, as the Exalted said in description of them:

> ﴾What caused you to arrive in the hell fire? They said: "We were not of those who prayed, nor did we feed the poor, and we used to dispute with the disputers and we used to deny the Day of Judgement until death came to us." The intercession of the intercessors shall not benefit them.﴿ (al-Muddathir: 42-48)
>
> So, because they are disbelievers, the benefit of the intercession of the intercessors is denied from them.
>
> **Two:** This is a negation of the intercession that is affirmed by the people of idolatry and those who resemble them among the people of innovation from the people of the book (the Jews and Christians), and the Muslims who believe that (some of) the creation have power from Allah whereby they are able to intercede without His (Allah's) permission—just as the people intercede among themselves, whereby the one from whom the intercession is sought accepts the intercession of the one seeking it due to his need for that person, be it willingly or unwillingly; just as the creation interact among themselves with mutual self interests. The idol worshippers used to take intercessors besides Allah among the Angels, the Prophets and righteous. They would produce images of them and seek intercession through them and say: 'These are the elite of Allah.'

I say: these are the words of Shaykh Ibn Taymiyya word for word. From these words, the reality of these verses become plainly clear—verses that are used as evidence by those who deny seeking intercession from the Prophet ﷺ in the life of this world or those who say that it is idolatry and misguidance.

The summary of his words is that the intended meaning of these verses is that the intercession will not benefit the idol worshippers. The verses are concerning that issue. Or (it is said) that what is meant is denial of the intercession that is affirmed by the people of idolatry, which is the belief that the intercessor possesses that without the permission of Allah ﷻ. What was mentioned here by the Shaykh is exactly what we believe as well, by the grace of Allah. We say: If the one seeking intercession from him ﷺ believes or thinks that he ﷺ intercedes without the permission of Allah, then this is idolatry or misguidance about which we have no doubt whatsoever. Allah forbid, Allah forbid, I repeat, Allah forbid that we believe or think that. We declare our innocence in front of Allah from that!

When we seek intercession, we believe completely that no one can intercede unless it is with His ﷻ permission, and nothing of this shall occur unless it is with His pleasure and support. This is only like seeking to enter paradise, seeking to drink from the lake fount, or seeking salvation upon the traverse. None of these things can be obtained unless it is with the permission of Allah and in its appropriate time that Allah the Exalted has decreed. Does anyone with intellect doubt this? Is this hidden to anyone with a modicum of knowledge or who has perused the books of the Salaf among the novice students of Sacred knowledge?

YOU ALONE WE WORSHIP AND FROM YOU ALONE WE SEEK ASSISTANCE

We clearly and unequivocally believe without any doubt that the basis for things like seeking aid and assistance, requests, calling out, and asking is that they are for Allah ﷻ, for He is the One who gives assistance and aid, and He is the One who responds. Allah the Exalted said: ﴾And do not call besides Allah that which can neither benefit you nor harm you, for if you do then surely you will be of the unjust. And if Allah should afflict you with harm, then there is none to remove it but He﴿ (Yūnus: 106-107) And He said: ﴾Seek provision from Allah and worship Him.﴿ (al- 'Ankabūt: 17) And He said: ﴾Who is more astray than the one who calls upon other than Allah; one who will not respond to him until the Day of Judgement?﴿ (al-Ahqāf: 5) And He said: ﴾Or, Who answers the distressed one and removes the evil when he calls upon Him?﴿ (al-Naml: 62)

So, worship in all of its forms, must be directed to Allah alone. It is not permissible to direct any of it to other than Allah no matter who it may be: ﴾Say, indeed my prayer and my sacrifice, my living and my dying are all for Allah, the Lord of the worlds—Him having no partner therein. With this I have been commanded and I am the first of those who submit (unto Him).﴿ (al-An'ām: 162-163)

So, there is no vow except that it is for Allah, no supplication except to Him, no slaughtering except for Him, there is no seeking of aid, help, or succour except through Him. There is no swearing except by Allah. There is no reliance except upon Him. Far removed is He from what the idol worshippers associate with Him. We believe Allah is the Creator of the servants and their deeds. There is no independent causation for anyone dead or alive except Him. There is no one who shares with Allah any action, leaving off (an action), provision, bringing of life, or bringing of death. There is no one from the creation who is capable of an act or the leaving off of an act by his own self volition, independent of Allah or along with Allah or less than that. The one who manages the affairs in the universe is Allah ﷻ, and no one possesses anything unless Allah bestows it upon him and gives him permission to utilize it. No one possesses the ability to bring benefit, harm, life, death, or resurrection to themselves, much less anyone else—unless Allah wills and allows for such. In that case, bringing benefit and harm would be limited with this limit and restricted with this restriction and its ascription to the creation would be by way of acquisition and means, not in the way of creating, bringing into being, causative and operative effect, or strength. So in reality, this ascription is figurative and not literal. The people however, differ regarding the ways of expressing these realities. Some of them go headlong into using figurative speech in a way that is nothing more than severe liberality, to the point where they fall into using doubtful expressions the outward purport of which they are innocent of while their hearts are sound and fastened upon correct *tawḥīd* and Divine transcendence of Allah.

There are some who hold extra fast to the literal wordings so much so that they go beyond the limits of balance, thereby falling into extremism, severity, and harming people by treating them according to the opposite of what they really believe and forcing them assent to what they do not believe, insisting on implications (of their words) that they do not intend, and judging them with matters that they are innocent of. What is obligatory is (for one) to be balanced and far removed from all of this, for it is safer for ones religion and more scrupulous in guarding the station of *tawḥīd*, and Allah knows best.

Shaykh Ibn Taymiyya mentioned a beneficial summary clarifying what is unique to the Real (Allah ﷻ), and this is exactly what we believe as well and worship Allah the Exalted by. Our creed is based off that of the Salaf, by the bounty of Allah, and our path is the Muḥammadan path and we also say as Ibn Taymiyya says (regarding this).

Shaykh Ibn Taymiyya said:

> Allah has made rights for Himself that none of the creation share with Him in, so it is not fitting that worship goes to other than Him, or that supplication is directed except to Him. There is to be no reliance except upon Him, no worshipful longing except for Him, no worshipful dread except of Him, and there is no source of safety and succour except unto Him, No one brings the good things but Him. No one removes the bad things except Him. There is no might or strength except through Him. ﴾And the intercession will not avail one from Him save for the one who He gives permission.﴿ (Sabā': 23) ﴾Who is he that shall intercede unto Him unless it is with His will?﴿ (al-Baqara: 255) ﴾There is nothing in the heavens and the earth save that it comes unto the Most Merciful as a slave. He has certainly encompassed them and taken count of them. All of them shall approach Him on the Day of Judgement alone.﴿ (Maryam: 93-95) And the Exalted said: ﴾And whoever obeys Allah and His Messenger and fears Allah and takes pious caution through Him, then indeed they are the successful.﴿ (al-Nūr: 52) So, He made obedience to be for Allah and the Messenger ﷺ, and for fear and piety for Him alone. Similarly, in the words of the Exalted: ﴾If only they were pleased with what Allah and His Messenger had given them and said: 'Allah is sufficient for us, indeed Allah and His Messenger shall give from His bounty. Indeed we are worshipfully longing for Allah.'﴿ (al-Tawba: 59) So here, (we see that) giving is for Allah and the Messenger. As for reliance and worshipful longing, they are for Allah alone.[64]

[64] *Al-Fatāwā*, 11:98.

Seeking Aid and Turning to the Prophet ﷺ in Request

We mentioned previously that we clearly and unequivocally believe without any doubt that the basis for things like: seeking aid and assistance, request, calling out, and asking, is that they are for Allah ﷻ, for He is the One who gives assistance and aid, and He is the One who responds. The Exalted said: ﴾And your Lord has said: 'Call upon Me, I shall respond to you.'﴿ (Ghāfir: 60) So, whoever seeks aid from one of the creation, seeks succour by him, calls upon him, asks him, or requests from him—be he dead or alive—while believing that he brings benefit and harm by himself and independent of Allah, then he has fallen into idolatry. With this however, Allah has allowed for the creation to seek help and succour from each other. He (also) ordered that the one from whom help is sought extend help to the seeker, and (ordered) the one from whom succour is sought to provide it, and the one who is called to respond. The Ḥadīth that speak of this are very numerous and all of them prove the meritorious nature of assisting the one in distress, helping the one in need, and removing the difficulties. The Prophet ﷺ is the greatest of those from whom help is sought unto Allah ﷻ in the removal of difficulties and fulfilment of needs. What severity is greater than the severity of the Day of Judgement, when the standing shall be lengthened, the crowding severe, the heat increased, and sweat shall reach wherever Allah wills? With the severity reaching its peak, the people shall seek assistance unto Allah through the best of His creation, as stated by the Messenger ﷺ: "While they are in that state, they shall seek the assistance of Ādam..." He used the expression *istighātha* (seeking assistance), and this is found in *Ṣaḥīḥ al-Bukhārī*. The companions, may Allah be pleased with all of them, used to seek his aid and assistance, and seek intercession through him ﷺ. They also used to complain to him of their affairs such as poverty, sickness, affliction, debt, and inability. They used to hasten to him in moments of severity and ask and request from him while believing that he is nothing more than an intermediary and means for benefit and harm, whereas the real doer is Allah.

Abū Hurayra Complains of Forgetfulness

Al-Bukhārī and others narrated from Abū Hurayra ﵁ that he once complained to the Prophet ﷺ about forgetfulness when he hears his noble Ḥadīth. He wanted an end to this, so he said ﵁: "O Messenger of Allah! I hear many Ḥadīth from you yet I forget them. I would love to not ever forget them." He ﷺ responded: "Open your garment." He (Abū Hurayra) then opened his garment, whereupon he ﷺ fanned air by his blessed hand inside the garment and said: "Close it." Abū Hurayra closed it. He later said: "I have not forgotten anything after that."[65]

So here is Abū Hurayra seeking from him ﷺ that he does not forget. This is something that is not possible except for Allah. He ﷺ did not censure him or accuse him of idolatry, because everyone knows that if a monotheist requests something from one who possesses rank with Allah, he does not intend thereby that he create something nor does he believe anything of the sort regarding him. He only desires that he acts as a means for him in what Allah gave him of ability in making supplications and whatever other matters Allah willed for him. Here you see that he ﷺ responded to his request and it is not reported in this story that he supplicated for him. All that is cited is that he ﷺ fanned air into his garment and ordered him to fasten it close to his chest. Allah made this happen as a bounty from Him, and a means for the fulfilment of his needs.

Likewise, he ﷺ did not say to him: "Why are you asking me when Allah is closer to you than I am?" It is well known to everyone that the deciding factor in the fulfilment of needs, is in He whose hands are the reigns of the affairs, and is based upon the closeness of the seeker to Him and the completeness of his position with Him.

Qatāda Seeks Aid with Him ﷺ to Heal his Eye: It is established that Qatāda b. al-Nuʿmān had an injury in his eye whereby his eyeball came out of its socket. They wanted to cut it off so he said: "No. Not until I seek the decision of the Messenger of Allah."

---

[65] Al-Bukhārī, 'The Book of Knowledge' section: 'Guarding Knowledge' #119.

He sought his decision and he ﷺ said: "No." Then, the Prophet placed the palm of his hand upon his pupil and gently pushed it and it returned to its original state and became his strongest eye. This was narrated by al-Baghawī, and Abū Ya'lā, and was cited by al-Dāraquṭnī, Ibn Shāhīn, al-Bayhaqī in *al-Dalā'il*, and was quoted by Ḥāfiẓ Ibn Ḥajar in *al-Iṣāba*[66] and al-Suyūṭī in *al-Khaṣā'iṣ al-Kubrā*.

Another Companion Seeks His Aid ﷺ in Removal of Large Cyst: From Muḥammad b. 'Uqba b. Shurayḥīl from his grandfather 'Abd al-Raḥmān from his father who said: "I went to the Messenger of Allah ﷺ with a large cyst on my hand. I said to him: 'O Prophet of Allah ﷺ! This cyst of mine has swollen and has prevented me from firmly grasping my sword and holding the reigns of my horse.' The Messenger of Allah ﷺ said: 'Come close to me.' I came close to him and he opened it, blew spittle into the palm of my hand then placed his hand on the cyst. He persisted in rubbing it with the palm of his hand until it was removed and I did not see any trace of it.' "[67]

Mu'ādh Requests Him ﷺ to Heal his Hand. During the Fighting on the Battle of Badr: 'Ikrima b. Abī Jahl struck Mu'ādh on the shoulder. Mu'ādh said: "He struck my arm and it was only hanging by the skin, but I was distracted away from it due to the fighting. In fact, most of the day I was dragging it around with me until it started to bother me, so I then placed my foot over it and pulled it off." In *al-Mawāhib* it states: "Mu'ādh b. 'Amr carried his hand around—the one that he struck 'Ikrima with—to the Messenger of Allah ﷺ, as mentioned by Qāḍī 'Iyāḍ from Ibn Wahb, whereupon the Prophet ﷺ spat upon it and it rejoined to his body. This story was mentioned by al-Zurqānī and ascribed it to Ibn Isḥāq from the route of al-Ḥākim.

Seeking Aid and Succour through Him ﷺ unto Allah: There are copious and numerous authentic texts stating that if there

---

[66] *Al-Isāba*, 3:225

[67] Narrated by al-Ṭabarānī and mentioned by Ḥāfiẓ al-Haythamī in *Majma' al-Zawāid*, 8:298.

was a drought and rain was withheld, the companions would hasten to him ﷺ, seeking intercession, performing *tawassul*, requesting, and seeking aid through him unto Allah. They would present their problems to him and complain of the afflictions and evil that had befallen them.

Take the Bedouin who called upon him while he was delivering the Friday sermon saying: "O Messenger of Allah! The wealth has been destroyed, and the paths have been severed, so supplicate to Allah that He sends us rain." He ﷺ supplicated to Allah, whereupon the rain fell until the Friday prayer of the next week and the Bedouin came back to him ﷺ and said: "O Messenger of Allah, the houses have been destroyed and the paths have been severed, and the grazing animals have been destroyed (from the large amount of rain)," so he ﷺ supplicated (to Allah) until the clouds were rent asunder and the rain poured on the outskirts of Medina.[68]

Abū Dāwūd narrated from 'Ā'isha with a sound chain that she said: "The people complained to the Prophet ﷺ of the torrential rains."[69]

It was narrated by Anas b. Mālik that a Bedouin came to the Prophet ﷺ and said: "O Messenger of Allah! I came to you because we do not possess a camel that can ride or a child whose hunger is satiated." Then he recited some lines of poetry:

We have come to you and the teats of the animals are bleeding
And the mother of the child is distracted away from her infant
The young man's shoulders are lowered
from the weakness of hunger
And he does not pass by or adorn himself
There is nothing for our people to eat
Save colocynth and washed 'ilhiz [70]

---

[68] Narrated by al-Bukhārī in 'The Book of Seeking Rain' section: 'The People asking the Imām for Rain when they suffer a Drought.'

[69] Abū Dāwūd, *Kitāb al-Ṣalāh*, section on seeking rain. This was also narrated by al-Bayhaqī in *Dalā'il al-Nubuwwa* from Anas with a chain containing no one that is accused of forgery. See *Fatḥ al-Barī*, 2:495.

[70] *'ilhiz*: a food eaten in times of famine and extreme scarcity, mixed with the blood and hair of camels.—**tr**

We have no other to flee to than you
And where shall the people flee to
other than to the Messengers?

So he ﷺ stood up dragging his upper garment until he ascended the pulpit, then he raised his hands and supplicated: "O Allah! Water us with a reliving rain that is abundant and dispersed, in the low and high valleys, beneficial and without harm. Send it quickly without delay, filling the utters with it, causing the crops to sprout, and bringing life to the earth after its death."

The narrator stated: "He did not lower his hands (from supplication) until the clouds gathered together and the people came out complaining about the immense amount of rain, so he ﷺ said: 'On our outskirts and not upon us,' after which, the clouds departed from Medina."

See how he ﷺ figuratively ascribed relief and benefit and its likes to the rain, and how he tacitly approved the statement of the poet when he said: "*We have no one to flee to save you...*" and did not consider him an idolater because the statement was an ascription. Were the words of Allah hidden from him ﷺ even though they were revealed to him? ﴾So flee unto Allah...﴿ (al-Dhāriyāt: 50)

What this means is to say that the fleeing whose benefit it is emphatically hoped for is to you (the Messenger of Allah ﷺ) and no other less than you, and to the Messengers and no other less than them. Hence, the Messengers are the greatest of those through whom *tawassul* is performed unto Allah ﷻ and they are the most tremendous of those on whose behalf and through whose hands, Allah fulfils the needs of those who turn to them and seek aid.

Contemplate deeply how he ﷺ was strongly affected by the words sung by the poet, and how he stood quickly to respond to their seeking of aid and request, to the point that he stood on the pulpit while dragging his upper garment—not even stopping to arrange it properly, all so he could respond and hasten to those who called him. May he and his family be granted the most virtuous of prayers and peace.

The Prophet ﷺ is our Pillar, Focal Point of Refuge, and Aid

Ḥassān b. Thābit called out to him and described him as the pillar upon which he relies and the focal point of refuge with whom he seeks aid. He said:

O you who are the sturdy pillar
and focal point of the one who seeks aid
And the useful refuge and close neighbour
O you who the Deity chose for His creation
And gifted him with the pure and clean character
You are the Prophet
and the best focal point of refuge for Ādam
O you who is generous like the effulgence of the bejewelled sea
Mīkāl and Jibrīl are both with you and they are
A source of your victory
from the One who is All Mighty and All Able[71]

Ḥamza is the Doer of Good and the one who Removes the Afflictions

There is a report from Ibn Shādhān from Ibn Masʿūd ؓ, in which he said: "We have never seen the Messenger of Allah ﷺ crying as severe as he was upon the death of Ḥamza b. ʿAbd al-Muṭṭalib. He placed him in the direction of the *qibla*, prayed the funeral prayer and wept until he was soaked. He said: "O Ḥamza! O uncle of the Messenger of Allah! O lion of Allah and lion of the Messenger of Allah! O Ḥamza! O doer of good! O remover of afflictions! O defender of the Messenger of Allah."[72]

There is No Difference Between Life and Death: If someone objects saying: 'Seeking aid through him ﷺ, complaining to him, seeking his intercession, aid, and everything else mentioned here is only correct when done during his life.

---

[71] Seel *al-Isāba*, 1:264 and *al-Rawd al-Ānif*, 2:91.
[72] *Al-Mawāhib al-Ladūniyya*, 1:212.

As for doing this after his death, it is disbelief (or he may be more easygoing and say that it is 'not legislated' or 'not allowed').' In response to this, we say: With regards to seeking aid and performing *tawassul*, if life is the factor affecting its validity as they say, then in that case, the Prophets are alive in their graves, as are others among the worshippers of Allah with whom He is pleased. If there were no proof for the jurist in proving the validity of *tawassul* and seeking aid through him ﷺ after his death save this analogy between *tawassul* and seeking aid through him during his life in this world, it would be sufficient. He is living in both of the two abodes and has constant concern for his Umma. He interacts in the affairs (of the world) with the permission of Allah and he is well informed of the conditions of the Umma. The prayers of those who pray among the Umma are presented to him and their salutations to him reach him despite their large number.

He who possesses expansive knowledge of the conditions of the souls, and the special qualities that they have been given—especially the lofty souls among them—his heart will be open to believe that (mentioned above), so how about the most superior soul among the souls and the most superior light among the lights, our Prophet, may prayers and peace be upon him.

If seeking intercession, seeking aid, and *tawassul* through him ﷺ was idolatry and disbelief—as they imagined—it would not be permissible under any circumstance, neither in the life of this world nor in death, and neither on the Day of Judgement nor before it. Idolatry is detested by Allah at all times.

A False Claim

As for the claim that the dead have no ability to do anything, this is false, because if this belief of theirs was a result of their belief that the dead become dust, then this is the peak of ignorance regarding what has been narrated from our Prophet ﷺ. Nay it is ignorance of what is mentioned by Allah regarding the life of the souls after their separation from their bodies and how the Prophet ﷺ addressed them on the day of Badr saying: "O 'Amr b. Hishām. O 'Utba b. Rabī'a. O so and so, we have certainly found the promise of our Lord to be true. Have you found the promise of your Lord to be true?" He ﷺ was asked about this and he replied: "You do not hear what I say better than they can."

Another example of this is when he sent his salutations and called out to the people of the graves: "Peace be upon you O inhabitants of this place."

Another example of this is the punishment and delight in the grave, and the affirmation of the souls coming and going, as well as other evidence Islam has brought which has been affirmed by philosophers both ancient and modern.

Let us suffice with this question. Do you all believe that the martyrs are alive with their Lord as stated by the Qur'ān or not? If they do not believe that then we have nothing more to say to them, because they have denied the Qur'ān wherein it states: ﴾And do not say regarding those who are killed in the way of Allah that they are dead. Nay, they are alive but you perceive not.﴿ (al-Baqara: 154) And: ﴾Do not consider those killed in the way of Allah as dead. Nay, they are with their Lord being provided for.﴿ (Āl 'Imrān: 169)

If they believe that, we say to them: the Prophets and many of the righteous Muslims were not martyrs—such as the major companions, and they are more virtuous than the martyrs without doubt. So if the life of the martyrs is established, then it is established *a fortiori* for those who are more virtuous than them, despite the fact that the life of the Prophets is explicitly stated in the authentic narrations.

We say: Since the life of the souls is established with decisive evidence, there is no room for us but to also affirm its unique qualities. This is because to affirm something obligates that its implications are affirmed as well, just as negating the implications of something necessitates negating that thing, as is well known.

What rational barrier is there to prevent seeking aid or succour from Allah through them (the souls), just as a man might seek the aid of the Angels in the fulfilment of his needs, or seek the aid of another man (and as the poet says: It is by your soul—not your body—that you are human)? The interaction of the souls is similar to the interaction of the Angels in that there is no need for spatial contact or tools. The souls are not bound by the laws of interaction that are known in this life of ours, nay it is a different life all together. ﴾They ask you concerning the soul. Say: "The soul is from the affair of my Lord."﴿ (al-Isrā': 85) So, what do they understand of the interaction undertaken by the Angels and Jinn in this world? There is no doubt that the souls possess a degree of freedom and ability to roam that enable them to respond to those who address them and aid those who seek their aid—just like the living—nay, even more so and to a greater degree.

So if they (the opponents) know nothing but the things found through sensory perception, and if they admit to nothing save those things that are physically observed, then this is the position of the naturalists and not that of the believers.

Let us compromise with them and concede that the souls cannot do anything after they are separated from their bodies. With that however, we say: If we assume this and agree for arguments sake, we are able to assert that the assistance and aid from the Prophets and saints to those who seek their aid is not from the category of the soul's intervention and interaction in this world. Rather, their aid to those who visit them or seek their aid is by supplicating for them, just as a righteous man supplicates for another. So, this is like the supplication of one who is good for one who is less good. At the very least, it is like a brother's supplication for his fellow brother. It is already known that they are alive and feeling, sensing, and knowing. Indeed, feeling is more complete, and knowledge is more comprehensive after (the soul's) separation from the body because it results in the veils of dirt being lifted and there are no conflict with the human base-desires.

It appears in the Ḥadīth that our deeds are presented to him ﷺ. If he finds good, he praises Allah. If he finds other than that, he seeks forgiveness for us. We are able to say: The one from whom aid and succour is sought is Allah, the Exalted, however, the one asking is asking while performing *tawassul* unto Allah through the Prophet ﷺ so that his needs are met. So the doer is Allah, however the questioner wanted to ask Him, the Exalted, by virtue of some of those who are close to Him and deemed noble. It is as if he is saying: '(O Allah), I am of those who love him, so have mercy upon me for his sake.' Allah shall bestow mercy upon many of the people because of the Prophet ﷺ and others of the

Prophets and saints. So in general, it is well known that Allah bestows His generosity upon some of the lovers of the Prophet ﷺ, for the sake of His Prophet, nay, He bestows (His generosity) upon some of the servants for the sake of other servants. Included in this are those who pray upon the dead and seek Allah's pardon and generosity for their sake by their statement: 'We have come to you as intercessors, so intercede for us (as well).'

IS IT IDOLATRY TO SEEK (FROM ONE) SOMETHING THAT ONLY ALLAH IS CAPABLE OF?

From the other false claims that are held to firmly by those who impute disbelief upon those who perform *tawassul* through the Prophet ﷺ or seek from him, is their statement: 'The people request things from the dead Prophets and righteous that only Allah is capable of and this request is idolatry.'

The response is that this is a faulty understanding of what the Muslims have been upon since the days of old till now. The people only request them to be a means unto their Lord in fulfilling what they seek from Allah, the Exalted and Sublime, in that He, the Exalted, fulfils it as a result of their intercession, supplication, and entreaties, as is authentically reported in the narration of the blind man and others who sought aid and performed *tawassul* through him ﷺ unto Allah, where he ﷺ then in turn, responded to their requests, soothed their thoughts, and caused their desires to materialize with His permission. He ﷺ did not say to any of them "You have committed an act of idolatry." This applies to everything requested of him in the form of preternatural phenomena such as healing a terminal illness without medicine, sending rain down from the heavens without clouds when there was a need for it, causing water springs to flow, water flowing from his fingertips, and causing food to increase etc. These things do not fall under the realm of what is customarily possible for humans, yet, he used to respond (to requests of that nature) and he did not say to them: "You have committed an act of idolatry so renew your Islam for you have sought from me that which none is capable of doing save Allah."

Are these (opponents) more knowledgeable of *tawḥīd* and that which expels one from Islam than the Messenger of Allah ﷺ and his companions? An ignoramus could not imagine such a thing, let alone a scholar!

The Glorious Qur'ān narrates the statement of Prophet Sulaymān ﷺ to the people of his gathering among the Jinn and men: ﴾O chiefs! Which of you is able to bring me her throne before they come to us in submission?﴿ (al-Naml: 38) So here, he is requesting them to bring a mighty throne from Yemen all the way to him in the Levant in a preternatural way in order that it might be a sign for its owner (the Queen) that invites her to faith. When the *'Ifrīt* (major Jinn) said: ﴾I can bring it to you before you stand up from you sitting place﴿ (al-Naml: 39), the Prophet of Allah, Sulaymān ﷺ said: "I want it faster than that." ﴾One of those who had knowledge of the book—one of the truthful ones from his gathering among the humans—said: I can bring it to you before you blink your eye.﴿ (al-Naml: 40) This means: before you lift your eyelid after you close it. He (Sulaymān) ﷺ said: "This is what I want." The man called out and lo and behold, the throne was in front of him.

Bringing the throne in this manner is something that none is capable of save Allah and it is not within the realm of what is possible for the human beings or Jinn customarily, yet Sulaymān requested this from the people of his gathering and that truthful man said to him: "I will do it." So did Sulaymān—the Prophet of Allah—fall into disbelief by this request of his, and did the truthful man commit an act of idolatry with his response? Far removed are they from such a thing. The ascription of the action in both statements is a form of logical metaphor that is not only allowed in the language, but very common.

Clearing up the obscurity of this—if it can be said that there is obscurity in this—is that the people only requested them to intercede with Allah in that—and this is something that Allah has enabled them to do and has given them possession of. So, the one who says: "O Prophet of Allah! Heal me!" or "Take care of my debt," only means (to say): "Intercede with me in getting healed, pray for me that my debt is paid, and entreat Allah concerning my affair." They have not sought anything from them save that which Allah has granted them and enabled them to do such as supplication and intercession.

This is what we believe concerning those who say this and this is what we take as our religion before Allah. The subject in the words of the people is logical metaphor that contains no harm for those who articulate it, and an example of which, are the words of the Exalted: ﴾Glorified and far removed from defect is the One who created in pairs all things that the earth produces.﴿ (Yā Sīn: 36) And his ﷺ statement: "Some of what the spring produces causes miscarriage or pain." This type of speech is very common in the speech of Allah and His Messenger ﷺ, and the commonality and elite. There is nothing that would forbid it. That it is spoken by a monotheist is an inference and proof of the intent and that it contains no ill manners. This has been elucidated in a special section in this book.

IF YOU ASK, ASK ALLAH, AND IF YOU SEEK ASSISTANCE, SEEK THE ASSISTANCE OF ALLAH

This is a portion of the well known Ḥadīth narrated by al-Tirmidhī from Ibn 'Abbās in *marfū'* form and declared rigorously authentic. Many people err in their understanding of this Ḥadīth, inferring from it that there is to be no request or seeking of aid in totality, from every angle or method, save from Allah, and they claim that requesting and seeking aid from other than Allah is an act of idolatry that expels one from the religion. With this (faulty understanding), they deny the (validity) of utilizing and taking help from means, and (by this) they demolish many of the textual proofs that have been cited in this area.

The truth is that this noble Ḥadīth does not mean it is forbidden to request or seek the aid of other than Allah as is indicated by its literal wording. What is intended by it is to prohibit heedlessness on the basis that whatever good that comes from the ways and means is from Allah. This Ḥadīth is a command to take notice that whatever bounty there is from the created things, then it is from Allah and by Allah.

This Ḥadīth means: if you want to seek the aid of any of the creation and it is a must, then you should rely entirely on Allah alone and by no means should you let the means veil you from seeing the One who enables the causes—the Exalted and Sublime. Do not be of those who only know the outward of the connections and relations between cause and effect in all of these things that are related to each other, while being heedless of the One who arranged linkages between them.

The Ḥadīth itself indicated this meaning when it mentioned that he ﷺ said at the end of this noble sentence: "Know, that if the Umma gathered together in order to benefit you with something, they would not be able to benefit you save with what was already decreed by Allah. And (know) that if the Umma gathered together in order to harm you with something, they would not be able to harm you save with what was already decreed by Allah for you." Here (in this Ḥadīth) as you see, he affirmed for them that there is harm and benefit in that which Allah decreed for the servant. So this clarifies his ﷺ intent.

How can we censure seeking aid with other than Him, when it has been commanded in many places in the Book and Sunna? The Exalted said: ﴾Seek aid with patience and prayer.﴿ (al-Baqara: 45) And He said: ﴾And prepare what you can against them of power.﴿ (al-Anfāl: 60) He, the Exalted mentioned the words of the righteous servant, Dhūl Qarnayn: ﴾So aid me with power...﴿ (al-Kahf: 95) The legality of the prayer of fear that is established in the Book and Sunna contains the legality of seeking aid with people seeking aid with each other. Similar to this, is His command for the believers to take their precautions against their enemy.

Similar to this also, is his ﷺ encouraging the believers to fulfil the needs of each other, to deal leniently with the one in dire circumstances, to remove difficulties, as well as his warning against neglecting all of this. This is found abundantly in the Sunna.

The two Shaykhs (al-Bukhārī and Muslim) narrated: "Whoever assists his brother, Allah with assist him."

Muslim, Abū Dāwūd and others narrated that he ﷺ said: "Allah will assist the servant as long as the servant is assisting his brother." He ﷺ also said: "Indeed Allah has servants who He created (to fulfil) the needs of the people, and the people rush to them for the fulfilment of their needs. They are the ones who shall be safe from the punishment of Allah." Look carefully at his words ﷺ: "...the people rush to them for the fulfilment of their needs."

He did not declare them to be idolaters, nay, neither (did he declare them) disobedient.

It has also been narrated in *marfū'* form: "Indeed, to Allah belongs bounties that He has placed among certain people as long as they fulfil the needs of the Muslims and are not bored with it. When they become bored with it, He moves (those bounties) to others." He (Abū Dāwūd) and Ibn Abī Dunyā narrated that he ﷺ said: "To Allah belongs people whom He has favoured with bounties for the benefits of the servants. These (bounties) stay with them as long as they spend freely of them. If they withhold them, He removes the best (bounties) of them to others." Ḥāfiẓ al-Mundhirī said: "If it was said that its chain is fair, then that is possible." He ﷺ said: "That one of you goes with his brother in order to fulfil his needs—then pointing with his finger—is better than him performing night retreat in this Masjid of mine.[73]

IF YOU ASK, ASK ALLAH

As for his statement ﷺ: "And when you ask, then ask of Allah." This (Ḥadīth) contains no evidence and has nothing (for them) to grab on to in their attempt to forbid asking or performing *tawassul*. Whoever understands from the literal wording (of this Ḥadīth) that it is completely forbidden to ask someone else, or that it is completely forbidden to perform *tawassul*, then he has missed the mark and engaged in outright sophism.

The one who takes the Prophets and saints as means unto Allah in order to obtain good from Him, the Exalted and Sublime, or to repel evil, is doing nothing more than asking Allah alone to facilitate for him what he requested or to repel from him what He wills, performing *tawassul* unto Him. By this, he is taking hold of the means that Allah placed in order for the servants to be successful in getting their needs fulfilled from Him, the Exalted and Sublime. Whoever takes a hold of the means that Allah

[73] Narrated by al-Ḥakim who said: "Its chain is *ṣaḥīḥ*."

ordered one to traverse upon to obtain His generosity, then he has not asked the means itself, rather, he has asked the One who placed the means (as a means).

When one says: "O Messenger of Allah! I want that you return to me my eye," or: "O Messenger of Allah! I want that you remove the affliction from me," or: "O Messenger of Allah! I want that you remove from me my sickness,' this means that he has sought these things from Allah through the intermediary of the Prophet's intercession ﷺ. It is similar to him saying: "Pray for me for such and such," or: "Intercede for me with such and such." There is no difference between them except that one is more explicit in stating his intent than the other.

Similar to both of these and ever more clear is the statement of the one performing *tawassul* when he says: "O Allah, I ask you by Your Prophet that You make such and such a thing easy (for me), of things that benefit or repel harm." So in all of this, the one performing *tawassul* has asked none but Allah, the Exalted and Sublime, for the fulfilment of his needs.

With this, we are of the view that seeking to prove the prohibition of *tawassul* with his ﷺ statement: "When you ask, then ask of Allah" is pure sophism in explaining the Ḥadīth in a manner that is clearly corrupt—explaining it as such that it is not allowed for anyone to ask anything from other than Allah. Whoever understands this from the Ḥadīth is clearly mistaken. It is sufficient in clarifying his error to point out that the Ḥadīth itself is nothing more than a response from him ﷺ to a question posed by the narrator of the Ḥadīth, Ibn 'Abbās after the Messenger of Allah ﷺ encouraged him to ask, saying: "Young man! Shall I not teach you some words that Allah will cause you to benefit from?" What encouragement to ask is more beautiful than this? Ibn 'Abbās said: "Of course," so he ﷺ responded with this Ḥadīth that contains this sentence.

If we were to go along with this conjecture (*wahm*), based on that, it would not be valid for an ignorant person to ask a scholar, for a person in mortal danger to ask for help from one who is the difference between his rescue or death, a person in debt to ask his debtor to absolve his debt, for one to seek out a loan from one who can loan money, and it would not be allowed for the people to ask the Prophets for intercession on the Day of Judgement, nor would it be valid for the Prophet of Allah, 'Īsā, to order the people to ask for the intercession of the Master of the Messengers ﷺ.

The proof they have for this conjecture is general and (proves the prohibition) of asking the things we mentioned as well as things we haven't mentioned. So, if they say: "What is prohibited is asking the Prophets and righteous among the people of the graves in their Isthmus (*barzakh*) life because they are unable (to respond)." This conjecture has been responded to in some detail. In general, the response is: They are alive and capable of interceding and supplicating. Their life is an Isthmus life that is appropriate to their station. By this, it is correct (to say) that they do benefit with their supplication and seeking of forgiveness. The least that can be said regarding the one who denies this is that he is ignorant of something that has almost reached the level of mass transmission from his ﷺ Sunna, the one who taught us that in the Isthmus life, the believers possess knowledge, hears, and possess the ability to supplicate. So what would you think about the major people of the Isthmus life among the Prophets and righteous?

In the Ḥadīth concerning the miraculous night journey that is rigorously authentic, nay, famous, there contains mention of what the Prophets—may prayers and peace be upon them—did with the best of them: Muḥammad ﷺ, such as: praying behind him, speaking with him, and supplicating for him in the heavens. The Umma did not succeed in having fifty prayers lightened to five prayers during the day and night due to his numerous intercessions ﷺ until that was indicated by the one to whom Allah spoke directly: Mūsā the son of 'Imrān—may the prayers and peace of Allah be upon both of them.

Based on this, the intent of the Ḥadīth is clear. It is not as thought erroneously by (the opponents), for that is clearly and explicitly false as has proceeded. The intent (behind the Ḥadīth) is nothing more than warning from covetously asking the people for their wealth without there being any need, and (encouraging) contentment in what Allah facilitates, even if it is small, (and this Ḥadīth is an encouragement) to have temperance and abstinence from (desiring) what is in the hands of people, and to seek sufficiency through asking Allah of His bounty.

Indeed, He loves those who are persistent in their supplication, whereas the people are the opposite of that.

The poet said:

Allah becomes angry if you leave off asking Him
Whereas if you ask from the children of Ādam
they become angry

The meaning of this Ḥadīth is: If you see wealth in the possession of anyone and it amazes you and causes your soul to aspire to it, do not ask him for what he possesses, rather, seek aid through asking Allah for His bounty as opposed to asking His servant. This Ḥadīth guides (one) to contentment and seeks to remove passionate longing (for the material).

How does this compare to asking Allah through His Prophets and righteous, or asking His Prophets to intercede for those who ask—something that Allah has placed their intercession in and is from the strongest of means for salvation? One the other hand, if a person embarks on the ship of desires, he will be shipwrecked in the proverbial island of conjecture and will lose serious understanding.

HELP IS NOT TO BE SOUGHT FROM ME

In a Ḥadīth it is mentioned that a man from the hypocrites was causing injury and annoyance to the believers, so Abū Bakr al-Ṣiddīq said: "Let us go and seek the help of the Messenger of Allah ﷺ against this hypocrite." The Prophet ﷺ said: "Help is not to be sought from me, rather help is to be sought from Allah."[74]

An inference might be made from this Ḥadīth by those who believe it is forbidden to seek the aid of the Messenger of Allah ﷺ. This inference however is false from its root. The reason for this is that, if this Ḥadīth were taken upon its literal wording, then it would mean that it is completely forbidden to seek his aid—as is apparent from the wording (of the Ḥadīth). This (false inference) is negated by the actions of the companions with the

[74] Narrated by al-Ṭabaranī in *al-Mu'jam al-Kabīr*.

Messenger of Allah ﷺ, for they used to seek his aid, seek rain through him, request his prayers for them, and he used to respond to all of that with delight and happiness. So with this, it is necessary to interpret this (Ḥadīth) in a manner that fits with the general Ḥadīth reports so that the textual evidence is organized appropriately. With this in mind we say: His intent behind what he said was to establish the reality of *tawḥīd* in the basis of faith, meaning that the one who gives aid in reality is Allah, the Exalted, and that the servant is nothing more than an intermediary in that. Or (it means) that he wanted to teach them that one should not request from the servant that which he is unable to do, such as gaining the triumph of Paradise, salvation from the fire, and guidance that is protection from hell and a guarantee of ending one's life with felicity.

This Ḥadīth does not prove that seeking aid and succour is restricted to the living and not the dead, and in no way whatsoever does it prove that distinction. Rather, its literal meaning indicates that it is prohibited to seek the aid of anyone besides Allah unrestrictedly—with no distinction being drawn between the living and the dead—and this is not what the (Ḥadīth) really means.

Shaykh Ibn Taymiyya indicated something close to this meaning when he said:

> There might be an expression in the words of Allah or His Messenger that contains a correct meaning, however some people understand differently than the intent of Allah and His Messenger—so this returns to this person's understanding. (An example of this) is what was narrated by al-Ṭabarānī in his *Mu'jam al-Kabīr*, that a man from the hypocrites was causing injury to the believers, so Abū Bakr al-Ṣiddīq said: "Let us go and seek the help of the Messenger of Allah ﷺ against this hypocrite." The Prophet ﷺ said: "Help is not to be sought from me, rather help is to be sought from Allah." The Prophet ﷺ only intended this second meaning with this, which is to seek from him that which only Allah is capable of.

> Otherwise, the companions used to request his prayers, and seek rain through him, as is found in *Ṣaḥīḥ al-Bukhārī* from Ibn 'Umar who said: "Perhaps I remembered the poet while I gazed upon the face of the Prophet when he sought rain as it was coming down until the fount came down:
>
> *A bright one seeking the rain clouds with his face*

Expressions Used: There are certain expressions used in praise of the Prophet ﷺ that have caused confusion for some, who as a result, judged those who use them with disbelief. This is like their statements:

- There is no one we seek refuge in save the Prophet ﷺ
- There is no one hoped for save him ﷺ
- I seek protection through him ﷺ
- Unto him (people) flee during afflictions
- If I hesitate, whom will I ask?

Their intent is: there is no one we seek refuge in—meaning from the creation, and there is no one hoped for—meaning from mankind, and unto him the people flee during afflictions—meaning, as opposed to the rest of the creation, due to his nobility with his Master and in order for him to turn to Allah and request from Him, and if I hesitate, who will I ask—meaning from among the servants of Allah?

Having said this, we do not use these expressions in our supplications or *tawassul*, nor do we invite to it or encourage it, so as to repel suspicions, be far removed from expressions that are differed over, and in order to hold fast to that which is apparent and without any differences therein. Despite this, we are of the view that ruling those who use these expressions with disbelief is hastiness that is not praiseworthy and it is an action that contains no wisdom. We must take into consideration that those who use these expressions are from the monotheists who testify that there is nothing worthy of worship but Allah and that Muḥammad is the Messenger of Allah, and they establish the prayer, and they believe in all of the pillars of the religion and believe in Allah as their Lord, Muḥammad as their Prophet, and as Islam as their religion. By this they have the protection (*dhimma*) of the people of the religion and the sanctity of Islam. Anas b. Mālik ﷺ said that the Messenger of Allah ﷺ said: "Whoever prays our prayer, submits in Islam, faces our *qibla*, and eats our slaughtered meat, then he is the Muslim who has the protection of Allah and His Messenger, so do not be shy with regards to Allah's guarantee of protection." (al-Bukhārī)

If we find in the speech of the believers, linkage to other than Allah ﷻ, it is obligatory upon us to consider it in light of logical metaphor. There is no way to impute them with disbelief because logical metaphor is used in the Book and the Sunna. That this linkage comes from a monotheist is sufficient in making it a linkage of logical metaphor. The correct belief is that Allah is the Creator of both the servants and their actions, and there is no independent affect from anyone besides Him—not for anyone living or dead. This belief is *tawḥīd*, as opposed to the one who believes other than this and as a consequence falls into idolatry.

There is no one among the Muslims who believes that anyone besides Allah possesses (independent) action, abandonment of action, bringing of life, or causing death.

With regard to these unclear and obscure expressions, the intent of those who say them is to seek intercession from Allah through that means—so the intent is Allah ﷻ. There is not a single person among the Muslims—neither far nor near—who believes that the one he requests or asks is independently capable of doing or leaving off an action without (the will of) Allah, the Exalted, or (that he is) a partner with Allah. We seek refuge with Allah from imputing a Muslim with idolatry or disbelief due to a mistake, ignorance, forgetfulness, or independent effort (*ijtihād*).[75]

We say: If people make mistakes in the way they express their requests for forgiveness, Paradise, healing, salvation, and their asking of the Messenger of Allah ﷺ directly, then their mistake is

---

[75] This reality has been mentioned repeatedly in this book of ours. We expounded upon it in a special area of research called: 'Logical Metaphor.' In it, many of the confusions and wrong understandings are made clear.

not in the realm of *tawḥīd*, because their intent is to seek the intercession unto Allah by this means. So, it is as if one is saying: "O Messenger of Allah! Ask Allah to forgive me and have mercy upon me. I perform *tawassul* through you unto Him for the fulfilment of my needs, the removal of my difficulties, and the attainment of my longing desire."

The companions, may Allah be pleased with all of them, used to seek help from him ﷺ, seek his aid, request his intercession, and complain of their conditions such as sickness, poverty, afflictions, debt, and inability as we have previously mentioned. It is well known that he ﷺ does not do that independently of his own accord or strength, rather, it is only by the permission of Allah and His command and power. He ﷺ is the servant who is commanded, and the one who possesses his station and rank with his Lord. He ﷺ possesses his honour and nobility by which the generality of the people approach Allah—those who believe in him ﷺ, believe in his message, and believe in his virtue and nobility.

We believe that whoever believes other than this has fallen into idolatry without any difference of opinion (in that).

It is for this reason that sometimes, you see him ﷺ drawing attention to this fact when it is made manifest to him through the medium of revelation or a particular state in which the one asking him or listening to him is deficient in belief. In one stance (we see that) he ﷺ informed that he is the Master of the children of Ādam, while in another stance, we see that he brought to their attention that the Master (in reality) is Allah. In one stance, we see that they sought his aid and he taught them how to perform *tawassul* through him, while in another stance, he said to them: "Help is only to be sought from Allah and help is not to be sought from me." In one stance, we see that they sought his aid, and asked of him so he could respond to their requests—nay, he would even give them a choice between two options (such as what is found in the Ḥadīth wherein he stated): being patient with an affliction and being guaranteed Paradise, or quickly removing the affliction—this being the choice he gave to the blind man and the women with seizures. He also gave Qatāda (a similar) choice when his eye was gouged.

In another stance, we see that he said to them: "When you ask, then ask of Allah, and when you seek help, seek the help of Allah. In one stance he said: "Whoever removes a difficulty from a believer..." while in another stance he said: "No one brings good but Allah."

So with this, it becomes clear to you that our belief—and to Allah belongs all praise—is the purest and cleanest of beliefs. The servant does not do any act (independently), no matter what his level or rank might be. Nay, not even the best of creation ﷺ. He only gives and withholds, harms and benefits, and responds and assists by Allah ﷻ. If aid or succour is sought from him, or if he is requested of something, then he only turns to the Exalted Master ﷻ and supplicates, seeks, asks, and intercedes, with his intercession being accepted and (his request) being responded to. He ﷺ never said to them (the companions): "Do not seek anything from me, ask anything from me, or complain of your circumstances to me! Rather, turn to Allah and ask Him, for His door is open and He is the One who is Close, the One who responds, the One who is in need of no one, and the One who has no veil or doorman between Him and the creation!"

The Stance of Shaykh Muḥammad b. 'Abd al-Wahhāb regarding these Expressions that they Claim to be Idolatry and Misguidance

Shaykh Muḥammad b. 'Abd al-Wahhāb had a mighty stance and wise opinion in this area, especially with regard to these expressions that are well known from the tongues—expressions that are alleged to be idolatry by the one who claims to safeguard and jealously watch over *tawḥīd*. Here is the Imām of *tawḥīd* and the head of the monotheists saying his upright words and with his rightly guided wisdom that caused his invitation to spread among the people and his way to become well known to the commonality and the elite alike. Listen to his words—may Allah have mercy upon him—in his work of creed found within his letter to 'Abdullāh Suhaym, who was the one in charge of commanding the good and forbidding the evil (*muṭawwa'*) of the people of al-Majma'a:

If this is made clear, then these (are) issues that he censured me for: From them is that which is pure slander, such as his words: that I invalidate the four juristic schools of thought, and that I say that for over six hundred years, the people were not upon anything, and that I claim *ijtihād* for myself, and that I am out of the realm of following qualified scholarship, and that I say that the differences among the scholars is a punishment, and that I impute disbelief upon those who seek a means of approach (*tawassul*) through the righteous, and that I impute disbelief upon al-Buṣayrī due to his statement: O *noblest of creation*, and that I say: if I were able to demolish the dome (over the grave) of the Messenger of Allah ﷺ, I would demolish it, and that if I was in authority over the Ka'ba, I would take the (golden) fount and (put in its place) a wooden fount, and that I forbid visitation of the grave of the Messenger of Allah ﷺ and that I deny visitation of the graves of (one's) parents and others, and that I impute disbelief upon those who swear by other than Allah, and that I impute disbelief upon Ibn al-Fāriḍ and Ibn 'Arabī, and that I burn *Dalā'il al-Khayrāt* and *Rawḍ al-Rayāhīn*, and that I call it: *Rawḍ al-Shayatīn*. My response to all of these issues is to say: ﴾Glorified are You this is indeed a mighty slander.﴿ (al-Nūr: 16) And before him, there was the one who slandered Muḥammad ﷺ, saying that he insulted 'Īsā b. Maryam and insulted the righteous. So their hearts resembled each other in inventing lies, and bearing false witness. The Most Exalted said: ﴾Only those who do not believe in the signs of Allah invent lies.﴿ (al-Naḥl: 105) The slandered him ﷺ, by saying that he says: 'The Angels, 'Isā, and 'Uzayr are in the fire.' So in response to that, Allah revealed: ﴾Verily those for whom the good has preceded from Us, they will be removed far there from (Hell)﴿ (al-Anbiyā': 101)

Conclusion

In summary, the one who seeks aid is not to be imputed with disbelief unless he believes that (things) besides Allah possess the independent ability to create and bring into existence. The distinction drawn between the living and the dead has no real meaning, because if someone believes that something other than Allah possess the ability to independently create, then they have disbelieved—with there being some difference of opinion regarding the Mu'tazila (sect) and their belief regarding the creation of actions. If someone believes in earning (of actions) and acquisition (*kasb*) then they are not to be imputed with disbelief.

You are aware that most people believe in with regards to the dead is that they are vehicles or means and earners, just like the living—not that they are creators bringing things into existence like the Deity (Allah).

It is not conceivable that the people's belief regarding them is anymore than their belief regarding the living, in that they do not believe they (the living) are anything more than acquisition and a means. If there is a blunder, then let it be in the belief in (the creation being) a vehicle of means and acquisition, because this is the most that a believing Muslim could believe regarding the creation, otherwise, he would not be a believer. The blunder in that is not idolatry or disbelief. We have not ceased repeating it to your faculties of hearing that it is not conceivable that belief regarding the dead should be more than that of the living—so actions are affirmed for the living by means of acquisition and means. That actions are affirmed for the dead by means of independent causality and bringing into existence is something inconceivable without a doubt.

The most that can be said regarding he who seeks aid in the dead—after having made all of these compromises—is that he is like someone who seeks help from one who is disabled, while not knowing that he is disabled. Who is able to say that this is idolatry? Rather, serving as a means has been decreed for the dead and it is within their capability to acquire it like the living, through supplication for us, as the souls do indeed supplicate for their close relatives.

It has been reported that the Prophet ﷺ said: "Indeed, your deeds are presented to your close relatives among the dead. If they (the deeds) are good, they take glad tidings in that. If it is other than that, they supplicate: 'O Allah, do not cause them to die until You guide them to what You have guided us.' This was narrated by Aḥmad and it has supporting chains of narration. See *al-Fatḥ al-Rabbānī, Tartīb al-Musnad*, 5/89, and *Sharḥ al-Ṣudūr* of al-Suyūṭī. It has been reported from Ibn Mubārak with his chain to Abū Ayyūb who said: "The deeds of the living are presented to the dead. If they see good, they take glad tidings and are delighted. If they see evil, they supplicate: 'O Allah, turn to them (in repentance).' "[76]

[76] See *Kitāb al-Rūḥ* of Ibn al-Qayyim.

PART II
PROPHETIC AREAS OF RESEARCH

CLARIFYING THE UNIQUE AND SPECIAL QUALITIES OF THE PROPHET ﷺ, THE REALITY OF PROPHETHOOD, THE REALITY OF HUMANITY, AND THE REALITY OF THE ISTHMUS LIFE

بسم الله الرحمن الرحيم

THE UNIQUE PROPHETIC CHARACTERISTICS AND THE STANCE OF THE SCHOLARS CONCERNING THEM

THE SCHOLARS have demonstrated great concern with the Prophetic characteristics, through authoring works, commentary, gathering, and conducting researches in individual issues. The most comprehensive and well known of these works is *al-Khaṣā'iṣ al-Kubrā* of the Imām, Ḥāfiẓ Jalāl al-Dīn al-Suyūṭī. There are a great number of characteristics—some of them have authentic chains, some do not, and others are differed over, with some (scholars) of the view that they are authentic, and others of the view that they are weak. These are matters of disagreement.

The discussions about these issues among the scholars, since the times of old, have always revolved around them being either correct or incorrect and authentic or invalid. The discussions have never revolved around disbelief and faith.

The scholars differ concerning many Ḥadīth and they refute each other in authentication, weakening, or rejecting them due to their differing views concerning the strength of the chains of narration and critique of the men (in the chain). Whoever among them authenticates that which is weak, weakens that which is authentic, establishes the authenticity of that which is rejected, or rejects that which is established—all with evidence, interpretation, or what resembles proof—then he has traversed the path of the scholars in research and investigation. That is his right as a human who possesses his own intellect and understanding. The sphere is open, the field is expansive, and the knowledge is spread among all.

This was encouraged by the Imām of the intelligent and Master of the scholars, the greatest Prophet and most noble Messenger, Muḥammad ﷺ, when he declared that the *mujtahid* (independent jurist) who is correct has two rewards, while the incorrect *mujtahid* has one reward. The scholars have not ceased being lenient when it comes to quoting (reports concerning) the Prophetic characteristics. Their view of them is that they are in (the same category) as virtuous actions. They have no relation to the lawful and unlawful.

Based on this, the scholars based their principle with respect to acting according to weak reports in virtuous actions as long as it is not fabricated or false—with its well known conditions that are given consideration in this area. They do not make it conditional that it is authentic according to the technical meaning of the word. If we were to take the view that this strange condition is a prerequisite, we would not be able to mention anything regarding the biography of the Prophet ﷺ, both before and after his Prophetic mission.

On the other hand, you see that the books of the Ḥuffāẓ which are relied upon and referred to in their field—from whom we learned what is allowed and not allowed to mention of weak Ḥadīth—their books are filled with (Ḥadīth reports) that are with severed chains, *mursal* reports, and narrations from soothsayers concerning the characteristics of the Messenger of Allah ﷺ because that is what is allowed to be mentioned in that area.

The Books of the Salaf and the (Prophetic) Characteristics: If we were to go back to the books of the Salaf, we would find many of the scholars of the Umma and Imāms of jurisprudence who mention samples of the (reports concerning) the Prophetic characteristics ﷺ and quote strange and amazing things. If the researcher was to base the acceptance of the report on merely the authenticity of its chain of narration, there would be but a very paltry amount of that which is clear in comparison the reports they quoted. This is based on what is well known regarding the principles of the scholars and their well established fundamentals in this area.

IBN TAYMIYYA AND THE PROPHETIC CHARACTERISTICS

Shaykh Ibn Taymiyya, who was well known for his strictness, quoted some statements concerning this subject—reports whose chains are not authentic—and he used them as examples for many issues and considered them reliable for the purpose of clarifying and strengthening the Ḥadīth that he was explaining.

An example of this is his statement in *al-Fatāwā al-Kubrā:*

> It has been narrated that Allah wrote his (the Prophet's ﷺ) name on the Throne, as well as the domes, doors, and leaves of Paradise. There are many reports narrated that agree with these well established Ḥadīth that clarify the exaltation of his name and elevating his mention...
>
> The wording of this Ḥadīth found in the *Musnad* from Maysara al-Fajr has already proceeded in which it was said to him ﷺ: "When where you a Prophet? He responded: 'When Ādam was between a soul and body."
>
> This was narrated Abū al-Ḥusayn b. Bushrān from Shaykh Abū al-Faraj b. al-Jawzī in *al-Wafā' bi-Faḍl al-Muṣṭafā* ﷺ, from Maysara who said: "I said: 'O Messenger of Allah! When where you (first) a Prophet?' He replied: 'When Allah created the earth ﴾Then He turned to the heaven, and fashioned it as seven heavens﴿ (al-Baqara: 29), and created the Throne, He wrote on the leg of the Throne: "Muḥammad the Messenger of Allah is the Seal of Prophets," then Allah created the Garden in which He made Ādam and Ḥawwā dwell, and He wrote my name on its gates, its tree-leaves, its domes and its tents, at a time when Ādam was still between the spirit and the body. When Allah, the Exalted, breathed life into him, he looked at the Throne and saw my name, whereupon Allah informed him that "He is the Master of all your

descendants." When Satan deceived them both, they repented and sought intercession to Allah with my name.' "[77]

Ibn Taymiyya and Miracles: The (Prophetic) special characteristics and miracles are from the same genus with respect to the rulings given to them, quoting them, and not being overly strict with reporting them like we are when it comes to quoting (reports on) legal rulings regarding the lawful and unlawful. All of these (reports on) miracles are in the sphere of these (reports on) virtuous actions and biographies.

Having said this, the position of Shaykh al-Islam Ibn Taymiyya concerning the miracles of the saints is the same as his position concerning the special Prophetic characteristics. He mentioned a good summary of miracles and preternatural phenomena that occurred in the early times.

If we were to research their individual chains, levels of strength, and routes of transmission, we would find that the reports contain that which is authentic, that which is *ḥasan*, that which is weak, that which is accepted, that which is rejected, and that which is irregular (*shādh*).

In this area (of research), all of this is acceptable and tolerated and quoted from the scholars. An example of such (from Ibn Taymiyya), is what he mentioned regarding the miracles of some of the companions:

- Umm Ayman went out to perform migration without any provision or water. She almost died of thirst while in her journey. While she was fasting, and the time of breaking the fast approached, she heard a sound above her head. When she raised her head, she saw a pitcher (of water) attached to a rope. She drank from it and never felt thirsty after that for the rest of her life.
- Safīna, the freed slave of the Messenger of Allah ﷺ informed the lion that he was the ambassador of the Messenger of Allah ﷺ, so the lion walked with him until he reached his destination.

---

[77] *Al-Fatāwā*, 2:151.

- Al-Barā' b. Mālik; When he would swear an oath in the name of Allah, Allah would fulfil it for him on his behalf. When the fighting would become severe for the Muslims during the *jihād*, they would say: "O Barā'! Swear an oath in the name of your Lord!" He would say: "O Lord! I swear an oath in Your name that You will sever their heads from their shoulders." Thereafter, the enemy would be defeated. During the battle of al-Qādisiyya he said: "I swear an oath in Your name that after You sever their heads from their shoulders, You will make me the first martyr." They were defeated and al-Barā' was killed as a martyr.
- Khālid b. al-Walīd surrounded a fortified castle and the inhabitants called out: "We will not surrender until you drink poison." He drank the poison and it did not harm him.
- When 'Umar b. al-Khaṭṭāb dispatched an army, he put them under the command of a man named Sāriya. When 'Umar was giving a sermon (in Medina), he started to shout while on the pulpit: "O Sāriya! The mountain! O Sāriya! The mountain! When the messenger of the army returned (to Medina), he was asked about this and he said: "O leader of the believers! We made contact with the enemy, and they while they were defeating us, a shouting voice called out saying: 'O Sāriya! The mountain!' So, we ascended the mountain and Allah defeated them."
- Al-'Alā' b. al-Ḥaḍramī was the governor of the Messenger of Allah ﷺ in Bahrain. He used to say in his supplication: "O All Knower, O Forbearing One, O Exalted, O Mighty!" When he would supplicate in this manner, his supplication would be answered. When he (and his forces) were without water for a long time, he prayed to Allah that they would receive water so they could drink and perform ablutions. His prayer was answered. When they were in pursuit of the enemy and were faced with crossing the sea with their horses and were unable, they walked on the water and the water did not even reach

the reins of their horses. He also prayed that if he died, that they would not see his body, and (after he died) they did not find his body in the burial niche (underground).

- Something similar happened to Abū Muslim al-Khawlānī when he was thrown into a fire. He and his accompanying soldiers walked over the Tigris river even though it was tossing wood and other sediments to and fro (from the severe waves). He looked at his companions and said: "Have any of you lost any personal belongings so that I can pray to Allah (concerning) it?" Some of them replied: "I have lost my helmet." He (Abū Muslim) said: "Follow me." The man followed him and soon found that the helmet had attached itself to something so he took it. When al-Aswad al-'Ansī claimed Prophethood, he called for him (Abū Muslim) to be brought forth. He (al-Aswad) said: "Do you testify that I am the Messenger of Allah?" Abū Muslim said: "I cannot hear." Al-Aswad repeated: "Do you testify that Muḥammad is the Messenger of Allah?" Abū Muslim replied: "Yes." Abū Muslim was then ordered to be thrown into a fire. After he was thrown in the fire, they found him standing up inside of it offering prayers and it had become full of coolness and peace for him. After the death of the Prophet ﷺ, he came back to Medina. 'Umar ؓ then sat him in between himself and Abū Bakr al-Ṣiddīq ؓ and said: "All praise belongs to Allah that He did not cause me to die until I saw from the Umma of Muḥammad ﷺ one whom (Allah) dealt with like He dealt with Ibrāhīm, the intimate friend of Allah." (It is also narrated) that a slave girl placed poison in his food in an attempt to kill him, yet it did not harm him. (It is also narrated) that a women attempted to sow discord between him and his wife, so he supplicated against her and she became blind, until she came to him and repented, after which he prayed to Allah for her and Allah returned her sight back.
- During the hot summer days, Sa'īd b. Musayyib used to hear the call to prayer issue fourth from the grave of the Messenger of Allah ﷺ during the times of the prayers,

even thought the Mosque would be empty.

- Once, when ‘Amr b. ‘Uqba b. Farqad was praying in the extreme heat, a dark rain cloud came over him. The beast of pray also used to look after him when he would act as a shepherd for the livestock of his companions—because during the expeditions, he would make it a condition that he would serve his companions.
- When Muṭarrif b. ‘Abdullāh b. al-Shikhīr used to enter his house, the cooking utensils would glorify Allah along with him. It is also reported that he, along with his companion, were once walking in the dark, when the tips of their riding whips would illuminate and glow.[78]

SHAYKH IBN AL-QAYYIM AND THE SEATING OF THE PROPHET ﷺ ON THE THRONE

The Imām, the ‘Allāma, Shaykh al-Islam Ibn al-Qayyim, quoted a strange and amazing unique quality that he referenced back to many of the Imāms of the Salaf ﷺ. He said:

> **Benefit:** Al-Qāḍī stated: “Al-Marrūdhī authored a book on the virtues of the Prophet ﷺ and mentioned that he ﷺ will be seated on the Throne.” Al-Qāḍī said: “It is the view of Abū Dāwūd, Aḥmad b. Asram, Yaḥyā b. Abī Ṭālib, Abū Bakr b. Ḥammād, Abū Ja‘far al-Dimashqī, ‘Ayyāsh al-Dawrī, Isḥāq b. Rāhawayh, ‘Abd al-Wahhāb b. al-Warrāq, Ibrāhīm al-Aṣbahānī, Ibrāhīm al-Ḥarbī, Hārūn b. Ma‘rūf, Muḥammad b. Ismā‘īl al-Sulamī, Muḥammad b. Mus‘ab al-‘Ābid, Abū Bakr b. Ṣadaqa, Muḥammad b. Bishr b. Shurayk, Abū Qilāba, Alī b. Sahl, Abū ‘Abdullāh b. ‘Abd al-Nūr, Abū ‘Ubayd, Ḥasan b. Faḍl, Hārūn b. al-‘Abbās al-Hāshimī, Ismā‘īl b. Ibrāhīm al-Hāshimī, Muḥammad b. ‘Imrān al-Fārisī the ascetic, Muḥammad b. Yūnus al-Baṣrī, ‘Abdullāh the son of Imām Aḥmad, al-Marrūdhī, and Bishr al-Ḥāfī.”

[78] Taken from *al-Fatāwā al-Kubrā* of Shaykh Ibn Taymiyya, 11:271.

Ibn al-Qayyim said: "I say: It is also the view of Ibn Jarīr al-Ṭabarī, and the Imām of all of these (above): Mujāhid, the Imām of Qur'ānic exegesis. It is also the view of Abū al-Ḥasan al-Dāraquṭnī who said about it in some of his poetry:

The Ḥadīth of the intercession has its chain, From Aḥmad to Aḥmad the Chosen One. There is also a Ḥadīth stating that he will be seated, On the throne, and we do not deny it. Pass the Ḥadīth along in its wording. And do not add to it that which will corrupt it (in meaning) Do not deny that he is seated, And do not deny that he shall be seated [79]

KASHHĀF AL-QINĀ' AND THE AMAZING UNIQUE QUALITIES

The jurist, 'Allāma, and Shaykh, Manṣūr b. Yūnus al-Bahūtī mentioned in his book *Kashhāf al-Qinā'*, a series of special Prophetic characteristics that are deemed odd by many whose intellects are far too short-sighted to grasp or understand these principles and fundamentals.

Among the characteristics that he mentioned: what is (normally) ritually impure, is pure when issued fourth from him ﷺ and the other Prophets—may Allah's prayers and peace be upon all of them. It is permitted to seek healing through his urine and blood, based on what was narrated by al-Dāraquṭnī, that Umm Ayman drank his urine, afterwards (the Prophet ﷺ) said: "Alas, your stomach shall not enter the fire." This report however, is weak.

It has also been narrated by Ibn Ḥibbān in his Ḍu'afā': '...that a boy once performed cupping upon the Messenger of Allah ﷺ. After he finished with the cupping, the boy drank his ﷺ blood. The Prophet ﷺ said: "Woe to you! What did you do with the blood?" The boy responded: "I concealed it in my stomach." The

---

[79] *Badā'i al-Fawā'id* of Shaykh Ibn al-Qayyim, 3:40 The early Salaf who held this view, believed that Allah would seat the Messenger ﷺ on the Throne. They did not believe that Allah sits or is settled upon the Throne.—**tr**

Prophet ﷺ responded: "Go, for you have saved yourself from the fire." Ḥāfiẓ Ibn Ḥajar said: "The secret behind that is what the two Angels did when they washed his ﷺ insides."

Another example of (these characteristics) is (when he said): "He did not cast a shadow from the Sun or the Moon because he is a being of light and a shadow is a type of darkness. This was mentioned by Ibn 'Aqīl and others and is attested to by (the narration stating) that he ﷺ, asked Allah to make all of his body parts and directions a light, and he ended (this supplication) by saying: "And make me light." The earth used to swallow his bowel movements—as mentioned in the report. Another example is when he said: "The lofty station is him being seated on the Throne. It is reported from 'Abdullāh b. Salām that (he will be seated on the footstool), and this was mentioned by al-Baghawī."

He also said: "He ﷺ did not yawn, and everything of the creation was presented to him, from Ādam until the end, just as (He, the Exalted) taught Ādam the names of everything—based on the Ḥadīth of al-Daylamī: "The earth was made in the likeness of water and mud and I was made aware of everything." His entire nation was presented to him to see, as reported in the Ḥadīth of al-Ṭabarānī: "Last night in my apartment, my nation was presented to me from the first to the last. They were made to appear to me as water and mud, so much so that I know more about a person among them than one of you knows about his companion." He was also shown what will occur with his nation until the last hour, as stated in the Ḥadīth of Aḥmad and others: "I was made to know what my nation shall go through and the blood that you shall shed amongst each other." Another example is when he said: "Visiting his grave is recommended for both men and women, based on the generality of what was reported by al-Dāraquṭnī from Ibn 'Umar who said: "The Messenger of Allah ﷺ said: "Whoever performs the pilgrimage and visits my grave after my passing, then it is as if he has visited me during (my worldly) life."[80]

---

[80] *Kashhāf al-Qinā'*;,5:30. Published by the decree of King Fayṣal b. 'Abd al-'Azīz—may Allah have mercy upon him.

From these special Prophetic qualities that he narrated is that which is authentic, that which is weak, and that which has no evidence whatsoever. Hence, I do not know what the opponent will say regarding these special characteristics that were reported by the major Imāms of Ahl al-Sunna—who did not oppose them with anything, rather, they passed them on and were lenient in reporting them, based on the principle of leniency when reporting virtuous acts. This is despite the fact that among these special characteristics are reports that, if the opponent or denier were to hear them, would judge the one saying it with that which is greater than disbelief. How is what we quoted here, compared to the report that our Master Muḥammad ﷺ will be seated by Allah on His Throne on the Day of Judgement—as the Imām, Shaykh Ibn al-Qayyim quoted from the major Imāms among the Salaf in his book *Badā'i al-Fawā'id*—with no authentic evidence from the Book or Sunna?

How are the special characteristics we quoted in comparison to that which was quoted in *Kashhāf al-Qinā'*, that the Prophet ﷺ is light and that he casts no shadow, and that bowel movements that issue fourth from him are swallowed up by the earth with nothing of them remaining on the surface? How are the special characteristics we quoted in comparison to the special characteristics quoted by Shaykh Ibn Taymiyya such as his statement: "His name ﷺ is written on the heights of the Throne, upon the leaves and trees of Paradise, on its doors, fruits, and domes"? So where are those with their footnotes? Where are the researchers? How did these issues pass them by without any critique and editing?

IF PARADISE IS UNDER THE FEET OF THE MOTHERS, HOW CAN IT NOT BE UNDER THE COMMAND OF THE PROPHET ﷺ

From the special Prophetic characteristics that have been researched among the people of knowledge, is the report stating that the Prophet ﷺ portions out the land in Paradise. This unique quality was mentioned by Ḥāfiẓ al-Suyūṭī, al-Qasṭalānī, and al-Zurqānī in his explanation of *al-Mawāhib al-Laduniyya*. It is well known that this portioning out will only be for those who deserve it from the people of *tawḥīd* and by the permission of Allah ﷻ, communicated by way of revelation, inspiration, or relation from Allah ﷻ (to him ﷺ). This was indicated in the words of the Prophet ﷺ: "I am only the apportioner; Allah is the Giver." If it is correct to say that Paradise is under the feet of mothers, how is not correct to say that Paradise is under his command, nay under his feet? The meaning is one, and it is known to the most novice student of knowledge that it is a figurative expression the means reaching Paradise is through kindness to parents and serving them, especially the mother. With respect to the Prophet ﷺ, it means through obedience to him, love of him and allegiance towards him. This special quality has many examples that testify to its correctness. We shall mention the most important among them:

The Prophet ﷺ Guarantees Paradise: The Prophets guarantee of (entering) Paradise for some is of the same meaning as portioning out Paradise. This (guarantee) is what occurred for the people who gave the oath of allegiance at al-'Aqaba. From 'Ubāda b. al-Ṣāmit who said: "I was among those who were present at the first al-'Aqaba..." In this (Ḥadīth) it states: "...so we pledged our allegiance to the Messenger of Allah ﷺ with the condition that we would not associate any partners with Allah, steal, commit fornication, kill our children, come with a mighty slander from in front of us or behind us, and that we would not disobey him in that which is good." He ﷺ said: "So if you fulfil (this oath), then Paradise is yours. If you betray (the oath) in anything of that, then your affair is with Allah. If He wills, He may forgive you, and if He wills, He may punish you." This was mentioned by Ibn Kathīr in the chapter concerning the beginning of the Anṣār's embrace of Islam.[81]

In the *Ṣaḥīḥ* (of al-Bukhārī) it was explicitly stated that this oath was conditioned upon entering the Paradise. 'Ubāda b. al-Ṣāmit said: "I am from the representatives who gave their oath of allegiance to the Messenger of Allah ﷺ." He said: "We gave our oath of allegiance to him on the condition that we will not associate any partners with Allah, steal, commit fornication, or

[81] *Al-Sīra*, 2:186.

kill a soul that Allah has forbidden except in right, with the return being that we enter the Paradise if we fulfil that." This was narrated by al-Bukhārī in the book concerning the virtues of the Anṣār, section: 'The Oath of Allegiance at al-'Aqaba.' In another narration it states that he ﷺ said: "Whoever fulfils (this oath), then Paradise is for him." [82]

From Qatāda it is narrated that they said: "O Messenger of Allah! What shall we have if we fulfil that?" He replied: "Paradise."[83]

It was narrated from Ibn Mas'ūd ﷺ that the Prophet ﷺ said: "If you act upon that then it is upon Allah, then me, that you (are granted) Paradise."[84] From 'Utba b. 'Amr al-Anṣārī it is reported that he ﷺ said: "If you act upon that then it is upon Allah then me that you (are granted) Paradise."[85] From Abū Hurayra ﷺ it is reported that the Messenger of Allah ﷺ gave him his sandals and said to him: "Go, and whoever you meet behind this wall who testifies that none has the right to be worshipped but Allah, then give them the glad tidings of Paradise."[86]

PROPERTY DEED FOR ENTERING PARADISE BY HIS HANDS ﷺ

It was narrated by Ibn 'Abbās ﷺ: the Messenger of Allah ﷺ said: "The Prophets will have pulpits made of light that they will sit upon. My pulpit will remain without me sitting on it—or he said: I will not sit on it—standing in front of my Lord out of fear that I am sent to Paradise while my nation remains behind. I shall say: 'O Lord! My nation, my nation!' Allah, the Sublime and Mighty shall say: 'O Muḥammad! What do you want me to do with your nation?' I shall say: 'O Lord! Hasten their reckoning.' They will be called fourth and called to reckoning. From them are those who shall enter the Paradise out of His Mercy, and some of them shall

---

[82] *Al-Bidāya*, 3:150.
[83] Ibid., p.162.
[84] Narrated by al-Ṭabarānī. See *Kanz al-'Ummāl*, 1:63 and *Majma' al-Zawā'id*, 6:47.
[85] Narrated by Ibn Abī Shayba and Ibn 'Asākir. See *Kanz al-'Ummāl*, 1:67.
[86] Narrated by Muslim in *Kitāb al-Īmān*.

enter the Paradise due to my intercession. I will not cease interceding to the point that that I give a (property) deed to men who were dispatched to the hell fire, so much so that the Angel guarding over the hell fire will say: 'O Muḥammad! You have not left any chastisement for your nation from the anger of your Lord!'

This was narrated by al-Ṭabarānī in *al-Kabīr* and *al-Awsaṭ*, as well as al-Bayhaqī in *al-Ba'th*. Al-Mundhirī said: "There is no one in this narration who is rejected (*matrūk*)."

The Prophet ﷺ Gives Paradise: In a narration from Jābir ؓ, he said: "We said: 'Upon what do we pledge our oath?' He ﷺ said: 'To hear and obey both in times of energy and sluggishness, and to spend in times of difficulty, and to command the good and forbid the evil. If you do so, then Paradise is yours.' " Al-Ḥāfiẓ Ibn Ḥajar said: "Aḥmad has another route from Jābir in which he states: 'Al-'Abbās was holding the hand of the Messenger of Allah ﷺ, and when we were finished, the Messenger of Allah ﷺ said: "I have taken and given." This means "I have taken the oath of allegiance and given the Paradise." '[87] I say: In another narration, it explicitly states it even more emphatically. Jābir said: "The Prophet ﷺ said to them: 'Take the oath of allegiance to me upon the condition of hearing and obeying...' until he said: 'And the Paradise is yours.' Jābir said: 'They said: 'By Allah! We shall never abandon this oath or detract from it,' so we gave him the oath of allegiance and he obliged us with (things) and placed conditions (upon us) in return for him granting us Paradise.' " Al-Haythamī said: "The authors of the *Sunan* narrated a part of this. It was narrated by Aḥmad, and al-Bazzār. The men of Aḥmad are men of the *Ṣaḥīḥ* (collection)."[88]

The Prophet ﷺ Sells Paradise and 'Uthmān Purchases it: Abū Hurayra ؓ said: "'Uthmān purchased Paradise from the Prophet ﷺ twice. Once, in his transaction with the Real (Allah) when he dug the well at al-Ma'ūna, and the other time, when he equipped the army in the time of difficulty." Narrated by al-Ḥākim in his

---

[87] *Fatḥ al-Bārī*, 7:223. Narrated by Aḥmad (*Majma' al-Zawā'id*, 6:48).
[88] *Majma' al-Zawā'id*, 6:46.

Mustadrak (3/107) who authenticated it. Every intelligent person knows that Paradise belongs to Allah ﷻ and that no one possesses it or can portion it out, no matter who they are or what level they possess—not an Angel, Prophet, or Messenger—however, Allah bestows Divine gifts upon His Messengers and gives them of His bounties that which distinguishes them from others.

This is due to their nobility and high status with Him. Based on this, these bestowed gifts are ascribed to them, and these interactions are attributed to them in the sense of honouring, lauding, respecting and giving preference to them. It is from this area, that the unique qualities are reported stating that the Prophet ﷺ portions out the land in Paradise, guarantees Paradise, sells Paradise, and gives glad tidings of Paradise—even though Paradise belongs to Allah ﷻ, and no one doubts that save an ignoramus possessing not one iota of knowledge concerning the smallest of knowledge based issues. O Allah! Enlighten our insights, open the hearing of our hearts, and show us the truth as truth and bestow upon us (the ability) to follow it.

What is Meant by the Saying that the Night of the Prophetic Birth is the Best Night? Some scholars mention that among the Prophet's unique qualities ﷺ is that the night of his birth ﷺ is better than the night of power (in Ramaḍān). Concerning this topic, there have been comparisons (compiled) between the two nights. What we desire to mention here at this juncture is that the night that is intended is the actual night of the Prophetic birth—which has passed hundreds of years ago, and without doubt, it was before the night of power was known or manifested. Not intended here is the anniversary night of the Prophetic birth that repeats year after year corresponding to his actual birth. The truth behind this matter is that researching this is without much benefit. There is no harm or danger to be associated with denying it or attesting to it. None of that goes against the fundamental tenets of faith.

The scholars have conducted researches into the most miniscule of issues and authored specialized works that do not equal anything in comparison to this issue. In summary, we believe that this preference is between the actual Prophetic birth and the night of power, and that the night in which he was born—the preference of which being researched—has already passed and no longer exists. As for the night of power, it exists and repeats itself year after year and it is for that reason the night of power is the best of nights based on Allah's words: ﴾Indeed, We have sent it down on the night of power. What would make you understand what the night of power is? The night of power is better than one thousand months.﴿ (al-Qadr: 1-3)

Research in this issue as well as other matters have taken place between the Imāms of knowledge and have been spoken about among the notables of the Salaf. Take the Shaykh and Imām, Ibn Taymiyya speaking about the preference between the night of power and the night of the ascension. He researched this with precision and mastery—even though it is not established that anyone before him either researched or spoke about this issue from the Imāms of the Salaf and the people of the first generation—not to mention the companions or the Messenger ﷺ.

The Legal Verdict of Ibn Taymiyya in this Matter:

The Imām and Shaykh, Ibn al-Qayyim said:

> Shaykh al-Islam—may Allah have mercy upon him—was asked concerning a man who says: "The night of the ascension is better than the night of power"—whereas another man says: "Rather, the night of power is better"—so which of the two are correct?
>
> He responded: All praise belongs to Allah. As for the one who says that the night of the ascension is better than the night of power, if by this he means to say that the actual night in which the Prophet ﷺ was taken on his night journey, *as well* as every corresponding date each year, is better for the nation of Muḥammad ﷺ than the night of power, in that standing in prayer and supplicating therein is better than the night of power, then this is false and no one among the Muslims has ever said this. Its falsehood is categorically known and it is not from the religion of Islam. If, on the other hand, he intends by this, that the particular night in which the Prophet ﷺ was taken on the night journey, and during

> which he obtained that which he did not obtain on other nights—without (this person) legislating that (this night) is to be singled out with special standing in prayer or worship, then this is correct.[89]

DO NOT EXAGGERATE ABOUT ME

Some people understand from his ﷺ words: "Do not exaggerate about me as the Christians exaggerated concerning 'Īsā b. Maryam," that it is prohibited to laud him ﷺ, and they consider that to be exaggeration and blameworthy extremism that leads to idolatry, and (they hold) that all of those who laud him ﷺ, elevate him above others of mankind, compliment him, and describe him with that which distinguishes him from all others, have innovated in the religion and opposed the Sunna of the Master of the Messengers ﷺ.

This is an evil understanding that illustrates their short-sightedness. The Prophet ﷺ prohibited that he be over praised like the Christians over praised 'Īsā b. Maryam when they said: "He is the son of Allah." What this means is that the one who exaggerates about him ﷺ and describes him as the Christians described their Prophet, then he has become like them.

As for the one who lauds him and describes him in a manner that does not take him outside of the reality of humanity—while believing that he is a servant of Allah and His Messenger and being far removed from the belief of the Christians, then without doubt he is from the most complete of people in *tawḥīd*.

Leave what the Christians have claimed for their Prophet
Thereafter praise him as you like, but do so well.
Ascribe to his essence what you wish of honour,
Attribute to his exalted status what you will of greatness!
Truly, the Messenger of Allah's bounty
Cannot be overstated by two lips and a tongue.
If a miracle could equal his stature in magnitude,
The mere mention of his name would revive decaying bones.

---

[89] See the introduction to *Zād al-Ma'ād* of Ibn al-Qayyim.

Allah has taken it upon Himself to laud His chosen Prophet ﷺ, hence He said: ﴾And indeed you are upon a lofty character.﴿ (al-Qalam: 4)

He commanded good etiquette with him when speaking and answering, hence He said: ﴾O you who believe! Do no raise your voices about the voice of the Prophet.﴿ (al-Ḥujurāt: 2) He also forbade us from interacting with him as we interact with each other, or that we call him as we call each other, hence He said: ﴾And do not make your address to the Messenger among yourselves as you address one another.﴿ (al-Nūr: 63) He condemned those who deal with him and speak to him on a level equal to that of others, hence He said: ﴾Indeed, most of those who call you from behind the apartments do not understand.﴿ (al-Ḥujurāt: 4) The noble companions used to laud the Prophet ﷺ.

Take Ḥassān b. Thābit who said:

A seal of Prophethood from Allah is upon him
That has emerged, is attested to, and witnessed
The Deity attached the name of the Prophet to His Name
When the caller to prayer says that he bears witness
when (calling for) the five (prayers)
He portioned out to him from His name,
in order that he be exalted
For He is the Possessor of the Throne, the one who is Praised and this is
Muḥammad (the oft praised one)
A Prophet who came to us after despair and a period
Between the (sending) of the Messengers
when the idols were worshipped

He also said:

O you who are the sturdy pillar
and focal point of the one who seeks aid
And the useful refuge and close neighbour
O you who the Deity chose for His creation
And gifted him with the pure and clean character
You are the Prophet, and the best focal point of refuge for Ādam

O you who is generous like the effulgence of the bejewelled sea
Mīkāl and Jibrīl are both with you and they are, A source of your victory,
from the One who is All Mighty and All Able [90]

Take Ṣafiyya b. 'Abd al-Muṭṭalib who lauded the Messenger of Allah ﷺ:

Alas, O Messenger of Allah you were our hope
You were kind to us and you were not coarse towards us
You were merciful; a guide and a teacher
So whoever shall cry, let him cry today over you
You were truthful; truthfully you conveyed the message
You threw the wooden cross in the serene daybreak
May my mother and aunt be sacrificed
for the Messenger of Allah
As well as my uncle, my fathers, my self and wealth
By your life, I do not cry over the Messenger of Allah
due to (our) loss of him
Rather; I cry because I fear the senseless killing that shall come
It is as if the remembrance of Muḥammad
is imprinted in my heart
And folded up so I do not fear any after the Prophet
If the Lord of mankind caused our Prophet to remain
We would be happy, however, His command comes to pass
Prayers and peace from Allah upon you
You have entered Gardens of 'Aden well pleased
I shall be weaned, May Allah,
the Lord of Muḥammad send His prayers
Upon the tomb that has found its dwelling place in Ṭayba there

Take Ka'b b. Zuhayr who praised the Prophet ﷺ with his well known metered song that contained:

Su'ād has gone, and as a result my heart today
has been rendered sick and weak
enslaved (to her) in her wake, and shackled (as if in chains),
with no escape

---

[90] Seel *al-Isāba*, 1:264 and *al-Rawd al-Ānif*, 2:91.

And he said:

I was informed that the Messenger of Allah promised me
And pardon from the Messenger of Allah is longed for
Indeed, the Messenger is a light
From whom illumination is sought
An unsheathed Muhannad, [91] *sword from the swords of Allah*
among a group from the Quraysh
Someone said from among them
inside Mecca when they embraced Islam and surrendered
They walk with the serenity and calmness of white camels,
protected by blows at a time
when the short dark ones seek an exit or escape

In the narration of Abū Bakr b. al-Anbārī it states that when he reached the following line of the poem:

Indeed, the Messenger is a light
from whom illumination is sought
An unsheathed Muhannad, sword from the swords of Allah

He ﷺ tossed him his outer cloak that he was wearing, and Mu'āwiya offered him over ten thousand dirham for it, to which he replied: "I am not about to prefer anyone over the Messenger of Allah ﷺ." When Ka'b died, Mu'āwiya sent twenty thousand (dirham) to his inheritors and acquired it from them.

Here is the Messenger of Allah ﷺ praising himself when he ﷺ said: "I am the best of the companions of the right." (He ﷺ said:) "I am the best of the foremost ones." (He ﷺ said:) "I am the most God-fearing of the children of Ādam and most noble of them in the sight of Allah—without boasting."[92] He ﷺ said: "I am the best of the first and the last—without boasting."[93] He said: "None of my forefathers ever committed fornication."[94]

[91] An Indian sword highly valued by the Arabs.—**tr**
[92] Narrated by al-Ṭabarānī and al-Bayhaqī in *al-Dala'il.*
[93] Narrated by al-Tirmidhī and al-Dārimī.
[94] Narrated by Ibn 'Umar al-'Adanī in his *Musnad.*

Jibrīl ﷺ said: "I searched through the east and west and did not find a man better than Muḥammad, and I did not see a clan better than the clan of Hāshim."[95]

From Anas ﷺ: "The Prophet ﷺ was brought to the heavens by the *Burāq* [96] on the night of ascension. When it hesitated, Jibrīl said to it: 'You do this to Muḥammad? There is no one who has ridden you nobler in the sight of Allah than him, so take off.' (al-Bukhārī and Muslim)

In the Ḥadīth of Abū Sa'īd he said: "The Messenger of Allah ﷺ said: 'I am the Master of the children of Ādam on the Day of Judgement—without boasting. (On that day) I shall have the banner of praise—without boasting. There shall be no Prophet that day—from Ādam on down—save that they will be under my banner. I am the first one for whom the earth will split open—without boasting.' "[97]

Anas said: "The Messenger of Allah ﷺ said: 'I am the first of the people to come out (of the grave) when they are resurrected. I am their leader when they are placed in delegations. I am their speaker when they become silent. I am their intercessor when they are detained. I am the one to give them glad tidings when they despair. The keys, nobility, and the banner of praise will be with me on that day.' " Also: "I am the most noble of the children of Ādam in the sight of my Lord. One thousand servants shall surround me appearing as if they are concealed eggs or opened pearls."[98] Abū Hurayra narrated that the Messenger of Allah ﷺ said: "I am the first person to have the earth split open and I shall be adorned with some of the adornment of Paradise. Then I shall stand on the right side of the Throne, and none of the creation besides me shall have that station."[99]

---

[95] Narrated by al-Bayhaqī, Abū Nu'aym, and al-Ṭabarānī from 'A'isha ﷺ.

[96] The riding animal that took the Prophet ﷺ on his miraculous night journey.

[97] Narrated by al-Tirmidhī who said: "It is *ḥasan ṣaḥīḥ*."

[98] Narrated by al-Tirmidhī and al-Dārimī.

[99] Narrated by al-Tirmidhī who said: "It is *ḥasan ṣaḥīḥ*."

THE PROPHETS ARE HUMAN, *HOWEVER...*

Some people think that the Prophets—may the prayers and peace of Allah be upon them—are just like other humans in all of their states and ways. This is a clear mistake and exposed ignorance that is refuted by sound evidence in the Book and the Sunna.

Even if they share with the rest of the children of Ādam in the reality of their nature—that being humanity, as attested to by His (Allah's) statement, exalted be His mention: ❮Say: I am only a man like yourselves.❯ (al-Kahf: 110)—still, they are different from them in many attributes and contingent qualities. If that was not the case, then what is their distinction? How can the fruit of their distinction and selection be manifested over others? In this area of research, we shall mention a portion of their attributes in the life of this world, as well as their unique qualities in the Isthmus (*barzakh*) life that have been affirmed for them in texts of the Book and the Sunna.

The Prophets are the Masters of Mankind: The Prophets are the specially selected and chosen ones among the servants of Allah. Allah honoured them with Prophethood, gave them wisdom, and provided them with intellectual prowess, sound opinion, and chose them to be the intermediaries between Him and His creation. The Prophets convey to mankind the commands of Allah ﷻ and warn them from His anger and chastisement. The Prophets guide their people to that which leads to their felicity in this life and the next. It was from the wisdom of Allah that the Prophets were humans in order for the people to gather with them, take from them, and follow them in their manners and spiritual practices. Their humanity is the sum of their miraculous nature because they are human, yet at the same time, they are distinguished from the rest of humanity with qualities that no others can share with them. This is why, seeing their normal humanity stripped of these other qualities is a view of the time of ignorance (*jāhiliyya*) and idolatry.

An example of this, is the statement of the people of Nūḥ concerning him that Allah mentioned about them when He said: ❮The chiefs of the disbelievers among his people said: "We see you but a man like ourselves..."❯ (Hūd: 27)

From that also is the statement of the people of Mūsā and Hārūn: ❮They said: "Shall we believe in two men like ourselves, and their people are obedient to us with humility (and we use them to serve us as we like)?"❯ (al-Mu'minūn: 47) From that also is the statement of the people of Thamūd: ❮You are but a human being like us. Then bring us a sign if you are of the truthful.❯ (al-Shu'arā': 154)

From that also is the statement of the people of Ayka to their Prophet Shu'ayb: ❮They said: "You are only one of those bewitched! You are but a human being like us and verily, we think that you are one of the liars!"❯ (al-Shu'arā': 185-186) From that also is the statement of the idolaters to our Master Muḥammad ﷺ, those who saw him in the light of mere humanity, free (from his special qualities): ❮And they say: "Why does this Messenger eat food, and walk about in the markets (like ourselves)?"❯ (al-Furqān: 7)

The Attributes of the Prophets: The Prophets—may Allah send upon them prayers and peace—are humans in that they eat, drink, feel healthy, get sick, marry women, walk about in the market place, and are exposed to the common human conditions such as weakness, old age, and death. Despite all of this, they are distinguished with special characteristics and described with tremendous and noble qualities. With respect to them, these qualities are inseparable from them and are necessary traits. These qualities are summarized as follows:

1. Truthfulness
2. Conveyance
3. Fulfilling the trust
4. Intelligence
5. Being free of loathsome defects
6. Infallibility

This is not the place to go into detail regarding these qualities. They have been covered in detail within the books of *tawḥīd*. Here, we shall mention some of the qualities by which the Master of the Messengers ﷺ is distinguished from the rest of mankind.

He ﷺ Sees from Behind just as He Sees from the Front: The two Shaykhs (al-Bukhārī and Muslim) narrated from Abū Hurayra that the Messenger of Allah ﷺ said: "Do you see my *qibla* here? By Allah, your bowing and prostration is not hidden to me. Indeed, I see you from behind me." Muslim narrated from Anas that the Messenger of Allah ﷺ said: "O people, indeed I am your Imām, so do not precede me with either bowing or prostration, for indeed I see you from the front of me and from behind me." 'Abd al-Razzāq in his *Jām'ī*, al-Ḥākim, and Abū Nu'aym narrated from Abū Hurayra that the Prophet ﷺ said: "Indeed I can look behind me just as I look in front of me." Abū Nu'aym narrated from Abū Sa'īd al-Khudrī who said that the Messenger of Allah ﷺ said: "Indeed I see from behind me."

He ﷺ Sees what we don't See and He Hears what we don't Hear: Abū Dhar said that the Messenger of Allah ﷺ said: "Indeed I see what you do not see and I hear what you do not hear. The heavens creak and it has every right to creak. By the One in whose Hand rests my soul, there is not a place in the heavens that is the width of four fingers except that there is an Angel placing its forelock there lying prostrate to Allah. By Allah, if you knew what I know, you would laugh less and cry more, and would not take pleasure with women in your beds, and would go out to open areas and seek protection from Allah." Abū Dhar said after mentioning this narration: "Would that I could be a bush that is chewed up."[100]

His Noble Armpits ﷺ: The two Shaykhs (al-Bukhārī and Muslim) narrated from Anas who said: "I saw the Messenger of Allah ﷺ raising his hands in supplication until I saw the whiteness of his armpits." Ibn Sa'd narrated from Jābir who said: "When the Prophet ﷺ would prostrate, the whiteness of his armpits could be seen."

There are numerous Ḥadīth from the companions mentioning the whiteness of his armpits ﷺ. Al-Muḥib al-Ṭabarī said: "From his unique characteristics is that the armpits of people are of a different colour than the rest of their body whereas his were the

[100] Narrated by Aḥmad, al-Tirmidhī, and Ibn Mājah.

same." Al-Qurṭubī said similar to this and added that along with this, there was no hair upon his armpits.

He ﷺ Never Yawned: Al-Bukhārī in his book of history, Ibn Abī Shayba in his *Muṣannaf*, and Ibn Sa'd, all narrated from Yazīd b. Asamm who said: "The Prophet ﷺ never yawned." Ibn Abī Shayba narrated from Muslima b. 'Abd al-Malik b. Marwān who said: "No Prophet ever yawned."

His Noble Sweat ﷺ: Muslim narrated from Anas ؓ who said: "The Prophet ﷺ came to us and then took a nap at our place. During this time, he began to sweat, whereupon, my mother came with a small bottle and collected his sweat inside of it. After this, the Prophet ﷺ woke up and said: 'O Umm Sulaym! What are you doing?' She replied: 'We place the sweat in our perfume and it is the sweetest of our scents.' "

Muslim also narrated a similar wording from Anas ؓ who said: "The Prophet ﷺ used to come to Umm Sulaym and take his naps at her house and she would lay out a mat for him to sleep on. He used to sweat a great deal, so she would gather his sweat and place it in perfume and bottles. He once said: 'O Umm Sulaym! What are you doing?' She replied: 'I add your sweat to my perfume.' "

His Height ﷺ: Ibn Khaythama in his book of history, al-Bayhaqī, and Ibn 'Asākir, all narrated from 'Ā'isha who said: "The Prophet ﷺ was neither exceedingly tall nor short. If he walked alone, he would be considered of average height, yet, there was never a time that he walked with a group of tall people, except that he would seem taller than the rest. Perhaps he would be around two tall people yet he would seem taller, and when he would walk away, he would seem of average height." Ibn Sab'a mentioned this in his collection of unique qualities and added to it that when he ﷺ would sit, his shoulders would be higher than the rest of those sitting.

His Shadow ﷺ: Al-Ḥākim al-Tirmidhī narrated from Dhakwān that the Messenger of Allah ﷺ did not cast a shadow from either the sun or the moon.

Ibn Sab'a said: "From his unique qualities is that he did not cast a shadow on the ground. He was light when he walked out in the sun or the moon and he had no shadow." Some of them said: "This is strengthened by the Ḥadīth wherein he ﷺ said: 'And make me a light...' "

Qāḍī 'Iyāḍ mentioned in his *Shifā'*, and al-'Azfī mentioned in his book on *mawlid*, that among his unique qualities ﷺ, is that flies would never descend upon him, Ibn Sab'a mentioned in his collection: "Flies never descended upon his clothes." He also mentioned that among his qualities is that lice never infested him.

His Blood ﷺ: Al-Bazzār, Abū Ya'lā, al-Ṭabarānī, al-Ḥākim and al-Bayhaqī, all narrated that 'Abdullāh b. Zubayr came to the Prophet ﷺ while he was getting a *ḥijāma*[101] performed. When he was finished, he said: "O 'Abdullāh! Take this excess blood and dispose of it in a place where no one will see you." 'Abdullāh then took it and drank it. When he returned, he ﷺ said to him: "O 'Abdullāh! What did you do?" 'Abdullāh replied: "I disposed of it in the most concealed place that I know of. It is hidden from the people." The Prophet ﷺ said: "Did you drink it?" He replied: "Yes!" The Prophet ﷺ then said: "Woe to the people from you and woe to you from the people." Afterwards, the people would see that he had extra strength due to the blood he drank.

His Sleep ﷺ: The two Shaykhs (al-Bukhārī and Muslim) reported from 'Ā'isha who said: "O Messenger of Allāh! Are you going to sleep before you pray the *witr* prayer?" He replied: "O 'Ā'isha! My eyes sleep whereas my heart sleeps not." The two Shaykhs reported from Anas b. Mālik ؓ who said: "The Messenger of Allāh ﷺ said: 'My eyes sleep, whereas my heart sleeps not.' " He ﷺ said: "The eyes of the Prophets sleep, whereas their hearts sleep not."

His Sexual Prowess ﷺ: Al-Bukhārī reported from the route of Qatāda from Anas who said: "The Prophet ﷺ used to take turns in visiting his wives (for conjugal relations), one after the other in one day, and they were eleven in number."

---

[101] I.e. bloodletting: cupping.

Qatāda said: "I asked Anas: Was he capable of such a thing? Anas replied: "We used to say that he was given the strength of thirty men."

The Prophet ﷺ was Protected from Having Wet Dreams: Al-Ṭabarānī reported from the route of 'Ikrima from Anas and Ibn 'Abbās, and al-Daynūrī in his work *al-Mujālasa*, reported from the route of Mujāhid from Ibn 'Abbās who said: "No Prophet ever had a wet dream and indeed, it is only from Satan."

His Blessed Urine ﷺ: Ḥasan b. Sufyān in his *Musnad*, Abū Ya'lā, al-Ḥākim, al-Dāraquṭnī, and Abū Nu'aym all narrated from Umm Ayman who said: "The Prophet got up one night and urinated in a bowl. During that night, I rose in the state of thirst so I drank whatever was in the bowl. In the morning I told Him what I had done, after which he smiled and said: 'Surely you will never have pain in your stomach.' "

'Abd al-Razzāq narrates from Ibn Jurayj who said: "I was told that the Prophet used to have a wooden bowl in which he used to urinate and it was placed under His bed. Once, he searched for it and found that it was empty. He then asked a woman named Baraka, who was the servant of Umm Ḥabība who came with her when she returned from Abyssinia. He asked: 'Where is the urine that was in the bowl?' She replied, 'I drank it.' The Messenger of Allah ﷺ then said: 'O Umm Yusuf! You will most certainly be healthy!' This (Umm Yūsuf) was her nickname. She never became ill after that day save the sickness that immediately preceded her death."

Ibn Daḥiyya said: "This story is different from the story of Umm Ayman, and this Baraka Umm Yūsuf is different from Baraka Umm Ayman.

A Beneficial Conclusion: Some have composed lines of poetry wherein they summarized the unique physical characteristics of the Prophet that distinguished him from everyone else:

Our Prophet was chosen with ten special qualities
Never did he have a wet dream and no shadow did he have
What is expelled from him the earth does indeed swallow

Just as the flies keep away from him
His eyes sleep whereas his heart sleeps not
He sees from behind just as he sees from the front
Never once did he yawn and this is the seventh quality
And he was born circumcised
The beasts know him when he embarks upon them
Quickly they approach him and they flee not
He towers over those around him when sitting in gatherings
May prayers and peace of Allah be upon him
both night and morning

In section two of our research concerning the Prophetic qualities, we mentioned some of the unique Prophetic qualities and our basic view concerning them; that these unique qualities are quite numerous. Some of them have authentic chains, some of them have weak chains, and some are differed over among the scholars—with some holding the view that they are authentic, and others holding the view that they are weak—therefore, these are issues of disagreement.

In the times of old, the words of the scholars concerning these reports centred around what is deemed as either correct or incorrect, or what is authentic or false. Never did their words centre around faith and disbelief. We have mentioned a sample of such unique qualities; some of which are authentic, some of which are not authentic. Some of them are acceptable, and some are not.

We mentioned these reports so they serve as examples showing the leniency of some Imāms in citation without checking or criticism. (Our) intent behind this was not to go into discussion regarding their authenticity or weakness, so understand this.

THE CORRECT UNDERSTANDING OF SEEKING BLESSINGS

Many people err in their understanding of the reality of seeking blessings (*tabarruk*) from the Prophet ﷺ, his personal relics, his family, and those who inherit from him among the scholars and saints, may Allah be pleased with all of them. They impute those who do these things with idolatry and misguidance—this being their standard response to anything new that proves difficult for them to understand or grasp.

Before we cite the evidence and examples that prove the permissibility—nay, the legality—of seeking blessings, we first must know that seeking blessings is nothing more than *tawassul* unto Allah ﷻ through the one from whom blessings are sought—be that a person, place, or personal relic. With respect to individuals, this (seeking of blessings) is due to the belief in their virtue and closeness to Allah ﷻ, while at the same time believing that they themselves are utterly incapable of bringing benefit or harm unless it is by the permission of Allah. With respect to personal relics, this (seeking of blessings) is done because these things are attributed to those individuals, hence, they are ennobled by the nobility of those individuals, and honoured, extolled and beloved due to those individuals. With respect to places, they have no innate virtue in and of themselves, however, they do have blessings when good and righteousness takes place in or at them, such as prayer, fasting, and all other types of worship that the righteous perform. From this, the effulgent mercies descend upon it, the Angels attend to it, and tranquillity engulfs it. These are the blessings that are to be sought from Allah in the places intended for such. These blessings are to be sought by embarking upon their proper places and turning to Allah, the Exalted, with supplication to Him, seeking His forgiveness, and remembering the major events and noble occasions that took place therein that move the souls and infuse them with high aspirations and energy to imitate the people of those places among the people of success and righteousness. Take some of these examples that are extracted from our separate essay on the subject of blessings:

Seeking Blessings with His Hair, Excess Water of Ablution, His Spit and Sweat ﷺ: Ja'far b. 'Abdullāh b. al-Ḥakam reported that Khālid b. al-Walīd once lost a hat during the battle of Yarmūk. He ordered the soldiers saying: "Look for it!" but they did not find it. He ordered them to look for it a second time whereupon they found it. When they found it, they discovered that it was an old hat, after which Khālid said: "Once, the Messenger of Allah ﷺ performed the 'Umra, thereafter shaving his head. The people then rushed to take the hair that was cut from his sides, however, I beat them to getting the hair that was cut from his front, after which I placed it inside of this hat. Never once did I witness a battle with this hat, except that I was given victory.

Ḥāfiẓ al-Haythamī said: "This was narrated by al-Ṭabarānī and Abū Ya'lā with the same wording. Their men are the men of the *Ṣaḥīḥ* collection. Ja'far heard from a group of the companions, however, I do not know if he heard directly from Khālid or not."[102] This narration was mentioned by Ḥāfiẓ Ibn Ḥajar in *al-Maṭālib al-'Āliya* and therein it states that Khālid said: "There was not a direction I turned except that it was opened up (conquered) for me."[103]

Mālik b. Ḥamza b. Abī Usayd al-Sā'idī al-Khazrajī narrated from his father who in turn narrated from his grandfather, Abū Usayd, that he had a well in Medina called the *Well of Biḍā'a* which the Prophet ﷺ once spat in and (Abū Usayd) would drink from it and rub his body with the water.[104]

'Urwa b. Mas'ūd Describes the State of the Companions Around the Messenger of Allah ﷺ: Imām al-Bukhārī mentioned his chain after which it said: "Then, 'Urwa glanced at the companions of the Prophet ﷺ and said: 'By Allah, never did the Prophet ﷺ spit, except that it would land in the hand of a man among them, who would then rub his face and body with it. When he would command them, they would hasten to carry out his command.

'When he would perform ablutions, they would almost fight each other to get his excess ablution water. When in his presence, they would speak with lowered voices. Out of awe of him, they would never stare directly at him.'

When 'Urwa returned to his people he said: 'What kind of people are these? By Allah, I have been in delegations sent to kings, delegations sent to Caesar, Chosroes and Negus, but I have never seen a king who is extolled by his companions like the

[102] *Majma' al-Zawā'id*, 9:349.

[103] *Al-Matālib al-'Āliya*, 3:90.

[104] Narrated by al-Ṭabarānī and its men are all reliable.

companions of Muḥammad ﷺ extol him. By Allah, he does not spit except that it falls in the hands of one of them, who then rubs his face and body with it. If he commands them, they hasten to carry out his order. When he performs ablutions, they almost fight to get his excess ablution water. When they speak in his presence, they lower their voices. Out of awe of him, they never stare directly at him.'[105]

The Commentary of Ḥāfiẓ Ibn Ḥajar upon this Story:

Ḥāfiẓ Ibn Ḥajar commented:

> This contains proof that spit and cut hair are both pure. It also contains proof for the (permissibility) of seeking blessings from the pure remnants of the righteous. Perhaps the companions did this in front of 'Urwa in an exaggerated fashion in order to dispel any notions he had that they were afraid. So, it was as if they were saying: 'Whoever loves his Imām in such a way, and who holds him in awe in such a way, how can it be imagined that he will run away from him and give him to his enemy?'
>
> Nay, they were more covetous of him, his religion and his victory than the tribes were of each other due to their mere blood relations. This story indicates that it is permissible to reach every aim with whatever permissible means are available.[106]

The Prophet ﷺ Instructs Them to Guard the Remnants of His Ablution Water: From Ṭalq b. 'Alī who said: "We set out as a delegation to the Messenger of Allah ﷺ, after which we pledged allegiance to him and prayed with him. We informed him that in our land we had a temple, so we requested that he give us the water from the remnants of his ablution. He called for water to be brought out and performed ablution and gargled it. He then poured it into a container for us and said: 'When you arrive in your land, demolish your temple and moisten its grounds with

---

105 Al-Bukhārī; 'The Book of Conditions', section: 'Conditions in *Jihād*' (*Fatḥ al-Bārī*, 5:330).

106 *Fatḥ al-Bārī*, 5:341.

this water and then turn it into a Mosque.' We said: 'Our land is very far away and the weather is very hot, so the water will evaporate.' He said: 'Dilute it with more water for it shall only increase it in sweetness.' "

This was narrated by al-Nasā'ī and is also found in *al-Mishkāt* (nr.716). This Ḥadīth is part of the well known and well considered foundations establishing the permissibility of seeking blessings through him ﷺ, his personal relics, and everything else that is ascribed to him. Here, we see that he took the excess water from his ablution, placed it in a container, and ordered them to take it with them—all in fulfilment of their request. There must indeed be a strong secret within them that encouraged them to request this water—even though Medina was filled with water, not to mention their own lands. So why all of this effort and struggle to carry this small amount of water from one distant land to another in the scorching heat?

Indeed, none of this concerned them in the least because the secret that was carried in that water made all of those difficulties seem paltry—that secret was seeking blessings through him, his personal relics, and everything that is ascribed to him that was not found or made available in their lands. Nay, this point is strengthened further by his support ﷺ for them and his pleasure in their action, when they said the water would evaporate because of the severe heat, to which he replied: "Dilute it with more water." He clarified that his blessings within the water would remain no matter how much more water they added to it, for those blessings are continuous and connected to it.

Seeking Blessings through His Hair after His Death ﷺ: 'Uthmān b. 'Abdullāh b. Mawhib said: "My family sent me with a container of water to Umm Salama, who then came out with a bell like object (*juljul*) of silver, encasing strands of hair from the Prophet ﷺ. Whenever someone would be afflicted with the evil eye or anything else, they would send someone to her with a pot. I looked inside the encasing and saw several strands of red hair.[107]

---

[107] Al-Bukhārī; 'The Book of Clothing', Section: 'What has been mentioned regarding Gray Hair.'

The Imām and Ḥāfiẓ Ibn Ḥajar said in *al-Fatḥ*:

> Wakī' clarified this in his collection. He said: "An encasement was made to preserve the hair of the Prophet ﷺ that was in the possession of Umm Salama. A *juljul* is similar to a bell in appearance and it is made out of either silver, brass or copper. It can be hollowed out in order to place within it whatever needs to be preserved."[108]

Imām al-'Aynī said:

> To explain this: Umm Salama had in her possession some strands of the Prophet's hair ﷺ that had turned red from being inside of the *juljul*. When people would fall ill, they would seek blessings and cure from it. They would take some of the hairs, place them in a container of water, and drink that water wherein the hairs were placed, thereby being healed. The family of 'Uthmān took some strands from her and placed them in a silver container and drank the water contained inside, thereby they were all healed. After this, 'Uthmān was sent to return the container to Umm Salama, where she then took it from him and placed (the hairs) back in the *juljul*. When she did that, 'Uthmān looked inside the *juljul* and saw numerous red strands of hair.
>
> The statement: "When people would fall ill..." till the end, are the words of 'Uthmān b. 'Abdullāh b. Mawhib. Al-Kirmānī explained it as: "In other words, my family used to..." Some of them said in explanation: "And it used to be (meaning with the people), that if someone (among them) was afflicted." What al-Kirmānī stated was more correct and it shows that if a person was afflicted with the evil eye or some other sickness, his family would send him to it—meaning the *mikhḍaba* (a type of pot), which is used for storing water. Water is placed inside of it along with some of the blessed hairs that float on it. They would be healed through this, and then the hair would be returned to the *juljul*.[109]

---

108 *Fatḥ al-Bārī*, 10:353.

109 *'Umda al-Qārī' Sharḥ Ṣaḥīḥ al-Bukhārī*, 18:79.

The Prophet ﷺ Distributes His Hair among the People: Muslim narrated from the Ḥadīth of Anas: "The Prophet ﷺ went to Minā, approached the stone pillar and cast his stones. Afterwards, he went to his resting place in Minā, sacrificed an animal, and said to the barber: "Take"—while pointing at his right and then left side. Afterwards, he started to give the hair to the people." Al-Tirmidhī also narrated from the Ḥadīth of Anas who said: "After the Messenger of Allah ﷺ cast his stones at the stone pillar, he slaughtered his sacrificial animal and then gave the right side of his head for the barber to cut. He then gave it (the hair) to Ṭalha. Then, he gave the left side of his head for the barber to cut and said: "Divide it among the people." The apparent meaning of al-Tirmidhī's narration is that the hair that he gave to Ṭalha to divide among the people was the hair from his left side. This has also been narrated by Muslim via Ibn 'Uyayna. As for the narration of Ḥafṣ b. Ghiyāth and 'Abd al-'Alā', it mentions that the hair divided among the people was from his right side—and both of these narrations are in Muslim's collection.

The Prophet ﷺ Distributes His Hair Strand by Strand: The narration of Ḥafṣ mentioned in Muslim states: "...He began with the right side and distributed it strand by strand, or two strands at a time among the people. Then, he did the same with his left side as he did with (the right side)." Abū Bakr said in his narration from Ḥafṣ: "He said to the barber: 'Here'—and he pointed with his hand to the right side of his head. After this, he distributed the hairs to those near him. Then, he got the attention of the barber and pointed to his left side, who then cut it, after which, the Prophet gave (the hair) to Umm Sulaym."

The People Compete to Acquire Strands of His Hair ﷺ: There is a narration in the *Musnad* of Imām Aḥmad which states that he ﷺ gave some of his hair from the right side of his head to Anas in order to take it to Umm Sulaym, who was the wife of Abū Ṭalha. In this narration, Anas states: "When the Messenger of Allah ﷺ had his hair cut at Minā, he took hold of the right side of his head with his hand (had it cut), and then gave it to me when he was finished. He said: 'O Anas! Go with this and give it to Umm

Sulaym.' " Anas said: "When the people saw what he had specially gifted to us, they started competing to acquire what was left to be cut on the other side. You could see one person taking from this, and another taking from that."

The Reality of the Words Mentioned on this Subject: As you see, the narrations differ on this subject. Some of them state that he gave Abū Ṭalha hair from the right side, while he distributed the hair that was cut from the left side. Other narrations state the opposite. In yet others, it states that he gave the hair from the right side to Umm Sulaym.

All of these narrations are reconciled by what was mentioned by the author of *al-Mufhim* (explanation of *Ṣaḥīḥ Muslim*) when he said:

> His statement: "When the Messenger of Allah ﷺ had the right side of his head cut, he gave it to Abū Ṭalha..." does not contradict what is stated in the second narration; that he distributed the hair cut from the right side among the people, and gave the hair from the left side to Umm Sulaym. She is the wife of Abū Ṭalha and the mother of Anas—may Allah be pleased with her.
>
> All of these narrations in sum mention that when the Prophet ﷺ cut the hair on his right side, he gave it to Abū Ṭalha to distribute among the people, and he (Abū Ṭalha) did so. He ﷺ then gave from his left side in order that it be with Abū Ṭalha—so all of that is authentically traced back to him—and Allah knows best.

Al-Muḥib al-Ṭabarī reconciled (these narrations) where possible, and chose some over others when he was unable to reconcile them. He said:

> What is correct is that it was (the hair) from the right side that was distributed among the people. He gave (the hair) of the left side to Abū Ṭalha and Umm Sulaym. There is no contradiction between the two narrations, because Umm Sulaym is the wife of Abū Ṭalha and he ﷺ gave it to them both. As a consequence, sometimes it is attributed to him and sometimes to her.

This Ḥadīth also shows proof for seeking blessings through his hair ﷺ and other personal relics and effects. May my mother, father and soul be sacrificed for him! In his *Musnad*, Aḥmad narrated up to Ibn Sīrīn who said: "'Ubayda al-Sulaymānī narrated it to me"—meaning this Ḥādīth—and then he said: "That I have just one strand of his hair is more beloved to me than possessing all of the gold and silver in and on this world." Many have mentioned that Khālid b. al-Walīd had some strands of his ﷺ hair inside of his hat, and that for this reason, no place did he go except that it was opened up to him (conquered). This is strengthened by what was mentioned by Mullā in his Prophetic biography that Khālid once asked Abū Ṭalha when he was distributing the hairs of the Prophet ﷺ among the people that he give him of the hairs of his forelock, so he gave some to Khālid. That the hairs he had were from the front of the forelock proved appropriate for him to conquer every land he travelled to.[110]

Seeking Blessings through His Sweat ﷺ: From 'Uthmān who reported from Anas who said: "Umm Sulaym used to spread a leather mat for the Prophet and he used to take his midday nap on it at her home." Anas added, "When the Prophet slept, she would take some of his sweat and hair and collect it (the sweat) in a bottle and then mix it with *suk* (a kind of perfume) while he was still sleeping." When the death of Anas b. Mālik approached, he advised that some of that *suk* be mixed with his *ḥanūt* (a burial perfume for use on the dead), and it was mixed with his *ḥanūt*.[111]

In another narration found in Muslim it states: "The Prophet ﷺ once visited us and took a nap, after which he started to perspire. My mother brought a bottle and started to collect the sweat. The Prophet ﷺ then woke up and said: 'O Umm Sulaym! What are you doing?' She replied: 'This is your sweat that we mix with our perfumes and it makes them the most fragrant of perfumes.' "

In the narration of Isḥāq b. Abī Ṭalha it states: "...he started to perspire and his sweat began to soak an old leather mat. She

[110] Ibid., 8:230-231.

[111] Al-Bukhārī; 'The Book of Permission,' chapter: 'Concerning those that visit People and take Naps at their Houses.'

(Umm Sulaym) began to collect the sweat into a bottle. When the Prophet woke up he said: 'What are you doing?' She replied: 'We hope for it to bless our young children.' He ﷺ replied: 'You are correct.' "

In a narration from Abū Qilāba it states: "She used to gather his sweat and place it in bottles and in perfumes. He ﷺ said: 'What is this?' She replied: 'It is your sweat that I use to sweeten my perfume.' "

All of these narrations show that the Prophet ﷺ saw what Umm Sulaym was doing and declared her correct in doing so. There is no contradiction between her saying that she would gather it in order to sweeten the perfume, and her saying that it was for blessing. It is understood that she did it for both of those reasons.[112]

Seeking Blessings through Touching His Skin ﷺ: From 'Abd al-Raḥmān b. Abī Laylā reported from his father who said: "Usayd b. Ḥuḍayr ؓ was a very pious and humorous man. Once, when he was with the Messenger of Allah ﷺ and the people, speaking to them and entertaining them, the Messenger of Allah ﷺ poked him in the waist. He (Usayd) said: 'O Messenger of Allah! You have caused me pain!' He ﷺ said: 'Retaliate.' Usayd said: 'O Messenger of Allah! You have a long shirt on and I don't!' The Messenger of Allah then lifted his shirt and held it with his arms and Usayd started to kiss his hip area and said: 'May my mother and father be sacrificed for you! This is all I wanted!' "

Al-Ḥākim said: "This Ḥadīth has an authentic chain and was not reported (by al-Bukhārī and Muslim)." Al-Dhahabī agreed with him and said: "It is *ṣaḥīḥ*." It was also narrated by Ibn 'Asākir from Abū Laylā ؓ in a similar wording, as found in *al-Kanz* (7/701). I say: This Ḥadīth is also found in the collection of Abū Dāwūd and al-Ṭabarānī from Usayd b. Ḥuḍayr as well, as found in *al-Kanz* (4/43).

Ibn Isḥāq narrated from Ḥibbān b. Wāsi', from elders among his people that once, the Messenger of Allah ﷺ was aligning the rows of his companions on the day of Badr and in his hand was an arrow to straighten them out. He passed by Sawād b.

[112] *Fatḥ al-Bārī*, 11:82.

Ghaziyya ﷺ—an ally of 'Adī Banū Najjār—who was out of the row, and poked him with the arrow. Sawād said: "You hurt me! Allah sent you with truth and justice so let me retaliate." He ﷺ exposed a part of his body and said: "Retaliate." He (Sawād) embraced him and kissed his stomach. The Messenger of Allah ﷺ said: "What motivated you to do that Sawād?" Sawād replied: "O Messenger of Allah! This large group you see has gathered, and it is my wish that the last thing I do is to have my skin touch yours." The Messenger of Allah ﷺ prayed for him to obtain good.[113]

'Abd al-Razzāq narrated from Ḥasan that once, the Messenger of Allah ﷺ met a man who had dyed his hair yellow. The Messenger of Allah ﷺ—who had a palm leaf stalk in his hand—said to the man: "Yellow dye?" and then struck him with the stalk and said: "Did I not forbid you from this?" The strike caused the man's stomach to bleed. The man said: "Retaliation, O Messenger of Allah!" The people asked: "Are you going to get even with the Messenger of Allah?" The man replied: "There is no one's body that is any better than mine." The Messenger of Allah ﷺ uncovered his stomach and said to the man: "Take retaliation." The man then kissed the Prophet's stomach and said: "I will leave it in order for you to intercede for me on the Day of Judgement."[114]

Ibn Sa'd narrated (3/72) from Ḥasan that the Messenger of Allah ﷺ saw Sawād b. 'Amr—and it was stated by Ismā'īl that he was: "covered up, and he ﷺ said: 'Line up straight,' then he poked him in the stomach with a stick or *siwāk* (tooth stick) that caused him pain, and the rest of the story is the same."

'Abd al-Razzāq also narrated from Ḥasan (as found in *al-Kanz* 15/19) that he said: "There was a man from the Anṣār who was called Sawāda b. 'Umar ﷺ. He used to pretend that he was bowlegged. When the Prophet ﷺ would see him, we would lower our gaze. Once, when he was pretending, the Prophet ﷺ came to him and struck him with a stick that was in his hand, thereby injuring him. He (Sawāda) said: "Retaliation, O Messenger of Allah!" The Prophet then gave him his stick and lifted the two shirts that he was wearing. The people were turning their heads

---

[113] *Al-Bidaya wa al-Nihāya*, 3:271.
[114] *Al-Kanz*, 15:91.

away from him until he had exposed the same area of his body where he struck Sawāda. At this point, Sawāda threw the stick and started to kiss him and said: "O Prophet of Allah! Rather, because of this, I will leave it for you to intercede for me on the Day of Judgement!"[115]

The Report of Zāhir: He ﷺ used to say regarding Zāhir: "Zāhir is our man from the desert and we are his city people." He ﷺ used to love him. Once, the Prophet ﷺ was walking to the market and saw Zāhir standing. He ﷺ came to him from behind and grasped him with his hand to his chest. Zāhir sensed that it was the Messenger of Allah ﷺ. He said: "I started to wipe my back that was on his chest in hope of gaining some blessings." In the narration of al-Tirmidhī in the *Shamā'il* it states that he ﷺ embraced him from behind where he couldn't see him. Zāhir said: "Let me go! Who is this?" He then turned his head and recognized that it was the Prophet ﷺ. He then tried his best not to press his back against the Prophet ﷺ. The Messenger of Allah ﷺ then started to say: "Who will purchase this slave?" Zāhir said to him: "O Prophet of Allah, you will find that I am non-saleable." The Prophet ﷺ replied: "Nay, you are expensive with Allah." Also, in the narration of al-Tirmidhī it states: "However, with Allah you are not non-saleable" or he said: "You are expensive with Allah."[116]

SEEKING BLESSINGS WITH THE BLOOD OF THE PROPHET ﷺ

The Report of 'Abdullāh b. al-Zubayr: From 'Āmir b. 'Abdullāh b. al-Zubayr ؓ who stated that his father narrated to him that once, he came to the Prophet while he was getting cupped (bloodletting). When he was finished he said: "O Abdullāh! Take this excess blood and dispose of it where no one can see you." When he departed, he then took the excess blood and drank it. When he returned, the Prophet ﷺ said: "O Abdullāh! What did you do with the blood?" He replied: "I disposed of it in most concealed place I know of that would hide it from the people."

---

[115] Al-Baghawī narrated a similar narration. See *al-Iṣāba*, 2:96.
[116] *Al-Mawāhib al-Laduniyya*, 1:297.

The Prophet said: "Perhaps you drank it?" He replied: "Yes." The Prophet ﷺ asked him: "Why did you drink the blood? Woe to the people from you and woe to you from the people." Abū Mūsā said: "Abū 'Āṣim said: 'They (the companions) used to believe that the strength he possessed was due to that blood.' " This is found in *al-Iṣāba* (2/310) and was narrated by al-Ḥākim (3/554) and al-Ṭabarānī as well.

Al-Haythamī said: "It was narrated by al-Ṭabarānī and al-Bazzār in summarized form. The men of al-Bazzār (his chain) are men found in the *Ṣaḥīḥ* collection, save for Humayd b. Qāsim who is reliable."[117] A similar report was narrated by Ibn 'Asākir as found in *al-Kanz* (7/57) along with the statement of Abū 'Āṣim. In another narration it states: Abū Muslima said: "They believed that the strength within Abū al-Zubayr was from the strength of the Prophets blood ﷺ."

In Abū Nu'aym's *Ḥilya* (1/33) there is a report from Kaysān, the freed slave of 'Abdullāh b. al-Zubayr ؓ in which he said: "Once, when Salmān entered upon the Messenger of Allah ﷺ, he found 'Abdullāh b. al-Zubayr holding a bowl and drinking its contents. 'Abdullāh then went to the Messenger of Allah ﷺ and he (the Prophet ﷺ) asked him ('Abdullāh): 'Did you empty (it)?' He ('Abdullāh) said: 'Yes.' Salmān inquired: 'What was that, O Messenger of Allah?' He replied ﷺ: 'I gave him the excess contents (of blood) from the cupping for him to dispose of.' Salmān said: 'By the One who sent you with the truth, he drank it!' He ﷺ asked: 'He really drank it?' Salmān said: 'Yes.' He ﷺ then asked Abdullāh b. al-Zubayr why, to which he replied: 'I wanted the blood of the Messenger of Allah to be inside of my body.' The Prophet ﷺ stood up and patted his head and said: 'Woe to you from the people and woe to the people from you. The fire shall not touch you save the strong oath (*qasam al-yamīn*).' ".

This was narrated by Ibn 'Asākir in a similar summarized form. Its men are all reliable. This is stated in *al-Kanz* (7/56). Al-Dāraquṭnī narrated a similar report in his *Sunan*. In yet another narration, it states that when Ibn al-Zubayr drank the blood of the Messenger of Allah ﷺ, he ﷺ said to him: "What motivated you to do that?" He replied: "I knew that your blood

[117] *Majma' al-Zawā'id*, 8:270.

would not be touched by the fire of Hell, so for that reason I drank it." He ﷺ said: "Woe unto you from the people and woe unto the people from you." In a similar narration in al-Dāraquṭnī from Asmā' it adds: "The fire shall not touch you."

In the book *al-Jawhar al-Maknūn fī Dhikr al-Qabā'il wa al-Buṭūn* it mentions that when he drank his blood ﷺ, the fragrance of musk emanated from Ibn al-Zubayr's mouth and remained with him until he was crucified.[118]

The Report of Safīna the Freed Slave of the Prophet ﷺ: Al-Ṭabarānī narrated from Safīna ؓ who said: "Once, the Prophet ﷺ was getting cupped. He said: 'Take this blood and bury it so as to conceal it from the animals, birds, and people.' I (Safīna) went to a concealed place and drank it. I (returned and) mentioned this to him ﷺ and he laughed." Al-Haythamī said: "The men of al-Ṭabarānī are all reliable." (8/280)

The Report of Mālik b. Sinān: In the *Sunan* of Sa'īd b. Manṣūr it is mentioned from the route of 'Amr b. al-Sā'ib who said that it reached him that when the Prophet's ﷺ noble face was injured during the battle of Uḥud, Mālik b. Sinān—the father of Abū Sa'īd al-Khudrī—sucked the blood from the wound until the injured spot was cleaned and its whiteness was apparent. After this, the Prophet ﷺ said to him: "Spit it out." He (Mālik) said: "I will never spit it out." Then, he (Mālik) swallowed it, so the Prophet ﷺ said: "Whoever wants to see a man from the people of Paradise, then let him look at this (man)." He (Mālik) was later killed in the battle. Al-Ṭabarānī also narrated this with the addition: "Whoever has my blood mix with his blood will not be touched by the fire." Al-Haythamī said: "I didn't see in its chain anyone whose weakness is unanimously agreed upon." Sa'īd b. Manṣūr also narrated that he ﷺ said: "Whoever would be delighted to see a man who has had my blood mix with his, then look at Mālik b. Sinān."

Another one Performing Cupping and Drinking His Blood ﷺ: Ibn Ḥibbān narrated in his *al-Ḍu'afā'* (weak) collection from Ibn

[118] *Al-Mawāhib al-Laduniyya.*

'Abbās ﷺ who said: "Once, a boy from among the Quraysh cupped the Prophet ﷺ. When he was finished, he took the excess blood with him behind a wall. He looked from his left and his right, and when he did not see anyone, he drank the blood till it (the container) was empty. He then returned and the Prophet ﷺ looked in his face and said: 'Woe unto you! What did you do with the blood?' He (the boy) said: 'I disposed of it behind the wall.' The Prophet ﷺ asked him: 'Where did you dispose of it?' The boy replied: 'O Messenger of Allah, your blood was too valuable for me to dispose of in the earth so it is in my stomach.' He ﷺ said: 'Go, for you have guarded yourself from the fire.' "[119]

The Report of Baraka the Servant of Umm Ḥabība: Ḥāfiẓ b. al-Ḥajar said: "It was narrated by 'Abd al-Razzāq from Ibn Jurayj who said: 'I was told that the Prophet ﷺ used to have a wooden bowl in which he used to urinate and it was placed under His bed. Once, he ﷺ searched for it but found that it was empty. He ﷺ then asked a woman named Baraka, who was the servant of Umm Ḥabība who came with her when she returned from Abyssinia. He ﷺ asked: "Where is the urine that was in the bowl?" She replied, "I drank it." The Messenger of Allah ﷺ replied: "O Umm Yusuf! You will most certainly be healthy!" This (Umm Yūsuf) was her nickname. She never became ill after that day save the sickness that immediately preceded her death." '[120]

I say: Both Abū Dāwūd and al-Nasā'ī narrated this in summarized form. Ḥāfiẓ al-Suyūṭī said: "It was completed by Ibn 'Abd al-Barr in *al-Isti'āb* and in it, it mentions that he ﷺ asked her about the urine that was in the container, to which she replied: 'I drank it, O Messenger of Allah...' "[121]

The Report of Umm Ayman: The Imām and Ḥāfiẓ, al-Qasṭalānī said in *al-Mawāhib*: "It was narrated by Ḥasan b. Sufyān in his *Musnad*, al-Ḥākim, al-Dāraquṭnī, al-Ṭabarānī, and Abū Nu'aym from the Ḥadīth of Mālik al-Nakha'ī from al-Aswad b. Qays from Nabīh al-'Anzī from Umm Ayman who said: 'Once, during the

---

[119] Ibid.

[120] *Talkhīs al-Ḥabīr fī Takhrīj Aḥādīth al-Rāfi'ī al-Kabīr*, 1:32.

[121] *Sharḥ al-Suyūṭī 'alā Sunan al-Nasā'ī*, 1:32.

night, the Messenger of Allah ﷺ woke up and went to the clay pot at the side of the house and urinated inside of it.

'Later, I woke up thirsty and drank what was inside of it, not realizing what it contained. When the Prophet ﷺ woke up he said: "O Umm Ayman! Get up and dispose of what is in the clay pot." I said: "By Allah, I drank what was inside of it." He ﷺ then laughed until his molar teeth showed and said: "By Allah, your stomach will never feel any pain." '

Ḥāfiẓ Ibn Ḥajar said in *al-Talkhīṣ*:

> Ibn Daḥiyya correctly stated that these are two separate incidents that occurred with two different women—and this is clear from the different contexts (of each report). It is clear that Baraka Umm Yūsuf is different from Baraka Umm Ayman, who was his freed servant.

Benefit: In the narration of Salmā the wife of Abū Rāfi' it states that she drank the bath water of the Messenger of Allah ﷺ, who as a result said to her: "Allah has forbidden your body from the fire." Al-Ṭabarānī in *al-Awsaṭ* has narrated this from her Ḥadīth and it contains some weakness.[122] Al-Qasṭalānī said: "This is the view of Shaykh al-Islam al-Bulqīnī, and these Ḥadīth contain proof that the Prophet's ﷺ blood and urine are both pure."

The Report of Sarra the Servant of Umm Salama ؓ: Al-Ṭabarānī narrated from Ḥakīma b. Umayya from her mother who said: "The Prophet ﷺ used to have a container from 'Aydān that he would urinate in (at night) and place under his bed. Once, he woke up and looked for it but could not find it. He asked: 'Where is the container?' They answered him: 'Sarra, the servant of Umm Salama that came with her from Abyssinia drank it.' He ﷺ said: 'She has been forbidden from the fire with a partition.' "

Al-Haythamī said: "Its men are all men of the *Ṣaḥīḥ* collection save for 'Abdullāh b. Aḥmad b. Ḥanbal and Ḥakīma, and both of them are reliable." (8/271)

---

[122] *Talkhīs al-Ḥābīr*, 1:32.

THE STATEMENTS OF THE SCHOLARS CONCERNING THIS SUBJECT

Imām Muḥyī al-Dīn al-Nawawī said in *Sharḥ al-Muhaddhab*:

> Those who were of the opinion that both (his blood and urine ﷺ) were pure, inferred such from two well known Ḥadīth, one, that Abū Ṭayba the cupper once cupped him ﷺ, and drank his blood and he ﷺ did not censure him for that, and (two,) the report that a women once drank his urine ﷺ and he did not censure her either. The Ḥadīth of Abū Ṭayba is weak and the Ḥadīth about the drinking of his urine is authentic and reported by al-Dāraquṭnī who said that it was a *ḥasan ṣaḥīḥ* narration. This is sufficient to use as evidence (concerning the purity) of all of his excretions by way of analogy. ...Qāḍī Ḥusayn said: "The most sound view is to positively assert that everything (from him ﷺ) is pure." '

Then he (al-Nawawī) said in his response to the query about why he ﷺ used to seek to avoid it (his excrements if they were pure) and he responded by saying that it was based on one of recommendation.[123] The Imām and 'Allāma, Badr al-Dīn al-'Aynī said in his well known explanation of al-Bukhārī (titled:) *'Umda al-Qārī* (2/35): "As for the hair of the Messenger of Allah ﷺ, it is honoured and glorified and is not a part of this (issue regarding purity)." I say: Māwardī said:

> As for the hair of the Prophet ﷺ, stating that the correct view is to positively assert that it is pure seems to allude to another view opposite of that. We seek refuge in Allah from that other view! Some of the Shāfi'īs crossed the limits and almost left the fold of Islam when one of them claimed: "Concerning the (purity) of the hair of the Messenger of Allah, there are two views." Far removed is the hair of the Messenger of Allah ﷺ from that! How could he have said this when it has been stated that his excrements ﷺ are pure—not to mention his noble hair?

[123] *Al-Majmū' Sharḥ al-Muhaddhab*, 1:233.

Al-'Aynī went on to say:

> Many Ḥadīth have been cited showing that a group of companions drank the blood of the Prophet ﷺ, from them: Abū Ṭayba the cupper, the young man from the Quraysh who cupped the Prophet ﷺ, and 'Abdullāh b. Zubayr who drank the blood of the Prophet ﷺ, as narrated by al-Bazzār, al-Ṭabarānī, al-Ḥākim, al-Bayhaqī, and Abū Nu'aym in the Ḥilya. It has also been reported from 'Alī ؓ that he drank the blood of the Prophet ﷺ, and it has been reported from Umm Ayman that she drank the urine of the Prophet as well, which was narrated by al-Ḥākim, al-Dāraquṭnī, al-Ṭabarānī, and Abū Nu'aym. Al-Ṭabarānī mentioned in his *al-Awsaṭ* collection in a narration from Salmā, the wife of Abū Rāfi', that she drank some of the excess water left over from the Prophet's bath. The Prophet ﷺ said to her: "Allah has made your body forbidden from the fire."

In *al-Mawāhib*, Ḥāfiẓ al-Qasṭalānī commented on Imām al-Nawawī's statement from Qāḍī Ḥusayn:

> The soundest view is that it is positively asserted that all of his excrements are pure. This is the view held by Abū Ḥanīfa as al-'Aynī stated. Shaykh al-Islam Ibn Ḥajar said: "The abundance of evidence shows that his excrements are pure ﷺ. The Imāms counted this to be among his unique qualities."

Seeking Blessings from the Place in which He Prayed ﷺ: From Nāfi' who stated that 'Abdullāh b. 'Umar relayed to him that the Prophet ﷺ once prayed in the small Mosque located near the Mosque in the heights of al-Rawḥā'.

'Abdullāh used to know the exact place in which the Prophet ﷺ prayed and he would say: "When you arrive at the Mosque to pray, turn to the right, and the Mosque is on the edge of the right side of the pathway if you are walking towards the direction of Mecca. Between it and the large Mosque is only a stones' throw away." (Narrated by al-Bukhārī)

Seeking Blessings from the Place that the Prophet's Mouth ﷺ had Touched: Imām Aḥmad and others narrated from Anas ﷺ that the Prophet ﷺ once entered upon Umm Sulaym, and there was a water skin container hanging on the wall. He ﷺ took it and drank from its spout while he (Anas) was sleeping. Anas said: "Umm Sulaym cut off the spout of the water skin and it is now with us."

The meaning of this is: Umm Sulaym cut off the spout of the water skin in order to keep it and derive blessings from where the Prophet drank from ﷺ. This was narrated by al-Ṭabarānī and in its chain there is al-Barā' b. Zayd who was not weakened by Aḥmad, and the rest of the men in the chain are men found in the *Ṣaḥīḥ* collections.

SEEKING BLESSINGS THROUGH KISSING THE HANDS OF THOSE WHO TOUCHED THE MESSENGER OF ALLAH ﷺ

From Yaḥyā b. al-Ḥārith al-Dhimārī who said: "I met Wāthila b. al-Ashqa' ﷺ and said to him: 'Was it with this hand of yours you gave the pledge of fealty to the Messenger of Allah ﷺ?' He said: 'Yes.' I said: 'Give me your hand so that I may kiss it.' He then gave me his hand and I kissed it.' " Al-Haythamī said: "It contains 'Abd al-Mālik al-Qārī whom I don't know, and the remainder of the men in the chain are reliable." [124]

From Abū Nu'aym in the *Ḥilya* it states on the authority of Yūnus b. Maysara who said: "Upon our return, we entered upon Yazīd b. al-Aswad, and saw as Wāthila b. al-Ashqa' ﷺ came to see him. When Wāthila looked at him, he extended his hand and Yazīd took it and wiped it over his face and chest because Wāthila gave the pledge of fealty to the Messenger of Allah ﷺ. Wāthila said to him: 'O Yazīd! How is your opinion of your Lord?' Yazīd replied: 'It is good.' Wāthila said: 'In that case, receive the good news, because I heard the Messenger of Allah ﷺ say: "Allah has said: 'I am as My servant thinks of Me. If it is good then it is good, and if it is bad, then it is bad.' " This is narrated in al-Bukhārī's *al-Adab al-Mufrad* (p.144) from 'Abd al-Raḥmān b. Razīn who said:

[124] *Majma' al-Zawā'id*, 8:42.

"We once passed by al-Rabdha and it was said to us: 'Salama b. al-Akwa' ﷺ is here. We approached him and gave him our salutations. He then extended his hand to us and said: 'I gave the pledge of fealty to the Prophet ﷺ with these two hands of mine.' He extended a large palmed hand like the hand of a camel and we kissed it.' "

Ibn Sa'd narrated a similar report from 'Abd al-Raḥmān b. Zayd al-'Irāqī. Al-Bukhārī also narrated in *al-Adab al-Mufrad* (p.144) from Ibn Jad'ān who said: "Thābit asked Anas ﷺ: 'Did you touch the Prophet ﷺ with your hand?' Anas replied: 'Yes.' Thereafter, Thābit kissed his hand.' " Al-Bukhārī also narrated in *al-Adab al-Mufrad* (p.144) from Ṣuhayb who said: "I once saw 'Alī kiss the hand and feet of al-'Abbās." Another report from Thābit states: "When I used to go to see Anas, he would inform me of my real rank. I would enter upon him, take his two hands, kiss them and say: 'By my father, these are the two hands that touched the Messenger of Allah ﷺ.' I would also kiss his eyes and say: 'By my father, these are the eyes that saw the Messenger of Allah ﷺ.' " This was mentioned by Ḥāfiẓ Ibn Ḥajar in *al-Maṭālib al-'Āliya*.[125] Al-Haythamī said: "It was narrated by Abū Ya'lā and its men are all men found in the *Ṣaḥīḥ* collections, save for 'Abdullāh b. Abī Bakr al-Maqdamī who is reliable, and al-Būṣīrī was silent regarding him."[126]

SEEKING BLESSINGS THROUGH HIS CLOAK ﷺ

It is reported that Asmā' bint Abī Bakr once took out a cloak made of Persian cloth with a hem of brocade, and sleeves bordered with brocade and she said: "This was the cloak of the Messenger of Allah ﷺ. It was with 'Ā'isha until she died, and when she died, I got possession of it. The Messenger of Allah ﷺ used to wear this, and we now wash it for the sick and seek a cure from it."[127]

---

[125] *Al-Maṭālib al-'Āliya*, 2:11.

[126] *Majma' al-Zawā'id*, 9:325.

[127] *Ṣaḥīḥ Muslim*, 'The Book of Clothing and Adornment', 3:140.

Seeking Blessings from Things that His Hands ﷺ Touched

From Ṣafiyya bint Majra'a who reported that Abū Maḥdhūra used to have a long lock of hair at the front of his head that was so long, it would reach the ground if he sat down. Some people once said to him: "Will you not cut this?" He replied: "The Messenger of Allah ﷺ touched it, so I shall not cut it until the day I die." This was narrated by al-Ṭabarānī and its chain contains Ayyūb b. Thābit al-Makkī. Abū Ḥātim said: "His Ḥadīth are not to be carried."[128]

From Muḥammad b. 'Abd al-Mālik b. Abī Maḥdhūra it is reported from his father that his grandfather (Abū Maḥdhūra) said: "O Messenger of Allah! Teach me the Sunna of the call to prayer." He ﷺ, touched the front of Abū Maḥdhūra's head and said: "Say: 'Allah is the Greatest, Allah is the Greatest, Allah is the Greatest, Allah is the Greatest—while raising your voice." In another narration it states that Abū Maḥdhūra would neither braid nor comb the hair on the front of his head because the Prophet ﷺ touched it. This was narrated by al-Bayhaqī, al-Dāraquṭnī, Aḥmad, Ibn Ḥibbān, and al-Nasā'ī with the same meaning.

Seeking Blessings With The Water Vessel and Mosque in which He ﷺ Prayed

From Abū Burda who said: "I arrived in Medina and was met by 'Abdullāh b. Salām. He said to me: 'Come to my house so I may give you drink from the water vessel that the Messenger of Allah ﷺ drank from, thereafter, you may pray in the Mosque that the Prophet ﷺ used to pray in.' I went with him and he gave me drink and fed me dates and I went on to pray in his ﷺ Mosque."

This was narrated by al-Bukhārī in the book on holding fast to the Book and the Sunna.

---

[128] *Majma' al-Zawā'id*, 5:165.

Seeking Blessings from the Footsteps of the Prophet ﷺ

In a Ḥadīth narrated by Abū Miljaz it states that once, when Abū Mūsā was travelling between Mecca and Medina, he stood up and prayed the nightfall prayer as two units (as a traveller). He then performed the *witr* prayer and read one hundred verses from *Sūra al-Nisā'*. After completing his prayers he said: "I did not want to neglect placing my feet exactly where the Messenger of Allah ﷺ placed his feet and to read exactly what the Messenger of Allah ﷺ read."[129]

Seeking Blessings from a Blessed Residence

From Muḥammad b. Sūqa from his father who said: "When 'Amr b. Ḥurayth built his house, I approached him in order to rent it from him and he inquired from me: 'What shall you do with it?' I replied: 'I want to conduct business in it and buy and sell.'

"He said: 'Let me relate to you something about this house. This house is blessed for the one who dwells in it, and it is blessed for the one who buys and sells in it as well. This is because I once came to the Prophet ﷺ and he had some money with him. He took it out with his hand, gave it to me and said: "Take these *dirhams*, 'Amr, until you see something you in which you can invest them." These are the *dirhams* of the Messenger of Allah ﷺ.

" 'I took the money and we lived normally until Allah willed. Afterwards, we moved to Kufa, and when I wanted to buy a house, my mother said to me: "O son! When you buy a house and get the money together to pay for it, please inform me." I did as she said.

" 'Afterwards, I came to her and called her when the money was gathered together. She then took something out and added it to the *dirhams* and mixed it in with her hands. I said to her: "O Mother! What is this?" She said: "O Son! These are the *dirhams* that you once brought to me and said that the Messenger of Allah ﷺ gave them to you with his own hand, so I know that this house

---

[129] Al-Nasā'ī, 3:243.

is blessed for whoever sits inside of it and that it is blessed for whoever buys and sells." '[130]

SEEKING BLESSINGS FROM THE PULPIT OF THE MESSENGER OF ALLAH ﷺ

Qāḍī 'Iyāḍ said: "Ibn 'Umar was seen placing his hands on the seat of the Prophets pulpit and then rubbing his face with them."

From Qusayṭ and al-'Utbī it is reported that, when the Mosque would be empty of people, the companions of the Prophet ﷺ would rub the pommel of the pulpit that was facing the direction of the grave with their right hands and then turn towards the *qibla* and supplicate.[131]

Shaykh Ibn Taymiyya also narrated from Imām Aḥmad that he allowed for the pulpit and pommel to be wiped. He also mentioned that Ibn 'Umar, Sa'īd b. al-Musayyib and Yaḥyā b. Sa'īd among the jurists of Medina use to do that.[132]

SEEKING BLESSINGS FROM HIS NOBLE GRAVE ﷺ

When death approached the leader of the believers, 'Umar b. al-Khaṭṭāb ﷺ, he said to his son 'Abdullāh: "Go to the Mother of the believers, 'Ā'isha, and say to her that 'Umar gives you his greetings. Do not say: 'The leader of the believers,' for today I am not the leader of the believers. Say to her that 'Umar b. al-Khaṭṭāb seeks permission to be buried alongside his two companions." 'Abdullāh then went out, sought her permission to enter and gave her the greetings. When he entered upon her, he found her crying and said to her: "'Umar gives you his greetings and seeks permission to be buried alongside his two companions." She said: "I wanted that for myself, however today I shall most certainly prefer him over myself." When 'Abdullāh

---

[130] Related by al-Ṭabarānī in *al-Mu'jam al-Kabīr*, and Abū Ya'lā as cited in *Majma' al-Zawā'id*, 4:111.

[131] Mullā 'Alī al-Qārī who explained Qāḍī 'Iyāḍ's *al-Shifā* said: "It was narrated by Ibn Sa'd from 'Abd al-Raḥmān b. 'Abd al-Qārī, 3:518.

[132] *Iqtiḍā' al-Ṣirāṭ al-Mustaqīm*, p.367.

returned, it was said: "'Abdullāh the son of 'Umar is back." 'Umar said: "Help me up." A man helped him up and he said to 'Abdullāh: "What news do you have?" 'Abdullāh replied: "News that you shall love, O leader of the believers! You have been given permission."

'Umar said: "All praise belongs to Allah. There was nothing more important to me than that. When I die, carry me there and say: "Umar seeks permission to enter.' If permission is granted to me, then place me inside. If I am refused, then bury me in the graveyard of the Muslims."

This was narrated in its entirety by al-Bukhārī in the book of funerals under the chapter heading: ' Concerning the Grave of the Prophet ﷺ', as well as in the book on the virtues of the companions under the chapter heading: 'The Story of the Pledge of Fealty.'

SEEKING BLESSINGS FROM THE PERSONAL RELICS OF THE RIGHTEOUS, THE PROPHETS AND THOSE OF THE PAST

From Nāfi' who said: "'Abdullāh b. 'Umar informed us that once while on a journey, the people descended upon al-Ḥijr, the land of the Thamūd, with the Messenger of Allah ﷺ, and they began to draw water from its wells to drink and prepare bread. The Messenger of Allah ﷺ ordered them to throw out the water they drew from the wells and to feed the camels with the bread they baked and give drink to the camels from the wells they previously did not want to drink from."

This was narrated in Muslims collection in the 'Book of Asceticism' under the chapter heading:[133] 'The Prohibition of Entering in the Land of al-Ḥijr'. Imām al-Nawawī said in his explanation: "Of the benefits found in this Ḥadīth is the permissibility of seeking blessings from the personal relics of the righteous."[134]

---

[133] All of the chapter headings in Muslim's collection were done by Imām al-Nawawī in his explanation of *Ṣaḥīḥ Muslim*.—**tr**

[134] *Sharḥ Ṣaḥīḥ Muslim*, 8:118.

Seeking Blessings from the Ark of the Covenant

Allah the Exalted mentioned the virtue of the ark in the Qur'ān when He said: ﴾And their Prophet said unto them: Indeed, the sign of his kingdom is that there shall come unto you the ark wherein is peace of reassurance from your Lord, and a remnant of that which the house of Mūsā and the house of Hārūn left behind, the Angels bearing it. Indeed, herein shall be a sign for you if you are believers.﴿ (al-Baqara: 248)

The summary of the story is: This ark was with the children of Israel and they would seek victory by means of it and perform *tawassul* unto Allah through the relics that it contained. This is the exact meaning of *tabarruk* that we mean and intend here. Allah informed us of the contents of the ark when He said: ﴾...a remnant of that which the house of Mūsā and the house of Hārūn left behind.﴿ This remnants left behind from the house of Mūsā and Hārūn were: the staff of Mūsā and some of his and Hārūn's clothes, as well as his sandals, the tablets of the Torah, and a bowl—as was mentioned by the scholars of Qur'ānic exegesis and the historians, such as Ibn Kathīr, al-Qurṭubī, al-Suyūṭī, and al-Ṭabarī, so you may go back and refer to them. These verses indicate many meanings. From among them: the permissibility of performing *tawassul* through the personal relics of the righteous, and preserving and seeking blessings through them.

Seeking Blessings from the Masjid al-'Ashār

From Ṣāliḥ b. Dirham who said: "We went on the Ḥajj and came upon a man who said to us: 'To your other side there is a village called al-Abila.' We said: 'Yes.' He said: 'Who among you can guarantee for me that he will pray two or four units of prayer in the Masjid al-'Ashār? I heard from Abū Hurayra, who said: "I heard my intimate friend Abū al-Qāsim (the Prophet ﷺ) say: 'On the Day of Judgement, Allah, the Exalted and Sublime, shall resurrect martyrs from those at the Mosque al-'Ashār who will not stand among the martyrs of Badr.' " The man said: 'This is the Mosque near the side of the river.' " [135]

[135] Reported by Abū Dāwūd.

The ‘Allāma and great scholar of Ḥadīth, Shaykh Khalīl Aḥmad al-Sahāranpūrī said in his book *Badhl al-Majhūd Sharḥ Sunan Abī Dāwūd:* "In this Ḥadīth there is evidence proving that the reward for bodily acts of obedience can reach others, and that the relics of the saints and those brought near are to be visited and blessings are to be sought from them."[136] The ‘Allāma and scholar of Ḥadīth, Shaykh Abū Ṭayyib, the author of *‘Awn al-Ma‘būd* (another explanation of Abū Dāwūd's *Sunan*) said: "The Masjid al-‘Ashār is a well known Mosque that is prayed in for the intent purpose of seeking blessings."[137]

WE ARE WITH THE BLESSINGS OF THE MESSENGER ﷺ

We often overhear people saying: "We are with the blessings of the Messenger ﷺ" or other phrases which indicate that we are with his blessings ﷺ. Shaykh al-Islam Ibn Taymiyya was asked about this and he replied:

> As for the one who says that "We are with the blessings of so and so," or "From the time of his arrival blessings are present,' these words are correct from one perspective and incorrect from another perspective. As for what is correct, if it means that (this person) has guided us, taught us, commanded us with good and forbidden us from evil, thereby through the blessings of following and obeying him we have obtained the good we have—in this case these words are correct. When the Prophet ﷺ came to the people of Medina, they were with his blessings because they believed in him and obeyed him. It was through the blessings of such obedience and following they achieved felicity in both the life of this world and in the hereafter. Nay, every believer who has faith in the Messenger and obeys him shall obtain—from the blessings of the Messenger due to his faith and obedience to him—of the good of the worldly life and hereafter what is not known to any but Allah. Also, if one intends by this phrase, that with the blessings of his ﷺ supplication and

[136] *Badhl al-Majhūd*, 17:225.
[137] *‘Awn al-Ma‘būd*, 11:422.

righteousness, Allah shall repel evil and cause us to obtain provision and victory, then this is truth, for the Prophet ﷺ said: "And are you given victory and provision except by means of the weak ones among you—through their supplications, prayers and sincerity?"

It is possible that the torment is warded off from the disbelievers and corrupt ones in order that harm does not befall the believers among them who do not deserve punishment. This is indicated in the words of Allah the Exalted: ﴾Had there not been believing men and believing women whom you did not know, that you may kill them, and on whose account a sin would have been committed by you without your knowledge, that Allah might bring into His Mercy whom He wills, if they (the believers and the disbelievers) should have been apart, We verily had punished those of them who disbelieved, with painful torment.﴿ (al-Fatḥ: 25) So if it were not for the sake of the weak ones residing in Mecca in the midst of the disbelievers, the disbelievers would have been punished. Similar to this is the statement of the Prophet ﷺ: "If it were not for the women and children in the houses, I would have ordered the prayer to be established, and gone out with other men carrying lit torches and set ablaze the houses of those who do not attend the congregational prayer with us."

On a similar note, the pregnant adulteress is not punished with stoning until she delivers her child. The Messiah a said: ﴾"And make me blessed wherever I may be."﴿ (Maryam: 31) So, the blessings of the righteous saints of Allah, in the sense of them benefiting the creation with their invitation to Allah's obedience, supplications for them, and the mercy Allah sends down and evil that he wards off because of them, is something true and existent. Whoever intends this by the word 'blessing' and was truthful in that, then his statement is correct.

As for the incorrect meaning, it is like the one who intends to associate partners (with Allah) from among the creation; such as the case in which there is man who is buried in a place, and it is thought by the people that Allah takes care of their affairs only for his sake—even if they themselves were not obedient to Allah and His Messenger. This is ignorance, for the Messenger of Allah ﷺ, the Master of the children of Ādam, was buried in Medina in the year of the drought, and the people of Medina experienced killing, plundering, and fear to a degree that is known only to Allah. All of this was because after the rightly guided Caliphs, they engaged in acts that brought this upon themselves. Before that, Allah would ward off harm from them due to the faith and piety of the rightly guided Caliphs. The punishment was also warded off because the rightly guided Caliphs commanded them with faith and piety. It was by the blessings of their obedience to the rightly guided Caliphs and the blessings of the deeds of the Caliphs with them, that Allah gave them aid and victory. Similar to this is the case of the intimate friend (*khalīl*, Prophet Ibrāhīm ﷺ) who is buried in the Levant: even though the Christians conquered those lands over one hundred years ago. This was because its inhabitants were upon evil. So whoever thinks that the dead can ward off harm from the living—even though the living are in disobedience to Allah—then he is grossly mistaken.

Likewise, whoever thinks that an individual's blessings return to the one who is associating him (as a partner with Allah) and who is not living in obedience to Allah and His Messenger—such as the one who thinks that the blessings of prostrating to other than Him, kissing the ground they are upon or other such things will cause him to obtain felicity, even if he is not acting in obedience to Allah and His Messenger, or, if he believes that this individual shall intercede for him and cause him to enter Paradise by the mere fact that he loves him and ascribes himself to him—these things and their likes which contain opposition to the Book and the Sunna are from the states of the pagans and the people of innovation and are false. It is not permissible to either believe in them or rely upon them.[138]

---

[138] *Majmū' al-Fatāwā*, 11:113.

Imām Aḥmad Seeks Blessings and Imām al-Dhahabī Supports him

'Abdullāh, the son of Imām Aḥmad said: "I saw my father take a hair that belonged to the Prophet ﷺ, put it on his mouth, and kiss it. I recall seeing him put it on his eyes. He also dipped it in water and drank the water to obtain cure. I saw him take the Prophet's ﷺ bowl, wash it in water, and drink from it. I saw him drink *zam zam* water in order to seek cure with it, and he wiped his hands and face with it." 'I (Dhahabī) say: "Where is the extremist critic who will censure Imām Aḥmad now? It is also authentically established that 'Abdullāh asked his father about those who touch the pommel of the Prophet's pulpit and touch the wall of the Prophet's room ﷺ, and he said: 'I do not see any harm in it.' May Allah protect both us and you from the opinion of the Khawārij (sect) and from innovations!" '[139]

Conclusion

The upshot regarding all of these reports and Ḥadīth narrations is that seeking blessings through him ﷺ, his personal relics, and everything ascribed to him is a lofty *sunna* and a praiseworthy and legislated path.

The actions of the notables among the companions—may Allah be pleased with all of them—and the Prophets support, nay command of this in one instance and allusion to it in another instance, is sufficient as a proof to establish its validity. By the textual evidence that we have cited here, it becomes clear the lie of he who claims that none of the companions took great concern (with the Prophetic relics), save Ibn 'Umar, and that none of the companions of the Messenger ﷺ agreed with him in that.

This is pure ignorance, a lie and deception. Many others besides him used to do that and many besides him took great concern with it.

---

[139] *Siyar 'Alām al-Nubalā'*, 11:212.

Among them are the rightly guided Caliphs—may Allah be pleased with them all—Umm Salama, Khālid b. al-Walīd, Wāthila b. al-Ashqa', Salama b. al-Akwa', Anas b. Mālik, Umm Sulaym, Usayd b. Ḥuḍayr, Sawād b. Ghaziyya, Sawād b. 'Amr, 'Abdullāh b. Salām, Abū Mūsā, 'Abdullāh b. al-Zubayr, Safīna the freed slave of the Prophet ﷺ, Surra the servant of Umm Salama, Mālik b. Sinān, Asmā' b. Abī Bakr, Abū Maḥdhūra, Mālik b. Anas and his teachers among the people of Medina such as Sa'īd b. Musayyib, and Yaḥyā b. Sa'īd.

PART III
MISCELLANEOUS AREAS OF RESEARCH

THE LEGALITY OF VISITING THE PROPHET ﷺ AND OTHER RELATED MATTERS SUCH AS SEEKING BLESSINGS THROUGH RELICS, VISITING SANCTUARIES, AND OBSERVING SPECIAL OCCASIONS

بسم الله الرحمن الرحيم

THE ISTHMUS LIFE IS A REAL LIFE

THE Isthmus (*barzakh*) life is a real life. This is proven by the clear Qur'ānic verses and well known and rigorously authenticated Ḥadīth. This real and actual life does not contradict the qualitative description of death that is applied to those who have died, as the Most Exalted said: ﴾And We have not given immortality to anyone before you.﴿ (al-Anbiyā': 34) (And He said:) ﴾Indeed you shall die just as they too shall die.﴿ (al-Zumar: 30)

When we say that the Isthmus life is a real life, we mean that it is not an imaginary or allegorical life (*wahmiyya* or *khayāliyya*), as is believed by some of the atheists whose rational faculties are not expansive enough to have faith in anything besides that which is seen with the eyes and observed with sensory perception—they are those who are unable to have faith in the matters of the unseen that the human intellect is incapable of fathoming and they are unable to admit that the modality of those things falls under the power of Allah ﷻ.

It takes only a short moment of reflection to realize that there is not the slightest obscurity at all when we say that the Isthmus life is real. This is apparent even to those whose understandings and tastes are lacking when it comes to perceiving nuanced meanings. The word 'real' is only to negate falsehood, expel conjecture, and negate the false imagining that might occur in the mind of one in doubt concerning the Isthmus world, the hereafter, and other worlds such as: the gathering, the quickening, spreading out, and the account. This explanation of 'real' is grasped by even the most simple minded of Arabs. They know that the word 'real' means that which stands exactly opposite of conjecture, imagination, and allegory. So when something is said to be real, it means that it is not conjectural, and this is precisely what is meant here. This is our conception and understanding of the issue.

By Allah, there are a large collection of Ḥadīth narrations and reports affirming that the dead can both hear and have sensory perception—be they believers or disbelievers. Among these Ḥadīth is the Ḥadīth of Qulayb found in the two *Ṣaḥīḥ* collections from many angles and reported by Abū Ṭalha, 'Umar, and his son 'Abdullāh. It states: "The Prophet ﷺ ordered that the bodies of twenty four of the Qurayshī notables slain on the day of Badr be thrown into a well whose interior was encased with stones. He then approached the well and began addressing them saying: 'O Abū Jahl b. Hishām! O Umayya b. Khalf! O 'Utba b. Rabī'a! O Shayba b. Rabī'a! O so and so! Have you not found what your Lord promised you to be true? We have certainly found what our Lord promised us to be true!' Upon hearing this, 'Umar said: 'O Messenger of Allah! Why speak to lifeless bodies that have no souls?' He ﷺ replied: 'By Him in whose hand is my soul, you do not hear my words better than they do, however they are unable to respond.' "

It was narrated in this manner from the two Shaykhs (al-Bukhārī and Muslim) from the Ḥadīth of Ibn 'Umar. Al-Bukhārī's narration is reported by Anas on the authority of Abū Ṭalha and Muslim's narration is from Anas on the authority of 'Umar. It was also narrated by al-Ṭabarānī from the Ḥadīth of Ibn Mas'ūd with a sound chain and from the Ḥadīth of 'Abdullāh b. Saydān with the following addition: "They said: 'O Messenger of Allah! Do they really hear?' He ﷺ replied: 'They hear just as you hear, however they do not respond.' " There is also the narration found in the collection of al-Bazzār and declared rigorously authentic by Ibn Ḥibbān, from the route of Ismā'īl b. 'Abd al-Raḥmān al-Suddī, from his father, from Abū Hurayra, from the Prophet ﷺ who said: "Indeed, the deceased hear the people's footsteps when they turn away to leave." Ibn Ḥibbān reported from the route of Muḥammad b. 'Amr, from Abū Salama, from Abū Hurayra, from the Prophet ﷺ a similar wording in a longer Ḥadīth.

In his *Ṣaḥīḥ* collection, al-Bukhārī titled his chapter: 'The Dead Hear the Squeaking of the Shoes.' He then narrated from Anas, from the Prophet ﷺ, who said: "After a servant is placed in the grave and his companions turn to leave, and he hears the squeaking of their shoes, the two Angels come to him and sit him upright." He (al-Bukhārī) then mentioned the Ḥadīth regarding the questioning in the grave, and this was also narrated by Muslim. The deceased's hearing the squeaking of shoes is cited in numerous Ḥadīth. Among these Ḥadīth are those who mention the questioning in the grave—and these are many and well known. These Ḥadīth reports explicitly mention the two Angels questioning the person in the grave and the answers provided by that person that are congruent to their state of either felicity or misery. Among these Ḥadīth reports are the ones in which the Prophet ﷺ legislated for his nation to send salutations to the people of the graves and address them with the phrase: "Peace be upon you in the abode of the believing people."

Ibn al-Qayyim said:

> This address is to one who is able to hear and understand. If that were not the case, this address would be synonymous with addressing that which is nonexistent or inanimate—and the Salaf are unanimous upon this. The reports from them attesting to the deceased's knowledge of the living visiting them and giving them glad tidings has reached the level of mass transmission..."

Ibn al-Qayyim went on to mention a collection of these reports in his book *al-Rūḥ*, so refer back to that.

I say: concerning this, 'Abd al-Razzāq narrated a Ḥadīth from Zayd b. Aslam who said: "Abū Hurayra and one of his companions both passed by a grave. Abū Hurayra said to his companion: 'Send your salutations.' His companion replied: 'Should I send my salutations to a grave?' Abū Hurayra replied: 'If that person saw you in the life of this world even if only for one day, then most certainly he will know you now.' "[140]

What we have stated above is the belief of the pious predecessors—may Allah be pleased with all of them. They are Ahl al-Sunna wa al-Jamā'a, hence, I do not know how the claimants to the way of the Salaf can be unaware of this reality.

Shaykh Ibn al-Qayyim reported extensively on this in his book *al-Rūḥ*, and it has proven to be sufficient and healing. Here, we wish to cite an esteemed legal verdict on this topic by Shaykh al-Islam, Imām Ibn Taymiyya, as found in *al-Fatāwā al-Kubrā*: The Shaykh was asked if the dead recognize and know the living when they visit them, and are the living informed of the state of the deceased if he was one of their relatives or anyone else?

Reply:

> All praise belongs to Allah. Yes! There are reports which speak of mutual meeting and inquiring and the actions of the living being presented to the dead—as has been narrated by Ibn al-Mubārak from Abū Ayyūb al-Anṣārī who said: "When the soul of a believer is taken, it receives the mercy of Allah's servants just as they would receive the bringer of good news in the life of the world. They come to him warmly and they ask each other questions. They say to each other: 'Here is your brother now relaxing. Certainly, he was going through severe difficulties.' They go to him and ask him: 'What did such and such man do? What did such and such woman do? Did she get married?' "
>
> As for the deceased person knowing the living person when the later visits him and send salutations, there appears in the Ḥadīth of Ibn 'Abbās who said that the Messenger of Allah ﷺ said: "There is no one who passes by

[140] *Muṣannaf* of 'Abd al-Razzāq, 3:577.

> the grave and sends salutations to his believing brother whom he knew in the life of this world, except that the deceased knows him and returns salutations to him." Ibn al-Mubārak said: "That is established from the Prophet ﷺ and it was declared rigorously authentic by 'Abd al-Ḥaqq, the author of *al-Ahkām*.[141]

In another area of his collection, he (Ibn Taymiyya) was asked: "Does the deceased person hear the words of the one visiting him, and does he see that person? Is the deceased's soul returned to his body at that time or does is levitate around his grave at that time or any other time? Does his soul meet with the souls of his family and relatives who passed away before him?

Reply:

> All praise belongs to Allah. Yes! In general, the deceased person hears, as is established in the two *Ṣaḥīḥ* collections from the Prophet ﷺ who said: "He hears the squeaking of their shoes when they depart from him..."
>
> ...(So), these texts and those like them show that, in general, the deceased hear the words of the living. It is not necessary that this hearing is at all times. Rather, the dead could hear at various times, and not hear at other times, just as this occurs with the living.
>
> The living might hear the one addressing him sometimes, and not hear him at other times due to some factor. This hearing is one of comprehension, and there is no reward attached to it, nor is it the hearing which is negated in His words: ﴾Certainly, you cannot cause the dead to hear.﴿ (al-Naml: 80)
>
> What is meant by that is the hearing of acceptance and compliance. This is because Allah made the disbeliever like a dead person who is unable to respond to the one who calls upon him, (and He has made him) like the animals that hear voices but do not understand the meanings. Even if the dead hear and understand the meaning of what they hear, they are still unable to respond to the caller, or comply with his command or

[141] *Al-Fatāwā al-Kubrā*, 24:331.

> prohibition. Hence, he is not benefited by that person's command or prohibition—just as the disbeliever does not benefit from the command or prohibition—even if they hear the address and understand its meaning, as Allah the Exalted said: ﴾And if Allah knew any good in them He would have caused them to hear.﴿ (al-Anfāl: 23) As for the dead seeing, there are reports concerning this from 'Ā'isha and others. As for the one who asks if the soul of the deceased is returned to his body during that time or if it levitates around the grave at that time or other than that time, the answer is: his soul is returned to his body during that time, as is mentioned in the Ḥadīth. It also returns to the body in other times as well.
>
> Along with this, the soul is attached to the body whenever Allah wills and such an attachment takes place in an instant—similar to the descent of Angels or the travelling of the sun's rays or waking up from sleep. There are numerous reports which state that the souls are in the outer courtyards of the graves. Mujāhid said: "The souls are in the outer courtyards of the graves for seven days after the day of burial not departing from that location." This occurs on occasion.
>
> Mālik b. Anas said: "It has reached me that the souls are free to roam around wherever they wish." And Allah knows best.[142]

In another place, Shaykh Ibn Taymiyya said:

> As with regards to the life and provision of the martyrs that Allah informed us about, and the rigorously authentic Ḥadīth that mentions their souls entering Paradise, some groups were of the opinion that this is particular to them only and not the truthful ones (*ṣiddiqūn*) and others. The correct view held by the Imāms and majority of Ahl al-Sunna is that this life, provision, and entering Paradise is not restricted to the martyr—as is proven by established textual evidence. The martyr was given special mention because it might be imagined by some that he (the martyr) has died—thereby causing them

[142] Ibid. 24:362.

> to withhold from engaging in *jihād*. They were informed of this (life of the martyr) in order to remove an obstacle that would keep them from going forward in *jihād* and in pursuit of martyrdom—just as it is forbidden for someone to kill their children out of fear of poverty, as is the reality, even if it is still forbidden to kill them without fear of poverty.[143]

Do not Annoy the Dead lest they Annoy You: The Messenger of Allah ﷺ once saw a man reclining on the side of a grave, so he said to him: "Do not annoy the inhabitant of the grave." This Ḥadīth was mentioned by Majd b. Taymiyya in *al-Muntaqā* [144] and he relayed it back to Aḥmad's *Musnad*. It was likewise mentioned by Ḥāfiẓ Ibn Ḥajar in *al-Fatḥ*[145] who said: "Its chain is rigorously authentic."

Al-Ṭaḥāwī also narrated it in his *Ma'ānī al-Āthār*[146] from the Ḥadīth of Ibn 'Amr b. Ḥazm with the wording: "The Messenger of Allah ﷺ saw me reclining on the side of a grave and he said to me: 'Get away from the grave lest you annoy the inhabitant of the grave and he annoys you' "[147]

The Meaning of the Isthmus Life: It is crucial for us to explain here that the life of the *barzakh* is an Isthmus life and is different from this life of ours. It is a special life that is appropriate for its inhabitants and the world in which they reside. At the same time, it is a must that we explain to the people that the Isthmus life is not like our life because our life is less, more degraded, weaker, and narrower. The person living in the life of this world revolves around worship, customary day to day practices, obedience and disobedience, and various other obligations and responsibilities for himself, family and Lord. Sometimes, this person is in a state of ritual purity, and at other times he is not. Sometimes, he is in the Mosque, and at other times he is in the bathroom—and he does not know in which of the two he shall meet his final end.

---

[143] Ibid. 24:332.

[144] *Muntaqā al-Akhbār*, 2:104.

[145] *Fatḥ al-Bārī*, 3:178.

[146] *Ma'ānī al-Āthār*, 1:296.

[147] *Majma' al-Zawā'id*, 3:61.

The person in this life might be a bows length from attaining Paradise, until his affair goes completely off track and he ends up being of the people destined for the hell fire. The opposite may also occur. As for the Isthmus life however, if its inhabitant is a believer, then he has gone beyond the measuring scale of tribulations in which none remain firm save the people of felicity, not to mention that he is no longer legally responsible. He has become a pure, contemplating and enlightened spirit that travels, floats, and visits the kingdoms and dominion of Allah ﷻ. That spirit has no pressing concerns, sadness, stress, or difficulties because it possess no worldly life; no house, no gold, and no silver—so there is no envy, hatred, or transgression. It goes without saying that if the person is not a believer, then it is the opposite of all of that.

THE UNIQUE QUALITIES OF THE PROPHETS IN THE ISTHMUS LIFE

The Prophets—may the prayers and peace of Allah be upon them all—have unique qualities in the Isthmus life that they are unrivalled in among mankind. Even if some of people share with them in some of those qualities, it is only by way of relative ascription. The uniqueness conferred to the Prophets in the Isthmus life is from two ways:

1. From the purity of origin
2. From the perfection conferred therein

Below are some of their unique qualities:

The Perfection of Their Lives: We previously mentioned that the Isthmus life is a real and actual life, and that the dead—be they believers or disbelievers—hear, sense, and know. We also mentioned that matters such as: life, provision, and the souls entering Paradise are not restricted to the martyr alone, as is proven by affirmed textual evidence. This is the correct view held by the Imāms and the majority of Ahl al-Sunna. After all of this, for it to be said that the Prophets are alive is almost extraneous speech that is as clear as the sun. There is no need for any separate (proof) to establish it. What is correct is for us to affirm that their life is more complete, more noble, more perfect, and more esteemed (than this life).

Similar can be said with respect to the people living in this world. The lives people live are at varying degrees, levels, and stations. Among them are the living dead: those who are dead but in the form of a living person. The Master (Allah) said concerning them: ❮They have hearts with which they do not understand, eyes with which they do not see, and ears with which they do not hear. They are like cattle, nay, they are even more astray. They are the heedless ones.❯ (al-A'rāf: 179)

Among the dead are those who He mentioned: ❮Certainly, the friends of Allah, no fear shall be upon them nor shall they grieve.❯ (Yūnus: 62) And among them are those who He mentioned: ❮The believers are certainly successful.❯ (al-Mu'minūn: 1) Up till when He said: ❮...They are the inheritors.❯ (al-Mu'minūn: 10) Among them are those who He mentioned: ❮Indeed, before that they were good doers. Very little did they sleep in the night, and in the early pre-dawn hours they would seek forgiveness.❯ (al-Dhāriyāt: 15-18)

So in a similar sense, the Isthmus life is of varying degrees, levels, and stations. ❮Whoever was blind in this world, then in the next world he will be blind and even more astray.❯ (al-Isrā': 72)

As for the Prophets—may peace of Allah be upon them—their life, provision, knowledge, hearing, comprehension, sensing, and feeling is even more complete, perfect, and loftier than that of others. The proof for this is in the words of Allah concerning the martyrs: ❮Do not consider those killed in the way of Allah as dead. Nay, they are alive with their Lord being provided for.❯ (Āl 'Imrān: 169)

If life only means that the soul remains without ceasing to exist or perish, then there is no unique characteristic that the martyr possesses that deserves any special mention. Certainly, the souls of all of the children of Ādam shall remain (after death) and none of them will cease to exist. This is the correct view held by the verifying scholars (*muḥaqqiqūn*) among the people of knowledge—as mentioned by Shaykh Ibn al-Qayyim in his book *al-Rūḥ*. So, it is essential that there be some clear distinguishing quality by which the martyrs are shown to be unique from everyone else. If this were not the case, then mentioning that they are alive would be extraneous speech without any added benefit—especially when we see that Allah forbade others from saying that they are dead.

He said: ﴾Do not say about those who are killed in the way of Allah that they are dead. Nay, they are alive, however you perceive it not.﴿ (al-Baqara: 154)

So we say that it is a must that their life be more complete and noble than that of others. This is the view which is aided by the apparent meaning of the texts. Their souls receive provision and visit the rivers of Paradise and eat of its fruits as the Most Exalted said: ﴾...With their Lord being provided for.﴿ (Āl 'Imrān: 169)

Their sensing of that food, drink, and delight is a complete sensing with full feeling and complete pleasure and real enjoyment, as mentioned in the Ḥadīth: "...when they find the delightful food, drink, and resting place, they will say: 'Would that our brothers know how Allah has treated us!' "[148]

Their souls have a greater amount of discretion and movement because they roam freely in Paradise wherever they will and take refuge inside of the lamps suspended under the Throne.

They hear speech and understand when addressed. In the *Ṣaḥīḥ* collection there is a report which states: "Allah, the Exalted, shall say to them (the martyrs): 'What do you desire?' They shall respond: 'We desire such and such.' They are then asked again and they answer back. They shall then seek to be returned to the life of this world in order to wage *jihād*. Afterwards, they shall ask Allah to convey a message from them to their brothers in the life of this world explaining what Allah has honoured them with. Allah shall say: 'I will convey it on your behalf.' "

So, if this is established for the martyrs, it is also established for the Prophets for two reasons:

One: This noble rank was given to the martyr as a divinely bestowed gift, and there is no rank higher than that of a Prophet. There is no doubt that the states of the Prophets are loftier and more complete than the states of all of the martyrs. It is

---

[148] Ibn Kathīr said: "Narrated by Aḥmad."

impossible therefore for the martyrs to obtain a perfection that is not obtained by the Prophets—especially this completion that brings about more closeness, intimacy, and bounty through the Exalted and Most High.

Two: The martyrs obtained this rank as a reward for their *jihād* and for sacrificing their souls for Allah, the Exalted, yet it was the Prophet ﷺ who made this (*jihād*) a *sunna* for us and invited and guided us to it with the permission and ability granted by Allah, the Exalted. He ﷺ said: "Whoever inaugurates a good Sunna then he shall have its reward and the reward of those who act upon it until the Day of Judgement." He ﷺ also said: "Whoever invites to guidance will have the reward of those who follow him without that decreasing their reward in the least. And whoever invites to misguidance shall incur sin like the sins of those who followed him, without that decreasing their sins in the least."

The rigorously authentic Ḥadīth reports concerning this are numerous and well known, therefore, whatever reward the martyr obtains, the Prophet ﷺ will obtain as well due to his striving—and life is itself a reward, so the Prophet ﷺ shall possess it.

The real Isthmus life of the Prophets—especially our Prophet—is so much more lofty and complete that what is imagined by the ignoramus or dolt who thinks that by life, we mean they are living as we do: eating and drinking, in need of food and drink, urinating and defecating, coming out of their graves to attend the gatherings of remembrance, attending Qur'ānic reading circles, taking part in the happy and sad occasions of the Umma, attending their *'īd* celebrations and other occasions, afterwards going back to their graves underground—that narrow hole covered by dirt! This is not an honour or virtue in the least! On the contrary, this is the worst affront that no one would be pleased for their own follower or maid (as a so called reward), not to mention Allah giving this to the best of His creation and His most noble slave!

This real Isthmus life is complete sensation, perfect comprehension, and true knowledge. It is a pure life containing supplication, extolling Allah, declaring His oneness, praising Him, and prayer.

The Prophets' Prayers and other Acts of Worship Performed in their Graves

Among the fruits of this Isthmus life are the prayers they offer within their graves. These prayers are real. They are not allegorical or imaginary. There are many Ḥadīth reports concerning this topic. From among them:

From Anas b. Mālik ﷺ: "The Messenger of Allah ﷺ said: 'The Prophets are alive and praying in their graves.' " This was narrated by Abū Ya'lā, al-Bazzār. The men of Abū Ya'lā are reliable.[149] The Imām and Ḥāfiẓ al-Bayhaqī mentioned in his slim volume on this subject:"In the narration from Anas ﷺ from the Prophet ﷺ who stated: 'The Prophets do not remain in their graves after forty nights, rather, they pray in front of Allah until the trumpet is blown.' "

Al-Bayhaqī commented: "If it is authentic with this wording, then it means—and Allah knows best—that they are not left in their graves without praying save for this amount of time. Afterwards, they pray in front of Allah, the Exalted...there are corroborating reports from authentic Ḥadīth narrations showing the Prophets to be alive after their death."

Al-Bayhaqī then went on to mention the following Ḥadīth with his chain of narration: "I passed by Mūsā while he was standing inside of his grave praying." And: "I saw myself among a group of the Prophets, and lo and behold, there was Mūsā standing and praying, and then there was a thin man with a reddish complexion resembling the men of Shanu'a—it was 'Īsā b. Maryam. He was also praying. The man who resembles him the most (among you) is 'Urwa b. Mas'ūd al-Thaqafī. Afterwards, there was Ibrāhīm who was standing and praying. The man who most resembles him is your companion."—meaning himself ﷺ. When the time for the congregational prayer arrived, I led them in prayer. When I finished the prayer, someone said to me: 'O Muḥammad! This is Mālik, the keeper of the fire. Send him your greetings.' I then turned to the side and he initiated the greetings.' "

---

[149] *Majma' al-Zawā'id*, 8:211.

I say: This was narrated by Muslim on the authority of Anas ﵁ (2/268), as well as 'Abd al-Razzāq in his *Muṣannaf* (3/577).

Al-Bayhaqī said in *Dalā'il al-Nubuwwa*: "And in the authentic Ḥadīth from Sulaymān al-Taymī and Thābit al-Banānī from Anas b. Mālik it states that the Messenger of Allah ﷺ said: 'I went to Mūsā on the night of the ascension and he was on a red hill, praying in his grave.' " I say: It is rigorously authentic and narrated in Muslim (2/268).

It has been established in such a manner that there is no further room for doubt, that the reason our prayers have been lightened from fifty to five is because of Mūsā a. He conveyed the message of his Lord and went to His company in the higher gathering. He was the means for much good reaching the Muḥammadan Umma when he requested our Prophet ﷺ to go back to his Lord. He (Mūsā) said: "Go back to your Lord and ask Him to lighten the burden, for your nation is unable to follow that." So, was it imaginary or allegorical when Mūsā asked him ﷺ to go back to his Lord? Was it during sleep in a dream state or was it during wakefulness? Is this story true or is it a lie? Did Mūsā die or did he remain alive until that time?

Al-Ḥākim narrated and authenticated a report from Ibn 'Abbās ﵁ that states: "Once, the Prophet ﷺ passed by a narrow mountain pass and asked: 'What is this?' someone said: 'It is such and such mountain pass.' He ﷺ said: 'It is as if I am looking at Yūnus upon a camel that has a fibre noseband. Yūnus is wearing a woollen cloak and saying: "To Your call O Allah I respond!" '[150] In another Ḥadīth it states: "I saw myself near the Ka'ba last night, and I saw a man with a whitish red complexion, the best you may see amongst men of that complexion, having long hair reaching his earlobes which was the best hair of its sort, and he had combed his hair and water was dripping from it. He was performing the *ṭawāf* around the Ka'ba while he was leaning on two men or on the shoulders of two men. I asked, 'Who is this man?' Somebody replied, '(He is) the Messiah, the son of Mary.' "

In another Ḥadīth it states: "Once, the Messenger of Allah ﷺ passed by *Wādī al-Azraq*. He said: 'It is as if I am looking at Mūsā coming down from the mountain pass calling Allah with the

[150] *Al-Durr al-Manthūr*, 4:334.

talbiyya (audible prayer recited in the Ḥajj).' Afterwards, the Prophet ﷺ came to another mountain pass and said: 'It is as if I am looking at Yūnus b. Mattā reciting the *talbiyya* (of the Ḥajj) upon a red camel, while wearing a woollen cloak and the nose ring of his camel is made of talon.' " In another Ḥadīth it states: "It is as if I am looking at Mūsā while he places his fingers in his ears."

As we have stated earlier, all of these Ḥadīth are rigorously authentic and they speak of Mūsā and 'Īsā and their standing in prayer and being led in prayer by the Prophet ﷺ. It is not to be said that this was all in a dream vision and that his ﷺ statement, "I was shown" indicates that it was during sleep. What occurred in the miraculous night journey was during a state of wakefulness according to the correct view held by the majority of the Salaf and those after them. Even if it was said to be a dream, still, the dreams of the Prophets are true. When he ﷺ said: "I was shown," it does not indicate it was during sleep, because he also said: "I saw myself in my apartment"—and that was during wakefulness as is proven in the remainder of the report.

Their Bodies Remain: In the Ḥadīth of Aws b. Aws he said that the Messenger of Allah ﷺ said: "The most virtuous of your days is Friday. It was the day in which Ādam was created, the day in which his soul was taken, the day the trumpet shall be blown, and the day of the deafening thunderclap. So, because of this, you must frequently send prayers upon me, for your prayers are presented to me." The companions said: "How can our prayers be presented to you when your body shall deteriorate?" He ﷺ replied: "Indeed, Allah has forbidden the earth from consuming the bodies of the Prophets."

This Ḥadīth was narrated by Sa'īd b. Manṣūr, Ibn Abī Shayba, Aḥmad in his *Musnad*, Ibn Abī 'Āṣim in his book of prayer, Abū Dāwūd, al-Nasā'ī, and Ibn Mājah in their *Sunan* collections, al-Ṭabarānī in his *Mu'jam*, Ibn Khuzayma, Ibn Ḥibbān, and al-Ḥākim in their authentic collections, al-Bayhaqī in his book *Ḥayāt al-Anbiyā'* and *Shu'ab al-Īmān*, and in other collections.

You should know that this Ḥadīth: "Indeed, Allah has forbidden the earth from consuming the bodies of the Prophets," has been transmitted from numerous routes. All of these routes were gathered by Ḥāfiẓ al-Mundhirī in a special volume. He also said in *al-Targhīb wa al-Tarhīb* that it was narrated by Ibn Mājah with a good chain, narrated by Aḥmad, Abū Dāwūd, Ibn Ḥibbān in his *Ṣaḥīḥ* collection, and al-Ḥākim who authenticated it.

Ibn al-Qayyim said in his book *al-Rūḥ*, quoting from Abū 'Abdullāh al-Qurṭubī:

> It has been authentically reported from the Prophet ﷺ that the earth does not consume the bodies of the Prophets. It has also been reported that the Prophet ﷺ gathered with the other Prophets on the night of miraculous ascension in Jerusalem and in the heavens—and in particular, met with Mūsā a. He was informed that "No Muslim sends greetings to him except that Allah returns his soul to his body in order that he may return the greeting," as well as other reports that, when taken all together, prove decisively that the death of the Prophets is only insofar as they are absent from us and we do not sense them—even though they are present and alive. This is similar to the state of the Angels, for they are alive and present even though we do not see them.

The words of al-Qurṭubī were also quoted and supported by Shaykh Muḥammad al-Safārīnī al-Ḥanbalī in his *Sharḥ 'Aqīda Ahl al-Sunna*. He said:

> Abū 'Abdullāh al-Qurṭubī said: "Our Shaykh, Aḥmad b. 'Umar al-Qurṭubī—the author of *al-Mufhim fī Sharḥ Muslim*—said: 'What shall remove this obscurity is to explain the matter as such: death is not complete non-existence, rather, it is moving from one state of being to another. The proof for this is that the martyrs are alive with their Lord in a state of delight and being provided for after they have died and were killed. This is the attribute of one who is alive in this world and, if this is the state of the martyrs, then the Prophets are deserving of it *a fortiori*.' "

Al-Qurṭubī mentioned that the souls of the martyrs do not deteriorate. There is a rigorously authentic report from Jābir in which he states that both his father and 'Amr b. al-Jamūḥ ﷺ were killed as martyrs at the battle of Uḥud and were buried in the same grave. After a flash flood, their grave was washed up and their bodies were found unchanged. One of them was injured and had placed his hand on the site of the injury, and was buried in that state. The people moved his hand from where he placed it before being killed, yet it returned to where it was. Forty two years had passed between this event and the battle of Uḥud. When Mu'āwiya had uncovered a large spring in Medina, around fifty years after the battle of Uḥud, and some of the dead were exhumed and moved from their burial sites, Ḥamza's foot was uncovered and blood was flowing from it. 'Abdullāh b. Ḥarām was found as if he had died the day before. The general community of Medina narrated that when the wall to the Prophet's house collapsed during the time of al-Walīd, they saw the foot of 'Umar b. al-Khaṭṭāb uncovered.

Shaykh Ibn Taymiyya mentioned that when the wall collapsed, 'Umar's foot, shin, and knee were uncovered. When 'Umar b. 'Abd al-'Azīz saw this, he became frightened. 'Urwa then came to him and informed him that it was the foot, shin, and knee of 'Umar, so he became happy.[151] The Imām and proof, Abū Bakr b. al-Ḥusayn al-Bayhaqī authored a special essay on this topic wherein he gathered all of the reports that prove the life of the Prophets and the remaining of their bodies. Likewise, Ḥāfiẓ Jalāl al-Dīn al-Suyūṭī authored a special essay on the same topic.

THE SPECIAL LIFE OF OUR PROPHET ﷺ

It has been established that our Prophet ﷺ has a special Isthmus life which is more complete and greater than that of others. He himself spoke about it, affirming his attachment to this Muḥammadan Umma, his knowledge of its conditions, awareness of its actions, his hearing of their words, and his response to the greetings he receives. The Ḥadīth reports concerning this are abundant. Among them:

From 'Abdullāh b. Mas'ūd ﷺ, from the Prophet ﷺ: "To Allah belongs Angels that travel around the earth conveying to me the

[151] *Iqtiḍā' al-Ṣirāṭ al-Mustaqīm*, p.365.

greetings of my Umma." Al-Mundhirī said: "Narrated by Nasā'ī and Ibn Ḥibbān who authenticated it."[152] I say: It was also narrated by Ismā'īl al-Qāḍī and others from different routes with authentic chains with no doubt up to Sufyān al-Thawrī from 'Abdullāh b. al-Sā'ib, from Zādhān, from 'Abdullāh b. Mas'ūd. Sufyān al-Thawrī explicitly mentioned directly hearing, hence he said: "'Abdullāh b. al-Sā'ib narrated to me..." This is found in the collection of Ismā'īl al-Qāḍī. As for 'Abdullāh b. al-Sā'ib and Zādhān, Muslim narrated from them both and they were declared reliable by Ibn Ma'īn, therefore the chain is rigorously authentic.

From Ibn Mas'ūd ﷺ, from the Prophet ﷺ: "My life is good for you, you will relate about me and it will be related to you, and my death is a good for you, for your actions will be presented to me. If I see goodness I will praise Allah, and if see other than that I will ask forgiveness of him for you." Ḥāfiẓ al-'Irāqī said in the book of funerals in *al-Tathrīb fī Sharḥ al-Taqrīb*: "Its chain is good." Ḥāfiẓ al-Haythamī said in *Majma' al-Zawā'id* that it was narrated by al-Bazzār and its men are men found in the *Ṣaḥīḥ* collection.[153] It was also authenticated by Ḥāfiẓ al-Suyūṭī in *al-Mu'ajizāt* and *al-Khaṣā'iṣ*, as well as al-Qasṭalānī who explained *Ṣaḥīḥ al-Bukhārī*. Al-Munāwī stated in *Fayḍ al-Qadīr*[154] that it is rigorously authentic, as well as al-Zurqānī in his explanation of al-Qasṭalānī's *al-Mawāhib*, as well as Shihāb al-Khafājī in the explanation of *al-Shifā*.[155] Mullā 'Alī al-Qārī said in his explanation of *al-Shifā*: "It was also narrated by al-Ḥārith b. Usāma in his *Musnad* with a rigorously authentic chain."[156] Ibn Ḥajar mentioned it in *al-Maṭālib al-'Āliya* as well. This Ḥadīth has also appeared in *mursal* form from Bakr b. 'Abdullāh al-Muzanī and was narrated by Qāḍī Ismā'īl in his book on prayer upon the Prophet ﷺ. Shaykh al-Albānī said concerning this Ḥadīth: "It is *mursal ṣaḥīḥ*."

[152] *Al-Targhīb wa al-Tarhīb*, 2:498.

[153] *Majma' al-Zawā'id*, 9:24.

[154] *Fayḍ al-Qadīr*, 3:401.

[155] *Sharḥ al-Shifā*, 1:102.

[156] *Sharḥ al-Shifā*, 'Alī al-Qārī (1:102).

Despite the extremism and severity of Ḥāfiẓ Ibn 'Abd al-Hādī in his work *al-Ṣarim al-Munkī*, even he declared this narration rigorously authentic. Hence, this Ḥadīth is sound and without flaw. It proves that the Prophet ﷺ knows our actions and that they are presented to him. He seeks forgiveness for us for any sins or ugliness that we commit. If this is the case, then it is obviously permissible for us to take him as a means unto Allah and seek intercession through him and by him. This is because he knows that, therefore he can intercede for us and supplicate for us for he ﷺ is the one who intercedes and the one whose intercession is accepted. Allah informed us in the Qur'ān that the Prophet ﷺ is a witness for his Umma and this implies that the Umma's actions are presented to him in order for him to act as a witness to what he has seen and known.

Ibn al-Mubārak said: "A man from the Anṣār relayed to us from al-Minhāl b. 'Amr who stated that he heard Sa'īd b. al-Musayyib say: 'There is not a day that passes except that the Umma is presented to the Prophet ﷺ in the morning and the evening. He knows their names and deeds, and for this reason he is a witness for them. Allah the Exalted said: ﴾How will it be when We bring every nation with a witness and bring you as a witness against these?﴿ (al-Nisā': 41)' " From 'Ammār b. Yāsir, who said that the Messenger of Allah ﷺ said: "Allah has placed an Angel at my grave to whom He has given the names of the creation. No one sends prayers upon me from now until the Day of Judgement except that he conveys it to me saying; 'So and so, the son of so and so sent prayers upon you.' "

This was narrated by al-Bazzār, Abū al-Shaykh, and Ibn Ḥibbān with the following wording: "Allah, the Blessed and Exalted, has entrusted and Angel to whom He has given the names of the creation. When I die, this Angel will be standing at my grave. There will be no one who sends any prayer upon me except that the Angel will say: 'O Muḥammad! So and so, the son of so and so sends prayers upon you.' For every prayer that man sends, Allah the Blessed and Exalted will send ten to him."[157]

---

[157] Narrated by al-Ṭabarānī in *al-Kabīr* with a similar wording. See *al-Targhīb*, 2:500.

From 'Amr b. al-Ḥārith, from Sa'īd b. Abī Hilāl, from Zayd b. Ayman, from 'Ubāda b. Nasī, from Abū al-Dardā' who said: "The Messenger of Allah ﷺ said: 'Send prayers upon me abundantly on Fridays, for indeed it is witnessed by the Angels. There is no one who sends prayers on me except that his prayers are presented to me until he is finished.' I said: 'And after death as well?' He ﷺ said: 'And after death as well. Allah has forbidden the earth from consuming the bodies of the Prophets.—so the Prophet of Allah is alive being provided for.' "

This was narrated by Ibn Mājah in his *Sunan*. In *al-Zawā'id* this Ḥadīth is declared rigorously authentic, however, there is a split in two places in the chain. 'Ubāda's narrations from Abū al-Dardā' are *mursal*—as stated by al-'Alā'—and Zayd b. Ayman from 'Ubāda is also *mursal* as stated by al-Bukhārī.[158] From Abū Hurayra ؓ: "The Messenger of Allah ﷺ said: 'There is no one who sends greetings to me except that Allah returns to me my soul in order for me to return the greeting.' "[159]

Shaykh Ibn Taymiyya said:

> This Ḥadīth is sound according to the conditions of Muslim...and in the *Musnad* of Ibn Abī Shayba from Abū Hurayra there is a report in which he said: "The Messenger of Allah ﷺ said: 'Whoever prays upon me I shall hear him, and whoever prays upon me from far away it will be conveyed.' "[160] In the collection of al-Nasā'ī and others there is a report that he ﷺ said: "Allah has placed Angels at my grave that convey to me the greetings of my Umma." And there are numerous other Ḥadīth on this topic.[161]

---

[158] *Sunan Ibn Mājah*, p.524.

[159] *Sunan Abī Dāwūd*. See *al-Targhīb*, 2:499.

[160] Narrated by al-Dāraquṭnī.

[161] *Iqtiḍā' al-Ṣirāṭ al-Mustaqīm*, p.324.

The Prophet ﷺ Responds to the One Who Calls Him, Saying: 'O Muḥammad'

In the Ḥadīth of Abū Hurayra ؓ in the collection of Abū Ya'lā, the Prophet ﷺ mentioned 'Īsā a: "And if he was to stand at my grave and call out to me saying: 'O Muḥammad', I would certainly respond to him." This was mentioned by Ḥāfiẓ Ibn Ḥajar in *al-Maṭālib al-'Āliya* under the heading: 'His Life ﷺ in the Grave'[162]

Greetings Delivered to the Prophet ﷺ by Post

From Yazīd al-Mahdī: "When I bid farewell to 'Umar b. 'Abd al-'Azīz he said to me: 'I need a favour from you.' I said: 'O leader of the believers! How could you need a favour from me?' He said: 'I suppose that when you arrive in Medina you shall see the grave of the Prophet ﷺ, so convey to him my greetings.' "

From Ḥātim b. Wardān: "'Umar b. 'Abd al-'Azīz used to send letters from the Levant to Medina asking others to convey his greetings to the Prophet ﷺ."[163] Both al-Khafājī and Mullā 'Alī al-Qārī mentioned in their explanations of *al-Shifā* that this was narrated by Ibn Abī al-Dunyā and al-Bayhaqī in *Shu'ab*.

Al-Khafājī said:

> It was from the manners of the Salaf, that they would send greetings to the Messenger of Allah ﷺ in this way. Ibn 'Umar used to (request others) to convey greetings to him ﷺ, Abū Bakr, and 'Umar. So, even though the greetings of the people reach him and they are far away, this still contains the virtue of (having someone) address him directly and having him ﷺ respond to the greetings.[164]

This was also mentioned by al-Fayrūzabādī in *al-Ṣillāt wa al-Bishr* (p.153).

---

[162] *Al-Maṭālib al-'Āliya*, 4:23.

[163] Mentioned by Qāḍī 'Iyāḍ in *al-Shifā* in the section on visitation, 2:83.

[164] *Nasīm al-Riyāḍ* of al-Khafājī, 3:516.

The Greetings and the Call to Prayer Heard in the Grave of the Prophet ﷺ

The Imām and Ḥāfiẓ, Abū Muḥammad ʻAbdullāh al-Dārimī narrated in his *Sunan* collection, a collection that is considered from the six foundational books of Ḥadīth: "Marwān b. Muḥammad informed us from Saʻīd b. ʻAbd al-ʻAzīz who said: 'During the days of the drought, neither the call to prayer nor the *iqāma* (second call to prayer) was called in the Prophet's Mosque ﷺ for three days. Saʻīd b. al-Musayyib remained in the Mosque for that time. He was unable to determine the time of the prayers save by the humming sound he heard emanating from the grave of the Prophet ﷺ.' "[165] This narration was mentioned by Shaykh Muḥammad b. ʻAbd al-Wahhāb in his essay on the rulings for wishing death upon oneself.[166] This narration was cited by the Imām, Majd al-Dīn al-Fayrūzabādī, the author of the famous dictionary *al-Qāmūs*, in his book *al-Ṣillāt wa al-Bishr* (p.104). Ibrāhīm b. Shaybān said: "I once performed the Ḥajj, and thereafter I went to Medina and went to the grave of the Prophet ﷺ. I greeted him and heard from within the confines of the apartment: 'And upon you be peace.' "

Ibn Taymiyya's Support for these Events

Shaykh Ibn Taymiyya mentioned these events when he was speaking on the issue of taking graves as Mosques and idols that are worshipped. He said: "This does not include the narrations mentioning some people hearing the greetings from the grave of the Prophet ﷺ or the graves of others among the righteous, or that Saʻīd b. al-Musayyib heard the call to prayer from the grave of the Prophet ﷺ during the nights of the drought, and so on."[167]

---

[165] *Sunan al-Dārimī*, 1:44.

[166] *Majmūʻa al-Muʼallafāt al-Shaykh*, 3:47.

[167] *Iqtiḍāʼ al-Ṣirāṭ al-Mustaqīm*, p.374.

The Affirmation of some of these Miracles for other than the Prophets

The people of knowledge have narrated some of these miracles that occurred with some of the pious predecessors after their death. This was relayed from them by way of reliable narrators who in turn received it from reliable narrators who witnessed these events with their own eyes. Here, we shall cite some of these reports that were mentioned by Shaykh Muḥammad b. ʻAbd al-Wahhāb—may Allah have mercy upon him. He said in his book: 'The Rulings for Wishing Death upon Oneself', found in his collection of works distributed by Imām Muḥammad b. Saʻūd university:

Prayer in the Grave: From Aḥmad's collection, from ʻAffān b. Ḥammād, from Thābit who said: "O Allah! If You are two give anyone the ability to offer prayers in their grave then give me the ability to pray in my grave!" Abū Nuʻaym narrated from Jubayr who said: "By Allah, besides whom there is no other god, I placed Thābit al-Banānī in his grave niche and with me was Ḥamīd al-Ṭawīl. After the both of us straightened out the wood boards, one of them fell out of place and I saw him (Thābit) praying in his grave."

Recital of the Qur'ān: Abū Nuʻaym and Ibn Jarīr both reported from Ibrāhīm b, al-Mahlabī who said: "Those who used to plaster the graves at night informed me saying: 'When we would pass by the grave of Thābit al-Banānī, we would hear the Qur'ān recited.' " In a narration from al-Tirmidhī—who declared it good—from Ibn ʻAbbās ﷺ, he said: "Some of the companions of the Prophet ﷺ once dug a hideout and did not realize it was a grave site. After opening it, they found someone reciting *Sūra al-Mulk* till the end of the chapter. Afterwards, the Prophet came and was informed of what happened and he ﷺ said: 'It is the impediment and giver of salvation from the punishment of the grave.' "

Al-Nasāʾī and al-Ḥākim narrated from ʻĀʾisha who said: "The Messenger of Allah ﷺ said: 'Once when I was sleeping, I saw myself in Paradise'—and in the narration in al-Nasāʾī it states: 'I entered Paradise'—'and heard the voice of a reciter. I asked: "Who is this?" I was told: "This is Ḥāritha b. al-Nuʿmān." ' The Messenger of Allah ﷺ said: 'This is how dutifulness is, this is how dutifulness is, this is how dutifulness is.' " Ḥāritha was most dutiful to his mother. Ibn Abī al-Dunyā narrated from Ḥasan who said: "It has reached me that if a believer dies having not memorized the Qur'ān, his Angels are ordered to teach him the Qur'ān in his grave so he may be resurrected on the Day of Judgement with its (the Qur'ān's) people. Ibn Abī al-Dunyā also narrated a similar report from Yazīd al-Raqāshī. It was also narrated by al-Silafī with a similar meaning in the *mursal* collection of Ibn ʿAṭiyya al-ʿAwfī.

The Inhabitants of the Graves Visiting Each Other: Ibn Abī Shayba narrated from Ibn Sīrīn who said: "Ḥasan used to love the burial shroud. He would say: 'The dead shall visit each other in their burial shroud.' " A report with a similar meaning is found in the *Musnad* of Ibn Abī Usāma from Jābir in *marfūʿ* form and it adds: "They vie with each other and visit each other in their graves." In the Ḥadīth of Muslim it says: "When one of you takes care of the burial of his brother he should shroud him well." Al-Tirmidhī, Ibn Mājah, and Muḥammad b. Yaḥyā al-Hamadānī in his authentic collection, all narrate from Abū Qatāda in *marfūʿ* form: "If one of you takes care of the burial of his brother, he should shroud him well because the dead visit each other in their graves."

A Letter from the Life of this World to the Isthmus Life with the Dead: Ibn Abī al-Dunyā narrated with his chain that is without fault, from Rāshid b. Saʿd who stated that a man's wife had died. The man later saw some women in his dream, but did not see his wife with them. He asked the women concerning her and they replied: "You all were negligent in your shrouding of her, so she is ashamed to come out with us." This man then went to inform the Prophet ﷺ, who in response said: "Is there any way for a reliable person?" He then went to a man among the Anṣār who was nearing death and he informed him of the man's dream. The Anṣārī said: "If there is anyone who will reach the dead, it will be me." The Anṣārī died shortly thereafter. He ﷺ brought two garments dyed with saffron and placed them with the shroud of the Anṣārī. When the night approached, the man saw the women again in his dream, and among them was his wife wearing those two yellow garments. Ibn al-Jawzī narrated from Muḥammad b. Yūsuf al-Faryābī, the story of the woman who saw her mother in a dream complaining about her shroud. This story was narrated to Muḥammad (b. Yūsuf) and they asked him about it. In this narration, it mentions that the mother said to her daughter: "Buy a shroud for me and send it with so and so."

Al-Faryābī said after mentioning this story: "They visit each other in their shrouds, so buy her a new shroud." The woman mentioned in the story (who was to be given the shroud) died that day, and they placed a shroud with her at the time of burial.

Light upon the Graves: Ibn Abī al-Dunyā narrated from Abū Ghālib—the companion of Abū Umāma—that there was a young man in the Levant who was upon his death bed. He said to his paternal uncle: "What do you think would happen if Allah was to give my mother disposal over my affair?" His uncle replied: "By Allah, she would enter you into Paradise." The boy said: "By Allah, Allah is more merciful to me than my mother," then he died. "I (Abū Umāma) entered the grave along with his uncle and we said: 'Let us prop up the wood casing.' As we were doing this, a piece of wood from the casing fell down. Suddenly, his uncle jumped up and away. I asked him: 'What is the matter?' He replied: 'His grave is filled with light.' Light stretched as far as the eye could see."

Abū Dāwūd and others narrated from 'Ā'isha who said: "When Negus died, we used to say to each other that light would continue to be seen upon his grave." In the history of Ibn 'Asākir, 'Abd al-Raḥmān b. 'Amāra said: "I attended the funeral prayer of al-Aḥnaf b. Qays. I was among those who lowered his body into the ground. After I aligned his body and arranged the grave, I saw it expand as far as my eye could see. I informed my companions of that but they did not see what I saw." Ibrāhīm al-Ḥanafī said: "When Māhān al-Ḥanafī was crucified on his door, we would see a glowing light emanate from his body at night time."

Please review the book 'The Rulings of Wishing Death upon Oneself' found in folio number 86/771 in the Saudi National

Library in Riyadh with the editing of Shaykh 'Abd al-Raḥmān al-Sadḥān and Shaykh 'Abdullāh b. Jibrīn in part two of the legal volume. In the beginning part of this collection, its authenticity and correct attribution to the Shaykh was established. This collection was distributed and published by the Muḥammad b. Sa'ūd University in Riyadh in its entirety after it was edited in relation to the 'Shaykh Muḥammad b. 'Abd al-Wahhāb week.'

DO NOT UNDERTAKE JOURNEY

Many people err in their understanding of the Ḥadīth: "Do not undertake journey except to three Mosques: the Masjid al-Ḥarām, this Masjid of mine, and the Masjid al-Aqṣā'." Many people infer from this Ḥadīth that it is prohibited to undertake a journey to visit the Prophet ﷺ. They consider this type of journey, one of disobedience. This inference of theirs is utterly rejected, because it is based upon a false understanding. As you shall see, this Ḥadīth is in one door, and that inference is in another door. To explain this, we say that this Ḥadīth: "Do not undertake a journey except to three Mosques..." employs a very well known Arabic literary style known to the linguists as the style of exception. This necessitates that there be an 'excluded' and an 'excluder'. That which is 'excluded' is what comes after the grammatical particle of '*illa*' (except). That which is the 'excluder' is what comes before the particle of '*illa*'. Both of these must be present—either physically present and explicit in the sentence, or estimated and implied in the meaning. This is mentioned and well known in the most basic books of grammar.

If we take a look at this Ḥadīth, we see that it clearly mentions the 'excluded', found in his statement: "...except to three Mosques..." This is what comes after the particle '*illa*'. The 'excluder' that comes before the particle '*illa*' was not mentioned, so it must be estimated. If we are to assume that the 'excluder' word here is 'grave', then the words attributed to the Prophet ﷺ would mean: "Do not undertake journey to a grave except to three Mosques." This structure of speech is obviously unorganized and it does not befit the pure Prophetic eloquence appropriate to the Prophet ﷺ. In this estimation, the 'excluder' is not within the same genus of the 'excluded'—which is the basis of this grammatical rule. No scholar who is wary of attributing to al-Muṣṭafā ﷺ what he has not said can feel contentment in his heart while ascribing this word 'grave' to the Messenger of Allah ﷺ, as it goes against the basis of the grammatical rules pertaining to exception. Since the word 'grave' is not fitting to be considered the 'excluder' here, let us suppose for arguments sake, that the estimated word is 'place'.

If this were the case, then the words attributed to the Prophet ﷺ would be: "Do not undertake a journey to any place except the three Mosques..." This would mean that we should not travel at all—not for business, knowledge, or good. To make this estimation would be raving madness and clearly false. This Ḥadīth mentions the 'excluded' without mentioning the 'excluder', therefore, by the consensus of the linguists there must be an estimated meaning. There are only three possible estimated words:

One: Grave: With this estimation, the Ḥadīth would mean: "Do not undertake journey to a grave except to three Mosques." This estimation is based upon the view of those who use this Ḥadīth as proof for the prohibition of visitation. Here you see how this estimation is cold and dismissed. It is not accepted by anyone who has the faintest taste of Arabic. It should not be attributed to the most eloquent of those who spoke the language of *ḍād*.[168] Far removed is he ﷺ from being pleased with this flimsy style of expression.

Two: Place: this estimation is clearly false, and there are no two people who disagree with this.

Three: The third possible estimation is the word 'Mosque'. Using that word in this context would mean: "Do not undertake a journey to any Mosque except three Mosques..." Here, you can plainly see that the words are both flowing and organized in accordance with the eloquent linguistic style. With this estimation, the other two incoherent possibilities run into hiding and the spirit of Prophecy shines. The heart is content to ascribe this to the Messenger of Allah ﷺ. Of course, this is all assuming that there are no other narrations of this Ḥadīth that explicitly mention the 'excluder'. If these narrations are found, then it is

---

[168] I.e. the Arabic language.

not permissible for anyone with religion to depart from it and hold to a mere possibility that does not find support in the eloquent language. All praise belongs to Allah, we have found other Prophetic narrations that explicitly mention the 'excluder'. Among them is the report narrated by Aḥmad from Shahr b. Ḥawshab who said: "I heard Abū Sa'īd say after I mentioned to him the idea of going to Mount Sinai to pray: 'The Messenger of Allah ﷺ said: 'It is not fitting for a traveller to undertake a journey to pray in a Mosque unless it be the Masjid al-Ḥarām, Masjid al-Aqṣā', or this Masjid of mine.' " Ḥāfiẓ Ibn Ḥajar said: "Shahr is good in Ḥadīth even if he contains some weakness." In another wording, it states: "It is not fitting for a traveller to undertake a journey to pray in a Mosque other than the Masjid al-Ḥarām, Masjid al-Aqṣā', or this Masjid of mine."[169] Ḥāfiẓ al-Haythamī said: "This contains Shahr, and there are some negative remarks about him, and his Ḥadīth is good."[170]

It is reported from 'Ā'isha that she said: "The Messenger of Allah ﷺ said: 'I am the seal of the Prophets and my Masjid is the seal of the Prophet's Mosques. The Mosques that are most deserving of being visited and journeying to are: the Masjid al-Ḥarām, and this Masjid of mine. Prayer offered in my Masjid is better than one thousand prayers offered elsewhere, except for Masjid al-Ḥarām."[171]

The words of the Messenger ﷺ regarding the Mosques, clarifies for the Umma that all other Mosques besides these three are equal in virtue, hence, there is no benefit in tiring out oneself in journeying to other than these three. As for these three, they have an added virtue. There is no mention of graves in this Ḥadīth whatsoever, so to include them as a part of the narration is a type of lie against the Messenger of Allah ﷺ. Along with this, visitation is recommended. Nay, many scholars mention it among the recommended acts in their books on the Ḥajj rites. This is in fact supported by numerous Ḥadīth. Among them are the following: From Ibn 'Umar, from the Prophet ﷺ who said: "Whoever visits my grave, my intercession will be guaranteed for

---

[169] *Fatḥ al-Bārī*, 3:65.
[170] *Majma' al-Zawā'id*, 4:3.
[171] Narrated by al-Bazzār. See *Majma' al-Zawā'id*, 4:3.

him." This was narrated by al-Bazzār. It contains 'Abdullāh b. Ibrāhīm al-Ghifārī who is weak. Ibn Taymiyya quoted this Ḥadīth and said that it is weak without judging it as being a fabrication or a lie.[172]

If there is a different ruling mentioned by him elsewhere, then it means that he was indecisive in his ruling upon it. It could also mean that he changed his opinion, and we do not know which view was his final view—if so then neither of them is relied upon.

From Ibn 'Umar who said: "The Messenger of Allah ﷺ said: 'Whoever comes to me as a visitor without any other need other than to visit me, then it is a right upon me that I act as his intercessor on the Day of Judgement." This was narrated by al-Ṭabarānī in *al-Awsaṭ al-Kabīr.* Its chain contains Muslima b. Sālim who is weak.[173] Ḥāfiẓ al-'Irāqī said: "It was authenticated by Ibn al-Sakan."[174]

From Ibn 'Umar, from the Prophet ﷺ who said: "Whoever performs the pilgrimage and visits my grave after my death, it is as if he had visited me in my lifetime." This was narrated by al-Ṭabarānī in *al-Awsaṭ al-Kabīr.* Its chain contains Ḥafṣ b. Abī Dāwūd al-Qārī'. He was declared reliable by Aḥmad and weakened by a group of the Imāms.

From Ibn 'Umar who said: "The Prophet ﷺ said: 'Whoever visits my grave after my death, it is as if he had visited me in my lifetime.' " Al-Haythamī said: "This was narrated by al-Ṭabarānī in *al-Ṣaghīr* and *al-Awsaṭ*. It contains 'Ā'isha b. Yūnus and I have not found anyone who listed a biography for her."[175]

The upshot of all of this is that the Ḥadīth reports regarding visitation have numerous supporting narrations—as mentioned by al-Munāwī in *Fayḍ al-Qadīr* from Ḥāfiẓ al-Dhahabī—especially given the fact that many scholars authenticated them or mentioned others who authenticated them, such as al-Subkī, Ibn al-Sakan, al-'Irāqī, Qāḍī 'Iyāḍ in *al-Shifā*, Mullā 'Alī al-Qārī who explained the *Shifā*, and al-Khafājī in *Nasīm al-Riyāḍ.* All of these scholars were Ḥuffāẓ in Ḥadīth and relied upon Imāms in its

---

[172] *Al-Fatāwā*, 27:30.
[173] *Majma' al-Zawā'id*, 4:3.
[174] *Al-Mughnī*, 1:265.
[175] *Majma' al-Zawā'id*, 4:2.

science. It is sufficient that the four Imāms—may Allah be pleased with them—and other luminary scholars and pillars of the religion supported the legality of visiting the Prophet ﷺ, as their students quoted from them in the relied upon works of jurisprudence. This is sufficient for them in authenticating the Ḥadīth regarding visitation and accepting it. This is because a weak Ḥadīth is strengthened by it being acted upon (by notables) and legal verdicts given in support of it—as is well known in the principles of the scholars of *uṣūl* and the scholars of Ḥadīth.

VISITING THE GRAVE IS EQUIVALENT TO VISITING THE MOSQUE ACCORDING TO SHAYKH IBN TAYMIYYA

Ibn Taymiyya has a valuable opinion that he mentioned in the context of visitation. He said, after speaking of the innovation of undertaking a journey to the grave of the Prophet Muḥammad ﷺ alone without visiting the Mosque:

> The opponent and his likes made travel to the graves of the Prophets a type of righteous act, then, after they saw what the scholars mentioned regarding the recommendation to visit the grave of our Prophet ﷺ, they supposed that other graves may be travelled to just as it is travelled to. They erred from two angles:
>
> **One:** In reality, travel to his grave is only travel to his Mosque—which is recommended by textual evidence and consensus.
>
> **Two:** The journey undertaken there is to the Mosque during the life of the Messenger ﷺ and after he was buried, and it is before he was buried in his apartment and after he was buried in it. Hence, it is a journey undertaken to the Mosque, whether the grave is present there or not, so it is not permissible for it to resemble travel to the grave alone...
>
> ...**Six:** Travelling to his Mosque—which is called travelling to visit his grave—is unanimously agreed upon by the Muslims, generation after generation. As for travelling to other graves, it is not known from any of the

> companions or those who followed them in goodness, nor those who came after them...
>
> What is meant here is that the Muslims have not ceased travelling to his Mosque while (at the same time) not travelling to the graves of the Prophets such as the grave of Mūsā and the grave of al-Khalīl (Ibrāhīm) a. It is not known from any of the companions that they undertook a journey to visit the grave of al-Khalīl (Ibrāhīm), despite the frequency of their travels to the Levant and Jerusalem—so how can anyone deem travel to the Mosque of the Messenger—that some people call visitation—equivalent to travel to the graves of the Prophets?

A very important benefit is deduced from the words of Shaykh Ibn Taymiyya. He was unable to imagine someone undertaking a journey with the sole intent of visiting the grave of the Prophet ﷺ alone, without entering the Mosque and praying in it to derive benefit from its blessings and increase the value of his prayers, as well as visit the garden of Paradise (*rawḍa*) contained in it. On the flip side, it is also unthinkable that someone would undertake a journey with the sole intent of visiting the Mosque alone, and then not pay a visit and stand at the noble grave in order to send greetings to the Prophet ﷺ and his two companions. Here you see the Shaykh indicating this meaning when he said: "...so how can anyone deem travel to the Mosque of the Messenger—that some people call visitation..." and: "In reality, travel to his grave is only travel to his Mosque" and: "Travelling to his Mosque—which is called travelling to visit his grave—is unanimously agreed upon by the Muslims..." This good and valuable opinion removes a huge problem that has been the cause of Muslims separating from each other, and a cause for some levelling charges of disbelief upon others and expelling them from the fold of Islam.

If those who claim to follow the path of the Salaf only took the path of Ibn Taymiyya—who was the Imām of Salaf in his times—and gave people the benefit of the doubt regarding their intentions, and had good opinions of them, a large group of people would be saved from entering the fire and would enter the permanent abode of Paradise. This is the truth that we take as our religion with Allah and believe in with all truthfulness—

whether we explicitly declare it or not. If someone among us was to say that he is travelling to visit the Prophet ﷺ or his grave, then in general, he intends to visit the noble Mosque. If he was to say that he is travelling to visit the Mosque, then in general, he intends to visit the grave as well. The most that can be said is that he neglected to explicitly state his whole intention because of the inseparable link between the Mosque and the grave—the grave being in reality an expression denoting the person of the Prophet ﷺ himself, because the one who undertakes a journey to the grave is in reality only undertaking a journey to the Prophet ﷺ.

As for the actual grave, the traveller does not intend it in and of itself, rather, we only undertake a journey and direct ourselves to him ﷺ, seeking closeness to Allah through that visitation. So in hindsight, it is necessary for all of the Muslims undertaking visitation to correct their outward expressions in order to be far removed from doubtful matters. They should say: "We are visiting the Messenger of Allah" or: "We are undertaking a journey to the Messenger of Allah." Based on this, Mālik said: "I detest that a man say: 'I visited the grave of the Messenger.' " This was explained by the Mālikī Imāms as an observance of proper manners in ones verbal expression. Were those undertaking journey only intending to visit the grave, you would not see the severe crowding at the ennobled *rawḍa* that you do. You would not have seen the people racing and shoving each other to the point of almost killing each other at the gates of the Prophet's Mosque. Those who are keen to pray in the Mosque and who race to reach the *rawḍa* are the same ones who undertake journeys and visit Muḥammad b. 'Abdullāh ﷺ.

A Beneficial Substantiation

The investigation of the 'Allāma and Shaykh Muḥammad 'Aṭiyya Sālim, the author of the completion of *Aḍwā' al-Bayān*. The 'Allāma and Shaykh, Muḥammad 'Aṭiyya Sālim, the judge in Medina, mentioned in his completion of the well known book of Qur'ānic exegesis *Aḍwā' al-Bayān* of the 'Allāma and exegete Shaykh Muḥammad al-Āmīn al-Shanqīṭī:

> Regarding this issue, I believe that were it not for the dispute between Shaykh al-Islam and other (scholars) on other topics, this issue would not have any place. However, they found it as a sensitive matter and it was a cause for emotions to flare up, and out of their love for the Messenger of Allah ﷺ, they stirred it up and judged him based on the implication of his words when he said: "Undertaking a journey should not be for the sake of visitation, rather, it is to be for the sake of the Mosque—which is the most noble visitation undertaken, as expressed in the Ḥadīth text." They put words in his mouth that he did not say. If only they were to understand his words as a negation and not as a prohibition, it would be agreed upon—meaning there would not have arisen any differences because he—may Allah have mercy upon him—did not forbid visiting the Prophet ﷺ or sending greetings to him. Rather, he counted these two acts among the virtuous acts that draw one near. All he did was stick strictly to the literal wording of the Ḥadīth which limits undertaking journeys to the Mosque and everything else, including sending greetings to the Messenger ﷺ, as is clearly mentioned in his books.[176]

He went on to quote the same words of Ibn Taymiyya that we quoted, after which he said:

> His words here—may Allah have mercy upon him—prove that visiting the grave and offering prayers in the Mosque are intimately linked. Whoever claims that they are separate from each other has opposed reality. If their intimate link is established, then the differing has dissipated and that which brought about the dispute is removed, and all praise belongs to Allah the Lord of all the worlds. In another place, on p.346, he (Ibn Taymiyya) mentioned the four opinions of Imām Aḥmad's companions regarding shortening prayers when undertaking a journey to visit the graves of the righteous. The third opinion of them was that the prayer may be

[176] *Aḍwā' al-Bayān*, 8:586.

> shortened if the journey was to visit the grave of the Prophet ﷺ...
>
> This is the clearest and most unequivocal declaration from him—may Allah have mercy upon him—that there is no real separation between visitation and prayer in the Mosque according to the generality of the scholars.

Concerning the ignorant one, he said:

> As for the one who is unaware of this, he might not intend anything but travelling to the grave. Even in his case though, he must pray in the Mosque, and hence, he will be rewarded for that. Whatever he did that was prohibited whilst he was unaware of its prohibition, he will not be punished for it—so the upshot is that he obtains reward and earns no sin.[177]

With this, it becomes clear that in all cases, the one who intends the grave is not denied of reward and recompense. Is it to be said then regarding him that he is an 'innovator', 'misguided', or a 'pagan'? Glorified are you my Lord, this is evident slander.

Imām Mālik and Visitation

Imām Mālik was of the staunchest of people in showing esteem for the Prophetic significance and stature. It was he who would neither walk in sandals, nor ride an animal, nor relieve himself in Medina out of his esteem and honour for the dust of Medina that the Messenger of Allah ﷺ walked upon. Once, he was addressing the leader of the believers, al-Mahdī, when the latter came to Medina. He said to him: "You are passing through Medina and you shall pass by people on your left and on your right who are children of the Muhājirūn and the Anṣār. Give them your greetings because there are no people on the face of the earth more virtuous than the people of Medina, and there is no better than Medina." Al-Mahdī said to him: "And what makes you say that O Abū 'Abdullāh?" Mālik replied: "Because there is no grave

---

[177] Ibid. 8:590.

of a Prophet on the face of the earth that is known except for the grave of Muḥammad ﷺ. Whoever has the grave of Muḥammad in their vicinity, then it is a must that their virtue is known."[178]

It was out of his strong veneration for Medina that he disliked that it be said "I visited the grave of the Prophet ﷺ." It was as if he wanted the person to say that he directly visited the Prophet ﷺ without using the word 'grave'. This is because a grave is something that is abandoned, as the Prophet ﷺ said: "Pray in your houses and do not make them into graveyards." Ḥāfiẓ Ibn Ḥajar said: "He only hated this expression out of proper observance of etiquette, not the basis of visitation itself, for it is from the most virtuous of actions and noblest of deeds that draw one close and allow one to reach the Possessor of Grandeur (Allah). Its legality is agreed upon by consensus with no dispute."[179] The Imām and Ḥāfiẓ, Ibn 'Abd al-Barr said: "Mālik only hated that it be said: "*Ṭawāf* of visitation," and "We visited the grave of the Prophet ﷺ" because people use the same phrases with reference to themselves with others—meaning among themselves—so he hated that the Prophet ﷺ be made to seem equal to the rest of the people by using these expressions. He loved that he ﷺ be specially mentioned by saying: "We greeted the Prophet ﷺ."

Also, visiting ordinary people is legally permissible, however, it is obligatory to undertake journey to his ﷺ grave. Here, what is intended by obligation is the obligation of recommended nature and strong encouragement, not the legal obligation (in Sacred Law). What seems more appropriate to me, is that Imām Mālik's prohibition and hatred of it (this statement) is due to its attribution to the grave of the Prophet ﷺ, and that if someone said: "We visited the Prophet ﷺ," he would not have detested it because he ﷺ stated: "O Allah! Do not make my grave into an idol that it worshipped. The anger of Allah is severe against those who took the graves of their Prophets as Mosques." So he (Imām Mālik) considered the attribution in this expression to the grave and the resemblance to the act of those people as a means of cutting off the ways and means and shutting the door

---

[178] *Tartīb al-Madārik* of Qāḍī 'Iyāḍ.

[179] *Fatḥ al-Bārī*, 3:66.

(*sadd al-dharīʿa*). I say: If the intent behind his statement was to declare it reprehensible to visit, he would have said: "I detest for a man to visit the grave of the Prophet ﷺ." However, what is apparent from his statement: "I dislike that a man say..." is that he only intended the actual expression.

THE RECOMMENDATION TO VISIT THE PROPHET ﷺ ACCORDING TO THE ḤANBALĪS AND OTHERS

Visiting the Prophet ﷺ is legislated, and was mentioned by many of the scholars of this Umma and Imāms of the Salaf. Mentioning the Ḥanbalīs separately here is only to dispel the false notions of some who claim that the Ḥanbalīs do not allow it. We must mention them separately to correct this lie. Otherwise, all of the books in Islamic jurisprudence are crammed full of discussions on this issue.

If you like, go review the works in Ḥanafī jurisprudence, Mālikī jurisprudence, Shāfiʿī jurisprudence, Ḥanbalī jurisprudence, Zaydī jurisprudence, Ibāḍī jurisprudence, and Jaʿfarī jurisprudence. You shall see that all of them compiled a chapter on visitation after their chapters in the rites of Ḥajj.

THE WORDS OF THE IMĀMS OF THE SALAF CONCERNING THE LEGALITY OF VISITING OUR MASTER THE MESSENGER OF ALLAH ﷺ AND UNDERTAKING JOURNEYS TO HIS GRAVE

Qāḍī ʿIyāḍ: Here, we shall mention the words of Qāḍī ʿIyāḍ regarding the legality of visiting the Prophet ﷺ according to the Salaf, as found in his explanation of the Ḥadīth narrated by Muslim from Ibn ʿUmar, from the Prophet ﷺ who said: "Indeed, Islam began as something strange, and shall return as something strange, and it shall seek refuge in the two Mosques just as a snake seeks refuge in his hole." Qāḍī ʿIyāḍ said:

> His statement ﷺ "...and it shall seek refuge in Medina..." means that *īmān* (faith) first and last shall take on this quality, because in the beginning of Islam, everyone

> sincere in his faith and correct in his Islam would come to Medina as either a migrant seeking residence, or someone longing to see the Messenger of Allah ﷺ and learn and draw close to him. Then, afterwards, it was the same during the time of the Caliphs. People would go out to them to learn the way of justice and to follow the way of the community of the companions—may Allah be pleased with them all. Then afterwards, it was the scholars who were the lamps of their time, the Imāms of guidance. People would go out to them to take the well known Sunna practices that were present there with them.
>
> All who were of firm faith and expansive breasts used to undertake journeys there. After that time and in every time and up to our time today, it is done by visiting the grave of the Prophet ﷺ, seeking blessings from his shrine, and the relics of his noble companions. No one come to it save the believer.[180]

Imām al-Nawawī: The Imām and Ḥāfiẓ, Muḥyī al-Dīn al-Nawawī, the author of the famous explanation of *Ṣaḥīḥ Muslim*, compiled a chapter in his well known book of Ḥajj rites called *al-Īḍāḥ* specifically on visiting the Prophet ﷺ. In it he said: "When the pilgrims and those performing the lesser pilgrimage depart from Mecca, they should go towards the direction of the city of the Messenger of Allah ﷺ to visit his grave, for it is of the most important of deeds that draws one close and of the most successful of endeavours."[181]

Imām Ibn Ḥajar al-Haytamī: The Ḥāfiẓ Ibn Ḥajar al-Haytamī said in his gloss upon *al-Īḍāḥ* of al-Nawawī, commenting on al-Nawawī's words:

> It was narrated by al-Bazzār and al-Dāraquṭnī with their two chains from Ibn 'Umar ؓ who said that the Messenger of Allah ﷺ said: "Whoever visits my grave, my intercession is guaranteed for him."

---

[180] *Sharḥ Ṣaḥīḥ Muslim* of al-Nawawī, p.177.

[181] It is also worthwhile to read his comments on the Ḥadīth: "Do not undertake journey..." in his commentary of *Ṣaḥīḥ Muslim*.

Al-Haythamī said: "It was also narrated by Ibn Khuzayma, al-Ṭabarānī, and Ibn al-Subkī who authenticated it with the wording: 'Whoever visits me with no other need other than to visit me, then it is a right upon me that I be an intercessor for him on the Day of Judgement.' In another narration it states: 'And it will be his right with Allah that I am his intercessor on the Day of Judgement.' His statement: '...with no other need other than to visit me...' means turning away from any motive that is not related to the visit."

As for what relates to it, such as intending retreat (*'itikāf*) in the Prophet's Mosque, performing many acts of worship inside it, visiting the companions, and other things, these are all recommended actions for the visitor to perform. These things will not taint his motive in acquiring the intercession for himself. Our companions (among the Shāfi'īs) and others have said that it is the Sunna for one to intend to draw close by undertaking a journey and praying the Prophet's Mosque just as one intends closeness by visitation, as mentioned by the author. This Ḥadīth also implies visiting him both in his ﷺ life and his death. It includes both men and women be they living far or near. It is used as evidence to infer the desirability of undertaking a journey for that purpose—hence, travelling with that goal is recommended because the means take the same rulings as the ends. Abū Dāwūd narrated with a rigorously authentic chain: "There is no one who sends greetings to me except that Allah returns my soul to me in order to respond to his greetings." So you should contemplate deeply on this tremendous virtue, for him ﷺ to respond to the greetings of a Muslim while he ﷺ is alive in his grave—like the rest of the Prophets, as indicated by the *marfū'* report that has been cited: "The Prophets are alive in their graves offering prayers." Having his noble soul returned to him means that he is given the ability to articulate at that moment in order to return the greetings.[182]

[182] From the gloss upon *al-Īḍāḥ*, p.488.

Ḥāfiẓ Ibn Ḥajar al-'Asqalānī: Ibn Ḥajar al-'Asqalānī, in his explanation of *Ṣaḥīḥ al-Bukhārī* when commenting on the Ḥadīth: "Do not undertake a journey except to three Mosques..." said:

> His statement: "...except to three Mosques," in this, the excluder is not mentioned (ellipsis), so the estimated speech is either general, thus meaning: "Do not undertake a journey to any place"—meaning for any purpose—except to three, or, the estimation is more restrictive.
>
> There is no way for the first option to be possible because it would sever the means of travelling for trade, family ties, seeking knowledge, and other matters. The second possibility becomes necessary. It is more appropriate that the estimated speech be that which is closer in relation, which in that case (the Ḥadīth) would mean: "Do not undertake a journey to a Mosque for the purpose of prayer except three Mosques." In this way, the view of those who prohibit undertaking a journey to visit the noble grave and the other graves of the righteous is made invalid. And Allah knows best.
>
> Al-Subkī said: "This matter confused some folks. They claimed that undertaking a journey for a visit to other than these three is included in the prohibition. This is a mistake, because the excluder can only be from the genus of the excluded, hence, this Ḥadīth means: "Do not undertake a journey to a Mosque or place for the sake of that place except the three mentioned." Undertaking a journey in pursuit of knowledge or for the sake of visitation is not to that specific place, rather it is to he who is in that specific place. And Allah knows best.[183]

Imām al-Kirmānī: who explained *Ṣaḥīḥ al-Bukhārī*. Shaykh al-Kirmānī said in his explanation of al-Bukhārī, under the Ḥadīth: "...except to three Mosques...":

> The exception here is absent (ellipsis), so if you said the estimated meaning is that one should not undertake a journey to any place or site, then this implies that it is not allowed to travel anywhere not excluded (in the Ḥadīth),

---

[183] *Fatḥ al-Bārī*, 3:66.

even travelling to visit Ibrāhīm the intimate friend a and others. Because the exception is absent, it must be estimated with that which is most general (inclusive). I say: what is meant by the 'most general' is what is appropriate for that which is excluded both in its type and description.

For instance, if you said: "I do not see but Zayd," its estimated meaning would be: "I did not see any man but Zayd" or "...anyone but Zayd." It would not mean that you saw nothing at all or not even an animal, but Zayd. Here, the estimated meaning is: "Do not undertake a journey to a Mosque except three." Many debates concerning this issue have taken place in our times here in the lands of the Levant and both sides have authored works, but this is not the appropriate time to discuss that.[184]

The Shaykh and Imām, Badr al-Dīn al-'Aynī: Shaykh al-'Aynī said in his explanation of al-Bukhārī:

> And al-Rāfi'ī has reported from the Qāḍī Ibn Kujj who said: "According to me, anyone who takes a vow to visit the grave of the Prophet ﷺ must fulfil it from one legal angle. According to me, if he takes a vow to visit the grave of someone else, there are two legal angles." Both Qāḍī 'Iyāḍ (from the Mālikīs) and Abū Muḥammad al-Juwaynī from the Shāfi'īs state that it is forbidden according to the prohibition (in the Ḥadīth), to undertake a journey to visit any other Mosque besides the three Mosques. Al-Nawawī said: "This is a gross error. What is correct according to our companions and what was preferred by Imām al-Ḥarāmayn and the verifying scholars (of the school) is that it is neither forbidden nor detested." Al-Khaṭṭābī said: "The phrase: 'do not undertake', Is a predicate and it means—by way of obligation—what a person vows upon himself such as vowing to pray in a certain place in which blessings are sought. This means that it is not necessary for him to fulfil any part of that oath, so there is no need for him to undertake a journey and travel long distances except to three: the Mosques of the Prophets—may Allah

[184] *Sharḥ al-Kirmānī*, 7:12.

bless them and grant them peace. If someone were to take a vow swearing to pray in other than these three, then he has a choice of either going to them or praying his prayers where he is at without undertaking a journey."

Our Shaykh, Zayn al-Dīn said: "The best way to interpret this Ḥadīth is to state that it only refers to the ruling upon these Mosques and that there is no undertaking of a journey to any Mosque but these three. As for going out on a journey without intending a Mosque, but rather in pursuit of knowledge, trade, a casual trip, visiting the righteous and the sanctuaries, and visiting the brethren etc, these are not included in the prohibition. In some routes of the Ḥadīth found in the *Musnad* of Aḥmad, this is explicitly mentioned: "Hāshim narrated to us: 'Abd al-Ḥamīd narrated to us: "Shahr narrated to me: 'I heard Abū (Sa'īd) al-Khudrī ﷺ say after I mentioned to him the idea of going to Mount Sinai to pray: "The Messenger of Allah ﷺ said: 'It is not fitting for a traveller to undertake a journey to pray in a Mosque unless it is the Masjid al-Ḥarām, Masjid al-Aqṣā', or this Masjid of mine.' " Its chain is good. Shahr b. Ḥawshab was declared reliable by a group of the Imāms.[185]

Shaykh Abū Muḥammad b. Qudāma: The Imām of the Ḥanbalīs and author of *al-Mughnī*, Shaykh Muwaffaq al-Dīn 'Abdullāh b. Qudāma said:

It is recommended to visit the grave of the Prophet ﷺ due to the report of al-Dāraquṭnī with his chain from Ibn 'Umar who said: "The Messenger of Allah ﷺ said: 'Whoever performs the pilgrimage and visits my grave after my passing, then it is as if he has visited me in my lifetime.' " And in another narration: "Whoever visits my grave, my intercession is guaranteed for him." The first narration was narrated as such: "From Sa'īd: 'Ḥafṣ b. Sulaymān narrated to us from Layth, from Mujāhid, from Ibn 'Umar. Aḥmad said in the narration of 'Abdullāh b. Yazīd b. Qusayṭ from Abū Hurayra, that the Prophet ﷺ said: 'There is no one who sends greetings to me at my

[185] *'Umda al-Qārī'*, 7:254.

grave except that Allah returns my soul in order to return the greetings.' "

If the one who has never performed Ḥajj before—meaning the one who is not travelling by way of the Levant—then he should not go straight to Medina because I fear for him having an accident on the way. He must first go to Mecca by way of the best and closest route and not get distracted with other things.

It is narrated from al-'Utbī who said: "As I was sitting by the grave of the Prophet ﷺ, a Bedouin Arab came and said: 'Peace be upon you, O Messenger of Allah ﷺ! I have heard Allah saying: ﴾If they had only, when they were unjust to themselves, come unto thee and asked Allah's forgiveness, and the Messenger had asked forgiveness for them, they would have found Allah indeed Oft-returning, Most Merciful﴿ (al-Nisā': 64) So I have come to you asking forgiveness for my sin, seeking your intercession with my Lord.' Then he began to recite poetry:

O best of those, whose bones are buried in the deep earth,
And from whose fragrance the depth
and the height have become sweet,
May I be the ransom for a grave which thou inhabit,
And in which are found purity, bounty and munificence!

Then he left, and I slept and saw the Prophet ﷺ in my sleep. He said to me: 'O 'Utbī! run after the Bedouin and give him glad tidings that Allah has forgiven him.' "[186]

Shaykh Shams al-Dīn Abū al-Faraj 'Abd al-Raḥmān b. Qudāma al-Ḥanbalī: Shaykh Abū al-Faraj, the Shaykh of the Ḥanbalīs and author of *al-Sharḥ al-Kabīr* said:

> **Issue:** When he is finished with the pilgrimage, it is recommended to visit the grave of the Prophet ﷺ, as well as the graves of his two companions...

Afterwards, Shaykh Ibn Qudāma mentioned the expression that is to be said when sending greetings upon the Prophet ﷺ:

---

[186] *Al-Mughnī*, 3:556.

'O Allah! You have spoken, and Your words are true: ﴾If they had only, when they were unjust to themselves, come unto thee and asked Allah's forgiveness, and the Messenger had asked forgiveness for them, they would have found Allah indeed Oft-returning, Most Merciful.﴿ (al-Nisā': 64) So I come to you (Muḥammad ﷺ) seeking forgiveness for my sins, seeking intercession through you unto my Lord. I ask you O my Lord, that you guarantee for me forgiveness for my sins just as you have guaranteed it for those who came to him during his lifetime. O Allah! Make him the first of the intercessors and the most successful of supplicants, and most noble of the first and last by Your mercy O You who are the Most Merciful of those who show mercy...' It is not recommended to wipe or kiss the wall of the Prophet's grave ﷺ. Aḥmad—may Allah have mercy upon him—said: "I do not know of this." Al-Athram (one of Aḥmad's companions) said: "I saw that the scholars from the people of Medina did not wipe the grave of the Prophet ﷺ. They would stand to the side and send their greetings." Abū 'Abdullāh (Imām Aḥmad) said: "This is how Ibn 'Umar used to act." He also said: "As for the pulpit, there is the narration of Ibrāhīm b. 'Abdullāh b. 'Abd al-Qārī who said that he once saw Ibn 'Umar placing his hands on the seat of the Prophet's pulpit ﷺ and wiping his face afterwards."[187]

Shaykh Manṣūr b. Yūnus al-Bahūtī al-Ḥanbalī: Shaykh Manṣūr b. Yūnus al-Bahūtī said in his book *Kashhāf al-Qinā' 'an Matn al-Iqnā'*:

Section: And when he has completed his pilgrimage, it is recommended for him to visit the grave of the Prophet ﷺ and the graves of his two companions: Abū Bakr and 'Umar, due to the Ḥadīth of al-Dāraquṭnī from Ibn 'Umar who said that the Messenger of Allah ﷺ said: "Whoever performs the pilgrimage and visits my grave after my passing, then it is as if he has visited me in my lifetime."

[187] *Al-Sharḥ al-Kabīr*, 3:495.

And in another narration: "Whoever visits my grave, my intercession is guaranteed for him." Sa'īd narrated the first wording.

Notice: Ibn Naṣrullāh said: "The recommendation to visit the grave of the Prophet ﷺ implies that it is recommended to undertake a journey to it as well. This is because one's visit for the pilgrimage is after the Ḥajj and it is not possible without undertaking a journey—so this is a clear and explicit recommendation to undertake a journey to visit him ﷺ.[188]

Shaykh al-Islam Muḥammad Taqī al-Dīn al-Futūḥī al-Ḥanbalī: Shaykh al-Futūḥī said:

> And it is a *sunna* to visit the grave of the Prophet ﷺ and the graves of his two companions. The visitor should send him the greetings while facing him, then he should face the *qibla* with the grave to his left and supplicate. It is forbidden to perform *ṭawāf* around it and it is detestable to rub it and raise one's voice there.

Shaykh Mar'ī b. Yūsuf al-Karmī al-Ḥanbalī: Shaykh Mar'ī b. Yūsuf said in his book *Dalīl al-Ṭālib*:

> It is the Sunna to visit the grave of the Prophet ﷺ and the graves of his two companions—may Allah be pleased with them. It is recommended to pray in his ﷺ Mosque, and it is equal to one thousand prayers elsewhere. In the Masjid al-Ḥarām, the prayers are equal to one hundred thousand prayers elsewhere, and in Masjid al-Aqṣā it is equal to five hundred prayers elsewhere.[189]

Shaykh al-Islam Majd al-Dīn Muḥammad b. Ya'qūb al-Fayrūzabādī: The author of *al-Qāmūs al-Muhīt* [a famous Arabic dictionary], said in his book *al-Ṣillāt wa al-Bishr*:

---

[188] *Kashhāf al-Qinā'*, 2:597.
[189] *Dalīl al-Ṭālib*, p.88.

Know, that sending prayers upon the Prophet at his grave is highly emphasized. It is recommended to set out on a journey with one's riding animal to obtain this tremendous success and noble rank. The Qāḍī Ibn Kujj (Qāḍī Yūsuf b. Aḥmad b. Kujj) said: "According to me, anyone who takes a vow to visit the grave of the Prophet ﷺ must fulfil it from one legal angle. According to me, if he takes a vow to visit the grave of someone else, there are two legal angles, and it is known that there nothing that binds him to vows save acts of worship. Among our companions (in the Shāfi'ī school) some explicitly stated that it is recommended: al-Rāfi'ī at the end of the chapter on Ḥajj, al-Ghazālī in the *Iḥyā'*, al-Baghawī in *al-Tahdhīb*, Shaykh 'Izz al-Dīn b. 'Abd al-Salām in his book of rites, Abū 'Amr b. al-Ṣalāḥ, and Abū Zakariyyā al-Nawawī—may Allah have mercy upon all of them. Among the Ḥanbalīs: Shaykh Muwaffaq al-Dīn, Imām Abū al-Faraj al-Baghdādī, and others. Among the Ḥanafīs: the author of *al-Ikhtiyār fī Sharḥ al-Mukhtār*. He authored a chapter in his book counting visitation among the most virtuous of recommended acts. As for the Mālikīs: Qāḍī 'Iyāḍ mentioned consensus from them upon this. In the book *Tahdhīb al-Maṭālib* of 'Abd al-Ḥaqq al-Ṣaqalī, he mentions from Shaykh Abū 'Imrān al-Mālikī who said that visiting the grave of the Prophet ﷺ is obligatory. 'Abd al-Ḥaqq commented on his words saying: "Meaning from the obligatory *sunnas*." In the words of al-'Abdī al-Mālikī in his explanation of *al-Risāla*: "Walking to visit the grave of the Messenger of Allah ﷺ is better than the Ka'ba and Jerusalem. Most of the expressions used by the jurists of the schools imply undertaking a journey to visit, for they believed it to be recommended for the pilgrim to pay a visit after his Ḥajj. From the necessary implications of that is undertaking a journey. As for visiting itself, the proofs for it are numerous.

Among these proofs, are the words of the Exalted: ﴾If they had only, when they were unjust to themselves, come unto thee and asked Allah's forgiveness, and the Messenger had asked forgiveness for them, they would have found Allah indeed Oft-returning, Most Merciful﴿

> (al-Nisā': 64) There is no doubt that he ﷺ is alive and that the deeds of his Umma are presented to him.

The Shaykh went on to mention numerous Ḥadīth regarding visitation.[190]

Shaykh Muḥammad b. 'Allān al-Ṣiddīqī al-Shāfi'ī: Shaykh Ibn 'Allān explained *al-Adhkār* (of Imām al-Nawawī). Commenting on al-Nawawī's words: "Visiting him is from the most virtuous of things that draw one near, and the most successful endeavour..."

He said:

> How could this not be the case, when the visitor has been promised a guarantee of his ﷺ intercession. This is not guaranteed save for the people of faith—so this indicates a glad tidings for one dying upon faith, not to mention the additional things attached to this act, such as him ﷺ hearing the greeting of the visitor without any intermediary. Abū al-Shaykh narrated the report: "Whoever sends prayers upon me at my grave I shall hear them, and whoever sends prayers upon me from afar I shall come to know of it." Al-Ḥāfiẓ said: "Some investigation is needed regarding its chain." Abū Dāwūd and others narrated from Abū Hurayra that the he ﷺ said: "There is no one that sends greetings to me except that Allah returns my soul in order that I return their greetings." Al-Ḥāfiẓ said: "This is a good Ḥadīth, narrated by Aḥmad, al-Bayhaqī and others." Shaykh al-Subkī mentioned in his work *Shifā' al-Siqām*: "A group of the Imāms relied upon this Ḥadīth in support of it being recommended to visit his grave ﷺ.
>
> This is the correct and relied upon position because if the visitor sends his greetings to him ﷺ, he will be responded to from up close, and this is a sought after virtue. I say: The Prophet's ﷺ response to him is also from himself, even if the visitor had nothing of closeness other than this address, it would be sufficient for him.

[190] *Al-Ṣillāt wa al-Bishr*, p.147.

> How can this not be so when it contains the greater intercession and the increase of value for the prayers offered in the lofty Ḥarām (of Medina). Taqī al-Subkī cited several of these Ḥadīth in *Shifā' al-Siqām*, as well as Ibn Ḥajar al-Haytamī in *al-Durr al-Munaẓẓam* and his student al-Fākihī in *Ḥusn al-Ishāra fī Adāb al-Ziyāra*.[191]

THE SALAFĪ VISITATION OF THE PROPHET ﷺ

It is well known that by visitation, it means the legislated visitation. Its etiquette and the proper behaviour visitors are bound by have been explained in the Prophetic Sunna. Shaykh Ibn Taymiyya explained the difference between the visitation of the people of *tawḥīd* and the visitation of the pagans:

> The visitation of the people of *tawḥīd* to the graves of the Muslims is composed of: greeting them and praying for them, which is similar to the funeral prayer recited over them. As for the visitation of the pagans, it is composed of: making the creation resemble the Creator, vowing to the dead, prostrating to them, praying to them, and loving them as they love the Creator. So with this, they have taken equals with Allah and made them like the Lord of the worlds. Allah has forbidden that the Angels and Prophets be taken as partners in worship.
>
> He (Allah) said: ﴾It is not fitting for any human being unto whom Allah had given the Scripture and wisdom and the Prophethood, that he should afterwards say to the people: Be slaves of me instead of Allah; but rather he says: Be Lordly scholars by virtue of your constant teaching of the Scripture and of your constant study thereof. And he did not order you to take the Angels and the Prophets as lords. Would he order you with disbelief after you are Muslims?﴿ (Āl 'Imrān: 79-80) And: ﴾Say: 'Call on those—besides Him—whom you will: they have neither the power to remove harms from you nor to change them.

[191] *Al-Futūḥāt al-Rabbāniyya 'alā al-Adhkār al-Nawawiyya*, 5:31.

> Those whom they call upon desire (for themselves) means of access to their Lord—even those who are nearest: they hope for His Mercy and fear His Wrath; the Wrath of your Lord is something to take heed of.﴿ (al-Isrā': 56-57)
>
> A group of the Salaf said: there were people who prayed to the Prophets such as the Messiah and 'Uzayr, as well as the Angels, so Allah informed them that they are themselves slaves who hope for His mercy, fear His punishment, and seek to draw near to Him with good acts.[192]

I say: Is our visit to the Prophet ﷺ based on anything but this methodology and upright way and straight path? Allah, His Angels, the carriers of the Throne, and the people in the heavens and earth all bear witness that in our visits to our Master and liege lord, the Messenger of Allah ﷺ, we do not believe that he is anything other than a human who received revelation. He is from the chosen servants of Allah who hopes for the mercy of his Lord, fears His punishment, and seeks to draw near to Him with good deeds—nay, he is the keenest of the people in that. He has the most piety towards Allah among us, and the most fear of Allah. It is through him that we obtained knowledge and gnosis of Allah. We do not make him resemble the Creator, nor do we vow to him, prostrate to him, pray to him, or take him as an equal or partner with the Lord of the worlds. We love him more than ourselves, our wealth and our families—just as he ﷺ commanded.

SHAYKH IBN AL-QAYYIM AND VISITING THE PROPHET ﷺ

Shaykh Ibn al-Qayyim mentioned how visitation should be performed and its proper etiquette in his well known rhyming poem known as the *al-Qaṣīda al-Nūniyya*. He spoke about how the visitor should feel as he stands in front of the noble gate (to the Prophet's ﷺ grave) and what he should sense in front of the one who is buried. At the end of this section of his poem, when speaking about visitation, and the feelings that are due, he mentioned that it is from the most virtuous of deeds.

---

[192] *Al-Jawāb al-Bāḥir fī Zuwār al-Maqābir*, p.21.

He said:

If it is to the Prophetic Mosque we visit
We pray the prayer of greeting first as two units
With the completion of its pillars and its due humility
And presence of heart,
such is the action of one possessing perfection

Then, in the course of the visit we intend
the noble grave—even if it is with eyelids
We stand in front of the grave submissively
humbling ourselves both internally and externally
It is as if he is in the grave, alive and speaking
So those standing in front of him have lowered necks
Awe has completely overcome them
So the lengthy standing has them stumbling
The eyes have erupted with the outpouring of their water
As long as they were lowered over time

The Muslims approaches and delivers greetings with awe
and respect; a possessor of knowledge and faith
Voices are not raised at his shrine
nay, and the necks do not prostrate
Nay, and there is not to be seen
one who is performing ṭawāf around the grave
It is as if the grave is a second house
Then he begins with his supplications, directing himself
to Allah, in the direction of the house possessing pillars
This is the visit of one who holds fast to the
Sacred Law of Islam and faith
This visitation is from the most virtuous of actions
And on the day of the gathering it will be on the scales[193]

Contemplate his words—may Allah have mercy upon him: "This visitation is from the most virtuous of actions," for Allah has blinded the inner vision of some readers of this poem and they denied it.

---

[193] *Nūniyya* of Ibn al-Qayyim.

Some people—may Allah correct their affairs and guide them to the straight path—look at the noble grave of the Prophet ﷺ from the perspective of it being a simple grave only. This being the case, it is no surprise to learn of all of the corrupt ideas that come to their minds and all of the evil thoughts and insinuations that appear in their hearts directed towards the Muslims who visit the Prophet ﷺ, set out intending him, and pray at his grave. You hear them saying: "Do not undertake a journey to his ﷺ grave. It is not allowed to supplicate at his grave." In fact, their extremism could lead them to declare that supplicating at his grave is paganism and disbelief, and that facing the grave is a blameworthy innovation or misguidance, and that frequently standing at the grave and going back to it is paganism or blameworthy innovation. They could believe that whoever says the grave is best place on earth—even better than the Ka'ba itself—has fallen into paganism or misguidance. Levelling charges of disbelief and misguidance like this, with such a reckless and shoddy criterion, and without insight and intelligence, is in opposition to the way of the pious predecessors—may Allah be pleased with them all.

When we speak about the grave, visiting the grave, the virtue of the grave, undertaking a journey to the grave, or calling upon Allah and entreating him in front of the grave, the intent behind all of that—which no two people differ about and over which no two goats butt heads—is only the one residing in the grave. Indeed, he ﷺ is the Master of the Messengers from beginning to end, he is the best of all of Allah's creation. He is the greatest Prophet and the ennobled Messenger ﷺ. Otherwise, what value would the grave have without him? Nay, what value would the Mosque have without him? Nay, what value would Medina have without him? Nay, what value would the Muslims themselves have without him? If it were not for him and his message, faith in him, love for him, and believing in the testimony of faith that is a condition, then they (the Muslims) would not be; they would not have been successful, and they would not have found salvation.

Ibn 'Aqīl al-Ḥanbalī was asked about the favouritism given to the grave over the Ka'ba, to which he replied:

> If you merely intend the grave itself, then the Ka'ba is better. If, however, you intend the grave on account of the one inside of it ﷺ, then no, by Allah, neither the Throne, its carriers, the Paradise of 'Aden, or the celestial constellations are better. This is because that grave contains a body that, if weighed against this life and the next, it would outweigh them all.[194]

This is what is meant by favouring the grave over other places, visiting it, and undertaking journey to it. Having said this, the scholars mentioned that it is not appropriate for one to say: "I visited the grave," rather one should say: "I visited the Prophet ﷺ." This is what the scholars determined to be the proper meaning of Imām Mālik's statement; "I detest that one say: 'I visited the grave of the Prophet ﷺ.' " This is because the one visiting is in fact visiting one who hears him, sees him, senses him, knows him, and responds to him. So the issue at hand here is not regarding a mere grave, rather, it is much greater, nobler, and higher than that.

If we are to look at the grave alone without considering who is contained inside of it, even still, we shall find that there are pure souls surrounding it from every side and an Angelic bridge stretching from the higher gathering (of Angels: *al-Mala' al-'Alā'*) all the way to the grave of Muḥammad ﷺ—an uninterrupted procession whose numbers do not cease and whose spiritual succour cannot be enumerated save by the Real (Allah), the Mighty and Majestic.

Al-Dārimī narrated in his *Sunan*: "'Abdullāh b. Ṣāliḥ narrated to us: 'Al-Layth narrated to me: 'Khālid—who is Ibn Yazīd—narrated to me from Sa'īd—who is Ibn Abī Hilāl—from Nabīh b. Wahb who stated: 'Ka'b went to see 'Ā'isha and they mentioned the Messenger of Allah ﷺ. Ka'b said: 'There is not a day that passes, except that seventy thousand Angels descend and surround the grave of the Prophet ﷺ. They strike their wings and send prayers upon the Messenger of Allah ﷺ until the evening time approaches, after which they ascend back to the heavens

---

[194] Quoted by Ibn al-Qayyim in *Badāi' al-Fawā'id*.

and another group of Angels come down and do they same as they did. This will continue until the day the earth is split asunder and he ﷺ comes out with the seventy thousand Angels surrounding him.' "[195]

I say: this report was also narrated by the Ḥāfiẓ Ismā'īl al-Qāḍī with his chain that is good as a follow up narration, a supporting narration, and in virtues of people and deeds.

I do not think anyone with intelligence and keenness for good would hesitate to offer prayers in the *rawḍa* which is around the grave and is a portion of Paradise, and around the pulpit which obtained the highest degree of honour through the beloved ﷺ, and shall be at his mighty pond ﷺ on the Day of Judgement, along with the date palm that yearned for him like one bereaved of a child, which shall be placed in the middle of all trees in Paradise—and it has been said that it was buried where it stood inside the Mosque. No one possessed of intelligence would hesitate praying in these places.

The Prophet's Grave ﷺ and Supplications

The scholars—may Allah be pleased with them—mentioned that it is recommended for the one who visits the Prophet ﷺ to stand for offering supplications, asking Allah, the Exalted whatever he likes of good and virtue, and that it is not necessary to face the *qibla* for that. If he doesn't face the *qibla*, his standing does not make him an innovator, misguided or pagan. The scholars have stated this textually (in their works), nay some of them even went so far as to say that it is recommended.

The basis regarding this is what has been reported from Imām Mālik b. Anas, when Abū Ja'far b. Manṣūr debated him the Prophet's Mosque. Mālik said to him: "O leader of the believers! Do not raise your voice in this Mosque, for Allah corrected some people when He said: ﴾And do not raise your voices above the voice of the Messenger.﴿ (al-Ḥujurāt: 2) And He praised others when he said: ﴾...Those who lower their voices in the presence of the Messenger of Allah...﴿ (al-Ḥujurāt: 3)

[195] *Sunan al-Dārimī*, 1:44.

And He condemned others when He said: ﴾Indeed, those who call you out...﴿ (al-Ḥujurāt: 4) Indeed, his sanctity in death is just like his sanctity in life." Abū Ja'far conceded to him and asked: "O Abū Abdullāh! Should I face the *qibla* when I supplicate or should I face the Messenger of Allah ﷺ?" Mālik replied: "And why would you turn your face from he who is your means and the means of your father Ādam ﷺ unto Allah, the Exalted, on the Day of Judgement? Rather, you should face him and seek intercession through him unto Allah, for Allah, the Exalted said: ﴾...and if only they had, after wronging themselves...﴿"

This incident was reported by Qāḍī 'Iyāḍ with his chain in his famous book *al-Shifā fī al-Ta'rīf bi-Ḥuqūq al-Muṣṭafā* ﷺ (The Healing by Identifying the Rights of the Chosen One) in one of the chapters on visitation. Many other scholars explicitly stated the same view.

Shaykh Ibn Taymiyya said: "Ibn Wahb stated—in what he narrated from Mālik: 'When one sends greetings to the Prophet ﷺ, he should stand while his face is toward the grave and not the *qibla*. He should come close, give the greetings, and supplicate. He should not rub the grave with his hand.' "[196]

This was also explicitly supported by al-Nawawī in *al-Adhkār*, in the chapter on visitation, as well as his *al-Īḍāḥ*, and in *al-Majmū'* (8/272).

Al-Khafājī, who explained *al-Shifā* said:

> Al-Subkī said: "Our companions (among the Shāfi'ī jurists) clearly stated that it is recommended to approach the grave while facing it with one's back toward the *qibla*, give the greetings to the Prophet ﷺ, then the two Shaykhs (Abū Bakr and 'Umar), and then one goes to where he began; standing and supplicating."[197]

---

[196] *Iqtiḍā' al-Ṣirāṭ al-Mustaqīm*, p.397.
[197] *Nasīm al-Riyāḍ*, 3:398.

The Opinion of Shaykh Ibn Taymiyya

Shaykh Ibn Taymiyya said, after quoting the views of the scholars on this issue: "So, they were in agreement regarding facing the *qibla*, but they differed regarding facing one's back to the grave while supplicating." This is the summary of Shaykh Ibn Taymiyya's view on the topic. This clearly proves that the one who stands in front of the grave and calls upon Allah, the Exalted, and asks of His bounty as He legislated, is upon a strong foundation that is given consideration and is supported by statements from the Imāms of the pious predecessors—may Allah be pleased with all of them. If the fair minded and intelligent person only contemplated the words of Ibn Taymiyya: "But they differed regarding facing one's back to the grave while supplicating," he would understand that which brings contentment to his heart, brings coolness to his eyes, and gives him glad tidings that those who stand for supplication at the grave after sending their greetings to the Messenger of Allah ﷺ are still upon *tawḥīd* and are still from the people of faith. This is because the issue is disputed over among the Salaf and their views over it being recommended or not are differed over, so should that lead one to say that it is paganism or misguidance? Glorified are you O Allah, this is manifest slander!

Analyzing the Words of Shaykh Ibn Taymiyya

What is understood from the words of Shaykh Ibn Taymiyya is that the prohibition lies in supplicating at the graves, or intending to supplicate at the graves, hoping for the prayer to be accepted there, or feeling that the supplication is more apt to be answered there than anywhere else. As for one calling upon Allah while he happens to be there passing by graves or visiting a grave and greeting its occupant, in that case, it is not necessary for him to turn to the *qibla* and it is not to be said regarding him that he is a pagan or an innovator. Take these quotes from the Shaykh on this topic.

In *Iqtiḍā' al-Ṣirāṭ al-Mustaqīm*, on p.336, he said:

And what is included in this is going to the graves to supplicate therein or for the ones therein. Supplication at the graves and other places are divided into two types:

One: That the supplication occurs in that place by coincidence, without there being a clear intention to supplicate in it, such as the one who calls upon Allah while walking and happens to pass by graves, or the one who visits graves and sends them greetings and happens to ask Allah to give himself well being as well as the deceased: as is according to the Sunna. There is no problem with this and what resembles it.

Two: that one sets out to these places in order to supplicate therein, in the sense that he feels that praying there is more apt to be responded to than in other places. This type is prohibited—either prohibited in that it is forbidden, or prohibited in that it is reprehensible, and it is closer to being prohibited in that it is forbidden, and the distinction between the two types is manifestly clear.
If someone embarks to supplicate at the site of an idol, cross, or church, hoping that his prayer is answered, then he has committed a gross enormity. Nay, if he embarked to supplicate at a house or a shop in the market place, or street corner, hoping that his prayer is answered, this would be from the forbidden evil acts, for there is no added virtue justifying supplications at these places. Embarking to supplicate at the graves is in this category, nay, it is more severe than other cases because the Prophet ﷺ forbade that graves be taken as Mosques, places of *'īd*, or prayer—as opposed to many of those other places.

...Embarking to supplicate at the graves, hoping that the supplication is answered there more than elsewhere is something not legislated by Allah or His Messenger, nor did any of the companions, followers, or Imāms of the Muslims do it, and it was not mentioned by any of the righteous early scholars.

...Whoever contemplates the books which gather the reports, and knows the state of the Salaf, he will come to sure certainty that they did not seek aid at the graves or embark to supplicate therein at all.

Rather, as we mentioned, they used to forbid the ignorant ones among them who did such acts."[198]

THE OPINION OF SHAYKH MUḤAMMAD B. 'ABD AL-WAHHĀB CONCERNING SUPPLICATION AT GRAVES: "SUPPLICATING AT GRAVES IS NEITHER INNOVATION NOR PAGANISM"

Shaykh Muḥammad b. 'Abd al-Wahhāb was asked about the statement of the jurists regarding *istisqā'* (seeking rain): "There is no problem with performing *tawassul* through the righteous," and the statement of Aḥmad: "*Tawassul* is to be performed through the Prophet ﷺ only" (and how this is joined with) the jurists' statement: "Help is not to be sought from the creation." He responded:

> The distinction (between the two) is very clear and has nothing to do with what we are speaking about. So, some give a dispensation for performing *tawassul* through the righteous and some give dispensation for performing *tawassul* through the Prophet ﷺ. Most scholars (however), prohibit it and see it as detestable. This issue is from the issues of jurisprudence. Even though what is correct according to us is the view of the majority: that it is detested, we do not censure the one who performs it for there is no censure in issues of *ijtihād*.
>
> Our censure is only against the one who supplicates to the creation more than he supplicates to Allah, and the one who goes out to the grave humbling himself in front of the shrine of 'Abd al-Qādir or other than him, seeking removal of difficulties, rescue from distress, and having his wishes granted. So where is this in comparison to the one who supplicates to Allah, being sincere to Him in the religion and not calling upon any other along with Allah while at the same time saying: "I ask You by Your Prophet" or: "By the Messengers" or: "Your righteous servants," or the one who goes out to a well known grave

---

[198] *Iqtiḍā' al-Ṣirāṭ al-Mustaqīm*, p.339.

or other than that, while supplicating at it however not calling upon any other than Allah: in sincerity to Him in the religion. So how does that compare to what we are discussing?[199]

Seeking Blessings through Kissing or Touching the Prophet's Grave ﷺ or Screen

You should know that it is not appropriate for the visitor of the noble grave to either rub it with his hands, or rub his stomach or back against the wall, the portioned cover (like the *kiswa* cloth at the Ka'ba) or the metal screen. All of that is detestable (*makrūh*) as it is against the proper etiquette that must be observed in his ﷺ presence. The intention of seeking blessings does not negate that it is detested because this is ignorance of the etiquette that should be observed. Do not become deceived by what most of the common folk do, for certainly, the correct view upheld and implemented by the scholars is opposite of this—as Imām al-Nawawī stated in his *al-Īḍāḥ*.

In *al-Mina wa al-Jawhar*, Ibn Ḥajar went into great detail supporting this view and strengthening it. In the *Iḥyā'* it states: "Touching and kissing the sanctuaries is a custom from the Jews and Christians."

Al-Fuḍayl b. 'Iyāḍ—may Allah have mercy upon him—said: "Follow the path of guidance and do not be harmed by the paltry numbers of its wayfarers. Beware of the paths of misguidance and do not be deceived by the large number of people who are destroyed."

Whoever has it cross his mind that touching with his hand is better for obtaining blessings, then it is only due to his ignorance and heedlessness. This is because blessings are only found in that which is in accordance with the Sacred Law, so how can one seek virtue in that which is in opposition to what is correct?[200]

---

[199] *Fatāwā* of the Shaykh, Imām Muḥammad b. 'Abd al-Wahhāb in *Majmū'a al-Mu'allafāt*, 3: 68, distributed by Imām Muḥammad b. Sa'ūd Islamic University during Muḥammad b. 'Abd al-Wahhāb week.

[200] See *Majmū' al-Fatāwā*, 8:275.

The Opinion of Imām Aḥmad b. Ḥanbal

Concerning this, there are some narrations from Imām Aḥmad that seem to affirm its permissibility, and other narrations that seem to withhold a ruling, and yet other narrations that make a distinction between the Prophet's pulpit and the Prophet's grave. In this third narration it states that touching the pulpit is permissible, whereas touching the grave is undecided whether it is allowed.

Regardless of what can be said about such differences, in no way does the ruling of one who does it reach the point of disbelief, misguidance, leaving the religion or innovating. The most that may be said about such an act is that it is differed over or that it is detestable. So what is meant here is to clarify in order that the common folk do not take it as a customary practice and believe that it is from the requirements and etiquette of visitation. Take the words of Aḥmad. In *Khulāṣa al-Wafā* it is stated:

> In the book *al-'Ilal wa al-Su'ālāt* of 'Abdullāh b. Aḥmad b. Ḥanbal he said: "I asked my father about a man touching the grave of the Prophet ﷺ, kissing and touching it for the sake of obtaining blessings, and doing likewise at the pulpit, hoping for the reward of Allah, the Exalted. He (my father) said: 'There is no problem with it.' "
>
> Abū Bakr al-Athram said: "I asked Abū 'Abdullāh (Imām Aḥmad): 'Can the grave of the Messenger ﷺ be touched and rubbed?' 'I am not aware of that,' he replied. 'What about the pulpit?' I asked. He replied: 'As for the pulpit, yes, for there is a report concerning it narrated from Ibn Fudayk from Abū Dhi'b from Ibn 'Umar stating that he used to rub the pulpit. A similar reported is cited from Sa'īd b. al-Musayyib about the pommel.' I say: it was also narrated by Yaḥyā b. Sa'īd that when he wanted to travel to 'Iraq, he approached the pulpit, wiped it, and supplicated—so I saw that he deemed it good...perhaps it was because of necessity or some other need."
>
> "It was said to Abū 'Abdullāh: 'They are rubbing their stomachs on the wall of the enclosure surrounding the grave.'

> "I said to him: 'I saw that the people of knowledge in Medina did not touch it. They would stand to its side and give the greetings.' Abū 'Abdullāh said: 'Yes, and this is how Ibn 'Umar used to do.' Abū 'Abdullāh then said: '...by my father and mother.' "

Shaykh Ibn Taymiyya said:

> Aḥmad and others narrated reports about rubbing the pulpit and the pommel and they did not give dispensation for rubbing the grave. Some of our companions (among the Ḥanbalīs) did narrate a report (from Aḥmad) allowing one to touch his grave, because Aḥmad once followed a funeral procession and placed his hand on the grave and supplicated for the deceased. The difference between the two cases is obvious.[201]

THE PROPHET'S GRAVE ﷺ IS DIVINELY PROTECTED FROM PAGANISM AND IDOL WORSHIP

Allah, the Exalted, has Divinely protected this grave that is ennobled by containing the greatest beloved and the most noble Messenger ﷺ. No polytheism takes place there or any other rites of worship that should only be directed to Allah. In no one's mind does it occur that he is an idol that is worshipped or a *qibla* to be turned to with worship. All of this is due to the blessings of his ﷺ supplication. He ﷺ prayed for this and Allah answered his prayers and fulfilled his desires. Shaykh al-Islam Ibn Taymiyya said: "In the *Muwaṭṭā'* of Mālik ؒ, from the Prophet ﷺ: 'O Allah! Do not make my grave an idol that is worshipped. The anger of Allah was severe against a people who took the graves of their Prophets as Mosques.' "

Allah answered his prayers. To Allah belongs all praise, it has not been taken as an idol as the graves of others have been. Nay, no one has been able to even enter inside his apartment after it was built up. Before that, no one would be allowed to go inside to

[201] *Iqtiḍā' al-Ṣirāṭ al-Mustaqīm*, 367; *al-Furū'*, Ibn Mufliḥ, 3:524.

supplicate, pray, or do anything else that is done at other graves. However, there are some ignorant folk who pray in the direction of the apartment, raise their voices, or speak words that are forbidden. All of this, however, is done outside of his apartment and not at his grave. To Allah belongs all praise, He answered his prayer, so no one has ever been able to enter into his grave and pray, supplicate, or associate him as a partner (with Allah in worship) as occurred with other graves which were taken as idols. During the life of 'Ā'isha, no one came in except to see her, and she never allowed anyone the chance to do anything forbidden at his grave. Afterwards, it was locked off until it was added to the structure of the Mosque, where its door was then sealed and a wall was built in its place. All of this was done in order to safeguard it from being taken as an idol or a place of *'īd*. Having said that, it is known that the people of Medina were all Muslims and no one would go there save Muslims, and all of them had great esteem for the Messenger ﷺ, and the graves of his individual followers are esteemed in the lands, so they did not do as they did so as to belittle his noble grave, rather, they did it in order that it not be taken as an idol that is worshipped or a place of *'īd*, or that it be treated as the people of the book treated the graves of their Prophets.

The noble grave in the apartment is covered with large gravel. It is not covered in elaborate stone or wood work, nor is it covered in mud plaster as was done to other graves. He ﷺ forbade that in order to seal off the ways and means (that lead to evil), just as he forbade offering prayers during the sunrise and sunset in order that it does not lead to paganism. He prayed to Allah that his grave not be taken as an idol that is worshipped, and Allah answered his ﷺ prayer.

His grave was not like other graves which were taken as Mosques. No one enters his grave in the first place, whereas in the case of the Prophets before him ﷺ, when their people would innovate in the religion, Allah would send them another Prophet, forbidding them from that. He ﷺ, is the seal of the Prophets with no other Prophet coming after him, so Allah safeguarded his nation from uniting upon falsehood, and He safeguarded his ennobled grave from being taken as an idol. If that were to take place—and Allah's refuge is sought—there would be no other

Prophet after him to forbid them from that and those who do it would overcome the Umma, and he informed us that there will never cease to be a group from his Umma who are victorious and upon the truth. They will not be harmed by those who oppose them nor by those who abandon them, until the Day of Judgement, hence, there is no way for the people of innovation to perform acts at his grave ﷺ similar to acts performed at the graves of others.[202]

FREQUENTING THE PROPHETIC RELICS AND RELIGIOUS SITES AND SEEKING BLESSINGS FROM THEM

Shaykh Ibn Taymiyya wrote valuable words on this topic. We shall quote some important benefits from it:

> As for the sanctuaries of the Prophets and righteous—being such places where they were located, moved to, or in which they worshipped Allah ﷻ, yet not being taken as Mosques—what has reached me concerning this matter is that there are two well known views held by the scholars:
>
> **One:** That it is forbidden and detested, and that it is not recommended to embark or intend a specific place for worship unless that is attested to by the Sacred Law. This specifically refers to the places where the Prophet ﷺ intentionally sought out to pray in, such as the prayer place of Ibrāhīm, or the places where he intentionally sought to avoid, such as churches. This is like the one who embarks to pray in the front row at the Mosque and its likes.
>
> **Two:** That a moderate amount of that is without problem, as has been narrated from Ibn 'Umar (that he used to seek out the places where the Prophet rested and sat, even if the Prophet ﷺ found those sites by chance and not intentionally looking for them). Al-Sindī al-Khawātīmī said: "We asked Abū 'Abdullāh (Aḥmad b. Ḥanbal) about a man who goes to these sanctuaries and what his opinion was about that. He replied: 'Considering the Ḥadīth of Ibn

[202] *Al-Jawāb al-Bāhir fī Zuwār al-Maqābir*, p.13.

> Umm Maktūm in which he asked the Prophet ﷺ to allow him to pray at home and take it as a prayer place, and what Ibn 'Umar used to do when he would seek out the places the Prophet ﷺ went, there is no problem with a man going to these sanctuaries, however, the people have gone overboard with it and frequented them too much.' "
>
> It was also narrated from Aḥmad b. al-Qāsim that he (Imām Aḥmad) was asked about a man who frequents the sanctuaries which are found in Medina al-Munawwara and other places. He replied: "Considering the Ḥadīth of Ibn Umm Maktūm and what Ibn 'Umar used to do when he would seek out the places the Prophet ﷺ walked to, to the point where he was seen pouring water on a spot and when asked about this, he replied: 'I saw the Prophet ﷺ pouring water here'—considering all this, there is no harm in it." He then said: "However, the people have gone to extremes in it and frequented them too much..." He then mentioned some of the things that occur at the grave of Ḥusayn.[203]

Shaykh Ibn Taymiyya further said:

> Abū 'Abdullāh gave details regarding the sanctuaries that are the sites which contain the relics of the Prophets and righteous yet are not Mosques—such as the sites in Medina. He made a distinction between that which is visited infrequently and not taken as an *'īd*, and that which is taken as an *'īd*. In this distinction, he gathered between the reports and statements of the companions, for it was narrated by al-Bukhārī in his *Ṣaḥīḥ* collection from Mūsā b. 'Uqba who said: "I saw Sālim b. 'Abdullāh seek out places in the road and pray there. He narrated that his father used to pray at these places saying that he saw the Prophet ﷺ praying there." Mūsā said: "Nāfi' narrated to me that Ibn 'Umar used to pray in these places." This is where Imām Aḥmad made concessions.
>
> As for what he detested, Sa'īd b. Manṣūr narrated in his *Sunan*: "Abū Mu'āwiya narrated to us: 'al-A'mash narrated to us from al-Ma'rūr b. Suwayd from 'Umar.

[203] Narrated by al-Khalāl in 'The Book of Etiquette.'

> "He said: 'We went out with him ('Umar) on pilgrimage. In the morning prayer, he led us reading: ❮Have you not seen how We dealt with the companions of the elephant?❯ in the first unit of prayer, and ❮For relief to the Quraysh...❯ in the second unit. After he completed his pilgrimage, he saw the people going to a Mosque, and he asked: 'What is this?' They answered: 'This is a Mosque in which the Messenger of Allah ﷺ prayed.' He said: 'The people of the book before you were destroyed in this way. They took the relics of their Prophets as temples. Whoever of you finds himself in the time of prayer, let him pray, and whoever does not find himself in the time of prayer, then let him move along.' " Hence, 'Umar ﷺ detested that the prayer place of the Messenger of Allah ﷺ be taken as a place of *'īd*. He explained that the people of the book were only destroyed due to similar actions.

Shaykh Ibn Taymiyya further said:

> The scholars—may Allah be pleased with them—differed among themselves about frequenting the sanctuaries. Muḥammad b. Waḍḍāh said: "Mālik and other scholars in Medina used to detest going out to those Mosques and relic sites in Medina, with the exception of Qubā and Uḥud. Sufyān al-Thawrī went to Jerusalem to pray without viewing the relics or praying at their sites."
>
> So these scholars detested it unrestrictedly due to the Ḥadīth of 'Umar ﷺ mentioned above, and because it resembles prayers offered at graves, hence, it is a means to taking them as places of annual gathering and resembling the people of the book. None of the companions agreed with what Ibn 'Umar did. It is not mentioned from the rightly guided Caliphs or any of the Muhājirūn or Anṣār that any of them would go out intending these places the Prophet ﷺ happened to stop at.

Then he said:

> Others among the later scholars recommended going (to these sites) and a group of authors from our companions (among the Ḥanbalīs) mentioned in their writings on the

> Ḥajj rites that it is recommended to visit these sanctuaries. They enumerated and named some of them as well. As for Aḥmad, he made concession for the ones that were mentioned in the reports, unless they were taken as sites of annual gathering (*'īd*), such as when it is recommended and people gather at those sites at a particular time. This is similar to his (Aḥmad's) concession allowing women to pray the congregational prayer in the Mosques—even if prayer in their homes is better—unless they uncover themselves. In that, he gathered between the reports and used the Ḥadīth of Ibn Umm Maktūm as evidence.[204]

The clear upshot from the words of Imām Aḥmad is that he allowed frequenting the relic sites, sanctuaries, and sites attributed to the Prophets and righteous. He was of the view that going out to these locations and giving them attention has a basis in the Prophetic Sunna and that it is not an innovation or misguidance—much less paganism or disbelief. He was critical of excessiveness in it and giving it too much attention. This is the summary of his view.

As for Shaykh Ibn Taymiyya, he understood from Imām Aḥmad's words that there is a distinction between that which is done frequently and that which is done infrequently. He understood that visiting the sanctuaries frequently is detested according to Aḥmad. He ruled that it was detested only and did not add any other words to that. He explained to what extent frequenting those sites and Prophetic relics is detested—and it is when those sites and relics are taken as places of annual gathering when people get together and celebrate at particular times.

From Shaykh Ibn Taymiyya's words it is also understood that the relic sites and places where it is established that the Prophets took as Mosques, or prayed therein, are not included in these details. This for one, establishes that the places and sites wherein it is confirmed that the Prophets prayed, have a distinction above other places and that they may be sought out for prayer and worship.

---

204 *Iqtiḍā' al-Ṣirāṭ al-Mustaqīm*, p.387.

This is explicitly clear from his words where he says in the beginning of the research (...however, they did not take them as Mosques...). Abū ʿAbdullāh gave details regarding the sanctuaries that are the sites which contain the relics of the Prophets and righteous yet are not Mosques—such as the sites in Medina. He made a distinction between that which is visited infrequently and not taken as an *ʿīd*, and that which is taken as an *ʿīd*.

The Meaning of the ʿ*Īd* that is Prohibited in the Ḥadīth: Shaykh Ibn Taymiyya defined the meaning of the prohibited *ʿīd* mentioned in the Ḥadīth of the Prophet ﷺ: "Do not take my grave as an *ʿīd*." He said:

> In general, what takes place at the graves is exactly what the Messenger of Allah ﷺ forbade when he said: "Do not take my grave as an *ʿīd*." Going out to a particular place at a particular time and getting accustomed to that annually at the turn of every year, month, or week, is the exact meaning of *ʿīd*. Thereafter, both the obvious and obscure of that is forbidden—as has proceeded from Imām Aḥmad's censure when he said: "However, the people have gone to extremes in it and frequented them too much..." and he then mentioned some of the things that occur at the grave of Ḥusayn.

In another place he said:

> As for taking their graves as places of *ʿīd*, it is from the things forbidden by Allah and His Messenger. Going out to these graves at a particular time and having a general gathering at a particular time, is what it means to take them as an *ʿīd*. I do not know of any difference of opinion regarding this among the people of knowledge from the Muslims. Hence, do not become deceived by the numerous corrupt customs, for that is all resemblance to the people of the book which the Prophet ﷺ informed us about saying that it would occur in his Umma.[205]

[205] *Iqtiḍāʾ al-Ṣirāṭ al-Mustaqīm*, p.377.

The Beliefs of this Author. By the grace of Allah ﷻ, what Shaykh Ibn Taymiyya mentioned here is exactly what we believe regarding this matter. It is what we invite to and encourage the people to uphold at every place and at every occasion. We forbid them from taking the grave of the Prophet ﷺ, or the sanctuaries and relics as places of *'īd*. We forbid them from setting aside any portion of worship for any other than Allah. We forbid them from setting aside a particular day for them to gather together and celebrate. This is what we believe and take as our religion with Allah. It is not a belief that we took today or yesterday, nay, it was inherited by the later ones from the Salaf, and sons from fathers, by the bounty of Allah ﷻ.

It is a duty upon us to consider these statements and these precise scholarly explanations that show good understanding taken from the true taste of knowledge. We must not hasten to level charges of disbelief, innovation, or misguidance upon the Muslims for their mere frequenting of the relic sites and their attention to the sanctuaries, shrines, and places associated with the Prophets and righteous. We must have good thoughts about them and know that the One intended is Allah ﷻ, and that these places are all means and causes for the souls to increase in faith and observe remembrance, engage in contemplation, and become attached to the ones (buried there) and their history.

They are the good examples for mankind, not to mention the fragrant effusions and blessings that one is exposed to in such places of goodness and guidance. The places that were filled with the people of goodness and piety remain places of pleasure and delight. Similarly, the places that were filled with the people of evil and corruption are places of Divine anger and displeasure. It is for this reason, the Messenger of Allah ﷺ forbade his companions from entering the dwellings of Thamūd unless they were crying, and forbade them from drinking the water there. Nay, he ordered them to throw out what they had taken and not eat what they had cooked with it. He also ordered them to move swiftly when they entered the well known valley called the valley of fire.

Attention Given to the Sanctuaries and Relics

Safeguarding the Prophetic relics is a mighty matter of heritage and history. It is the history of this Umma in which we take pride. It indicates our nobility and the nobility of our notables and Imāms who established this nation's glory and honour and produced our leadership in every field. Neglecting these relics is nothing more than effacing the evidence of our Islamic civilization and distorting our historical and natural roots. It is a crime against the most valuable and prized things we possess as a nation, a mark of disgrace upon us, and a splinter in our eye that clouds our vision and deprives us of great good that shall never be replaced. It will change the signposts of our religion and efface its boundary markers—with nothing remaining after it that would cause one to recognize the religion.

If it is argued that some people may take these relics and sites as places of *'īd* and associate partners with Allah therein, or that they might make *ṭawāf* around them, tie strings and paper there, or sacrifice animals, we reply: We are neither pleased with any of that nor do we agree with it. We forbid it and warn others from it—as it is from ignorance that must be fought. Those who do such actions believe in Allah and testify to His oneness and that there is no god but He, however they are doing incorrect actions and are ignorant about what is right. It is obligatory to educate them and guide them. That being said, none of their actions call for us to neglect, efface, or remove these sites, using such a cold reasoning and excuse. This is unacceptable to the scholars and those possessing intelligence. It is possible to eliminate such actions if they are found, by preventing people from doing them, watching them closely, commanding the good and forbidding the evil, inviting unto Allah with wisdom and goodly preaching, and observing good character—all the while leaving our sites intact and safeguarded so as to protect the roots of this nation, fulfil the historical trust that is upon our necks, and safeguard the splendid history that includes the history of our Prophet Muḥammad ﷺ.

Today, intellectuals safeguard the historical relics of cursed and punished nations gone past, such as the people of Thamūd and 'Ad.

So is it correct for us to safeguard those historical sites, show great concern for them, and strive for the sake of their preservation, while at the same time, letting the relics of the most noble of creation ﷺ go to waste and ruin—the relics of he who caused the servants and lands to be illuminated and by whom Allah honoured the Umma?

THE ATTENTION GIVEN IN THE QUR'ĀN TO THE RELICS OF THE PAST PROPHETS

In His Mighty Book, Allah ﷻ mentioned the story of the ark of the children of Israel that He made as a sign of Ṭālūt's kingship over them. He said: ﴾And their Prophet said to them: "A Sign of his authority is that there shall come to you the Ark of the covenant, with (an assurance) therein of security from your Lord, and the relics left by the family of Mūsā and the family of Hārūn, carried by Angels. In this is a symbol for you if you have faith."﴿
(al-Baqara: 248)

The status of this ark and its affair is mighty indeed. The children of Israel used to bring it to the frontlines during their battles and they would gain victory due to the blessings of *tawassul* to Allah through its contents. They would never go to battle with any of their enemies except that this ark was with them. In this Qur'ānic verse, Allah informed us of its contents, saying that it contained Divine security and Prophetic relics.

He said: ﴾...the relics left by the family of Mūsā and the family of Hārūn...﴿ These relics left by Hārūn included: the staff of Mūsā and Hārūn, their clothes and sandals, and two tablets of the Torah.

This is mentioned in the exegesis of Ibn Kathīr (1/313). It also contained a golden goblet that was used to wash the chests of the Prophets.[206]

Because of these esteemed relics that are attributed to the chosen ones of Allah's servants, Allah Himself caused the ark to be esteemed, safeguarded, of high rank, and He looked after it with a special Divine protection. After the children of Israel were defeated because of their disobedience and after having proven

[206] *Al-Bidāya wa al-Nihāya*, 2:8.

themselves undeserving and unworthy of safeguarding the ark, Allah punished them by taking it from them and bringing it back to them after a time in order to prove the validity of Ṭālūt's kingship over them. It was returned to them in the most spectacular and glorious manner: by way of Angels descending with it to them. So what care and concern is greater than this?

THE FOUR RIGHTLY GUIDED CALIPHS AND THEIR SAFEGUARDING OF THE PROPHET'S RING

Imām al-Bukhārī narrated with his chain from Ibn 'Umar ﵄: "The Messenger of Allah ﷺ acquired a silver ring that he used to wear. Afterwards (after his death), it was worn by Abū Bakr, then 'Umar, then 'Uthmān—until it fell from his hand into well of Arīs. The ring's engraving said: *Muḥammad the Messenger of Allah.*

Imām al-Bukhārī narrated it in his *Ṣaḥīḥ* collection in the book of clothing, chapter: 'The Ring of Silver'. Ḥāfiẓ Ibn Ḥajar said: "In a narration found in al-Nasā'ī; A search was made for it yet it was not found."

In a narration found in Ibn Sa'd: "It was in 'Uthmān's hand for six years."[207] Al-'Aynī said: "The well of Arīs is located in a garden near Mosque al-Qubā.' "[208]

I say: today, this well is known as the well of the ring—referring to the ring of the Messenger of Allah ﷺ that fell inside it during the reign of 'Uthmān. He tried to extract it from the well for three days, but was unable to find it. Refer to *al-Maghānim al-Muṭāba fī Ma'ālim Ṭāba* of al-Fayrūzabādī.

THE FOUR RIGHTLY GUIDED CALIPHS AND THEIR SAFEGUARDING OF THE PROPHET'S SPEAR

Imām al-Bukhārī narrated with his chain to Zubayr ﷛ who said: "On the day of Badr, I confronted 'Ubayda b. Sa'īd b. al-'Āṣ who was wearing a helmet with a face plate with only his eyes visible.

---

207 *Fatḥ al-Bārī,* 10:313.

208 *'Umda al-Qārī'*, 22:31.

His *nom de guerre* was Abū Dhāt al-Kirsh. He used to exclaim: 'I am Abū Dhāt al-Kirsh.' I attacked him with my short tipped metal spear, stabbing him in his exposed eye and killing him." Hishām said: "I was informed that Zubayr said: 'I placed my foot on his head in order to pry my spear out of his skull, but it took much effort to do so, and when it finally came out, its two ends were upturned and bent.' " 'Urwa said: "The Messenger of Allah ﷺ asked him for it and he gave it to him. When the Messenger of Allah ﷺ died, Zubayr took it back. Abū Bakr then asked him for it and he gave it to him. When Abū Bakr died, he took it back yet again until 'Umar asked him for it and he gave it to him. When 'Umar died, he took it back until 'Uthmān asked him for it and he gave it to him. When 'Uthmān was killed, the spear was in the possession of the family of 'Alī. 'Abdullāh the son of Zubayr sought it from them and it was in his possession until he was killed."

This was narrated by al-Bukhārī in the book of battles, chapter: 'The Angels Witnessing the Battle of Badr.' They upshot of this story is that Zubayr killed 'Ubayda during the battle of Badr by stabbing him in the eye with his metal spear, and the Prophet ﷺ asked to borrow the spear, and he gave it to him. When he ﷺ died, Zubayr took it, then Abū Bakr asked to borrow it, and he gave it to him and it remained with him until he died. After this, Zubayr got the spear back until 'Umar sought to borrow it from him. It remained with 'Umar for the remainder of his life, then Zubayr got it back. Afterwards, 'Uthmān asked him for the spear and it remained with him. When 'Uthmān was killed, 'Alī got possession of it until (Abdullāh b.) Zubayr requested it back—and it remained with him until he was killed.[209] We should ask: why all this major concern and keenness for the spear even though spears were abundant? Perhaps there were even spears of better quality around. Who showed such keenness for the spear? It was the four rightly guided Caliphs, who were the Imāms of the religion, exemplary pillars of *tawḥīd* and trustworthy ones.

---

[209] *Fatḥ al-Bārī*, 7:314; *'Umda al-Qārī'*, 17:107.

‘Umar b. al-Khattāb’s Safeguarding of al-‘Abbās’ Canal because the Prophet ﷺ Placed it where it was

From ‘Abdullāh b. al-‘Abbās ﷺ: “Once while going to the Mosque to lead the Friday prayer, ‘Umar passed by a canal (*mizāb*), which was in the way, and the dirty water from the canal sullied his clean clothes. He became angry and moved the canal out of the way, went back home, dressed up again and went to Mosque. In the Mosque, the Prophet’s ﷺ uncle, al-‘Abbās confronted him and said: ‘That canal was put there by the Messenger of Allah, as I saw with my own eyes.’ When ‘Umar heard that, he immediately left the Mosque with al-‘Abbās and went where the canal was, bent himself like in bowing and said to al-‘Abbās: ‘O uncle of the Messenger of Allah! Climb on my back and put the canal back where the Messenger of Allah put it!’ ”[210]

Imām Abū Muḥammad ‘Abdullāh b. Aḥmad b. Muḥammad b. Qudāma said in *al-Mughnī*:

> **Chapter:** It is not permissible to remove water canals to the main road or to smaller trails without the permission of their owners. Abū Ḥanīfa, Mālik, and al-Shāfi‘ī said that it is permissible to move them to the main roads because ‘Umar ﷺ passed by al-‘Abbās’ residence who had placed a canal there and he moved it out of the way, after which, al-‘Abbās said: “How can you move it when the Messenger of Allah placed it there with his own two hands?” ‘Umar replied: “By Allah, it will not be returned to where it was save with me carrying it upon my back.” He then bent down, placed it on his back and returned it to its original place.[211]

---

[210] *Kanz al-‘Ummāl*, 7:66.

[211] *Al-Mughnī*, 4:554.

Ibn ʿUmar was not the Only One with the Relics

Ibn ʿUmar was well known for his keenness to follow and safeguard the relics. Shaykh Ibn Taymiyya said:

> Imām Aḥmad was asked about a man who frequents the sanctuaries. In his answer he said: "...and what Ibn ʿUmar used to do when he would seek out the places the Prophet ﷺ walked to, to the point where he was seen pouring water on a spot and when asked about this, he replied: 'I saw the Prophet ﷺ pouring water here.' "

Al-Bukhārī narrated in his *Ṣaḥīḥ* collection from Mūsā b. ʿUqba who said: "I saw Sālim b. ʿAbdullāh seek out places in the road and pray there. He narrated that his father used to pray at these places saying that he saw the Prophet ﷺ praying there." Mūsā said: "Nāfiʿ narrated to me that Ibn ʿUmar used to pray in these places."[212]

Ibn ʿUmar was not alone in this matter. Nay, many other companions shared his keenness to follow the Prophetic relics and safeguard them. We have already mentioned the actions of the four rightly guided Caliphs who were the Imāms in the religion, and whose actions the Prophet made a *sunna* and an extension of his guidance and Sunna that is to be followed. It is known that their *sunna* is his ﷺ Sunna because they have no words, opinions or independent effort over his ﷺ words that are sound and established. In the chapter on seeking blessings, we mentioned a large portion of texts that are connected to this chapter. With this, it becomes clear that the companions would seek blessings from his personal relics—both Ibn ʿUmar and others as well. The truth is that this chapter and the previous one are interconnected and spring fourth from one base. This is because seeking blessings from the personal relics is a kind of safeguarding and concern for them. The second kind relates more closely to history and civilization, whereas the first kind relates to love, attachment, and faith.

---

[212] *Iqtiḍā' al-Ṣirāṭ al-Mustaqīm*, p.385.

Ibn 'Abbās and the Ancient Relics

When 'Abdullāh b. al-Zubayr wished to demolish the Ka'ba (and rebuild it according to its original foundations), he gathered the companions in order to seek their council. Ibn 'Abbās proposed to him that he not demolish all of it, and that he should rather repair certain parts of it so that which is intact from it remains intact as it was during the time of the beginning of Islam—the time in which the pledge of fealty was given to the Messenger of Allah ﷺ.

Aṭā' said: "When the house (the Ka'ba) caught fire during the time of Yazīd's reign after the raid of his troops from the Levant, Ibn al-Zubayr left it as it was and decided to wait until the people came for the Ḥajj in order to rouse them for battle against the people of the Levant. When the people arrived, he said to them: 'O people! Advise me! Should I demolish the Ka'ba and rebuild it from anew, or should I only repair the damaged parts of it?' Ibn 'Abbās said: 'I have already given my opinion regarding it, that you should only repair that which is damaged from it and leave the rest of the house and its stones as it was when the people embraced Islam in front of it and gave their pledge of fealty to the Messenger of Allah ﷺ.' "[213]

'Umar's Jealousy over the Prophetic Relics

Our Master 'Umar ؓ was strongly jealous over the Prophetic relics and had much concern and attention given to them. Once, he saw some people gathering under a tree that some claimed to be the tree under which Allah's good pleasure was earned in the pledge of *riḍwān*, which Allah mentioned: ﴾Allah was certainly pleased with the believers when they gave you the pledge of fealty under the tree.﴿ (al-Fatḥ: 18)

Upon seeing this, and knowing with surety that the tree under which the pledge was given is unknown—not only its exact location, but also the general area—he went and chopped the tree down. Even the companions who were present and

---

213 *Ṣaḥīḥ Muslim* with the explanation of al-Nawawī: chapter: 'The Demolishment of the Ka'ba and Building It from Anew', 9:92-94.

witnessed the pledge with their own eyes did not know where the tree was, so how could anyone else know? This was explicitly mentioned in the two *Ṣaḥīḥ* collections from Ibn 'Umar ﷺ. It states that the year after the pledge of *riḍwān*, they went out to look for the tree and no one was able to find it.

Musayyib, the father of Sa'īd said: "I saw the tree but was caused to forget its location so I do not know now." Ṭāriq b. 'Abd al-Raḥmān said: "Once, on the way to Ḥajj, I passed by some people who were praying. I asked: 'What is this Mosque?' 'This is the tree under which the Messenger of Allah ﷺ gave the pledge of *riḍwān* they replied. Afterwards, I approached Sa'īd b. al-Musayyib and informed him of what I saw. He said: 'My father informed me that he was among those who gave the pledge of fealty under the tree. He (my father) said: "We went out the year after and looked for it but we forgot its location, so do you know its location and are you more knowledgeable than us?" '

In another narration he stated: "It mysteriously disappeared from us." See *Ṣaḥīḥ al-Bukhārī*: the book of battles, chapter: 'The Battle of *Ḥudaybiyya*', and in *Ṣaḥīḥ Muslim* in the 'Book of Leadership', chapter: 'The Recommendation to Follow the Imām'.

So no two men agreed on its exact location. If this was the situation only one year after the pledge was given—even though the companions who attended it were all present—what would you think about a tree that became known during the time of 'Umar's Caliphate years later?

It was a different era and most of those who attended the pledge had passed on. The people differed regarding the location of the blessed tree that was ennobled by the Muḥammadan pledge of fealty—the pledge that was one of the great stances of sacrifice and *jihād*—a pledge that caused the heavens and the earth to shake, a pledge that the noble Angels witnessed and one that was recorded in the Qur'ān: ﴾Allah was certainly pleased with the believers when they pledged their fealty to you under the tree. He knew what was in their hearts and caused tranquillity to descend upon them and gave them a manifest victory.﴿ (al-Fatḥ: 18)

It was under this tree that one of the unique characteristics and praiseworthy qualities of the Prophet ﷺ was mentioned:

﴾Those who pledge their fealty to you are only pledging their fealty to Allah. Allah's Hand is above their hands.﴿ (al-Fatḥ: 10)

'Umar did not chop down the tree in order to prevent others from seeking blessings from relics or because he felt it was wrong. Nay, nothing of the sort even crossed his mind in the first place.

This is proven by the fact that he ﷺ is reported to have sought blessings from relics, such as when he sought the Prophet's spear that was in the possession of Abū Bakr, as well as his safeguarding of the Prophet's ring and other items. The Prophet ﷺ had borrowed the spear from Zubayr—as is mentioned in *Ṣaḥīḥ al-Bukhārī* in the chapter titled: 'The Angels Witnessing the Battle of Badr.'

THE ATTENTION GIVEN TO THE PROPHET'S SANDALS ﷺ AND THE STUDIES CONDUCTED REGARDING THEM

The sandals of the Prophet ﷺ have been the subject of many scholars' attention and concern. In fact, there have been many detailed studies regarding the description, make, and colour of them. The intent behind all that is the one who used to wear the sandals—the greatest Prophet and most noble Messenger ﷺ.

If we show great concern and spend great sums in acquiring the relics, clothing, garments, and property of famous individuals, and build special museums for these items, staffing them with their own specialists, then, he ﷺ—may my mother and father be sacrificed for him—is more deserving of that. If we were to spend out everything we have in pursuit of this for his ﷺ sake, it would be cheap.

THE CONCERN SHOWN BY THE (SAUDI) KINGDOM FOR THE RELICS

Allah has given success to our Sunni government here in showing great concern for the relics, and they have been keen to guard our noble heritage and protect the signposts of our civilization. The government formed a council dedicated to the preservation of historical relics under the name: 'Committee for the Preservation of Historical Relics', a special administrative order under royal decree number M/26-23/1396.[214] A special committee was formed to look into matters related to historical relics, called 'The High Committee for Historical Relics.' The council of ministers issued a declaration (number 235) on 2/21/1398, forming the members of this council under the leadership of the Ministry of Information and including members from the Ministries of Finance, Ḥajj, Interior, Endowments, Media, and (of) Historical Relics.

SAFEGUARDING HISTORICAL RELICS

In article six of the declaration it states:

> The high committee for historical relics shall cooperate with other national agencies and bodies in safeguarding and preserving historical sites and relics, and it shall determine the status of possible relics and historical sites that should be registered. The registration of such sites means that the government has determined that they possesses historical or artistic value and that steps should be taken to insure their protection, study, and display in the most appropriate manner.

THE MOSQUES AND PLACES OF WORSHIP ARE THE MOST IMPORTANT RELICS

In article seven of the declaration it states:

> Relics are two kinds: immovable relics, and movable relics. Immovable relics are the relics attached to the earth such as: natural and manmade caves used by ancient peoples, rock formations that have been painted, written on, or engraved, ancient urban ruins, subterranean structures, or other historical buildings

---

[214] This record may be found in; 'The Administrative Decree regarding Historical Relics' published by the Ministry of Finance 1399.

> such as Mosques, places of worship, castles, citadels, fortresses, gates, playgrounds, bath houses, burial sites, water canals, dams, and the interior remnants of houses such as doors, windows, pillars, balconies, ladders, roofs, curtains, crowns and their likes. Movable relics are by their nature movable objects which may be relocated elsewhere such as: sculptures, coins, engravings, manuscripts, textiles, and crafts, no matter what it may be and no matter how it was put to use.

URBAN PLANNING, RECONSTRUCTION AND HISTORICAL RELICS

In the declaration, it states:

> One must be warned from altering historical relics—whether done by the families (in whose possession the relic is found) or by way of urban planning and development. In article eleven it states: "It is forbidden to deface historical relics—be they movable or immovable—alter, damage, or otherwise change by way of inscription, engraving, or changing its features." It is similarly forbidden for families in whose possession are these historical relics to place notices and advertisements upon registered historical sites and relics.

In article twelve it states:

> When urban development plans are drawn up for the purpose of enlarging or beautifying an area, it is necessary to safeguard the historical sites and their sign posts. It is not permitted to approve urban development plans located within historical sites until the committee for the preservation of historical relics gives its agreement. It is necessary for the committee to pinpoint the sites of historical relics and to keep urban planners abreast with information on their exact locations.

It is known that along with the historical sites mentioned by the committee—particularly the Mosques and places of worship—the religious relics attributed to the Prophet ﷺ or his noble companions are included among them in the highest order. These are the historical relics that truly deserve to be honoured and favoured, for they are the pride of the believers and they remind the sons of their fathers and remind the later generation of their ancestors.

THE PROPHET'S HOME ﷺ AND THE NOBLE MOSQUE

Some rabble rousers once wanted to change the status of the Prophet's home ﷺ by removing the noble grave from the Mosque. When King Khālid b. 'Abd al-'Azīz got wind of this, he became infuriated and his strong religious sentiments were triggered, causing him to rebuke the one who suggested that sinful and disgraceful idea. Those who were in attendance heard this from him, and perhaps some of them are still alive till this day. May Allah have mercy upon the righteous king, and may He make the king's stance a treasure store for him with Allah and an honour for our Master, the Messenger of Allah, and may he obtain his intercession on the Day of Judgement for his stance—Allah willing.

THE LEGAL VERDICT OF SHAYKH MUḤAMMAD B. 'ABD AL-WAHHĀB REGARDING THE PROPHET'S HOME ﷺ

Some people of sedition and evil have attributed a view to Shaykh Muḥammad b. 'Abd al-Wahhāb in which he allegedly said that the Prophet's home should be removed from the confines of the Mosque. He denied that and disavowed both it and the one who holds that view. In his letter that was written for the people of al-Majma'a he said:

> If this is made clear, then these (are) issues that he censured me for: From them is that which is pure slander, such as his words:
>
> From it, his statement that I invalidate the four juristic schools of thought, and that I say that for over six hundred years, the people are not upon anything, and

> that I claim *ijtihād* for myself, and that I am out of the realm of *taqlīd*, and that I say that the differences among the scholars is a punishment, and that I impute disbelief upon those who perform *tawassul* through the righteous, and that I impute disbelief upon al-Buṣayrī due to his statement: *O noblest of creation*, and that I say: if I was able to demolish the dome (over the grave) of the Messenger of Allah ﷺ, I would demolish it, and that if I was in authority over the Ka'ba, I would take the (golden) fount and (put in its place) a wooden fount, and that I forbid visitation of the grave of the Messenger of Allah ﷺ and that I deny visitation of the graves of (one's) parents and others, and that I impute disbelief upon those who swear by other than Allah. So, these are twelve issues, and my response to all of them is to say: ﴾Glorified are You, this is a manifest slander.﴿ (al-Nūr: 16)[215]

THE OPINION OF SHAYKH MUḤAMMAD B. 'ABD AL-WAHHĀB REGARDING THE GREEN DOME

As for the green dome, some have said that Shaykh Muḥammad b. 'Abd al-Wahhāb believed it should be removed and demolished. The Shaykh however—may Allah have mercy upon him—strongly rebuked that and negated it in numerous places in his writings. In the first part of his correspondence letter to the people of Qaṣīm he wrote:

> This is a brief summary of my creed that I composed under a busy schedule, in order that you may read it and see what views I hold. Allah is the Trustee over what we say. It is not hidden to you that it has reached me that Sulaymān b. Suhaym's letter reached you and that some of the people ascribed to knowledge among you have confirmed and believed its contents.
>
> Allah knows that this man has invented things against me that I have not said, most of which have never even crossed my mind.

[215] *Al-Rasā'il al-Shakhṣiyya*, 5:63.

> From them: That I impute disbelief upon the one who performs *tawassul* through the righteous, that I impute disbelief upon al-Buṣayrī due to his statement: *O noblest of creation*, and that I burn the (book) *Dalā'il al-Khayrāt*. My response to all of this is to say: "Glorified are you my Lord, this is a manifest slander." [216]

In another letter of his addressed to the people of 'Iraq that he sent to al-Suwaydī—an 'Irāqī scholar who had sent him a letter inquiring about what the people have said about him. He responded:

> ...Among those things are slander that any intelligent person would be ashamed to relate—much less make it up in the first place. Among these slanders are the ones you inquired about: that I declare all of the people disbelievers save the ones who follow me, that I claim their marriages are annulled. How amazing! How can this enter in the mind of any intelligent person? Does a Muslim or a non-Muslim, or a sane or insane person say this?
>
> Similar to this is their statement alleging that I said: "If I was able to demolish the dome of the Prophet ﷺ I would do so." As for what is attributed to me regarding the book *Dalā'il al-Khayrāt*, then there is a reason for that. I indicated this in my advice to the brethren saying that there should be no book that becomes more valuable in their hearts than the Book of Allah—thinking that reading such a book is more noble than reading the Qur'ān. As for burning it and forbidding others to send prayers upon the Prophet ﷺ in whatever expression it takes, then this claim is nothing but slander.[217]

This stance of Shaykh Muḥammad b. 'Abd al-Wahhāb is the exact display of wisdom, correctness, and legal oversight that is necessary for all scholars, Shaykhs, and guides to take when they command, forbid, exhort and guide others. The Shaykh—may Allah have mercy upon him—was extremely keen to negate the

---

[216] Ibid.
[217] Ibid.

false claims of the liars and to refute the view of the rabble rousers who attributed this wretched statement and vile opinion to him.

Due to its extreme danger, and the tribulations, evil and harm that it leads to that we do not need, you see him negating it in numerous places in his various writings.

How does this compare to the one whose view of the Islamic sciences was so narrow, that he found no other topic to write about or research except the issue of the Green Dome. How foolish he is indeed whose intellect leads him to that, and how stupid he is indeed whose knowledge leads him to that. We have a separate research dedicated to this topic, and we ask Allah that He makes its completion and publication easy with His assistance and bounty.

SAFEGUARDING THE PROPHETIC RELICS TAKEN FROM THE LETTER OF HIS MAJESTY KING FAHD B. 'ABD AL-'AZĪZ

This is a noble stance that deserves to be preserved and recorded for history's sake. Once, when his majesty, King Fahd b. 'Abd al-'Azīz was debriefed regarding the plans to expand the building of Mosque of al-Qubā', and it was shown that the original demarcations of the original structure would be removed, his majesty ordered the project to be cancelled until new plans were drawn up that would keep the original demarcations, the pulpit and prayer niche, and expand it from the left and right sides, and the back—all the while preserving the front part of the Mosque in its original structure, so the Muslims in the coming generations may know the original part of the Mosque and in order to preserve the noble Prophetic relics.

His majesty said: "It is good for us to *increase* the Mosques of Allah not to *decrease* them." This noble and lofty stance of his majesty left an indelible impression upon us, for it showed us his safeguarding of the historical Islamic sites. Details of this incident were reported in several Saudi newspapers. Among them: *al-Madīna* paper, and *al-Nadwa* (corresponding to the 17th of the month Safar, 1405 H.).

The Correct Understanding of Gathering

It is customary for us to gather together to commemorate several historical occasions, such as the birth of the Prophet ﷺ, the miraculous night journey (*al-isrā' wa al-mi'rāj*), the night of the fifteenth of (the month of) Sha'bān, the Prophet's ﷺ migration, commemorating the revelation of the Qur'ān, and the battle of Badr. We consider this to be a mere customary practice that has no connection with the religion—hence, it is neither to be described as being legislated or a *sunna*, nor does it go against a fundamental of the religion. The only danger is believing something to be legislated that is not so. It is my opinion that nothing is to be said regarding these customary practices more than saying they are beloved or detested acts to the Lawgiver—and I believe that this is agreed upon by all.

Some people claim these occasions that people attend to commemorate are lacking because of there being no agreed upon time for them. They say: "People are accustomed to gathering together on the twenty seventh in order to commemorate the miraculous night journey, or the twelfth of (the month) *Rabī' al-Awwal* to commemorate the Prophet's birth ﷺ—despite the fact that the scholars have not agreed upon the exact date of the two events." In response, I say: The disagreement regarding the precise dates is irrelevant because we do not believe that it is legislated to specify a precise time for the gathering. As we have mentioned, it is a customary matter only. What concerns us is seizing the opportunity found in the gathering to guide others to good. It is on these occasions that many people gather together. No matter if the people were correct or mistaken regarding the precise timing, their gathering together for the remembrance of Allah and love for the Messenger of Allah ﷺ is sufficient a cause for obtaining the mercy and bounty of Allah. I firmly believe that as long as the people are gathering for Allah's sake and by Allah, then it is acceptable to Allah, even if the people were mistaken in the precise timing of the event. To explain this, let me strike a similitude: Suppose that a man invites others to his wedding party on a particular day, and some of the invited guests arrive at his house early, mistakenly believing that the wedding party is at that time. Do you suppose that the host of the wedding party will kick them out and coldly and coarsely refuse them, saying: "Get out of here! This is not the right time for the wedding party to which you were invited?" Do you suppose that he will behave like this, or do you suppose that he will warmly welcome them and thank them for their visit, and open his door and invite them inside and then invite them once again to come at the correct time? This is what I imagine and it is befitting the bounty of Allah and His generosity.

When we come together and gather for the commemoration of the miraculous night journey, the Prophet's ﷺ birth, or any other historical occasion, it does not concern us if the time is exactly precise. If it so happens that our gathering corresponds to the correct time, then all praise belongs to Allah. If it does not, we believe that Allah will not throw us out or close His door from us. According to me, seizing the opportunity of such gatherings by supplicating, directing oneself to Allah ﷻ, being open to His Divine outpouring of grace, goodness, and blessings, is better than the benefit obtained from the mere occasion itself. Taking advantage of the people gathering together in order to remind them, guide them, advise them, and direct them to goodness is more appropriate than preventing them, turning them away, and censuring them for their gathering in a way that is worthless. It is observed time and time again that such behaviour has no benefit, rather, the people only increase in their desire and firmness (to attend these gatherings) with every time they are censured—so it is as if the one forbidding them from it is ordering them to attend whereas they perceive not. The intelligent ones from among the educated thinkers and inviters hope with all of their hearts to find a place wherein people gather together, so they may espouse their views and gain people to their side. It is for this reason you seem them frequenting clubs, associations, and general meeting places to gain supporters. We see the Umma gather together to commemorate several different occasions with desire and longing, so what is our duty with respect to them? For us to busy ourselves with censuring them and going back and forth regarding the legal ruling of their gathering is foolishness, nay it is ignorance and stupidity, because by this behaviour, we waste so many good opportunities that are not found in any other time outside of these occasions.

THE CORRECT UNDERSTANDING OF THE *MAWLID* CELEBRATION

Many people err in their understanding of the real nature of the *mawlid* celebration that we call to and encourage others to attend. They have many false conceptions of it that they use to base their issues and long winded arguments that waste their time and the time of their readers. All of their arguments are specious because they are based upon false premises.

We have written a great deal about the *mawlid* celebration and we have spoken about it on radio programs and general gatherings, so our views regarding the noble *mawlid* are clear. We say now as we have said before: Gathering for the sake of the *mawlid* celebration is a customary matter. It is not an act of worship in itself. This is what we believe and take as our religion with Allah. Whoever wishes to imagine the reality of the *mawlid* celebration as something else, then they may do so, for each person is only responsible for what he believes and no one else.

In every gathering and celebration we say: "This celebration and occasion is a customary matter. It is not an act of worship at all." After this, is there any room for someone to censure or oppose? The biggest catastrophe is the lack of proper understanding, as Imām al-Shāfiʿī said: "I have never debated a scholar except that I defeated him, and I have never debated an ignoramus except that he defeated me." The most novice student of knowledge knows the difference between that which is customary and that which is worship and the reality of the two. If someone says that something is an act of worship with its particular modality, we retort: "What is your proof?" If someone says that something is a customary act we say to him: "Do as you like, because the real danger and tribulation that we fear is that an innovated and unlegislated act is covered in the garment of worship—although it is only the product of someone's *ijtihād*. We are not pleased with this. We wage war against it and warn from it."

The upshot of all of this is that even if gathering for the commemoration of the *mawlid* is a customary act, it is nevertheless from the customary acts of goodness that are composed of various benefits for the people because they are composed of acts which, when taken individually, are found to be sought after and legislated.

Among the corrupt notions that some people have is that we call for the celebration of the *mawlid* on a specific night as opposed to other nights of the year. This simpleton does not realize that in both Mecca and Medina, gatherings in commemoration of the *mawlid* are held every day of the year and whenever someone has a celebration or special occasion. There is not a day or night that passes in Mecca and Medina, except that there is a gathering in commemoration of the *mawlid*—this occurs; whoever knows it, knows it, and whoever is ignorant of it, is ignorant of it.

Whoever claims that we only remember the Prophet ﷺ in one night only, and that we are heedless of him for the other 364 nights of the year, then he has invented a falsehood and come up with a grievous lie. By the bounty of Allah, these gatherings commemorating the *mawlid* of the Prophet ﷺ occur on every night of the year. Hardly a day or night passes, except that there is a gathering here, or a celebration there. We always say that to restrict *mawlid* gatherings to one night only is of the greatest of offenses to the Messenger ﷺ, and for this reason, the people accept our council in this regard and to Allah belongs all praise. Likewise, whoever claims that we restrict the commemoration of his *mawlid* ﷺ to the city of Medina only is either ignorant or feigning ignorance. There is nothing we can do for such a person besides asking Allah to give him insight and to uncover the veils of ignorance so he may see that the *mawlid* is not restricted to Medina or a particular night in a particular month—rather, it is general for every time and every place.

Nothing is valid in the intellect
If the bright day is in need of an apodictic proof

The upshot of all of this is that we do not say it is a *sunna* to celebrate the *mawlid* on a specific night. On the contrary, whoever believes that has innovated in the religion. Remembering him ﷺ, and being attached to him is obligatory at all times and it must fill the souls.

Of course, in the month of his birth there is a stronger motive for the people to hasten to its commemoration, gather together, and sense the Divine outpouring due to the anniversary. In such times, the people remember the past and their thoughts move from the present to the past.

These gatherings are of the best means of inviting unto Allah, and they are golden opportunities that should not be missed. It is a duty upon all scholars and callers unto Allah to remind the Umma of the Prophet ﷺ, his morals, etiquette, spiritual states, life, interactions, and worship. They must advise the Umma and guide them to goodness and success as well as warn them from sedition, innovation, evil, and tribulations.

It is by the grace of Allah that we invite to that and say to the people that the intent behind such gatherings is not gathering together for its own sake and for its outward trappings—rather, that is only a noble means to a noble goal. Whoever doesn't find benefit in his religion from these gatherings then he is deprived from the noble *mawlid*. We will not exhaustively mention all of the evidence, arguments, and proofs we have inferred in support of this issue. Readers may refer to my separate work on this subject titled: 'Concerning Celebration of the noble *mawlid*.' Here, we shall suffice with mentioning the story of Thuwayba's manumission because of all of the controversy surrounding it.

THE STORY OF THUWAYBA'S MANUMISSION

In the books of Ḥadīth and Prophetic biography, the scholars have mentioned the story of Abū Lahab freeing his female servant, Thuwayba after she informed him of the Prophet's ﷺ birth. The story mentions that al-'Abbās once saw Abū Lahab in a dream after his death and inquired about his state. Abū Lahab replied: "I have not found any good after you save that I am given drink due to setting Thuwayba free, and on every Monday, my punishment is lightened." I say: this report was narrated by a number of Imāms in Ḥadīth and Prophetic biography such as: Imām 'Abd al-Razzāq al-Ṣan'ānī, Imām al-Bukhārī, Ḥāfiẓ Ibn Ḥajar, Ḥāfiẓ Ibn Kathīr, Ḥāfiẓ al-Bayhaqī, Ibn Hishām, al-Suhaylī, Ḥāfiẓ al-Baghawī, Ibn al-Dayba', al-Ashkhar, and 'Āmirī.

Imām ʻAbd al-Razzāq al-Ṣanʻānī narrated it in his *Muṣannaf* (7/478). Imām al-Bukhārī narrated it in his *Ṣaḥīḥ* collection with his chain up to ʻUrwa b. al-Zubayr in *mursal* form in the ʻBook of Marriage, chapter: ʻRegarding Allah's Words: ﴾And your mothers that weaned you.﴿' As for Ibn Ḥajar, he mentioned it in *al-Fatḥ* and said:

> It was narrated by al-Ismāʻīlī from the route of al-Dhuhalī from Abū Yamān. It was also narrated from ʻAbd al-Razzāq from Maʻmar who said: "This Ḥadīth proves that righteous action may benefit a disbeliever in the next life, however it goes against the clear texts in the Qur'ān wherein Allah the Exalted said: ﴾And we bring them to that what they did and they find it as scattered dust particles.﴿" It has been retorted that this report is *mursal* by way of ʻUrwa who did not mention who narrated it to him. Given the possibility that the chain is intact, the actual contents of the report are the product of a dream and dreams are not considered evidence. Perhaps the one who narrated it had not yet embraced Islam at the time of seeing the dream—so it cannot be used as evidence.
>
> Secondly: even considering that it is accepted, it carries the possibility of being something that is unique for the Messenger of Allah ﷺ, as was mentioned with regard to the narration of Abū Ṭālib in which it states that his punishment was lightened and he was moved from the deepest flames to the shallowest of them. Al-Bayhaqī said: "What has been narrated regarding the disbelievers not possessing any good is understood to mean that they will not find any way out of the hell fire and nor will they enter Paradise. It is possible that the punishment that they deserve for their sins and crimes besides disbelief be lightened for them on account of good they previously did." As for ʻIyāḍ, he stated: "It is agreed upon by way of consensus, that the disbelievers will not benefit from their good actions or receive their rewards for them by way of delight or lightening of punishment—even if some of them shall receive more punishment than others."
>
> I say: This does not negate the possibility that al-Bayhaqī mentioned, for everything narrated on this subject has to do with the sin of disbelief. As for the sins

that are less than disbelief, what is to prevent their punishment being lightened on account of them? Al-Qurṭubī said: "This lightening is restricted to those explicitly mentioned in the texts." Ibn al-Munīr said in his gloss: There are two issues here:

"**One:** That which is impossible, namely, to consider the obedience of the disbeliever to be of benefit when coupled with his disbelief—this is because the condition for obedience is that it takes place with the correct intention, which is not found in the case of the disbeliever.

"**Two:** That the disbeliever, out of Allah's pure generosity, is rewarded for some good actions he did. This is not rationally impossible. Once this is established, Abū Lahab's manumission of Thuwayba is a strong circumstantial element (*qarīna*) that should be well considered.

"It is rationally possible for Allah to bestow His generosity upon him in any way He wills, just as He did with Abū Ṭālib. What is to be followed in this matter are the Divine texts, both in affirmation and negation."

I say: In supplement to this; the above mentioned generosity may be shown to the disbeliever who did a good act, and Allah knows best.[218]

As for Ḥāfiẓ Ibn Kathīr, he narrated the story in al-*Bidāya wa al-Nihāya* and commented: "...This is because when Thuwayba gave him the good news of the birth of his nephew: Muḥammad b. 'Abdullāh, he immediately freed her and on account of that act he was rewarded with this."[219]

As for Ḥāfiẓ Ibn Dayba' al-Shaybānī, the author of *Jāmi' al-Uṣūl*, he narrated the story in his biography of the Prophet ﷺ and commented: "I say: the lightening of his punishment is only in deference to the Prophet ﷺ, just as the punishment was lightened for Abū Ṭālib. So, it was for this reason, and not because he freed (Thuwayba), as the Exalted said: ﴿And he annulled their actions and what they did was void.﴾"[220]

---

218 *Fatḥ al-Bārī*, 9:145.

219 *Al-Sīra al-Nawawiyya*, 1:224.

220 *Ḥadā'iq al-Anwār fī al-Sīra*, 1:134.

As for Ḥāfiẓ al-Baghawī, he narrated it in *Sharḥ al-Sunna* (9/76). As for Imām al-ʿĀmirī, he narrated it in his work *Bahja al-Mahāfil*. Al-Ashkhar who wrote an explanation of this work said: "It has been said that this is unique for him out of deference to the Prophet ﷺ, just as Abū Ṭālib's punishment was lightened because of him. It has also been stated that there is nothing to prevent every disbeliever who did good works from having his punishment lightened."[221]

As for al-Suhaylī, he cited this story in *al-Rawḍ al-Anif* in his explanation of Ibn Hishām's Prophetic biography.

After citing it he said:

> So that benefited him even though he is in the fire, just as his brother Abū Ṭālib was benefited by his defence of the Messenger of Allah ﷺ, and as a consequence, he is the one with the lightest punishment in the fire. It has already preceded in the chapter on Abū Ṭālib that this benefit is only through the lightening of his punishment, for all of the good deeds of the disbelievers are invalid and there is no difference of opinion regarding that. This means namely that there are no good deeds on their scales and they will not enter Paradise on account of them.[222]

THE SUMMARY OF THIS RESEARCH

The upshot is that this story is well known in the books of Ḥadīth and Prophetic biography. It was cited by Ḥuffāẓ who were both relied upon and well considered. Al-Bukhārī's citing of this Ḥadīth in his *Ṣaḥīḥ* collection—which all agree on its rank and greatness—is sufficient to establish its authenticity. Everything within it that possesses a chain is authentic without dispute. Even the *muʿallaq* and *mursal* reports in it do not leave the fold of acceptable reports and enter into the realm of rejected narrations. This is known by the scholars who busy themselves with the science of Ḥadīth and its nomenclature: those who know

---

[221] *Sharḥ al-Bahja*, 1:41.

[222] *Al-Rawḍ al-Anif*, 5:192.

the meaning of *mu'allaq* and *mursal* and their ruling if they appear in the *Ṣaḥīḥ* collection.

If you wish, you may read more about this in the *Alfiyya* of al-Suyūṭī and al-'Irāqī with their accompanying commentaries, as well as in *Tadrīb al-Rāwī*. In these works, they mentioned this issue and explained the value of the *mu'allaq* and *mursal* reports found in the *Ṣaḥīḥ* collection and explained that they are acceptable according to the verifying scholars.

In addition to this, this issue is related to virtuous traits, miracles, and virtuous actions that the scholars mention in the works dealing with the unique characteristics and biography. They are somewhat relaxed when it comes to citing reports of this nature and they do not stipulate that each report is *ṣaḥīḥ* as is understood in Ḥadīth nomenclature. If we were to stipulate such an odd condition it would not be possible for us to cite anything in the Prophetic biographies that relate to the Prophet ﷺ before he was entrusted with the Message. In the books of the Ḥuffāẓ—those who are the reliable pillars in this science, from whom we have come to know what is allowable to mention and what is not regarding Ḥadīth—we find them filled with narrations with severed chains and *mursal* reports, along with reports narrated from soothsayers and their likes on the topic of the Prophet's unique characteristics. These are permissible to mention in such circumstances.

As for the one who says that this report contradicts the words of Allah: ﴾And We brought them to what they did and made their actions as dust scattered in the wind.﴿ This view is rejected based on what we previously quoted from the scholars.

The decisive word on this matter is to state that this Qur'ānic verse proves that the deeds of the disbelievers are not looked at. This verse does not imply that all disbelievers share in equal punishment and that some of them cannot have their punishment lightened, as is affirmed by the scholars.

Similarly, the consensus cited by 'Iyāḍ is with respect to the generality of the disbelievers. Nowhere does it imply that Allah cannot lighten the punishment of some of the disbelievers on account of a good action they did. It is for this reason Allah created the hell Fire (*jahannam*) in multiple descending levels, where the hypocrites are in the lowest level therein.

In addition to this, the consensus goes against a clear-cut decisive and authentic text, and no consensus is valid if it contradicts a clear-cut text, as is known to all students. It is established in the *Ṣaḥīḥ* collection of al-Bukhārī that the Messenger of Allah ﷺ was asked: "Did you benefit Abū Ṭālib with anything, for he used to protect you and defend you?" He replied: "I found him in a deep portion of the fire and I took him out to a shallower portion."

This is Abū Ṭālib who was benefited through his defence of the Prophet ﷺ. For that reason, the Prophet ﷺ took him out of the deep portion of the fire to a shallower portion. Hence, the lightening of punishment given to Abū Lahab is similar to this and there is nothing objectionable in that. This Ḥadīth shows that the Qur'ānic verse is regarding the one who possessed no actions that would call for his punishment to be lightened. In a similar way, the reported consensus is to be understood.

In the Ḥadīth of Abū Ṭālib there is clear evidence that the Prophet ﷺ interacts with the creation both now and before the Day of Judgement in matters related to the next life, and that he intercedes with those who defend him and are attached to him.

As for the one who says that this report is a dream and dreams are not sufficient to establish legal rulings, we say that this person—may Allah guide him to what is correct—has not distinguished between legal rulings and other matters. As for legal rulings, there does in fact exist a difference of opinion among the jurists regarding the question: is it permissible to extract legal rulings and authenticate reports from dreams of the Prophet ﷺ or not? When it comes to relying upon dreams for other matters unrelated to the above (legal rulings or authentication of reports), then there is nothing blameworthy in it. The Ḥuffāẓ have relied upon dreams and mentioned such reports of the dreams seen by the people in the pre-Islamic time of ignorance (*jāhiliyya*) giving warning of a Messenger who will eradicate paganism and the corruption in which they were involved. The books of the Sunna are filled with such reports.

At the forefront of such books is the book *Dalā'il al-Nubuwwa*. The scholars considered such dreams to be *irhāṣāt* (miracles shown before the advent of a Prophet), and there is no problem in inferring such things from dreams, otherwise, the scholars would not have mentioned these reports in the first place.

The one who says that the dream of al-'Abbās is not evidence and that it cannot establish a ruling or be used as a report has departed from the established practice of the Ḥuffāẓ and others. His only motive is to browbeat his opponent and this is not the proper way an objective researcher should go about seeking the truth. His affair is left to Allah.

As for the one who says that al-'Abbās saw this dream while in a state of disbelief and that the testimony and report of a disbeliever is unacceptable—then his statement is rejected. There is not the slightest fragrance of knowledge emanating from this statement. It is clearly false because no one said that dreams are in the same category as testimony. Dreams are nothing more than glad tidings and they are not stipulated by faith or religion. On the contrary, Allah mentioned the miracle of Yūsuf ﷺ when he interpreted the dream of the king—who was a pagan not knowing any heavenly religion in the first place. Notwithstanding his paganism, Allah made his dream a sign of Yūsuf's Prophethood and virtue and mentioned it in his story. If such dreams do not prove Prophethood, then Allah would not have mentioned it because it was the dream of a pagan idol worshipper that contains no benefit in either supporting or opposing something. For this reason, the scholars mention that the disbeliever may see Allah in his dreams in a manner that communicates warning, censure and rebuke to him.

What is utterly and completely amazing is that this person says al-'Abbās saw this dream while in a state of disbelief and that the disbelievers' testimonies and reports are not accepted. This statement show their utter lack of knowledge in the science of Ḥadīth, for it is affirmed in the works of Ḥadīth nomenclature that if a companion or anyone else carries a Ḥadīth while in a state of disbelief, and thereafter narrates that report after they embrace Islam, then that report is accepted from them and acted upon. For examples of this, see the books of Ḥadīth nomenclature, so you may see the vast distance between the one who holds this strange view and real knowledge. It is only vain desires that motivate such a person to enter into that which he is not qualified to enter into.

Conclusion

This is what has been made easy for us to write concerning these topics in which we wanted to clarify our understandings and views. Whatever is correct, then to Allah belongs all praise. Whatever is other than that, then know that I am a mere human; I am correct and I err. All of us may have our statement accepted or rejected except for the Divinely protected and infallible Master ﷺ who does not speak from his own desires—rather only speaking that which is Divinely revealed. I seek refuge with Allah from vain disputes, argumentation and bickering, and I seek refuge with Allah from knowledge that does not benefit, supplications that are not answered, and a heart that is not submissively humble. I seek refuge with Allah from every evil, wrong, affliction, paganism, and innovation, and I openly disavow myself from that which the Messenger of Allah ﷺ disavowed himself from and I testify and have conviction in that to which he testified.

I ask Allah to make me firm with that until I die upon it as a Muslim, singling Him out in worship, and believing in Allah; in the lands of Allah; among the believers and monotheists who have witnessed that there is no god but Allah and that Muḥammad is the Messenger of Allah since the time Muḥammad b. 'Abdullāh ﷺ brought the message and followed by his companions, followers and their followers from the pious predecessors—may Allah be pleased with them all. May I die under the shade of the Imāms of *tawḥīd* and the callers to goodness from amongst our noble government—may Allah give them success in giving victory to the truth and bringing good to the lands and the servants under their reign—and all praise it to Allah the Lord of all the worlds. May Allah send His prayers and peace upon our Master Muḥammad, and upon his family and companions.

—Written and dictated by Muḥammad b. 'Alawī b. 'Abbās, the Mālikī in his juristic school, the Salafī in creed, Meccan in domicile, and Ḥasanī in lineage—may Allah pardon him, the servant of knowledge in the two Sacred Sanctuaries.

Appendix I

بسم الله الرحمن الرحيم

Responses and Replies to Certain Incorrect Notions

Shaykh Muḥammad ʿAlawī's statement (p.78): "This was reported by al-Ḥākim in his *al-Mustadrak* who authenticated it."

When al-Ḥākim says that a Ḥadīth has a rigorously authentic chain, it indicates that he has declared it rigorously authentic. He mentioned this in the beginning of his *al-Mustadrak*, in which he took it upon himself to cite what is rigorously authentic. So, whatever it contains is rigorously authentic according to his conditions, and thus, it is permissible for one quoting him to say "authenticated by al-Ḥākim." Furthermore, it is established in the science of the fundamentals of Ḥadīth that when a reliable Ḥadīth master (Ḥāfiẓ) rules a chain to be rigorously authentic, it is permissible to apply that to the Ḥadīth text (*matn*) as well, even if there is no inherent link between the two.

In his *Alfiyya* in Ḥadīth nomenclature, al-ʿIrāqī said:

> And judging a chain to be authentic or good without judging the text has been reported. If it is applied unrestrictedly, those who are relied upon have accepted it if they did not follow it up with criticizing its weakness.

Al-Suyūṭī said in his *Alfiyya*:

> And judging a chain as authentic or good as opposed to the text is for the people of critique. Due to a hidden defect or an irregularity. And judge the main text [as authentic or good] if a Ḥadīth master uses a general expression.

Al-Suyūṭī also said in *Ṭal'a al-Anwār*: "And accept it if one who is relied upon judges the chain as authentic or good."

The scholars of Ḥadīth who cited from al-Ḥākim said: "It was authenticated by al-Ḥākim," such as al-Qasṭalānī, al-Zurqānī, and al-Subkī. This illustrates that it is a well known usage found in the methodology of many scholars of Ḥadīth.

Shaykh Muḥammad 'Alawī's statement (p.78): "[Narrated by] Ḥāfiẓ al-Suyūṭī in his *Khaṣā'iṣ* who authenticated it,..."

Al-Suyūṭī mentioned this Ḥadīth in his Qur'ānic exegesis, *al-Durr al-Manthūr*, as well as in *al-Khaṣā'iṣ* and *al-Riyāḍ al-Anīfa fī Sharḥ Asmā' Khayr al-Khalīqa*. On p.49 of his latter work, al-Suyūṭī said: "This was narrated by al-Ḥākim in *al-Mustadrak* and was authenticated by al-Bayhaqī in *Dalā'il al-Nubuwwa*." Al-Suyūṭī said that it was a lone narration (*tafarrud*) from 'Abd al-Raḥmān who is weak. In his *Khaṣā'iṣ*, he cited a supporting narration from Ibn 'Abbās and said: "This was narrated by al-Ḥākim and authenticated by him." As for al-Suyūṭī's statement in *Manāhil al-Ṣafā* that it is weak, he meant that it was weak from the route of Ibn 'Umar, as he explicitly stated: "Narrated by Ibn 'Umar with a weak chain." So the upshot of this is that the Ḥadīth is rigorously authentic when taking into consideration its multiple chains and supporting narrations.

Shaykh Muḥammad 'Alawī's statement (p.78): "[Narrated by] al-Bayhaqī..."

After narrating it he said: "It was singularly reported from 'Abd al-Raḥmān b. Zayd who is weak." The author did not quote [al-Bayhaqī's] exact words; rather, he sufficed himself with mentioning the summary of what al-Bayhaqī said afterwards, in which he mentioned the different opinions regarding the strength of the Ḥadīth. This is more than enough to dispel any ill suspicions toward the author in his citations.

Shaykh Muḥammad 'Alawī's statement (p.78): "It was also authenticated by al-Qasṭalānī, and al-Zurqānī..."

Al-Qasṭalānī authenticated it in numerous places in his book *al-Mawāhib*. His final citation of it is found in 2:392, in the Dār al-Kutub al-'Ilmiyya edition. This illustrates the error of the one who claims that al-Qasṭalānī did not authenticate it.

As for al-Zurqānī, he authenticated it in several places in his commentary on *al-Mawāhib* and from multiple routes. Al-Zurqānī mentioned it after citing the narration in which Abū Ja'far asked Imām Mālik about facing the grave of the Prophet during supplication, to which Mālik said: "And why would you turn your face from he who is your means and the means of your father Ādam ﷺ unto Allah the Exalted on the Day of Judgement?" Al-Zurqānī said [regarding the Ḥadīth of Ādam's *tawassul*]: "This was narrated by al-Qāḍī 'Iyāḍ in his *Shifā* with a chain without problem; nay, it has been said that it is rigorously authentic." (*Sharḥ al-Mawāhib*: 8:314)

Note al-Zurqānī's comment on the Ḥadīth of Ibn 'Abbās: "This contains a strong supporting narration. It was authenticated by al-Ḥākim and supported by al-Subkī in *Shifā al-Siqām* and by al-Bulqīnī in his *Fatāwā*. Such things cannot be said on the basis of mere opinion, so the ruling is that it is a raised (*marfū'*) narration." There are other places that testify that this was al-Zurqānī's opinion from beginning to end and that he called to it and aided it.

Shaykh Muḥammad 'Alawī's statement (p.78) regarding the disagreement over the strength of this Ḥadīth.

This is the meaningful summary that has gathered the research from all angles and given it the correct ruling that is far from every type of desire and bigotry. Some of those who have written on this topic missed the mark. They did not take notice of this summary that illustrates the author's fairness and trustworthiness in the field of knowledge, and his distance from all forms of deception and concealment. He clearly explained and stated that there is disagreement regarding this Ḥadīth. By his statement, the author repelled the words of those who went about speaking on the men in the Ḥadīth and its chain, as if to make it seem to their readers that the author intentionally neglected to mention those facts, for the sake of deceiving the people and saying that the Ḥadīth is rigorously authentic by agreement.

The author has a detailed and research and deep study of this Ḥadīth, so may Allah give him the best of rewards on behalf of Islam and its people.

Shaykh Muḥammad 'Alawī's statement (p.79): "This proves that according to Ibn Taymiyya, the Ḥadīth is suitable for using as evidence."

Some have arrogantly refused and denied this assertion. They say: "Ibn Taymiyya said the Ḥadīth was fabricated." This could be correct, however here, in this citation, Ibn Taymiyya mentioned two Ḥadīth reports, used both as supporting evidence, and used them to explain authentic Ḥadīth and strengthen his own words. He was explicit in this, so was Shaykh al-Islam, the masterful scholar of Ḥadīth and knower of its principles, ignorant of the fact that it is impermissible to use a false or fabricated Ḥadīth as a supporting evidence, a follow up narration, or to explain [other reports], or be used as a supporting narration—even if he quoted it with its chain in full? Glorified are You O Lord, this is manifest slander!

Some went out of their way to find false interpretations for what Ibn Taymiyya did, but all of that was contrived and never would a fair student of knowledge cling to such interpretations. The truth of the matter is that someone citing a Ḥadīth in any place or circumstance is proof that the Ḥadīth in question is suitable for that, and it follows that such a person is not to be rebuked or held in contempt. If he cites a Ḥadīth in one place and in another place says that it is fabricated, then this indicates either a contradiction or a change in independent scholarly judgement (*ijtihād*). If it is shown to be a contradiction, then both views [of the person] are void. If it is shown to be a change in independent scholarly judgement, then neither of the two views is given precedence over the other because it is not know which of the two views came first or last. What concerns us here is that the author was correct in what he mentioned regarding Ibn Taymiyya's words. As for whether there was a contradiction, then that is left for another research.

Shaykh Muḥammad 'Alawī's reference to al-Bayhaqī and Ibn Kathīr (p.97).

See how the author mentioned that it was cited by al-Bayhaqī and did not say that he authenticated it. This is the peak of fairness. In addition to this, see how he said: "It was mentioned by Ibn Kathīr in *al-Bidāya wa al-Nihāya.*" On p.78, he added that Ibn Kathīr did not judge that it was fabricated. Anyone possessing the slightest familiarity with the science of Ḥadīth knows what this means. Here, the author's fairness and scholarly integrity are made clear. He mentioned here and elsewhere throughout the book that there is disagreement over this Ḥadīth.

Shaykh Muḥammad 'Alawī's statement (p.87): "Ibn 'Abbās said: 'The Jews of Khaybar were fighting the tribe of Ghatfān. When they met in battle, the Jews were defeated so the Jews supplicated with this supplication: "Indeed we ask You by the right of the unlettered Prophet..." ' "

This statement of Ibn 'Abbās is well-known in the relied upon books of Qur'ānic exegesis. It was cited by the Imāms of Qur'ānic exegesis from the reliable scholars of Ḥadīth such as Ibn Abī Ḥātim, al-Ṭabarī, al-Baghawī, al-Ālūsī, and al-Shawkānī. It was also cited by Ibn Kathīr in *al-Bidāya* without objection. This narration is acceptable in Qur'ānic exegesis—especially in the circumstances behind revelation (*asbāb al-nuzūl*). It was narrated by al-Bayhaqī in *Dalā'il al-Nubuwwa,* and he did not narrated fabrications, as he mentioned in his introduction.

Shaykh Muḥammad 'Alawī's statement (p.89): "Al-Mundhirī said: 'It was narrated by al-Ṭabarānī, and he said after mentioning it: "It is *ḥasan ṣaḥīḥ*." ' "

Ḥāfiẓ al-Mundhirī said in *al-Targhīb wa al-Tarhīb*: "After mentioning its routes of transmission, al-Ṭabarānī said: 'The Ḥadīth is rigorously authentic.' " This clearly shows that al-Ṭabarānī authenticated the Ḥadīth from all of its routes which were cited, which also includes the route mentioning the story. According to him, it was authentic and without criticism. The narrator of both the story and the Ḥadīth is one individual: 'Uthmān b. Ḥunayf. Al-Ḥākim also authenticated the story.

He said: "This was followed up with Shubayb b. Sa'īd from Rawḥ b. al-Qāsim with additional wordings in the text and chain. The statement within it is Shubayb's; he is reliable and trustworthy." (*al-Mustadrak*: 1:526) I say: al-Dhahabī did not object to this in any way, hence it is also his tacit approval as well. One scholar has written an essay on this Ḥadīth, its routes of transmission, and its story, and called it: *al-Manār al-Munīf fī Ḥadīth 'Uthmān b. Ḥunayf*. It is currently being published.

Shaykh Muḥammad 'Alawī's statement (p.106): "And the remaining people in the chain are narrators found in the authentic collections (of al-Bukhārī and Muslim)."

This is the author's own extrapolation from al-Haythamī's words regarding the Ḥadīth. This illustrates the peak of fairness and dispels the notions of those who claimed that the author attributed the authentication to al-Haythamī. Rawḥ b. Ṣalāḥ was declared reliable by Abū Ḥātim and Ibn Ḥibbān. Ibn Ḥibbān was from the rank of the scholars of Ḥadīth about whom al-Dhahabī mentioned: "If any of them declare someone reliable (*thiqa*) you should grasp his statement with your molar teeth." This was mentioned in al-Dhahabī's essay: *A Mention of Those Whose Statements are Relied Upon in Criticism and Praise* [of Ḥādīth narrators], printed with the checking of Shaykh 'Abd al-Fattāḥ Abū Ghudda. The conclusion is that there is no contradiction in the author's citation from al-Haythamī, rather the contradiction is in the comprehension of the critic.

Shaykh Muḥammad 'Alawī's statement (p.106): "It was also narrated by Ibn 'Abd al-Barr from Ibn 'Abbās, and Ibn Abī Shayba from Jābir. It was also narrated by al-Daylamī..."

He meant that they narrated the original story. This is not deception on his part. This is the way of the scholars of Ḥadīth in narration and citation, as was done by the authors of the *Mustakhrajāt* [collections in which the compiler adds newer chains to previously collected narrations]. This topic is long and detailed in the books of Ḥadīth nomenclature. The author explained the words of al-Haythamī regarding the Ḥadīth and that it contains Rawḥ b. Ṣalāḥ, so he fulfilled his duty. It was said by some that this Ḥadīth was narrated from other routes that do not contain this supplication and that it is only found in this route. This however, is not a defect (*'illa*), because additional wordings are neither strange nor rejected. Supplication with this meaning [found in this narration] has been cited in many other Ḥadīth reports, such as the Ḥadīth of 'Uthmān b. Ḥunayf, which the Ḥadīth masters concurred upon its authenticity. A supplication with a similar meaning is also found in the Ḥadīth of Abū Sa'īd al-Khudrī: "...by the right of those who ask..." This was mentioned by Ḥāfiẓ Ibn Taymiyya in *al-Kalim al-Ṭayyib*. The Ḥadīth: "...I ask You by the right of this walking of mine..." is another example. It was mentioned by Muḥammad b. 'Abd al-Wahhāb in *Ādab al-Mashī ilā al-Ṣalāt*.

The Ḥādīth of Abū Sa'īd al-Khudrī: "O Allah, I ask You by the right upon You of those who ask." (p.107)
This Ḥadīth was quoted by Muḥammad b. 'Abd al-Wahhāb in *Ādab al-Mashī ilā al-Ṣalāt* and he encouraged its use. After Ibn Khuzayma's declaration that this Ḥadīth is rigorously authentic and good, and being followed by others, all the way to the Imām of invitation—may Allah have mercy upon them all—there is nothing left for the objectors to say. May Allah grant us safety from misunderstandings.

Shaykh Muḥammad 'Alawī's statement (p.111): "Ibn Ḥajar said: 'Its chain is authentic.' "
Some have claimed that this is a lie and that Ibn Ḥajar did not authenticate the chain. This objection is high-handed and bereft of good manners. This is obvious to whoever refers back to Ibn Ḥajar's words in *al-Fatḥ*. The critic, however, was hasty and missed what was said in the beginning. Ibn Ḥajar authenticated the report before that and said: "It was narrated by Ibn Abī Shayba with a rigorously authentic chain..."

After mentioning the story in full, Ibn Ḥajar said:

> Sayf narrated in *al-Futūḥ* that the one who saw the aforementioned dream was one of the companions, Bilāl b. al-Ḥārith.

So, both the story and the chain are one, and both are rigorously authentic.

Ibn Ḥajar's statement that the chain is rigorously authentic is a slap in the face the one who claims that Ibn Ḥajar did not authenticate the report. The opponent wished to infer that Ibn Ḥajar declared the report weak, but would that he had followed up on Ibn Ḥajar's views on these matters. Ibn Ḥajar supported *tawassul* and undertaking journeys to visit the Beloved Chosen One ﷺ. Ibn Ḥajar's statement that the chain is rigorously authentic also includes the Ḥadīth text as we explained earlier—even if it is denied by those who do not possess knowledge in this science.

A MANIFEST ERROR FROM SOME OF THOSE WHO POSSESS INCORRECT NOTIONS

One of them claimed that the report authenticated by Ibn Ḥajar is in fact weak because its chain contains al-'Amash who is *mudallis* [conceals the name of the one on whose authority he narrates]. In response we say: How would the critic know that al-'Amash was *mudallis*, if not for Ibn Ḥajar and his books such as *al-Taqrīb wa al-Tadhīb* and others? This is such an obvious example of contradiction regarding Ḥāfiẓ Ibn Ḥajar; defending him one moment and critiquing him the next! Furthermore, this critic made a huge blunder that is not fitting for the novice students of this science, much less those who put themselves forward to authenticate and weaken Ḥadīth reports. The critic said that this Ḥadīth contains al-'Amash from Abū Ṣāliḥ al-Samān, and that it is agreed that al-'Amash was *mudallis*, and that the report of a reliable *mudallis* is not accepted unless he explicitly mentions from who he heard the report. Unfortunately, the critic neglected to mention that this principle is general, save for those excluded by the scholars, especially those who [are known to] both mention and conceal the name of their narrator, such as Ibn al-Musayyib, and like al-'Amash here.

This was clarified by Ḥāfiẓ al-Dhahabī in *Mīzān al-'Itidāl:*

I say: he conceals (*yudallis*), and perhaps he conceals someone who was weak whilst not knowing. Hence, whenever he says: "He narrated to us..." there is no problem, whereas if he says: "From..." there is a possibility of concealment, except from his Shaykhs from whom he took frequently, such as Ibrāhīm b. Abī Wā'il and Abū Ṣāliḥ al-Samān. His narrations in this manner are considered to be fully connected.

Shaykh Muḥammad 'Alawī's statement (p.112): "Ḥāfiẓ Ibn Kathīr mentioned that the rallying cry of the Muslims at the battle of Yamāma was: 'O Muḥammad' (*Yā Muḥammadā*)."
Some criticized this issue, claiming that issues of doctrine and *tawḥīd* cannot be taken from historical works, but this is fallacious reasoning. Shaykh al-Islam Muḥammad b. 'Abd al-Wahhāb clarified in his legal verdicts that *tawassul* is an issue of jurisprudence and not doctrine.

Shaykh Muḥammad 'Alawī's statement regarding the story of al-'Utbī (p.118): "It was narrated..."
This is correct and there is nothing wrong with it. The statement "narrated" is used for everything cited by the scholars, be it Ḥadīth, reports, or narrations that are *marfū'* (raised), *mawqūf* (stopped), or *munqaṭi'* (severed). This is the practice of the scholars; however, none know this but its people. Some opponents claimed that "the word 'narrated' can only be said for one who narrated a Ḥadīth and mentioned its chain from his Shaykhs to its end." We have no idea from where they got this principle which has no basis or precedent. It is well known to the scholars that the fundamentals are not through independent scholarly effort or invention.

Moreover, the scholars have narrated many reports and mentioned them in their written works without chains, such as the *mu'allaq* narrations of al-Bukhārī and the dissevered and attached (*balaghāt*) narrations of the *Muwaṭṭā'*. Some of these narrations are without the first part of their chains; others among them are without chains all together. With that, however, people say regarding them: "Narrated by al-Bukhārī" and "Narrated by Mālik." This is how al-Nawawī wrote in his book *al-Adhkār*.

Shaykh Muḥammad 'Alawī's collection of the names of scholars who believed in *tawassul* (p.143-144).

In this chapter, Shaykh Muḥammad 'Alawī gathered the names of many scholars who believed in *tawassul*. After mentioning each name, he mentioned the source for their view, cited explicitly by them, or implicitly. This is an extrapolation from the author and independent judgement in its appropriate place. It would have been deception on his part had he just mentioned the scholar's names without showing the source of their statements. May Allah be pleased with fairness and may He protect us from ignorance and bigotry.

Moreover, this extrapolation is correct according to the author and those who agree with him, because according to the critic, *tawassul* is an issue of doctrine, so how could those Imāms cite the Ḥadīth of Ādam's *tawassul* and the Ḥadīth of al-'Utbī, both of which prove *tawassul* and explicitly call to it, and encourage it? How could those Imāms cite such things without forbidding them and how could they not warn from them in their appropriate place? That is either negligence on their part (Allah forbid), or it is indicative of their approval—the latter being the view of the author. These quotes are authentic and established in their proper places from those who said them. The author has a separate essay concerning *tawassul* in which he presents the texts and statements of the scholars in detail.

Many of those same scholars whom the critic sought to use in criticism of the Ḥadīth reports on *tawassul*, were themselves believers in *tawassul* and carried its banner and defended it, such as al-Qāḍī 'Iyāḍ, al-Suyūṭī, Ibn Ḥajar, al-Qasṭalānī, al-Zurqānī, and al-Khafājī. The critic fell into a clear and inexcusable error when he denied this from al-Nawawī, al-Khafājī, and al-Qasṭalānī.

As for al-Nawawī, he explicitly mentioned it in his book *al-Īḍāḥ*, printed in a large size twenty-four font. Nay, he ordered the visitor to perform *tawassul* and seek intercession from the possessor of the praiseworthy station ﷺ. What lie is more ugly than this denial by the critic? As for al-Khafājī, he explicitly mentioned it and authenticated the Ḥadīth. He said: "It is rigorously authentic." (*Nasīm al-Riyāḍ*: 3:398) As for al-Qasṭalānī, he explicitly mentioned it in a special chapter and vigorously defended *tawassul* with all the means in his disposal.

(*al-Mawāhib*: 2:392 Dār al-Kitāb edition) In this hasty research, we are unable to cover all of the details. We only wished to provide some examples that emphasize the truth of what we call to and believe in and illustrate the falsehood of what is propagated by the opponents.

Shaykh Muḥammad 'Alawī's statement (p.166): "It is also the view of Abū al-Ḥasan al-Dāraquṭnī who said about it in some of his poetry: '*Do not deny that he is seated and do not deny that he shall be seated.*' "

Undoubtedly, this citation is correct according to those who believe in it, however we believe that the author only cited this narration to illustrate the laxity of some of the Imāms in Ḥadīth in quoting reports about the unique Prophetic characteristics. Allah forbid that the author, our brother, the 'Allāma al-Mālikī believes this. Having said this, in his annotation of [al-Subkī's] *al-Sayf al-Ṣaqīl*, Shaykh Muḥammad Zāhid al-Kawtharī denied the ascription of this report to al-Dāraquṭnī, as did Muḥammad Nāṣir al-Dīn al-Albānī in his summary and annotation of al-Dhahabī's book, *al-'Ulū*. He [al-Albānī] said: "This is a lie against al-Dāraquṭnī."

Shaykh Muḥammad 'Alawī's mentioning of the reports about seeking blessings from the Prophet ﷺ (p.185 and onwards).

These reports clearly establish and prove that the blessings of the Prophet ﷺ can transfer from his person to other concrete objects. These reports also show the people's efforts and keenness to obtain those blessings: from a hand that touched him, a container from which he drank, a mouthpiece of a water skin where he placed his mouth, dirhams touched by his hand, a cloak that he wore, and a place in which he stood for prayer and placed his feet. All of these details are explained in their appropriate place. The point behind all of this is to show that his blessings ﷺ transferred from his noble person to other concretes without distinction between them. This includes places and times without doubt. The clearest proof for this is found in the Ḥadīth of 'Utbān b. Mālik who requested that the Prophet ﷺ pray in his place so he could pray there as well.

The lovers see nothing from that save a request for blessings from Allah in the place in which the Chosen One ﷺ prayed. This is the meaning of seeking blessings from his places. Those who do not love the blessings of the Prophet ﷺ have different interpretations for this report, all of which are false and corrupt. We seek refuge in Allah from that. Listen to the words of the ʻAllāma and scholar of Ḥadīth, the jurist and Shaykh of the scholars of his epoch, Imām al-Nawawī. He said in his commentary upon this Ḥadīth: "There are many benefits to be found in this Ḥadīth of ʻUtbān. Among them: seeking blessings from the righteous and their personal effects, praying in the places in which they prayed, and seeking blessings from them." (*Sharḥ Ṣaḥīḥ Muslim*: 5/161, see also: *ʻUmda al-Qārī* of al-ʻAynī and *ʻAwn al-Bārī* of Shaykh Ṣiddīq Ḥasan Khān)

Shaykh Muḥammad ʻAlawī's statement (p.231): "Ḥāfiẓ al-ʻIrāqī said in the book of funerals in *al-Tathrīb fī Sharḥ al-Taqrīb*: 'Its chain is good.' "

Al-ʻIrāqī said this in his *Ṭarḥ al-Tathrīb* (3:297). In his Ḥadīth verification of *al-Iḥyā'* he said: "It was narrated by al-Bazzār from the Ḥadīth of Ibn Masʻūd and its men are men of the *Ṣaḥīḥ* collection except for ʻAbd al-Majīd b. Rawād who, even though he was mentioned by Muslim and was declared reliable by Ibn Maʻīn and al-Nasā'ī, was still weakened by many."

This contradicts what he said in *Ṭarḥ al-Tathrīb*, which is more reliable because it is one of his final works, which shows that al-ʻIrāqī's final judgement is his relied upon view. The ʻAllāma and Ḥadīth master, Shaykh Abū al-Faḍl ʻAbdullāh al-Ghumārī authored a separate essay on this issue. He titled it: *Nihāya al-Āmāl fī Ṣiḥḥa wa Sharḥ Ḥadīth ʻArḍ al-ʻAmāl.*

Shaykh Muḥammad ʻAlawī's statement regarding the disagreement of the scholars of Medina about seeking blessings from places (p.256)

This shows the peak of fairness from the author, for he truthfully and faithfully cited the words of the scholars concerning this issue and clarified those who allowed it and those who did not.

What remains after that is declaring the more preponderant of the two views according to independent scholarly judgement (*ijtihād*). Some of the critics closed their eyes and pretended not to notice this fairness and these quotes. They sought to change words from their proper places in order to mislead people into thinking that the author either neglected to mention them or feigned ignorance of them in order to aid his opinion—an opinion held by him and the majority of the Umma who seek blessings from the Master of the Messengers ﷺ, his personal relics, and the places which he visited. Regrettably, this is a prejudice against the way of truth and a detraction from scholarly integrity.

APPENDIX II

COMMENDATIONS BY VARIOUS ISLAMIC SCHOLARS

بسم الله الرحمن الرحيم

COMMENDATION BY THE GREAT SCHOLAR, JURIST AND HISTORIAN, SHAYKH MUḤAMMAD AL-KHAZRAJĪ, MINISTER OF JUSTICE, ISLAMIC AFFAIRS AND ENDOWMENTS, UNITED ARAB EMIRATES

All praise belongs to Allah, He of all laud and munificence, He who favours His servants as He wills; and I send prayers and peace upon the Best of the Prophets, and upon his noble family and companions.

I have examined the book that the great, diligent and noble scholar, Sayyid Muḥammad b. ʻAlawī al-Mālikī al-Ḥasanī, branch of the Prophetic tree, and scion of the Hāshimī line, has compiled, authored, and named *Notions That Must Be Corrected.*

In this work, the author has told things as they are, avoiding any kind of bias or impartiality on either side. He has corrected many dubious notions, and offered advice to his Muslim brethren, supported by sound arguments and decisive proofs, in order that they might follow in the footsteps of their righteous predecessors, and abide by the example of the virtuous people who came before them.

The book is concerned with three issues: areas of research that pertain to doctrine, areas of research that pertain to the Prophet ﷺ, and areas of research that pertain to the Isthmus (*barzakh*) life, and the legality of undertaking visitation and celebrating religious occasions. The Muslim community today is in dire need of sound knowledge of the issues that these researches cover; for much confusion has arisen concerning them, and too often have legal opinions been issued concerning them by ignorant people, who are lacking in understanding of the Book of Allah ﷻ and the principles of the Prophetic Sunna.

Now detailed clarification has come, so that they might avoid the pitfalls of misguidance, and become fine examples of those who have been granted Divine grace, in their words and their deeds. I ask Allah to bless the author with His kindness, and His support, and to keep and protect him.

May Allah bless our Master Muḥammad, and his family and companions and may He send peace upon all Messengers; and all praise belongs to Allah, the Lord of the worlds!

Muḥammad b. al-Shaykh Aḥmad b. al-Shaykh Ḥasan al-Khazrajī
Minister of Justice, Islamic Affairs and Endowments, United Arab Emirates
President of the Committee of Artefacts and History
Former Qāḍī of Abu Dhabi
United Arab Emirates

Commendation by the Great Scholar, Shaykh Muḥammad al-Ṭayyib al-Najjār, President of the National Centre of Sunna and Prophetic Biography and Former President of al-Azhar University

All praise belongs to Allah, and peace be upon our liege lord and Master, the seal of the Prophets; our Master Muḥammad b. ʿAbdullāh, and upon his family and companions, and upon all those who take up his call until the Day of Judgement.

The life of the eminent scholar, Sayyid Muḥammad ʿAlawī al-Mālikī al-Makkī al-Ḥasanī, is akin to the life of a good tree planted in good soil, grown in a sound environment, and cared for and protected until its shade spreads out, and its fruits ripen, and the people partake of its abundant goodness and blessing.

This should not come as a surprise, for his eminent father, Sayyid ʿAlawī al-Mālikī (may Allah grant him peace and the finest of abodes) was one of those prominent scholars who dedicated themselves to sacred knowledge, acting as its diligent custodians, noble scribes, and who acted in accordance with the knowledge they procured. His house in Mecca, adjacent to the noble Kaʿba, was frequented by the elite scholars of the Muslims, who gathered there to listen to the noble verses of the Qur'an, and lessons from the pure Prophetic Sunna, studying them in depth and great detail. Their gatherings would end with the recitation of poems dedicated to praising the Prophet ﷺ composed by the host, a Knower of Allah, who authored them in clear Arabic, with a pious heart and pure faith. Small wonder, then, that the eminent Shaykh and doting son, Sayyid Muḥammad ʿAlawī al-Mālikī turned out to be the very image of his father, living his life according to his father's example in his learning, decorum, and religion: *He who resembles his father does no wrong.*

The book that lies before us now is only one of the religious and scholarly works that Sayyid Muḥammad has authored; Allah be praised, each one of them is full of beneficial knowledge, sound opinion, and sagacious reasoning, and by means of them Allah has benefited millions of Muslims. This is of the bounty of Allah; and Allah is of infinite bounty.

As for this work, which the author has named *Notions That Must Be Corrected*, it is truly a lucid exposition of some of the notions that people believe in, imagining that any denial of them is falsehood and untruth.

The esteemed author's learning demanded that he correct these inaccurate notions, and speak the truth concerning them, sincerely for the sake of Allah alone. With this courageous act, he willingly risked any unfortunate reprisals that might have occurred—all for the sake of the noblest of ends, and the finest of devotions. May Allah reward him with the best of rewards for his services to scholarship and the religion.

And all aid is from Allah, and all success is through Him.

Dr. Muḥammad al-Ṭayyib al-Najjār
Former trustee of al-Azhar Mosque
Former President of al-Azhar University
Member of the Islamic Research Academy, Egypt
Member of the Arabic Language Academy, Egypt
Member of the Special National Council
Member of the Committee for the International King Faiṣal Prize

Commendation by the Great Scholar of Morocco, the Diligent Ḥadīth Scholar, Prof. ʿAbdullāh Guenon al-Ḥasanī, President of the Moroccan League of Scholars and Member of the Islamic World League, Mecca

All praise belongs to Allah, and peace be upon our liege lord and Master, the Messenger of Allah; and his family, companions, and all who follow him.

My brother for the sake of Allah, the great and eminent scholar Sayyid Muḥammad ʿAlawī al-Mālikī, has shown me this book, which he has named *Notions That Must Be Corrected*. He has divided the work into three sections: the first is concerned with tenets of faith, the second with Prophethood, and the third with visitation.

The author does not mean to examine the origins of these issues in the Sacred Law, or to give a comprehensive exposition of them; rather, he wishes to discuss those matters upon which scholars past and present have been divided, just as they differed concerning issues of jurisprudence. No clear unambiguous text exists concerning these issues, and so the reasoning of each of these scholars led them to the conclusions that best satisfied them; yet none of them criticised others, or denied the validity of where their own reasoning led them. Scholarly reasoning (*ijtihād*) always leads to several conclusions, not to one single conclusion, and so all who engage in it are deserving of reward. Reward is only granted for good deeds, not blameworthy ones.

We used to say that the difference of opinion in these matters was over and done with, just as the difference of opinion in matters of jurisprudence was, when at the Islamic conference held in Jerusalem in 1931, the Muslims prayed behind the Shīʿite Imām al-Ṭabāṭabāʾī despite their different juristic schools, and the multiple prayer niches were removed from the Umayyad mosque and al-Azhar and others, and the Muslims began to pray behind one Imām, in one mosque, with one prayer niche, without asking about his juristic school or his creed. They did this just as the companions did, praying behind al-Ḥajjāj b. Yūsuf in Basra, and behind other people in other places. Satan, however was not satisfied except that he should again stir up this issue between the Muslims, at a time when they most needed to be in agreement, putting aside conflict and standing up to those who showed enmity to their religion, as Allah ﷻ commanded them with His word: ﴾And fight the idolaters entirely, as they fight you entirely.﴿ (al-Tawba: 36) The discord of the Ash'arī vs. Salafī dispute over tenets of faith returned, and the Muslims were divided, accusing one another of heresy, or disbelief.

The Ash'arī school was only established when anthropomorphism took hold of the common people, and they no longer correctly understood Allah's transcendence. The school turned to figurative explanation (*ta'wīl*) in order to rescue the creed.

Figurative explanation is undeniably a permissible course to take, by evidence of the Qur'ānic text: ﴾It is He who has revealed unto you the Book, wherein are plain verses, which are the foundation of the Book; others are unclear. As for those in whose hearts is deviation: they seek out that which is unclear of it, seeking mischief, and seeking its explanation—yet none know its explanation save Allah, and those who are of sound knowledge.﴿ (Āl-'Imrān: 6)

Al-Ash'arī was one of those who possessed sound knowledge, as was Abū al-Ma'ālī al-Juwaynī, the Imām of the Two Sanctuaries, and Abū Ḥāmid al-Ghazālī, the Proof of Islam, and other great scholars of the Ash'arī school, which offered three distinct opinions regarding the allegorical verses: Firstly, the way of the early Muslims (*salaf*), which was to believe what was indicated by the outward expression, while at the same time maintaining Allah's transcendence and denying His having any likeness; secondly, figurative explanation according to lexical and metaphorical usage, which was the way of the later generation (*khalaf*); thirdly, the opinion to which al-Ash'arī himself leaned after having previously employed figurative explanation, which was to affirm that these allegorical phrases represented attributes of Allah ﷻ, the reality of which we cannot comprehend, but in which we believe as they are. As we said, those who used figurative explanation did so out of a desire to protect the laity from erring in their understanding of allegorical phrases.

For this reason, there were few of them who returned in the end to simply leaving the matter to Allah (*tafwīḍ*), so much so, that one of them used to say: "O Allah, grant us faith like the faith of old women!"

The important thing is that they are all Ahl al-Sunna wa al-Jamā'a, believers in all that came to them from Allah and His noble Messenger, as He ordered—so how could they be accused of being disbelievers or heretics?

It is nothing but bigotry and small-mindedness, if not political. Indeed, in Morocco, when al-Mahdī b. Toumart returned from his travels seeking knowledge in the East, meeting many great Ash'arī scholars like al-Kiyā al-Harrāsī, he proceeded to disseminate the school throughout Morocco. When he claimed to be the Mahdī, and established the Almohad state, he obliged the population to adhere to the school, and fought against the school of the early Muslims, dismissing the previous Almoravid state as "anthropomorphists", when they actually were upon the way of the early Muslims in their beliefs. He called his own dynasty *Muwaḥḥidūn* ("Monotheists"). He also opposed the Mālikī school and the scholars of Morocco and Andalusia who adhered to it. In this way, enmity developed between the two groups; and the inherent cause was political.

What has been said about this issue, which the first section of the book handles, can also be said about the issue of the celebration of the Prophet's ﷺ birthday in the second section, and the issue of visitation in the third.

Although people did not celebrate the Prophet's ﷺ birthday in the past, there are many things that we do not do that they did not, and al-Fārūq ('Umar ؓ) did not accept this argument from al-Siddīq (Abū Bakr ؓ) when he bade him compile the Qur'an, and Abū Bakr eventually changed his mind, and compiled it.

The like of this occurred when 'Umar b. 'Abd al-'Azīz ordered the scholars of the Muslims world to write down the Ḥadīth reports. In the past, they had abstained from doing so, but they acquiesced to him, none of them saying: "Would you do that which the earlier generations did not?" The same thing can be said for the adding of diacritics to the written text of the Qur'ān, and the development of prayer niches in the mosques and the building of minarets, until it reached the point where no mosque was built without them—yet this was not done in the Prophet's ﷺ time. The list goes on; the point is that if someone is overwhelmed by love of al-Muṣṭafā, the Prophet of Mercy, and the Intercessor of the Umma (May Allah bless him, give him peace, ennoble him, honour him, laud him, and magnify him), and so celebrates his birth, it is better that we let him be, not criticise him and make a song and dance over an issue the least of which can be said is that it is permissible.

More incredible still is that a believer could somehow be opposed to the visitation of the Prophet's ﷺ grave, when he himself told us to visit graves—any grave—to derive admonishment and reflection therefrom, and to visit the graves of our parents, forebears and relatives as a means of maintaining family ties, and to pray for them. It is narrated that he ﷺ sought his Lord's permission to visit his mother's grave, and He gave him leave to do so. How could we not visit the grave of the noblest of Messengers, by whose means Allah guided us to the straight path, when he is the most gracious of humanity to us, and the most beloved, more beloved to us than our parents and our children, and our own selves? There is no doubt that to omit to visit his grave, especially in the case of those who perform Hajj and comes a stone or two's throw from Medina, is the gravest kind of shunning, whether or not the Ḥadīth "Whoever performs Ḥajj and does not visit me, has shunned me" is authentic. Leave people and their faith alone, O you who seek to criticise! If your own emotions are not moved by these matters, keep to yourselves, and do not seek to prevent Allah's servants from opening themselves to His Divine grace, which He grants to whom He wills. The issue is exactly as the Truthful, Honest One ﷺ put it: 'I am only an apportioner; Allah is the giver.' Thanks are due to the venerable Sayyid Muḥammad 'Alawī for producing these studies, and correcting these notions. I believe that he has gone as far as can be gone with them, so there is no need for him to busy himself with debating them any further. The Ḥadīth says: 'Whoever leaves off arguing whilst he is in the right, Allah shall build for him a palace in the upmost part of Paradise. Whoever leaves it when he is in the wrong, Allah shall build for him a palace in the outskirts of Paradise.'

This is because the role of scholars in our times is to awaken emotion and zeal in the souls of the Muslims, and to encourage their leaders and rulers to stand up to the enemies of Islam who are enslaving the defenceless believers in Palestine, Eritrea, Afghanistan, and the Philippines. Whoever concerns himself with these issues, dividing the ranks of the believers, is only doing so in order to hide his inadequacy and his avoidance of what is incumbent upon him, and it in no way endears him to Allah. Islam has no land of its own today, and the Muslims are humiliated everywhere. They will never retain their strength, or be released from this humiliation, until they volunteer themselves for the defence of Islam and the protection of its essence, alongside the people of influence and authority. ﴾And Allah is predominant over His affairs—yet most people know it not.﴿ (Yūsuf: 21)

Fes, 2 Shaʿbān 1405

ʿAbdullāh Guenon al-Ḥasanī
General Secretary of the Moroccan League of Scholars
Member of the Islamic Research Academy, Egypt
Member of the Arabic University
Member of the Academy of the Kingdom of Morocco
Member of the Founding Council of the Islamic World League
Member of the Advisory Council to the Throne, Morocco

Commendation by the late Dr. Hāshim al-Ḥusaynī, Trustee of al-Azhar and General Secretary of the Islamic Research Academy

All praise belongs to Allah, and peace be upon our liege lord and Master, the Messenger of Allah; the one sent as a mercy to the worlds.

I present to the Islamic world this book *Notions That Must Be Corrected,* authored by the eminent teacher and Islamic preacher, the lover of Allah ﷻ and His Messenger ﷺ, Sayyid Muḥammad 'Alawī al-Mālikī al-Makkī al-Ḥasanī, the servant of knowledge and its folk at the two Sacred Sanctuaries.

Prof. Muḥammad 'Alawī al-Mālikī is a scion of the Prophetic household; Allah ennobled him and his family by granting them a family tie with the Messenger of Allah ﷺ. Al-Mālikī's household is characterised by knowledge and guidance, and anyone with any connection to the two Sacred Sanctuaries knows well the standing of the Mālikī household in respect to guidance and leadership, and calling to Allah ﷻ with wisdom and fine counsel, and the connection of the students in their circles with the most important and beneficial means of education: love for Allah ﷻ, and love for His Messenger ﷺ. The nation of the call to Islam was not established, nor attained to its immense success, except by means of the love that the Messenger of Allah ﷺ instilled in the hearts of the Emigrants and the Helpers.

Love for Allah and His Messenger, and love for the Muslims entire, was manifested in brotherhood that arose between the Aws and the Khazraj, and between the Emigrants and Helpers.

Allah blessed the Muslims by granting them the way of love. He showed them that it was a favour from Allah ﷻ when He said: ﴾And remember the favour of Allah upon you: how you were enemies, and He brought your hearts together, and by His favour you became brothers.﴿ (Āl-'Imrān: 103)

And He extolled the virtue of love, saying: ﴾Say: If you love Allah, then follow me: Allah will love you, and forgive you your sins.﴿ (Āl-'Imrān: 31)

The Mālikī household embraced this Islamic guidance, and focused on it. I myself saw the father of Sayyid Muḥammad ʿAlawī give lessons in the Sacred Mosque, teaching Qur'ānic exegesis and Ḥadīth, as well as jurisprudence, connecting all of this with love for Allah and His Messenger ﷺ.

His son Sayyid Muḥammad followed the same path, teaching exegesis, Ḥadīth, and linguistics, always connecting it to the love of Allah and His Messenger ﷺ. Because of this, hearts were drawn to the Mālikī household, and seekers of knowledge flocked to it from all over the Islamic world, that they might learn both knowledge and action, and the love of the Allah and His Messenger ﷺ. And Allah granted acceptance to this blessed household.

Whoever reads the book that we now present, will find within it a scholarly methodology that demonstrates the highest standard of academic study and meticulous research. It also demonstrates a sincere call to the love of Allah and His Messenger ﷺ. The book discusses a number of important issues, which may be summarised as follows:

The first section comprises an examination of tenets of faith, including a discussion of the incorrect criterion upon which accusations of disbelief and misguidance are based today.

The second section comprises an examination of issues related to Prophethood, including the unique characteristics of the Prophet ﷺ, the reality of Prophethood and humanity, and the correct understanding of seeking blessings from the Prophet ﷺ and his relics.

The third section comprises examinations of diverse topics, including the Isthmus life, the permissibility of visiting the Prophet's grave ﷺ, and other related issues.

This work sums up the issues that are destroying the Muslims' unity and achieves this by clearly showing the right way and speaking the truth, so that the Muslims can unite on what is good and right.

Finally, we ask Allah, Most High and Mighty, to benefit the Muslims with this upstanding work, and that He decree goodness and success for its author, and all who read it.

And Allah alone grants success.

Dr. Hāshim ʿAbd al-Majīd al-Ḥusaynī
Trustee of Al-Azhar
Former General Secretary of the Islamic Research Academy

3/6/1405

Commendation by the Virtuous Professor, Dr. Ra'ūf Shiblī, Trustee of al-Azhar University

All praise belongs to Allah, and peace be upon our liege lord and Master, the Messenger of Allah, our liege lord Muḥammad the son of 'Abdullāh, may the prayers and peace of Allah be upon him, his household, his companions, and all who follow his guidance with goodness until the last day.

The virtuous Shaykh and Professor, Muḥammad 'Alawī al-Mālikī al-Makkī al-Ḥasanī is from the best of the scholars of Islam and the most upright of them in decorum and the best of them in character. We have known him since he was a student at the department of higher studies at the University of al-Azhar: that fortress of Arabic, lair of invitation, and refuge of the Sacred Law.

Through al-Azhar, Allah has safeguarded the nation of the Arabs from idolatry in the religion, and through it, He has safeguarded the Arabic language from incorrect diction and grammar, and kept others from blocking the path of Allah. Al-Azhar has carried the banner of pure monotheism, defended Islam, and carried its banner across all corners of the world. We will not find a town or village small or large anywhere in the world except that it contains a scholar who has graduated from al-Azhar, heard from its Shaykhs, and carries its license.

Shaykh Muḥammad 'Alawī is one of these noble scholars who has been brought up in the confines of al-Azhar. He, along with the scholars of al-Azhar, has carried the banner of defending true monotheism and virtuous morals. He has been gifted with upright character and a well mannered style that is not insulting or abusive to those who have deviated from the truth, all the while claiming Islam.

It is a must for those who engage in *jihād* in Allah's way to adopt the ettiquette of Islam. They must observe the standards of good character that our liege lord Muḥammad came to complete, and be above pointless disputation, argumentation, gossip, and asking too many questions, for our beloved ﷺ forbade us from gossip, asking too many questions, and wasting wealth. It is also a must for those who engage in *jihād* in Allah's way to adopt everything that will unite the Muslims and bring them together.

They must not cause separation and disunity, because indeed, *jihād* is a tiresome and difficult effort; he who elects to wage it must adorn himself with the character of the companions of the Messenger of Allah ﷺ.

This book of Shaykh Muḥammad 'Alawī, *Notions That Must Be Corrected*, is one of the delightful and well written works that foils the plots of those who attempt to put blinders on the eyes of the Muslims for their own selfish motivations or sick political reasoning that is known to the Muslims the world over. The Muslims have rejected such people, and whoever has true Islamic sentiments and love for Allah, His Messenger, and the general body of the Muslims rejects them as well.

The noble and respected Shaykh—and we purify none above Allah, for He is enough for him and shall take him to account—is from the minority of scholars who wage *jihād* in the path of the truth with true insight and guidance and he is in no need of introduction. I ask Allah to protect him in his upright character and sincere *jihād*, and to guard him and lift from him all afflictions and evil, and allow him to be a means for spreading the word of truth and the upright religion. May Allah send His prayers upon our liege lord Muḥammad, and upon his household and companions.

Dr. Ra'ūf Shiblī
Trustee of al-Azhar University

Commendation by the Scholar and Caller unto Allah, Sayyid Yūsuf Hāshim al-Rifāʿī, Member of the National Council and Former Head of Ministerial Affairs in Kuwait

All praise belongs to Allah, and may prayers and peace be upon our liege lord, intercessor, example, and Imām, the Messenger of Allah ﷺ, and upon his household, companions, allies and those who love him.

Considering the vast sea of the Islamic awakening that has spread throughout the Islamic world today, and the confusion and turmoil of arguments, disputes, and vehement discussions that are witnessed in the mosques, institutes, schools, and universities concerning the essence of the way of the great bulk of Ahl al-Sunna, the Islamic library and Muslim youth are in dire need of this book *Notions That Must Be Corrected*. Allah has certainly given success to its author, our noble brother and Sayyid, Dr. Muḥammad ʿAlawī al-Mālikī—may Allah preserve him—and brought out a bright lamp for every seeker.

There is no doubt that every seeker of the truth will be delighted by this valuable book, and that by it, every obstinate opponent will have his evidence rebuffed and his proof invalidated. Sayyid Muḥammad ʿAlawī brought forth clarity, relying upon the Book of Allah, the Sunna of His Messenger, our liege lord the Messenger of Allah ﷺ, and the statements and reports from the pious predecessors of this noble Muḥammadan nation. I ask Allah, the Exalted, that people return to the truth after reading this wonderful book. Such is the focus of the believer, and as it says in the report: "Wisdom is the lost property of the believer; wherever he finds it, he takes it."

Undoubtedly, when confronting the enemies of Islam and the enemies of Ahl al-Sunna who attack us in every place, we must be firm in complying with the commands of the Sacred Law and we must show resoluteness, wisdom, and intelligence. We must cooperate and come together; we must love one another and think good thoughts about one another. It is important that our motto be: "*We cooperate and work together in those things in which we agree and pardon each other in that which we disagree*." If we observe this, we will be able to sail the ship of Islam to the coast of honour, dignity, and safety. And by Allah is all success.

May Allah send his prayers and peace upon our liege lord Muḥammad, and upon his household and companions.

Sayyid Yūsuf Hāshim al-Rifāʿī
Member of the National Council
Former head of Ministerial Affairs in Kuwait
Head of the Council on Islamic Minorities at the Islamic Congress

Commendation by the Scholar and Professor, Dr. ʿAbd al-Fattāḥ Baraka, General Secretary of the Association of Islamic Research in Cairo

All praise belongs to Allah who is Overpowering over His servants and All Wise and Well Aware. May prayers and peace be upon the witness, the bringer of glad tidings, and the warner, and upon his household and companions—the holders of the lofty station—and those who follow them and take them as allies until the last day.

I have examined the book *Notions That Must Be Corrected* by the scholar and verifier, Sayyid Muḥammad ʿAlawī al-Mālikī. He is the son of my teacher and Shaykh, Sayyid ʿAlawī al-Mālikī—may Allah have mercy upon him and reward him on behalf of the practicing scholars for his contributions to knowledge and its carriers, and the call and its callers.

I know that I have nothing more to add to the words of the esteemed scholars concerning the virtues of this book and its author, and the goodly effort he expended in solving problems, approximating detailed issues, going into precise subsidiary matters, and linking them with the fundamentals. Nonetheless, I am moved to add my name to that goodly group and add my voice to their lofty call to the clear truth. I raise my voice alongside theirs and I increase their ranks and take delight in giving aid to the truth and encouraging it with them.

Truthfully, it must be said that the Islamic nation has enough concern with its external enemies. Its enemies lie in wait for it and plot and plan day and night; they hatch plans and create justifications for pouncing upon it and casting it into the murky depths of darkness. If that were all, then things might be a bit easier to handle, and we could find within ourselves the strength to counter their plots and conspiracies and plunge their arrows into their chests. The problem is larger than that, unfortunately. Among the enemies' plots is their busying and occupying the Muslims among themselves, and igniting the flames of discord, hatred, name calling, and disunity between them. To a large degree they have been successful in this within every field and they have injected their poison into the thought of this nation.

It is easy to offer treatment and remedy to groups that fall outside of religious thought. If, however, a group relies upon investigative principles and fundamentals of thought, it is exceedingly difficult to find a healing cure for them, especially if differences have crept into the fundamentals and extended to doctrinal beliefs. When that occurs, minds become confused, tribulations are stirred up, and guidance is lost.

Every person who is sincere in his religion and protective over his Umma, must see to it that he steers clear of these pitfalls and saves himself from its fires. He must guard his Umma from its evils, or be a scholar who observes firmness and possesses insight into his own self and in calling to Allah with wisdom and goodly preaching. He must possess insight in countering misconceptions and eliminating the causes of differing. He must refer issues back to their pure origin and disavow himself from the things that lead to disunity and splitting. All of this is a must if we wish to return the Umma to a state of health and equilibrium, protect its unity, and make it ready for the means that will bring back its honour and dignity.

This valuable book is a great effort from a precise and verifying scholar. This book of his seeks to unite the Muslims and remove the effects of bigotry in branch issues of independent scholarly judgement (*ijtihād*) in which there are differences of opinion—especially those matters that cause Muslim groups to accuse one another of disbelief or idolatry. In this book, he also dealt with matters related to some of the Muslim groups, such as the Ash'arīs and modern day Salafīs. In addition to that, he has handled other issues, such as logical metaphor and being aware of it when judgements are made regarding disbelief or faith, the meaning of intercession, visiting the grave of the Messenger ﷺ, and other sensitive topics.

This book focuses upon three areas of research: research about doctrine and its criterion, research related to the Prophet ﷺ, and research related to the Isthmus *barzakh* life, the legality of visiting [the Prophet ﷺ], and celebrating religious occasions.

The Muslims are in great need of mending fences and uniting upon a common word by which a Muslim can pardon his brother—as much as is religiously possible—in matters of disagreement and independent judgement (*ijtihād*) and advise him with patience and truth so as to confront our real enemies who plot against Islam and wish to extinguish its light with their mouths—and Allah shall complete His light even if the disbelievers hate it.

It is hoped that this wonderful book can have a blessed share in removing the causes of differing, and that it can bring about the causes of unity and affability among the Muslims. Allah is the Knower of intentions, and our final call is: All praise belongs to Allah, the Lord of the worlds. May prayers and peace be upon the seal of all the Prophets and Messengers, and upon all of his household and companions

Dr. ʻAbd al-Fattāḥ Baraka
General Secretary of the Association of Islamic Research in Cairo

Commendation by the Head of the Ḥadīth Department at al-Azhar and some of its other Scholars

All praise belongs to Allah, the Lord of the worlds, and may prayers and peace be upon the noblest of Messengers, our liege lord Muḥammad, and upon his household and companions.

This is a testimony from the scholars in the faculty of Ḥadīth sciences at al-Azhar University in Cairo regarding the book that has reached both us and the Muslims, titled: *Dialogue with al-Mālikī.*[223] Now we have always known the Kingdom of Saudi Arabia to be the cradle of knowledge and site of the revelation. We have always known its faithful government and the family of Sa'ūd to be people of faith and sincerity, and true callers to unity and Islamic solidarity, and they remain so, all praise belongs to Allah. They shall continue to uphold the banner of truth, unity, and solidarity, and safeguard the Holy sites and serve the two Sacred Sanctuaries.

Both we and many of our colleagues who have taught in different institutions in the Kingdom have known of the respected Shaykh and Professor, Sayyid Muḥammad 'Alawī al-Mālikī. When one of us would go to the Sacred area in Mecca and enter the al-Salām gate, he would witness the largest gathering of sacred knowledge dedicated to the Prophetic Ḥadīth being presided over by the Shaykh. As scholars who used to teach there and go to the Sacred area in Mecca, we would witness this great scholar whom Allah had destined to serve the noble Prophetic Ḥadīth, as his father was destined to do so before him. This household possesses an undisputable virtue, influence, and honour. They specialize in the verbal transmission of Prophetic Ḥadīth, the authentic and connected chains of which go from this noble scholar, Sayyid Muḥammad 'Alawī al-Mālikī, to his father, and on to his Shaykh and the Shaykh of his Shaykh, all the way to the Messenger of Allah ﷺ. This is in addition to his splendid written works, his sagacious knowledge, and his many students and those who love him all around the Islamic world.

---

[223] This is in reference to a calumnious refutation of Shaykh Muḥammad 'Alawī al-Mālikī and this book.—**tr**

This noble scholar is to be considered a valuable treasure store of knowledge and spirituality, and a leader in Islamic culture, and an Imām among the Imāms of Ḥadīth who were known for their works and sincerity in addition to their knowledge. This is how we consider him, and we purify none above Allah. We only bear witness to what we know.

It is unfortunate that some people have maligned this noble scholar and Imām of Ḥadīth and were far from correct. Nay, those who objected to his views fell into grievous error when they attempted to expel him from Islam, despite the fact that all of his opinions and views were held by well-esteemed Imāms before him, such as Imām al-Suyūṭī, Ibn Ḥajar, al-Subkī, and others.

If only his opponents had reviewed the sources from which he took his views, they would have found that his views are correct and with a basis in the Sunna, and that many of the past Imāms and scholars held them as well. As for some of the aberrant opinions they have attributed to him that he is free from, it is nothing but deceit, for they are not his opinions. They have only distorted words from their proper places, so how can they judge him with disbelief? Have they opened his heart?

We have read his books and written works, and found nothing that was mentioned by the author of *Dialogue with al-Mālikī* save beneficial knowledge and clear guidance. The esteemed Shaykh, Muḥammad 'Alawī al-Mālikī is a scholar who specializes in the Prophetic Ḥadīth. And he has obtained the highest degrees from the oldest and most prestigious Islamic University, al-Azhar. He has written books on the Sunna, legislation, and the Prophetic biography ﷺ, and he has students and followers everywhere. We have read his books at his own request, we have listened to his words, and we have observed his character, prayers, and gatherings of knowledge. We have found him to be a man who is a nation unto himself; he leads his followers with knowledge and action and compiles books with veracity and trustworthiness.

He is one of the greatest scholars the Kingdom of Saudi Arabia can boast of. Nay, he is one of the greatest scholars the Muslims—laity and scholars alike—can boast of.

We adjure the author of *Dialogue with al-Mālikī* and his ilk to repent to Allah, the Exalted, for they have come forward with an enormous sin, maligning, accusing, and slandering this great Imām and scholar of Ḥadīth. Islam has forbidden a Muslim from accusing his brother of disbelief, because the locus of both faith and disbelief is the heart and none know the contents of the heart save the Knower of the Unseen. The Messenger of Allah ﷺ rebuked Usāma b. Zayd for killing a man who inclined to peace, and Islam has commanded us to be certain and investigate the facts. Allah, the Exalted, said: ﴾O you who believe! When you go forth to fight in the cause of Allah, investigate and do not say to one who gives you a greeting of peace: 'You are not a believer', aspiring for the goods of the worldly life...﴿ (al-Nisā': 94) The Messenger of Allah ﷺ did not accept Usāma's excuse, rather he said to him: "Did you split open his heart?"

The Messenger of Allah ﷺ said: "If a man says to his brother: 'O disbeliever', it [the statement] falls upon one of them." In another narration it states: "Whoever calls a man a disbeliever or an enemy of Allah while he is not, it will come back to him." [Muslim] He ﷺ also said: "There are three things from the fundamentals of faith: withholding harm from one who says: 'There is no god but Allah', not imputing anyone with disbelief due to a sin, and not expelling anyone from Islam due to ignorance." [Abū Dāwūd and Sa'īd b. Manṣūr with supporting narrations]

This is the judgement of Islam according to the text of the Qur'ān and the Sunna, so what permitted the author of the *Dialogue* and his ilk to fall into this slander and enmity? ﴾Indeed Allah does not love the transgressors.﴿ (al-Baqara: 190) How could they accuse this scholar with disbelief, he whose fame is wide-spread and whose books and writings have been distributed the world over? Glorified are you O Lord! This is but a manifest slander! We sincerely adjure those who fell into this grievous error and enormity to return to their senses and repent to Allah, the Exalted, and to repeat the testimony of Divine unity and sincerely regret what they have done.

This book of Ibn Manī' includes slander and transgression against the person of Sayyid Muḥammad 'Alawī al-Mālikī, as well as transgression against his knowledge, noble lineage, and other insults. The Messenger of Allah ﷺ said: "Insulting a Muslim is corruption and fighting him is disbelief."

The Book *Dialogue with al-Mālikī* is an aid to Zionism and the Enemies of Islam

As scholars of al-Azhar, our opinion is that the book *Dialogue with al-Mālikī* and its likes must be resisted and should not be read by Muslims because they divide their unity. The opinions of Shaykh al-Mālikī that the author tried to belittle are knowledge based and well respected views that have a basis within the Qur'ān and Sunna and were held by scholars and Imāms who have their own weight. Books like this are one of the biggest factors leading to the disunity of Muslims and they only aid zionism, communism, and the enemies of Islam.

This book, *Dialogue with al-Mālikī* serves as one of the greatest means in undermining the unity of Muslim scholars, which is a tremendous danger to the Islamic call and Islamic solidarity. There are many different opinions expressed in the books of jurisprudence and the juridical schools, and in Qur'ānic exegesis and commentaries on the Sunna: each view has its proof and method, yet no one belittled the other and no one accused the other of disbelief, because none know the contents of the heart save the Knower of the Unseen.

This book and the position of its author and his ilk against the scholar and caller, Shaykh Muḥammad 'Alawī al-Mālikī, only aid and assist the machinations of international zionism, communism, atheism, and all other enemies of Islam who use every means at their disposal to separate and split the Muslims. It is the greatest wish of the enemies of Islam for the scholars to divide and impute one another with disbelief. The old method of colonialism was to divide and conquer; the new method of cultural colonialism and ideological warfare is to strike at Islamic culture by attacking the individual scholars and callers, so in that regards, this book is a strike to the core of unity for Muslim laity and scholars alike.

The Book *Dialogue with al-Mālikī* is a Strike against Islam

The author of this book and his ilk have taken it upon themselves to split the ranks and widen the differences between the Muslims. If international zionism, communism, and colonialism expand efforts to split the Muslims' ranks while some Muslims wage *jihād* against them, what are the Muslims to do when they see scholars declaring some ignorant and others disbelievers? The plan of the secularists—who are in cahoots with the communists—is to separate religion from daily life by arguing that Islam does not benefit the Muslims. The way they hope to achieve this—in the view of the senior communists—is to sow doubts about Islam itself. There is no way for them to sow doubts about Islam unless they sow doubts about the scholars of Islam and its major callers who enjoy wide support from the people. Once the people lose confidence in these scholars, they will lose confidence in what they say, and when this happens, the enemy will have achieved its goal.

The book *Dialogue with al-Mālikī* and its likes represent this attempt to shake the confidence people have in this major scholar and reliable scholar of Ḥadīth who struggles for the sake of spreading knowledge by personal example before his words. Are you, Ibn Manīʿ, aiding the enemies of Islam by attacking the scholars of Islam? It is better for you and your cohorts to struggle against the enemies of Islam who have waged war against our faith, and to struggle against the atheists, the zionists, the freemasons, the Bahāʾīs, the Qadiyānīs, the communists, and others. You should not stand in the way of a scholar whose fame has spread far and wide and who has served Islam with his character, knowledge, and written works.

Muslim unity is a sacred duty, and it is obligatory upon the Muslims to stop whoever seeks to undermine it, because such a person wants to split the Umma and create disunity within its ranks. This book, *Dialogue with al-Mālikī*, includes such insults and false accusations that, if the ruling of the Sacred Law was applied on him, the author would be lashed eighty times and his testimony would never be accepted after that again.

We strongly urge the scholars of Islam around the world in general, and the scholars in the Kingdom in particular, to put an end to this disunity and separation. We have always known the Kingdom of Saudi Arabia to be a land of Islamic solidarity and the site of the revelation, the cradle of knowledge, and Islamic thought that unites and does not disunite.

We have great hope that his majesty and his faithful government will punish those who seek to undermine the unity of the Islamic Umma and cause separation between the scholars. We adjure them to bring together both the senior scholar and caller, Sayyid Muḥammad ʻAlawī al-Mālikī and the Muslim scholars, students and those who love him in the Sacred Precinct of Mecca, so as to ensure more benefit from him and his knowledge. May Allah send prayers and peace upon our liege lord Muḥammad and his household and companions.

Dr. ʻUmar Hāshim
Former head of the Department of Ḥadīth sciences, al-Azhar University
Dean of the faculty of Uṣūl al-Dīn at al-Zaqāzīq

Shaykh Muḥammad al-Sinrāwī
The first superintendent of al-Azhar
Religious advisor, Fayoum province

Dr. ʻAbd al-Ghanī al-Rājiḥī
Prof. of higher studies at al-Azhar

Commendation by the Jurist and Scholar, Shaykh Muḥammad Sayyid Aḥmad al-ʿAwaḍ, Muftī of Sudan and Head of the Council of Islamic Legal Verdicts

All praise belongs to Allah, the Lord of the worlds, the Master of all bounties who brought creation into being from nothingness, and may the prayers and peace be upon the greatest of Allah's creation, our liege lord Muḥammad the son of ʿAbdullāh—who was sent by his Lord as a mercy unto all the worlds—and upon his household and companions.

I had the good fortune and opportunity (and all praise belongs to Allah) to read this book by the verifying scholar and noble Sayyid, Muḥammad ʿAlawī al-Mālikī al-Makkī al-Ḥasanī—the servant of knowledge in the two Sacred Sanctuaries. This book is called *Notions That Must Be Corrected*, and these notions are handled in three sections within the book. The first section deals with areas of research related to Islamic doctrine. In this section, he clarified the proof and evidence showing the inherent corruption found in the criterion of imputing disbelief and misguidance today. In the second section, he dealt with areas of research related to the Prophet ﷺ, including the unique qualities of the Prophet ﷺ, the reality of Prophethood and humanity, the correct understanding of seeking blessings (*tabarruk*) from the Prophet ﷺ and his relics. In this section, he brought incontrovertible evidence and proofs from the companions and those after them from the noble scholars of this Umma. In the third section, he spoke about the Isthmus *barzakh* life and the legality of visiting the Prophet, and other related matters such as historical relics, shrines, religious occasions, and so on. In this section, he was precise, verified the truth, and corrected mistaken notions.

Those who take it upon themselves to advise the Muslims concerning the religious commands and prohibitions have mixed up the scales in charging others with disbelief or misguidance. They have rushed headlong, recklessly imputing Muslims with disbelief and describing them with manifest idolatry. That is based upon the belief that whoever does anything mentioned in the three above mentioned sections in the book has left the religion.

In this book *Notions That Must Be Corrected*, the great teacher and noble scholar, the servant of knowledge in the two Sacred Sanctuaries, Sayyid 'Alawī, corrected these notions and removed the obscurity from them. He explained them in a plain and simple manner based upon the Divine texts of the Book and the Sunna, in addition to the commentary of the scholars of this religion.

Those who take it upon themselves to advise the Muslims and teach them the affairs of their religion must see to it that they read this valuable book in order to gain complete knowledge of these facts. They must not rush headlong and recklessly accuse the people of this upright religion and clear proof with disbelief or misguidance. May Allah reward the author with the best reward, for he has done well: ﴾Those who do good will have good and more.﴿ (Yūnus: 26)

May Allah send prayers and peace upon our liege lord Muḥammad—the greatest Prophet—and upon his noble and generous household and companions.

Sayyid Aḥmad al-'Awaḍ Madanī
Supreme Court Judge, Republic of Sudan
Head of the Council of Islamic legal verdicts

15th Rabī' al-Awwal, 1407
December 17th, 1986

Commendation by the Shaykh of Ḥadīth, President of al-Ashrafiyya University and Amīr of Jam'iyya 'Ulamā' al-Islām in Pakistan

All praise belongs to Allah, the Lord of the worlds, and the good end is for the pious. May Allah send prayers and peace upon the seal of the Prophets and Messengers, and upon his household and companions.

I have examined this valuable and delightful book *Notions That Must Be Corrected*, by the virtuous 'Allāma and teacher, Shaykh Sayyid Muḥammad 'Alawī al-Mālikī al-Ḥasanī. In reality, this book contains within it a novel subject and possesses lofty content that is needed by all scholars and seekers. The sensibilities and high thought found in this work unravel and solve many problematic areas in the fundamentals of the religion. There is no doubt that this book removes the veil from many discreet and hidden points that are far from the eyes of the scholars. May Allah reward him with the best reward and shower upon him His bounties both internally and externally. We ask Allah, the Exalted, to allow the Muslims—and in particular, the scholars—to benefit from him and his knowledge always: from East to West. That is not difficult for Allah—Amīn O Lord of the worlds!

Muḥammad Mālik al-Kāndahlawī—may Allah forgive him
Shaykh of Ḥadīth at al-Ashrafiyya University, Lahore Pakistan

Confirmed by:
Shaykh Muḥammad 'Ubaydullāh Muftī
President of al-Ashrafiyya University

Shaykh 'Abd al-Raḥmān
Vice President of al-Ashrafiyya University

Shaykh Ḥāmid Miyāh b. Muḥammad Miyāh
Amīr of Jam'iyya 'Ulamā' al-Islām, Karachi
Successor of Shaykh al-Islām Ḥusayn Aḥmad al-Madanī

Commendation by the Director of Education at Jāmi'a al-'Ulūm al-Islāmiyya, Karachi, Pakistan

All praise belongs to Allah, the Lord of the worlds. May the prayers and peace be upon the most noble of the Prophets and Messengers, and upon his household and companions.

I have read what was written by the virtuous Shaykh, Sayyid Muḥammad 'Alawī al-Mālikī—may Allah protect him—and the commendations of the scholars. I agree with what was written by the Shaykh and 'Allāma, Muftī Ḥasanayn Muḥammad Makhlūf—may Allah protect him—and it is my opinion that the time has come to unite the word of the scholars of truth, and for them to be one rank like a solid structure in the face of a common enemy which seeks with all its might and power to destroy this upright religion and its adherents, and which transgress against the sacred Islamic sites. The time has come for the scholars to pardon each other in the matters that are within the realm of *ijtihād* for independent scholars, lest they lose their power through infighting. It is obligatory upon them to utilize their strength in spreading this upright religion and defending it.

I have observed the virtuous Shaykh, Sayyid Muḥammad 'Alawī al-Mālikī, during his days of study here with us when he visited Karachi and lived for some months. I found him very keen and eager to attend the gatherings of the people of truth and *tawḥīd* from the senior scholars such as: the 'Allāma and noble scholar of Ḥadīth, Shaykh Muḥammad Yūsuf Binūrī and the 'Allāma and noble Muftī, Shaykh Muḥammad Shafī'—may Allah have mercy upon them both.

I ask Allah, the Exalted, to grant him success and correctness

Dr. 'Abd al-Razzāq Iskandar
Director of Education and General Secretary, Jāmi' al-'Ulūm al-Islāmiyya, Karachi Pakistan

Confirmation:
Muḥammad b. Yūsuf al-Binūrī: Vice President of the University

Commendation by the Head of the Scholars' Council of Pakistan

All praise belongs to Allah, and may prayers and peace be upon he after whom there is no prophet, and upon his household, companions, and followers.

I, Sayyid Muḥammad 'Abd al-Qādir Āzād, president of the Scholars' Council of Pakistan, say independently from my own accord and on behalf of the Scholars' Council of Pakistan and its members who are—by Allah's grace—located in every city inside Pakistan and outside of it, and whose numbers include more than twenty thousand scholars: We have examined the book *Notions That Must Be Corrected*, by the virtuous 'Allāma, the Sayyid and Sharīf, Muḥammad 'Alawī al-Mālikī al-Makkī. We found it to contain that which Ahl al-Sunna wa al-Jamā'a have been upon from the time of the Salaf up until now. In this work of his, he has benefited and done extremely well in presenting Qur'ānic proofs and Ḥadīth evidence. We hope that Allah ﷻ will unite the word of the Muslims upon the plain truth. We are with the author in his struggle in calling unto Allah and aiding the people of truth: Ahl al-Sunna wa al-Jamā'a.

May Allah send prayers, abundant peace, and blessings upon our liege lord and Master Muḥammad, and upon his household, companions and followers.

Sayyid Muḥammad 'Abd al-Qādir Āzād
Head of the Scholars' Council of Pakistan
Head preacher at al-Masjid al-Malaki, Lahore
1/5/1408 Hijrī

Confirmation:
—Nafīs al-Ḥusaynī: Successor of Shaykh 'Abd al-Qādir Rāi'būrī
—Muḥammad 'Abd al-Ghanī: al-Jāmi'a al-Madaniyya, Lahore, Pakistan
— 'Alī Aṣghar Khaṭīb: Punjab Province, Pakistan
—Muḥammad 'Abd al-Wāhid: preacher at al-Jāmi' al-Islāmī, Sialkot, Pakistan

Commendation by Dr. Ḥasan al-Fattāḥ Qarībullāh, Principal of al-Jāmi‘a al-Islāmiyya

All praise belongs to Allah, the Lord of the worlds, and may prayers and peace upon the noblest of Messengers, our liege lord Muḥammad, and upon his household and companions and those who follow his guidance, take his example, and follow his way until the last day.

Undoubtedly, the household of Sayyid Muḥammad ‘Alawī al-Mālikī is well-known and possesses a high standing. Its members have spread knowledge and good character, and work hard to invite others unto Allah using the method of the Holy Qur’ān and purified Sunna. They are adorned with a lofty lineage that connects them with the Messenger of Allah ﷺ. They are distinguished by their deep love of the Holy lands and their respect and homage to those in charge over them, at the head of them, the servant of the two Sacred Sanctuaries.

The Prophetic household have ascended to the heights of glory and have dedicated their lives to the religion and its defence. They also defend the Kingdom against the transgressors—and how lowly they are—as well as the ignorant friends who adorn themselves with the garments of knowledge and religion—and how dim-witted they are! This research the author has elected to write is nothing less than a proof attesting to the truth of what I say. This work has been embarked upon by a senior scholar of Islam who has corrected notions regarding matters that were almost effaced by ignoramuses. In this work, he clarified realities and facts that were almost enshrouded in deep fog by others. In addition to all this, he was able to connect the Kingdom with the scholars and avoid the isolation that some wished to impose upon him.

In this work, the author clarified the corruption found within the criterion used to impute others with disbelief and misguidance: a false criterion spit out by the false claimants to knowledge who wish to take pride in a small number of Muslims and who do not wish take pride in their large numbers; those who wish to spread tribulation in the Muslims’ ranks, sometimes on account of external matters, and at other times on account of issues in which the scholars have differed, thereby causing them to add their dissenting voice and ideas.

Certainly, Sufism has been wronged by these false claimants. They have accused it and its adherents with things from which they are innocent—things which more aptly fit the false claimants. Given this situation, it was an absolute must that a scholar who knows how to argue and fight enters the arena of conflict. Indeed, commanding the good and forbidding the evil is not carried out in issues in which there are scholarly differences of opinion, nevertheless, if a minority faction has reason to observe bigotry, then the overwhelming majority of the Muslims have a greater reason to solidify their correct understandings that are based upon a deep understanding of the Book of Allah and the Sunna of His Messenger—upon him be the best prayers and must purified salutations.

As the author said, we believe Sufism to be a collection of knowledge based schools, all of them, with their various methods, programs, and paths, representing the highest peak of Islamic thought and the most beautiful side of its manners and examples. It represents perfection in *īmān* and perfection in every matter of life. It represents the pure summary of every Lordly invitation. It is truthfulness, fulfilment of trusts, loyalty, preference to others over oneself, generosity, and assistance to the weak, rescue of the distressed, assistance to one another in piety and righteousness, encouragement to truth and patience, and racing to perform acts of good that represent correct and upright character. It is by this, that the Islamic personality became manifest in its most exalted condition, complete manner, and highest example.

As for the people of Sufism, they are as Imām al-Ghazālī said in *al-Munqidh min al-Ḍalāl* (Deliverance from Misguidance):

> I knew with certainty that the Sufis were the true spiritual travellers in the path to Allah, the Exalted, and that their way was the best of ways and that their path was the most correct of paths and that their character was the best of character.

> Nay, were one to combine the insight of the intellectuals, the wisdom of the sages, and the knowledge of the scholars versed in the secrets of the Sacred Law, in order to change a single item of Sufi conduct and character and replace it with something better, there would be no way to do so! For all their motions and stillness, interiors, and exteriors are derived from the light of the niche of prophecy. Beyond the light of prophecy there is no light on earth from which illumination can be obtained.

That is the Sufism known by the *salaf.* That is the conduct of the Sufis as known by the latter generations. The outward form of Sufism was—and remains—love for the Messenger of Allah ﷺ, exaltation of him, visitation of him, and seeking blessings from his relics and the relics of those who followed him. As for the inward reality of Sufism, it is for one to worship Allah as though he sees Him and if he doesn't see Him then he knows that Allah sees him.

It is in light of this understanding based on the Book and the Sunna that the author moulded his book. For the scholars it is a proof; for the learners, a light and illumination. A distinguishing characteristic of this book is that it follows a sound knowledgeable method, a pleasant and gentle style, and contains valuable pieces of knowledge, clear proofs and incontrovertible evidence. May Allah increase the author in success and may He increase the readers in guidance and may He further increase its detractors in disgrace.

In closing we say: ﴾And why should we not believe in Allah and what has come to us of the truth? And we aspire that our Lord will admit us [to Paradise] with the righteous people.﴿ (al-Mā'ida: 84)

Prof. Dr. Ḥasan al-Fātiḥ Qarībullāh
Principal of al-Jāmi'a al-Islāmiyya, Omdorman, Republic of Sudan

Commendation by the Great Scholar and Man of Letters, Aḥmad ʿAbd al-Ghafūr ʿAṭṭār, one of the Masters of Arabic Literature in the Kingdom of Saudi Arabia and Winner of the King Fayṣal Prize for Arabic Literature

All praise belongs to Allah, the Lord of the worlds, and may prayers and peace be upon the noblest of the Messengers, our liege lord Muḥammad, and upon his household and companions.

A very close friend of mine gifted me with the book *Notions That Must Be Corrected*, which is the latest book of the virtuous ʿAllāma, Sayyid Muḥammad b. ʿAlawī b. al-ʿAbbās al-Mālikī. My friend requested that I offer my opinion regarding the book, so in response to his request I will offer a few words.

It is more than enough that commendations for this book have been written by scholars who possess lofty and high religious positions, sagacious and beneficial knowledge, and who struggle for the sake of the truth, such as the Ustādh ʿAbdullāh Guenon al-Ḥasanī, the president of the scholar's league of Morocco, Shaykh Aḥmad al-Khazrajī, Minister of Endowments and Islamic Affairs in the United Arab Emirates, and Shaykh Muḥammad al-Shādhilī al-Nayfur, the Dean of the faculty of Sacred Law in Tunis, Shaykh Muḥammad Sālim ʿAddūd, Chief Supreme Court Justice in the Islamic Republic of Mauritania, and Shaykh Ḥasanayn Muḥammad Makhlūf, who wrote the foreword to this book, the former chief Muftī of Egypt and member of the Council of Senior scholars at al-Azhar. Their commendations are more than enough; nevertheless, my friend wished to hear my opinion—which he heard from me after I read this book—and read it in written form and I allowed him to give it to the author to do with as he pleases—and this I have done. I am most delighted that my opinion is given as much consideration as my written works are by the readers, for I write nothing but the truth that I take as my religion.

I read the book *Notions That Must Be Corrected* and observed that its author, the ʿAllāma and astute researcher, did not write it for the sake of arguing with those who oppose him in some of his views (those who oppose him to the point of accusing him of disbelief), rather, the author only wrote his book for the sake of establishing the truth.

He adopted a wise and pleasant style, and did not embroil himself in insults and slanders against his opponents. There is not a single insulting or disparaging word found in his book. It is more a presentation of his knowledge than a presentation of his own particular viewpoints.

In his knowledge-based Islamic research, the virtuous and upright author did not intend to impose his opinions on the reader, and for this reason, he did not supplant it with his own personal views—despite their correctness and his right to do so—because personal opinions can be correct or incorrect. For the sake of guaranteeing objectivity in his book, the author turned away from mere personal judgements and built it upon the truth that comes from the Book and the Sunna; in matters of Sacred Law, creed, morals, society, character, and knowledge.

In Islam, this right is not closed off nor is it anyone's exclusive right to monopolize upon. It is the right of the people of knowledge to research it and derive rulings from it. It is only natural that view-points will differ in matters related to the understanding of certain Qur'ānic verses and Ḥadīth.

We find among the notable Imāms much differing about the obligations of ritual ablution. For example, according to the esteemed Ḥanbalīs, eating camel meat nullifies one's ablution, whereas according to the rest of the Muslims it does not. All of the Muslims—with the exception of the Ḥanbalīs—perform prayers after eating camel meat, and prayer is the central foundation of the religion and the greatest pillar of Islam after the testimony of faith. If we take the view of the Ḥanbalī legal school that was rejected by the other three Imāms: Abū Ḥanīfa, Mālik, and al-Shāfi'ī—may Allah have mercy upon them and Aḥmad b. Ḥanbal—then both the prayers and ablutions of the Muslims would be invalid.

This strong difference did not lead the Imāms to accuse one another of disbelief, and there are many different examples of disagreement that must not cause us to exchange insults, false charges, and accusations of disbelief.

The noble 'Allāma, Sayyid Muḥammad 'Alawī al-Mālikī al-Ḥasanī did well with this valuable book *Notions That Must Be Corrected*. One of the most distinguishing qualities of the author is his wise style that is far removed from insults; he choose instead to call to truth, goodness, beauty, and virtue with a delightful and resplendent style that springs from the character of the Prophetic household and the noble and pious family.

In summary, my opinion about this book is that it is a clear explanation of the truth and it clarifies both the methodology of the author in religious thought, as well as the valuable treasure-store of religious thought itself. The author has done well in authenticating certain understandings that the scholars have always met with honour and acceptance; two things that are clear from all of the commendations that bear witness on behalf of the author and his work. We share with them in their attestation and the honour which they deserve. We are gracious to the noble 'Allāma and great Islamic caller, Sayyid Muḥammad 'Alawī al-Mālikī al-Ḥasanī for his blessed efforts in the service of Islam and its Messenger, the Master of creation, Muḥammad—upon him be the best of prayers and purest salutations—just as we are gracious to him for his struggle in calling unto Allah; the effort of which has served to solidify Islam in East and South Asia and elevate the word of Allah in many parts of the Islamic and Arabic speaking world. May Allah reward him with every good and allow others to benefit from his lofty character and splendid knowledge and virtue.

Aḥmad 'Abd al-Ghafūr 'Aṭṭār
Mecca

Commendation by the Great Scholar, Shaykh Yūsuf b. Aḥmad al-Ṣiddīqī, Deputy Chief Judge of the Appellate Court of Bahrain and Member of the Islamic World League, Mecca

All praise belongs to Allah, the Lord of the worlds. May abundant prayers and peace be upon the Master of the Messengers and leader of those who perform ablutions, our liege lord and beloved intercessor, the doctor of our hearts, as long as the night turns into the day, and upon his purified household and chosen companions.

I have examined a mighty book by the name *Notions That Must Be Corrected*, by a noble author and member of the splendid and purified Prophetic family, the virtuous 'Allāma, Sayyid Muḥammad 'Alawī al-Mālikī. I found it to be a book filled with lofty meanings possessing high goals, and containing clear proofs, especially in his discussions on the permissibility of seeking blessings from the noble relics, performing *tawassul* with the Muḥammadan essence, and undertaking journey to his exalted Mosque and thronging in front of his noble and esteemed grave. He strengthened his book with evidence from the Book, the Sunna, and statements of the distinguished scholars from both early times and latter times.

May Allah reward its author with the best of rewards and give him recompense both in this life and the next. May Allah grant both him and us love for His noble Prophet and following in his upright footsteps. May He allow us to die upon his Sunna and unite us with him under this banner on the Day of Judgement.

May Allah send His prayers upon our liege lord Muḥammad and upon his household, companions, and followers until the Day of Judgement.

Yūsuf b. Aḥmad al-Ṣiddīqī
13 Sha'bān, 1405
Deputy Chief Judge of the Higher Appeals Court of Bahrain
Member of the Islamic World League, Mecca

Summary of Commendations by some of the Scholars of Yemen

All praise belongs to Allah, the Lord of the worlds. May prayers and peace be upon the noblest of the Messengers, our liege lord Muḥammad, and upon his household and companions.

The scholars of Yemen examined the book *Notions That Must Be Corrected*, by the author, the ʻAllāma and proof, the virtuous Sayyid, Muḥammad ʻAlawī al-Mālikī. They consented to it, acknowledged it, commended it, and found it to be the best written work expounding upon its subject matter. Its author clarified the creed of the Salaf and those after them, explained some of the more ambiguous matters that confuse people, and addressed what people have been wondering about in their minds. It is a resplendent jewel on the necklace of Sunni books, both old and new, poetry and prose. It is rare and unique in its genre, it fulfils the hopes of the seekers, and is in accordance with the doctrine of Ahl al-Sunna in which faith is a duty. May Allah reward him with the best reward on behalf of Islam and the Muslims.

—Muftī of the Republic of Yemen: Sayyid Aḥmad b. Muḥammad Zabāra
—Muftī of Taʻiz province: Sayyid Ibrāhīm b. ʻUmar b. ʻAqīl
—The head of the scholars in Zabīd: Shaykh Asad b. Ḥamza b. ʻAbd al-Qādir
—Shaykh Aḥmad Dāwūd
- President of the Islamic Salvation party of Yemen: Sayyid ʻAbd al-Hādī ʻAjīl
—Head of the Islamic Centre of Taʻiz: Muḥammad Ḥazzām al-Muqrimī
—Governor General of Zabīd: Shaykh Aḥmad ʻAlī al-Waṣābī
—Muftī of Zabīd: Sayyid Muḥammad b. Sulaymān
—Shaykh ʻAbd al-Karīm b. ʻAbdullāh
—Shaykh Ḥusayn b. ʻAbdullāh al-Waṣābī
—Shaykh Sayyid Muḥammad ʻAlī al-Baṭṭāḥ
—Muftī of Hudayda province: Muḥammad ʻAlī Mukrim
—Director of al-ʻIlmiyya Institute of Sanaʼa: Shaykh Muḥammad b. ʻAlī al-Manṣūr

Commendation by the Great Scholar, Ḥadīth Expert, and Investigative Jurist, Shaykh Muḥammad al-Shādhilī al-Nayfur, Former Dean of the Faculty of Sacred Law in Tunis and Member of the Islamic World League, Mecca

In our day and age, the Islamic world is facing numerous attacks by the opponents of Islam. The severest of these attacks are the ones hatched by the zionists, in which they employ means to penetrate into the body of the Muslims like the woodworm bores into wood. It is not obvious to the eyes—that, in addition to their offences in Palestine that penetrate deeply.

From another angle, the fierce zionist attacks against Islam around the world work day and night to place Islam in the tightest corner or to destroy it completely, and both the zionist and the crusaders assist other forces as well. So, there are a great number of violent attacks the Muslims are facing, to the point where the enemy has confused some and led them to their ideas, just as one is led to take poison thinking that it is a remedy. It is not enough for those who scream in the name of reform and progress to be poisoned, rather they wish to force the Muslims take the poison when the opportunity arises for them to take power, and they wish to raise their voices in inviting to what they call reform and progress so as to allure and seduce the Islamic world.

It is a fierce war that robs one's sleep and brings tears to the eyes. Most of us are heedlessly unaware and occupied with each other—as is seen in the hot wars between the Muslims and the cold wars among nations and misguided and poisoned individuals. Our painful reality forces us to resist these onslaughts and save ourselves from these immediate dangers instead of fighting amongst ourselves and with ourselves. A case and point of this is the attacks against the Ashʿarīs. There is no justification for that, because if we look at the Ashʿarīs, we see that they are upon the Sunna that our Prophet ﷺ left us with, the night of which is like its day. May Allah have mercy upon Imām Ibn ʿAsākir who took it upon himself to clarify the real face of the Ashʿarī school when he wrote his book *Tabyīn Kadhib al-Muftarī fī mā Nasaba lī al-Imām Abī al-Ḥasan al-Ashʿarī* (Clarifying the Lies of the Slanderer in what He Attributed to Imām Abū al-Ḥasan al-Ash'arī). He explained that it was in the middle path—and the best of all affairs are those in the middle—between extreme negation [of the attributes of Allah] and giving them resemblence [to the creation]. Allah inspired al-Ash'arī to give aid to the Sunna using rational proofs, allowing the people to affirm for Allah ﷻ what He affirmed for Himself of names and attributes, and to negate from Him that which does not befit His majesty. It has been said about the Ash'arīs:

The Ash 'arīs are a folk given success in reaching the truth
In their doctrine they have not departed from the Sunna or the Book

It is sufficient to establish the authenticity of his school by the fact that most if not all of the outstanding scholars were Ash'arīs, which was the case even before his appearance, because they were upon the way of the Sunna. After his appearance they followed his school.

This was mentioned by Ibn 'Asākir in *Tabyīn Kadhib al-Muftarī* in the chapter: "Mention of a group of his most famous companions." Since the virtue of a follower shows the virtue of the one who is followed, it is sufficient to mention that among his followers were Qāḍī Abū Bakr b. al-Ṭayyib b. al-Bāqillānī al-Baṣrī, the author of well known works refuting the opponents. Abū al-Ḥasan al-Tamīmī al-Ḥanbalī used to say to his companions: "Hold fast to this man, for the Sunna can never be without need of him!"

Among his other outstanding men: al-Ḥākim al-Naysabūrī, the author of *al-Mustadrak 'alā al-Ṣaḥīḥayn*, Ibn Fūrak, Abū Isḥāq al-Isfarāyīnī, Ḥāfiẓ al-Aṣfahānī, Abū Muḥammad al-Qāḍī 'Abd al-Wahhāb al-Baghdādī, the Mālikī jurist whose books are extremely famous, one of which was given great attention by Imām al-Māzirī in his book *al-Talqīn*. Other followers include the well known scholar of Ḥadīth, Ḥāfiẓ Abū Dharr al-Harawī al-Mālikī, Ḥāfiẓ Abū Bakr al-Bayhaqī, Ḥāfiẓ Abū Bakr al-Khaṭīb al-Baghdādī, Imām Abū al-Ma'ālī al-Juwaynī, Abū al-Ḥasan al-Ṭabarī, al-Kiyā al-Harrāsī, and the famous Imām and proof of Islam, Abū Ḥāmid al-Ghazālī. His followers among the people of the Maghreb include the two famous Imāms:

Abū al-Ḥasan al-Qābisī and Imām al-Māzirī. To follow up on the names of all of these scholars would entail knowing all of the scholars of the Muslims. If all of these are upon misguidance, then the Umma has gathered upon misguidance, and this entails a denial of the Ḥadīth of the Messenger of Allah ﷺ narrated by our liege lord Anas ؓ that the Messenger of Allah ﷺ said: "My Umma shall not gather upon misguidance, so if you see differences, see to it that you stick with the great majority." (Narrated by Ibn Mājah)

Another example of infighting, is the attack against the Prophet's birthday. If we were to soundly investigate the matter, we would find that it is not an innovation, and that rather, it is for the sake of exalting the day of the Prophet's birth and following in his footsteps as he exalted the day in which Mūsā was saved: on the day of 'Āshūra'. In order to avoid adding another *'īd* to the Muslims' *'īds*, the Muslims did not call his birthday an *'īd*. Rather, they called it the day of his *mawlid*, so may Allah reward them for that. The doubts concerning the *mawlid* were responded to by the noble Imām al-Suyūṭī in his book *Ḥusn al-Maqsad fī 'Amal al-Mawlid.*

These and other notions must be corrected, and this is what was done by the virtuous 'Allāma, Prof. Muḥammad 'Alawī al-Mālikī, in his lavish book *Notions That Must Be Corrected*. He has corrected many false notions that have been the cause of attacks and has clarified the correct understanding in them. This book deserves to be reviewed by those who wish to ascertain the correct positions—such as the two issues I mentioned above.

It is our hope that these attacks will end after the false notions have been corrected, and that the pens will turn their attention to the attacks against Islam, so as to rescue those who have been misguided by false ideas and allow us to be among those who defend Islam with their pens and thoughts.

We ask Him ﷻ to make us all from those who listen to the words and follow the best thereof.

Muḥammad Shādhilī al-Nayfur
Former Dean of the faculty of Sacred Law in Tunis
Member of the National Council, Tunis
Member of the Islamic World League, Mecca

Commendation by the Great Scholar and Jurist, Shaykh Muḥammad Fāl al-Banānī, General Secretary of the Mauritanian Islamic League and Member of the Islamic World League, Mecca

All praise belongs to Allah, the Lord of the worlds, Who said in His Clear Book: ﴾And assist one another upon piety and righteousness and do not assist one another upon sin and transgression﴿ (al-Mā'ida: 2) and: ﴾And do not backbite one another. Would one of you like to eat the flesh of his dead brother? You would detest it.﴿ (al-Ḥujurāt: 12) and: ﴾The believing men and women are allies to one another.﴿ (al-Tawba: 81)

May prayers and peace be upon the noblest of the Messengers and leader of those who performed ablutions and who narrated from him: "The believer means much to his brother" and "The believer is the brother of his fellow believer; he does not oppress him or surrender him to one who will oppress him" and "The example of the believers in their mutual love and mercy is like a single body; when one part of it falls ill, the rest of the body is affected by sleeplessness and fever" and "The believers are like a solid structure supporting one another" and "Do not envy one another, do not hate one another, and do not vie with one another [in the market place]; be slaves of Allah and brothers" and other such narrations that encourage mutual love, brotherhood, closeness, and good thoughts about Allah and the servants of Allah.

I examined with much attention and detail the book *Notions That Must Be Corrected* by the 'Allāma and man of letters, the scholar of Ḥadīth and skilful linguist, the father of notable children of high pedigree and father of esteemed heads, the Sharīf and son of noblemen, Sayyid Muḥammad 'Alawī al-Mālikī, the Meccan by domicile and birth. I found the book extremely articulate in the issues which he examined. He brought such proofs and texts that leave no room for doubt for anyone who possesses even the slightest iota of knowledge and fairness. This should come as no surprise, for he is a cluster of knowledge and its post, the son of a cluster of knowledge and its post.

His splendid style and arrangement of the topics, and his realisation of the subject matter drove me to write this commendation. I do this in order to take part in bringing the opponents back to what is correct and caution them from accusing the Muslims of disbelief due to issues in which there is no consensus. The scholars unanimously agreed that if a Muslim says or does something that carries the possibility of being apostasy from ninety-nine angles, yet carries the one possibility [of it not being apostasy], recourse is to be taken in that one angle lest a Muslim is expelled from the faith.

It is my view—and Allah knows best—that after reading the book *Notions That Must Be Corrected*, the opponents can do nothing more than submit to what it contains, because its contents are almost unanimously agreed upon by those in the past and those today. This was clarified by the notable Imāms and the relied upon Ḥadīth masters in the Islamic religion; may Allah reward them and the author of this book with the best reward on behalf of Islam. May He allow his book to remain as a treasure for the Muslims who want no more than the ascendency of the truth. May He bless him and have mercy upon his righteous and knowledgeable predecessors who acted upon what they knew. May he reward them for the knowledge they disseminated and conveyed among the Muslims around the world: knowledge of Qur'ān, Sunna, and the auxiliary sciences.

I bear witness that the author's father whom I met, Shaykh Sayyid 'Alawī 'Abbās al-Mālikī, played his role in the field of invitation, guidance and in relaying the religious sciences. I would often attend his gatherings, year after year: lessons in the Sacred Masjid on the Qur'ān and its exegesis, Ḥadīth and its jurisprudence, Divine Unity and doctrine, and other such things that led to a large number of students and attendees in his circles—may Allah have expansive mercy upon him and preserve his inheritor in knowledge and successor in teaching, the young pious and believing Sayyid, Muḥammad 'Alawī al-Mālikī, his good son, the one delivered from error, and the lover of Allah and His Messenger.

The one who absolves from himself all claims to power and might:

Muḥammad Fāl al-Banānī
General Secretary of the Mauritanian League for the defence of Islam and member of the Islamic World League, Mecca

20th Rajab, 1405
April 11th, 1985

Commendation by the Great Scholar, Jurist, and Expert in the Fundamentals of Jurisprudence, Shaykh Muḥammad Sālim ʻAddūd, Former Chief Supreme Court Justice of Mauritania, Member of the Fiqh Council of the Islamic World League, Mecca

Correct notions the people have neglected
Notions covered in confusion and separation
This is a precise and deep research without
Mixing matters up, conjecture or prevarication
In it al-ʻAlawī al-Mālikī showed us
That which the understandings of the clever have not obtained
It is a gathering, a clarification, an explanation, and exposition
From him, even if they argue and disclaim
Four things assisted him in his pursuit:
Divine texts, analogy, the leaving of things [to Allah] and inspiration
He turned away the fingers that were pointing at him;
Insulting fingers on hands without thumbs
It then became clear that the things they spread
And claimed were nothing but conjecture and superstitions
If any other than our Creator deserved prostration
We would fall to the son of ʻAbbās in prostration
With this I commend this research and hope
That it is an arrow of mine in aid of the truth

Muḥammad Sālim b. Muḥammad ʻAlī b. ʻAbd al-Wadūd " ʻAddūd "
Former Chief Supreme Court Justice of Mauritania
Minister of Culture and Islamic Affairs
Member of the Fiqh Council of the Islamic World League, Mecca

Commendation by the Great Scholar and Caller, Shaykh Muḥammad ʿAzīz al-Raḥmān al-Ḥaqqānī al-Hazārawī

All praise belongs to Allah alone, and may prayers and peace be upon he who there is no Prophet after, and upon his household and companions and those who follow his guidance.

I have examined the book *Notions That Must Be Corrected*, by the virtuous ʿAllāma, Sayyid Muḥammad ʿAlawī al-Mālikī al-Ḥasanī al-Makkī. We have found it—and whatever Allah wills comes to pass, and there is no might but through Allah—to be a valuable book in which the author gathered numerous benefits in a splendid style, showing respect to the scholars and following the path of the wise sages—so may Allah reward him with good.

We have found that—generally—everything in it is in accordance to the way of the majority of Ahl al-Sunna wa al-Jamāʿa, from both early and latter times. It is what we found our Shaykhs upon, from the scholars of Ḥadīth, the Qur'ānic exegetes, and the verifying jurists, such as the Ḥadīth master of India, Imām Shāh Waliyullāh al-Dahlawī al-Fārūqī, and his pupils and their students.

In addition to him, there is the Amīr and Mujāhid fighter, the Imām and knower of Allah, Shaykh Imdādullāh al-Fārūqī al-Muhājir al-Makkī and his compatriots, the two bright suns, the proof of Islam, Imām Qāsim al-Nānotwī, and the Pole of guidance, Imām Rashīd Aḥmad al-Gangohī. There is the sage of the Umma, Imām Shāh Ashraf ʿAlī al-Thanvī al-Fārūqī, Shaykh al-Islam Imām Sayyid Ḥusayn Aḥmad al-Madanī al-Ḥusaynī, the Pole of poles and blessing of the epoch, Shaykh al-Ḥadīth, Muḥammad Zakariyyā al-Kāndahlawī, and al-Muhājir al-Madanī—may Allah sanctify their secrets—and others among the notable scholars of Ahl al-Sunna wa al-Jamāʿa in the Indian Subcontinent.

Most of their books and essays are crammed full of these issues, especially the valuable tract *al-Muhannad ʿalā al-Mufannad* by the verifying Imām and noble ʿAllāma and scholar of Ḥadīth, Shaykh Khalīl Aḥmad al-Sahāranbūrī al-Anṣārī. His book was commended by the generality of the major scholars in this day and age.

The majority of the tract's contents are about the same issues mentioned in *Notions That Must Be Corrected*, even if the expressions differ and the writing styles are not the same, the end goal is one and they possess the exact same meaning, as the poet said:

Our expressions are varied and your beauty is one
And all point to that beauty

We hope that the Generous Originator [Allah] will gather the Muslims upon the manifest truth and unite their ranks, for they have never been in more need of unity than they are today, where they are surrounded by their enemies from among the Jews, Hindus, Christians, communists and atheists of both east and west, in addition to the deviant sects such as the Qādiyānīs, Bahā'īs, Ismā'īlī Bāṭinīs, and the Rāfiḍa.

The Sunnis are sleeping, and those among them who are awake are scattered in their efforts and dispersed in their strength and their hearts are divided. Simple matters in which the scholars have differed from the beginning have distracted them away from the major issues, immediate dangers, and clear corruptions that threaten the Umma from every side. If only they would come to their senses, those scholars who ascribe themselves to the victorious group (Ahl al-Sunna wa al-Jamā'a) and accuse the Muslims of disbelief and misguidance due to matters in which there is difference of opinion. Would that they expand their efforts in uniting the Muslims and helping them return to their religion and obey their Lord and follow their Prophet. How can such matters ever come to fruition without love, wisdom, and an open chest, goodly exhortation, and leaving aside the matters over which there is disagreement, and leaving off extremism and harshness? The All Mighty, All Wise, and Well Informed said to the best of His Messengers, the seal of His Prophets, and His Beloved and Chosen One: ﴾And if you had been rude in speech and harsh in heart they would have disbanded from about you.﴿ (Āl-'Imrān: 159)

May Allah reward the efforts of the 'Allāma, Sayyid Muḥammad 'Alawī al-Mālikī al-Ḥasanī, and increase him in success and acceptance. In this book of his, he maintained proper manners with his opponents who unjustly accused him of disbelief and misguidance. He did not mention a single one of them with a bad word, nay; he did not even mention their names to begin with. Rather, he brought manifest evidence from the Sacred Law and clear proofs from the Book of Allah, the Sunna of His Messenger ﷺ, and the statements of the Imāms of knowledge and religion. This is the way things should be and must be without argument. This is what was hoped for from him, may Allah protect him and grant him success for all good.

We used to always see that our Shaykh, the Imām and Pole, Muḥammad Zakariyyā al-Kāndahlawī al-Madanī—may Allah sanctify his secret—loved him a great deal and considered him as one of his own sons. The author is also among the greatest of those who loved our Shaykh during his life and after his death. In addition, the author possesses great love and respect for his Shaykhs and ours whose knowledge he benefited from and whose blessings poured upon him, such as the Imām of our time, the noble scholar of Ḥadīth, Sayyid Muḥammad Yūsuf al-Binūrī al-Ḥusaynī; the Imām and great scholar of Ḥadīth, Sayyid Fakhr al-Dīn al-Murādabādī; Shaykh al-Ḥadīth at Dar al-'Ulūm Deoband, Imām Muftī Muḥammad Shafī' al-Deobandī, chief Muftī of Pakistan; and the Imām, caller and scholar of Ḥadīth, Shaykh Muḥammad Yūsuf al-Kāndahlawī and others like them—may Allah sanctify their secrets.

"Souls are like conscripted soldiers; those whom they recognize, they get along with, and those whom they don't recognize, they do not get along with." We ask that He ﷻ accept this book, cause His servants to benefit from it, and to make it a way and means of guidance and uprightness. May Allah send prayers upon our liege lord and Master Muḥammad, and upon his household and companions. All praise belongs to Allah, the Lord of the worlds.

Muḥammad 'Azīz al-Raḥmān al-Ḥaqqānī al-Hazārawī
Preacher and Imām at Masjid al-Ṣiddīq al-Akbar, Rawalpindi
Pakistan
Successor to the Imām and scholar of Ḥadīth, 'Allāma
Muḥammad Zakariyyā al-Kāndahlawī al-Madanī

Commendation by the Virtuous Shaykh, Abū Zayd Ibrāhīm Sayyid, Arabic Language Consultant in the Republic of Egypt

Your book is a Sun

Your book is a sun radiating the facts
It is a light that gleams from the luminous glow of prophecy
You have risen in the morning with it as it breaks upon the horizon
Emitting lights of guidance and correct belief
You have radiated ideas and with its guidance
Minds have been enlightened
and its lights penetrate the depths of the deep sea
It is a lighthouse and guide for understanding;
Correcting among them that which goes against the Sacred Law
The Sayyid is well-known for knowledge and intelligence
That manifests in his sagacious knowledge of the Book and the Sunna
He intended none other than Allah, the Exalted and Majestic
And nothing other than uniting the ranks of the Muslims
He said: "Come to the One who is worshipped in truth
and come to His law;
We have had enough of enmity and separation!
Indeed, the sons of Islam are one body entire;
If one part of it suffers then all of it suffers fever
Yes! May Allah, the All Merciful bless a noble Shaykh
Who is honoured to be a branch in the 'Alawī family tree
O Lord! Give victory to the guardians of Islam
And help the protectors of the truth in every locality!

Commendation by the Virtuous Shaykh, Muḥammad ʿAbd al-Wāḥid Aḥmad, Trustee of the Ministry of Endowments in the Republic of Egypt

All praise belongs to Allah who enlightened us with the truth and guided us to it, who led us to what is correct and assisted us with it. Indeed, to Him belong the creation and the command; blessed is Allah, the Lord of the worlds. May prayers and peace be upon the noblest of His creation and best of His Messengers, Muḥammad b. ʿAbdullāh—may Allah send prayers and peace upon him, his household, and companions.

Allah, the Blessed and Exalted, gave success to a group of the scholars of this Umma, sincere scholars who are guides and rightly-guided. They safeguarded their deep-rooted heritage and dedicated themselves to refuting misconceptions and responding to confusing ambiguous matters and ascertaining the principles upon which the groups of Ahl al-Sunna are established. They are the possessors of lofty aspirations, pure thoughts for the sake of observing good behaviour towards their Prophet, loyalty in fulfilling his rights upon them and seeking the pleasure of their Lord. They are the best followers of the esteemed nobles who fulfilled the trust their Lord placed upon them and who honoured them by allowing them to ascribe themselves to it and defend it; reviving the noblest of matters with enthusiasm and strength.

Among these rightly-guided guides and hard working scholars is the knower of Allah and defender of Allah's religion, the strong lover of the Messenger of Allah, the trustworthy in every word, the virtuous Sayyid, Shaykh, and Sharīf, Muḥammad ʿAlawī al-Mālikī al-Ḥasanī—may Allah be good to him and give him strength in the religion, increase him in certainty, and honour him through Islam, and honour Islam through him as well as those with him among the people of guidance and sincerity, whom Allah entrusted with the honourable task of defending His religion and manifesting its lofty place upon which it was established by His Messenger and seal—upon by the best of prayers and purest salutations.

The author has defended the truth, called with truthfulness, and reminded us of the unique characteristics that Allah bestowed upon His greatest Messenger and the Divine gifts He gave him. Love for the Chosen One ﷺ has mixed with his soul and entered the depths of his heart, and as a result, he has revived the Sunna of our Prophet and established gatherings dedicated to sending prayers and peace upon him. He has perfumed his gatherings and assemblies with lauding the noblest of creation, the best Messenger, and the most beloved creation to Allah, our liege lord Muḥammad b. ʿAbdullāh—upon him be the prayers and peace of Allah from the time of his birth, the time of his being sent, and the time permission is granted to him for interceding on the plains of judgement before the Lord of the worlds and Most Wise of judges, the Exalted and Sublime.

May prayers and peace be upon our liege lord Muḥammad and upon his household and companions.

Muḥammad ʿAbd al-Wāḥid Aḥmad
From the scholars of al-Azhar and trustee of the Ministry of Endowments

Commendation by the Virtuous Shaykh, Ibrāhīm al-Dasūqī Mar'ī, Former Minister of Endowments, Egypt

All praise belongs to Allah, the Lord of the worlds. May prayers and peace be upon the seal of the Prophets, our liege lord Muḥammad, and upon his household and companions and those who call with his call until the last day.

I was fortunate to receive this valuable book *Notions That Must Be Corrected* by its author, the virtuous Sayyid, Dr. Sayyid Muḥammad 'Alawī b. 'Abbās al-Mālikī al-Ḥasanī. I realized from the title of this book, the extent of the author's love and exaltation of the Prophet of humanity and the mercy unto all the worlds, our liege lord Muḥammad ﷺ, as well as the author's protective jealousy over his religion and his mercy toward his Muslim brothers. This should come as no surprise, because this is the character of a true Muslim, not to mention that the author is from the Prophetic household; those who were purified by their Lord: ﴾Allah intends only to remove from you the impurity [of sin] O people of the household, and to purify you with extensive purification.﴿ (al-Aḥzāb: 33) Allah intended for them to be the prime examples, exemplary models, and callers unto the truth—a thorn in the necks of its enemies, and a sincere force in defence of this religion.

As long as I have served as a soldier in the field of Islamic invitation, I have always felt that the Islamic society has been in need of this book and its likes, so that the Umma can be safeguarded against the attacks that seek to sow doubt, and in order to announce to all that this religion possesses sincere soldiers who will defend it until the Last Day. They will not be harmed by those who oppose them or by those who abandon them until Allah makes victorious the truth or His command [the Last Day] comes.

All praise belongs to Allah, this book fulfils this to the utmost and has provided everything we hoped for. The author presented the correct opinions strengthened by proofs and the views of the Imāms in every epoch regarding the most important issues that have—or almost have—shaken the unity of this Umma and divided its ranks.

At the forefront of these issues is that of doctrine. This book presents things that have been said against the doctrine, and it mentions the proofs that invalidate and refute the views of the extremists and the falsehood around them—extremists who have taken it upon themselves to act as judges, charging whom they wish with disbelief and judging others with faith, all the while feigning ignorance of the Prophet's words: "Insulting a Muslim is corruption and fighting him is disbelief," and pretending to be ignorant of the fact that the unique quality of Islam is its tolerance and ease. How beautiful was the answer of 'Alī—may Allah ennoble his countenance—when he was asked about his opponents: "Are they disbelievers?" He responded: "No. It was from disbelief that they were fleeing." He was then asked: "So, are they hypocrites?" He responded: "No. The hypocrites do not remember Allah but a little." He was then asked: "So what are they?" He replied: "They are a folk who were afflicted by a trial, and thus they became blind and deaf."

The Prophet ﷺ said in a rigorously authentic Ḥadīth: "If a man says to his brother: 'O disbeliever', it [the statement] falls upon one of them." In addition to this, the Qur'ān has instructed us to purify ourselves from saying bad things even to the pagans. The Exalted said: ﴾Do not insult those whom they call upon besides Allah, lest they insult Allah in enmity and without knowledge.﴿ (al-An'ām 108) and He said to Mūsā and Hārūn when He dispatched them to Pharaoh: ﴾So say to him a kind word. Perhaps he will take the reminder or fear [Allah].﴿ (Ṭāhā: 44)

In the second section of his book the author responds to the claims of those who wrongfully accuse others with disbelief, those who level charges against those who know the Messenger's rank and whose hearts are filled with love for him, and who exalt and respect him. The wrongful accusers seem to forget that Allah exalted the Prophet, elevated his remembrance, and ordered us to observe etiquette with him in verses from the Holy Qur'ān whose recitation is a form of worship. There is no doubt that with the people of faith, his virtue, station, and rank with his Lord is continuous, both during his life and after he joins with his Lord. In the same section, the author speaks about Sufism and how it represents the highest peak of Islamic thought and the most beautiful side of its manners and perfections, and that it is innocent of superstitions, falsehoods, and charlatanism, and that the Poles of Sufism spoke of the Sacred Law which emphasizes their strict and complete adherence to all that it has come, within their acts of worship, interactions with others, and all other things.

He also speaks about *tawassul* and how it is one of the ways of supplication and a door from the doors of having hope in Allah, the Exalted and Sublime. He mentions that there is nothing that legally or rationally prohibits one from performing *tawassul* through the Prophet ﷺ during his life or after his death, not to mention the evidence the author provides for this. If the agreed upon type of *tawassul* is *tawassul* through one's righteous actions, then there is nothing to prevent *tawassul* through the righteous among this Umma. Similar to *tawassul* is seeking aid and help and other such things; in all of that, the believer sees none but his Lord.

He also speaks about intercession, celebrating the Prophet's birthday ﷺ, and seeking blessings from his personal relics ﷺ and the relics of the righteous. He presents evidence establishing that this is a lofty Sunna and a legislated path confirmed by the Messenger of Allah ﷺ and done by his companions after him.

In the third section of the book, the author speaks about visiting the Prophet ﷺ and the views of the scholars concerning it, and visiting the Prophet's grave and its legality, and visiting the relics and mausoleums and the views of the Imāms concerning that.

In conclusion, this book has come to quench the thirst of those desirous of the realities and longing for the facts in a time in which the forces of evil have come together to attack Islam and its teachings and kindle the flames of hatred and enmity among its adherents. By the bounty of Allah, this book is a cry of truth repelling falsehood and, lo and behold, it is pulverized. The light of faith extinguishes and drives away the darkness of doubt and guides unto the straight path. May Allah reward its author with good on behalf of Islam and the Muslims. May He allow us to benefit from what he has brought forth.

May He grant us sincerity in our beliefs and success in following the example of our Prophet and the one whom He loves and whom the righteous love, and those who are guided by his guidance and who follow him.

We also ask Him to bless the efforts of the sincere ones among the scholars who act upon what they know, and to grant them His succour and assist them with a spirit from Him, so as to allow the word of Allah to be uppermost so there is no tribulation and the religion is all for Allah.

With Allah is all success.

Ibrāhīm al-Dasūqī Mar'ī
Former Minister of Endowments, Egypt

21st Rabī' al-Awwal, 1407
December 4th, 1985

Commendation by the Virtuous Shaykh Ḥusayn Maḥmūd Mu'awwaḍ, from the Senior Scholars of al-Azhar

May Allah, the Most Compassionate and Merciful, send prayers and peace upon our Master Muḥammad, and upon his companions and family. All praise belongs to Allah, the Lord of the worlds. We praise You, O Lord, with everything by which You are praised, both that which we know and that of which we are unaware; we thank You with the gratitude of one whom You have encompassed with Your largesse and bestowed Your gifts. None can encompass the praise that You deserve; You are as You have praised Yourself. Honoured is the one close to You and exalted is Your mention. We send our prayers and peace upon our Master Muḥammad, the one sent as a mercy unto the worlds—with prayers unravelling that which is bound and by which difficulties are alleviated—by whose noble face rain is sought.

To commence: I have perused the book of the noble scholar and scion of the Prophetic line, Muhammad 'Alawī al-Mālikī, which he named *Notions that Must be Corrected*. I have found it full of precious knowledge and sound understanding. May Allah reward him good on behalf of Islam and the Muslims for what he has produced for us in this book, one that is bursting with lights shining between its lines. May Allah increase him in knowledge and understanding.

The true scholar is one who brings new insights into sacred knowledge, enlightening the people regarding issues that previously escaped their understanding and attention. Anyone who examines this book will clearly see that its author has filled it with illuminating proofs that leave no room for doubt with respect to its contents, and illustrate lucid realities that only a misguided person could have reservations about. No one swerves from the path outlined in this book save one who deviates from the straight path. The Messenger of Allah ﷺ said: "This religion is powerful so practice it with forbearance. No one goes to extremes in the religion except that it overcomes him. Instead, try to be near to perfection and receive the good tidings that you will be rewarded; and gain strength by worshipping in the mornings and in a portion of the night." This Ḥadīth clearly indicates that every extremist in the religion will perish.

Allah is free of all imperfections! Despite the diversity of people's natures and dispositions, when clarity comes and matters are explained properly, there is no choice but for the intelligent person to retract his own mistaken position and adopt that which is correct. Those who lived during the golden age of Islam and the Muslims truly exemplified this attitude. Take the case of 'Alī—may Allah be pleased with him and ennoble his face—who said: "This is an issue for which there is no Abū al-Ḥasan [i.e., I am unable]. He said that despite the testimony of his contemporaries who stated that "Knowledge is a city and 'Alī is its gate." This praiseworthy state of affairs was not restricted to the Prophetic period alone; the Prophet ﷺ testified to the purity of those who were to come after him, too. Regarding al-Shāfi'ī it is reported: "O Allah! Guide the Quraysh, for the knowledge of a scholar that comes from them will encompass the earth."

Abu Hurayra ؓ reported that the Prophet ﷺ went to a graveyard and called out: "Peace be upon you, O abode of a believing people! Certainly we will—Allah willing—be joining you soon. I wish that we were able to behold our brethren." Some of the companions asked: "O Messenger of Allah! Aren't we your brothers?" The Prophet ﷺ replied: "You are my companions; my brothers are those who are yet to come." Some of the companions asked further: "O Messenger of Allah! How do you know those of your *Umma* who are yet to come?" He replied: "Don't you see how a man with a horse with white streaks can recognize it if it is in the midst of dark horses?" The companions replied: "Of course." He said: "They will come with the effects of their ablution glistening and I shall meet them at my Basin; however, some people will be pushed away from my Basin just as a camel pushes away its fetcher. It will be said: 'They altered [the religion] after you,' and I will say: 'Be gone, be gone!' " (Muslim)

The Prophet ﷺ mentioned, in an authentic Ḥadīth, the diverse ranks of people: "People are mines like mines of gold and silver. The best of them in the times of ignorance are the best of them in Islam, provided they gain understanding in the religion. Souls are like conscripted soldiers; those whom they recognize, they get along with, and those whom they do not recognize, they will not get along with."

My dear brother's book discusses the following issues: [1] Charging some Muslims with disbelief because they swear, for instance, in the name of the Prophet ﷺ, even though it is known that the jurists allowed swearing by the Ka'ba, the Qur'ān, or the Prophet ﷺ. Allah has magnified these three things and there is no harm in us magnifying, by swearing, that which Allah Most High has magnified. This in no way contradicts the Ḥadīth: "Whoever wishes to swear must swear by Allah or abstain" for the one who swears by these things swears by them insofar as they are magnified by Allah. [2] Logical metaphor in the Qur'ān, [3] the intermediary between the Creator and the creation, [4] intercession, [5] the concept of seeking aid, and [6] seeking blessings with the personal effects and relics of the righteous, and more.

In conclusion, I find it shocking and repulsive that anyone with a connection to Sacred Knowledge could charge a fellow Muslim with disbelief, when the Qur'ān and the Sunna are unanimous on this point. Allah Most High says: ﴾And He forgives for less than that whom He wills.﴿ (al-Nisa':48) This means that Allah forgives everything less than disbelief. How can anyone charge a Muslim with disbelief due to an enormity when Allah Most High says: ﴾Say: "O My servants who have wronged their own souls! Do not despair of Allah's mercy. Indeed, Allah forgives all sins. Indeed, He is the Most Forgiving, the Merciful."﴿
(al-Zumar: 53)

Commendation by the Knowledge Council in the City of Marrakesh

All praise belongs to Allah who adorned the scholars with fear of Him, and bestowed them with the bounty of proximity. May He send prayers and peace upon the best of creation, and upon his household, companions, and offspring.

Knowledge is an overflowing sea without a shore and it leads to Allah, the Exalted. The real beneficial knowledge is that which accompanies action. It cannot accompany boasting or seeking to get one up on someone else, and it cannot be for the sake of turning people's heads to its possessor.

Busying oneself with knowledge, by both teaching and writing books, is an act of worship and it is a sufficient honour. It is the trade plied by the Prophets; and the scholars are the inheritors of the Prophets as is mentioned [in the Ḥādīth narration]. So, well done for the one who imparts it to others, teaches it, writes books concerning it, or explains to the people that which they need. Among the guiding notables who have taught, written books, and strived hard in the path of imparting goodness to this Umma, is the Sharīf of noble Ḥasanī lineage, Sayyidī Muḥammad 'Alawī al-Mālikī, who wrote the book *Notions That Must Be Corrected.* This book has come as a service to Islam; it hones understandings and removes confusions. It is one of the best books written in this era on the subject matter at hand.

When this book was presented to the Gnostic scholars, they met it with acceptance and lauded its author who fulfilled on their behalf an obligation that was on their necks toward Allah and His Messenger and the Umma. Nay, perhaps the pens of many are now barren since the emergence of this book. For this reason, the members of the Knowledge council in Marrakesh—under the auspices of its president—after examining this book and reading and reviewing some of its chapters and what they contain, are in complete agreement with it. We thank him for his great effort and bless his beautiful work.

And may peace, mercy and the blessings of Allah be upon you.

'Abd al-Salām Jibrān
President of the Knowledge Council, Marrakesh

Commendations we were Unable to Publish

A large group of senior scholars among the Muslims were kind enough to write about these notions and aid them, and write commendations and praise for our book. May Allah reward them with the best reward. Unfortunately, due to their length, we were unable to publish them in full, so here we shall suffice by mentioning some of them. The summary of their well-respected opinion is that of complete agreement and full support.

1. The Imām, scholar of *uṣūl,* and linguist, Shaykh Sayyidī al-Fārūqī al-Raḥḥālī, Shaykh of the scholars and president of the Scholar's Council, Marrakesh, Morocc
2. The virtuous and great scholar, jurist, and Ḥadīth expert of the Maghreb, nay the entire world, Shaykh Sayyid 'Abdullāh b. Muḥammad b. al-Ṣiddīq al-Ghumārī
3. The virtuous and great scholar, Ḥadīth expert, and master of *uṣūl al-fiqh*, Sayyid 'Abd al-'Azīz b. Muḥammad b. al-Ṣiddīq al-Ghumārī
4. The virtuous teacher and caller unto Allah, Sayyid Muḥammad b. 'Alī al-Ḥabashī, President of the Islamic Centre of Indonesia
5. The virtuous Imām, the great scholar, the knower of Allah, the caller unto Him, Ḥabīb 'Abd al-Qādir al-Saqqāf, Muftī of Hadramawt and the Shaykh of its scholars

Qur'ānic Exegesis
Ibn Kathīr, Ismā'īl b. 'Umar, *Tafsīr al-Qur'ān al-'Aẓīm*
Al-Qurṭubī, Muḥammad b. Aḥmad, *Tafsīr al-Qurṭubī*
Sālim, Muḥammad 'Aṭiyya, *Aḍwā' al-Bayān (Mutammima)*
Al-Suyūṭī, Jalāl al-Dīn, *Al-Durr al-Manthūr*

Ḥadīth and its Ancillary Disciplines
Al-'Aynī, Badr al-Dīn, *'Umda al-Qārī Sharḥ Ṣaḥīḥ al-Bukhārī*
Al-'Aẓīmabādī, Abū Ṭayyib, *'Awn al-Ma'būd*
Al-'Irāqī, Zayd al-Dīn, *Al-Mughnī 'an Ḥaml al-Aṣfār fī al-Asfār*
Ibn 'Umar al-'Adanī, *Musnad*
Bakkār, Zubayr b., *Al-Ansāb*
Al-Bazzār, Aḥmad, *Musnad*
Al-Bayhaqī, Aḥmad b. Ḥusayn, *Dalā'il al-Nubuwwa*
——*Kitab al-Ba'th*
——*Ḥayāt al-Anbiyā'*
——*Shu'ab al-Īmān*
Al-Bukhārī, Muḥammad b. Ismā'īl, *Al-Jāmi' al-Ṣaḥīḥ*
——*Al-Adab al-Mufrad*
——*Al-Tārikh al-Kabīr*
Al-Būṣīrī, Shihāb al-Dīn, *Miṣbāḥ al-Zujāja Zawā'id Ibn Mājah*
Al-Darāquṭnī, 'Alī b. 'Umar, *Sunan*
Al-Daylamī, *Musnad al-Firdaws*
Al-Dārimī, Abū Sa'īd, *Sunan*
Abū Dāwūd al-Sijistānī, Sulaymān b. al-Ash'ath, *Sunan*
Al-Hamadānī, Muḥammad b. Yaḥyā, *Ṣaḥīḥ*
Al-Haythamī, Nūr al-Dīn, *Majma' al-Zawā'id*
Al-Hindī, 'Alā' al-Dīn, *Kanz al-'Ummāl*
Ibn Ḥajar al-'Asqalānī, *Fatḥ al-Bārī Sharḥ Ṣaḥīḥ al-Bukhārī*
——*Talkhīs al-Ḥabīr fī Takhrīj Ahādīth al-Rāfi'ī al-Kabīr*
Ḥanbal, Aḥmad b., *Musnad*
Al-Ḥākim, Muḥammad b. Muḥammad, *Al-Mustadrak*
Ibn Ḥibbān al-Bussī, *Ṣaḥīḥ*
Al-Kirmānī, Shams al-Dīn, *Sharḥ al-Bukhārī*
Ibn Khuzayma, *Kitāb al-Tawḥīd*
Majd b. Taymiyya, *Muntaqā al-Akhbār*
Manṣūr, Sa'īd b., *Musnad*

Ibn Mājah, al-Qazwīnī, *Sunan*
Muslim b. al-Ḥajāj al-Naysabūrī, *Ṣaḥīḥ Muslim*
Al-Munāwī, Zayn al-Dīn b. 'Abd al-Ra'ūf, *Fayḍ al-Qadīr Sharḥ al-Jāmi' al-Ṣaghīr*
Al-Mundhirī, 'Abd al-'Aẓīm, *Al-Targhīb wa al-Tarhīb*
Al-Nawawī, Muḥyī al-Dīn, *Al-Adhkār*
——*Sharḥ Ṣaḥīḥ Muslim*
Abū Nu'aym al-Aṣfahānī, *Dalā'il al-Nubuwwa*
Al-Qasṭalānī, Aḥmad b. Muḥāmmad, *Irshād al-Sārī lī Sharḥ Ṣaḥīḥ al-Bukhārī*
Al-Rāzī, Ibn Abī Ḥātim, *al-Jarḥ wa al-Ta'dīl*
Ibn Sa'd, *Al-Ṭabaqāt al-Kubrā*
Al-Sahāranpūrī, Khalīl Aḥmad, *Badhl al-Majhūd Sharḥ Sunan Abī Dāwūd*
Sufyān, Ḥasan b., *Musnad*
Al-Suyūṭī, Jalāl al-Dīn, *Al-Khaṣā'iṣ al-Kubrā*
——*Sharḥ Sunan al-Nasā'ī*
——*Tadrīb al-Rāwī*
——*Alfiyya*
Ibn Abī Shayba, 'Abdullāh b. Muḥammad, *Muṣannaf*
Al-Shaybānī, Ibn Dayba', *Jāmi' al-Uṣūl*
Al-Ṣan'ānī, 'Abd al-Razzāq, *Muṣannaf*
Al-Ṣiddīqī, Ibn 'Allān, *Al-Futūḥāt al-Rabbāniyya 'alā al-Adhkār al-Nawawiyya*
Al-Tirmidhī, Aḥmad b. 'Isā, *Sunan*
Al-Ṭabarānī, Sulaymān b. Aḥmad, *Al-Mu'jam al-Kabīr*
——*Al-Mu'jam al-Awsaṭ*
——*Al-Mu'jam al-Ṣaghīr*
Al-Ṭaḥāwī, Muḥammad, *Ma'ānī al-Āthār*
Ibn Abī Usāma, *Musnad*
Abū Ya'lā, *Ṣaḥīḥ*

Biography, History, and Hagiography

Ibn 'Asākir, *Tārikh Dimashq*
Qāḍī 'Iyāḍ al-Yaḥṣūbī, Abū al-Faḍl, *Tartīb al-Madārik*
Ibn 'Abd al-Barr, *Al-Istī'āb*
Daḥlān, Aḥmad Zaynī, *Al-Sīra al-Nabawiyya*
Al-Dhahabī, Muḥammad b. Aḥmad, *Mīzān al-'Itidāl*

——*Siyar 'Alām al-Nubalā'*
Ibn Ḥajar al-'Asqalānī, *Al-Maṭālib al-'Āliya*
——*Al-Iṣāba*
——*Natā'ij al-Fikr*
Ibn Ḥibbān al-Busṭī, *Kitāb al-Ḍu'afā' wa al-Matrūkīn*
Ibn Kathīr, Ismā'īl b. 'Umar, *Al-Bidāya wa al-Nihāya*
Abū Nu'aym al-Aṣfahānī, *Ḥilya al-Awliyā'*
Al-Zurqānī Muḥammad b. 'Abd al-Bāqī, *Al-Mawāhib al-Laduniyya*

Jurisprudence, Legal Verdicts, and Doctrine

Al-Ājūrī, Abū Bakr, *Al-Sharī'a*
Al-Baghawī, Mas'ūd b. Muḥammad al-Farrā', *Sharḥ al-Sunna*
Al-Bahūtī, Manṣūr b. Yūnus, *Kashhāf al-'Qinā'*
Al-Bulqīnī, Aḥmad b. Muḥammad, *Al-Fatāwā*
Al-Ghumarī, 'Abdullāh, *Itḥāf al-Adhkiyā'*
——*Miṣbāḥ al-Zujāja fī Ṣalāt al-Ḥāja*
Al-Haytamī, Ibn Ḥajar, *Ḥāshiyā 'alā al-Īḍāḥ*
Ibn 'Abd al-Hādī, *Al-Ṣarim al-Munkī*
Al-Karmī, Mar'ī b. Yūsuf, *Dalīl al-Ṭālib*
Al-Nawawī, Muḥyī al-Dīn, *Al-Majmū' Sharḥ al-Muhaddhab*
——*Al-Īḍāḥ*
Ibn Qudāma al-Maqdisī, Muwaffaq al-Dīn, *Al-Mughnī*
Al-Safārīnī, Muḥammad, *Sharḥ 'Aqīda Ahl al-Sunna*
Al-Subkī, Tāj al-Dīn, *Shifā al-Siqām*
Al-Shawkānī, Muḥammad b. 'Alī, *Al-Durr al-Naḍīd fī Ikhlāṣ Kalima al-Tawḥīd*
Ibn Taymiyya, Taqī al-Dīn Aḥmad, *Majmū' al-Fatāwā*
——*Majmū 'a al-Rasā'il wa al-Masā'il*
——*Al-Jawāb al-Bāḥir fī Zuwwār al-Maqābir*
——*Iqtiḍā' al-Ṣirāṭ al-Mustaqīm*
——*Qa'ida Jalīla fī al-Tawassul wa al-Wasīla*
——*Al-Fatāwā al-Kubrā*
Ibn 'Abd al-Wahhāb al-Tamīmī, Muḥammad, *Aḥkām Tamannī al-Mawt*

Miscellaneous Works

Al-'Alawī, Sayyid 'Alī b. Yaḥyā, *Hidāya al-Mutakhabbiṭīn*

Qāḍī 'Iyāḍ al-Yaḥṣūbī Abū al-Faḍl, *Al-Shifā' bi-Ta'rīf Ḥuqūq al-Muṣṭafā*

Al-Būṣīrī, Sharaf al-Dīn, *Al-Kawākib al-Durriyya fī Madḥ Khair al-Bariyya*

Al-Dimyāṭī, Sharaf al-Dīn, *Al-Muttajir al-Rābiḥ*

Ibn Abī al-Dunyā, *Mujābī al-Du'ā'*

Al-Fayrūzabādī, Abū Ṭāhir b. Ibrāhīm Majd al-Dīn, *Al-Qāmūs al-Muḥīṭ*

——*Al-Ṣillāt wa al-Bishr*

——*Al-Maghānim al-Muṭāba fī Ma'ālim Ṭāba*

Al-Jawzī, Shihāb al-Dīn Muḥammad b. Muḥammad b. al-Dimashqī, *Al-Ḥiṣn al-Ḥaṣīn*

Ibn al-Jawzī, Abū al-Faraj, *Al-Wafā' bi-Faḍl al-Muṣṭafā* ﷺ

Al-Haytamī, Ibn Ḥajar, *Al-Jawhar al-Munaẓẓam*

Al-Ḥaddād, Sayyid Aḥmad Mashhūr, *Miftāḥ al-Janna*

Al-Khafājī, Aḥmad Shihāb al-Dīn, *Nasīm al-Riyāḍ*

Ibn Qayyim al-Jawziyya, *Kitāb al-Rūḥ*

——*Badā'i al-Fawā'id*

——*Zād al-Ma'ād*

——*Al-Qaṣīda al-Nūniyya*

Al-Qārī', Mullā 'Alī, *Sharḥ al-Shifā*

Al-Suhaylī, 'Abd al-Raḥmān b. 'Abdullāh, *al-Rawḍ al-Unuf*

Al-Suyūṭī, Jalāl al-Dīn, *Tanwīr al-Ḥalak fī Ru'ya al-Nabī wa al-Malak*

——*Sharḥ al-Ṣudūr*

Al-Shawkānī, Muḥammad b. 'Alī, *Tuhfa al-Dhākirīn*

Ibn Taymiyya, Taqī al-Dīn Aḥmad, *Al-Kalim al-Ṭayyib*

Ibn 'Abd al-Wahhāb al-Tamīmī, Muḥammad, *Majmū'a al-Mu'allafāt al-Shaykh al-Imām Muḥammad b. 'Abd al-Wahhāb*

——*Rasā'il al-Shakhṣiyya*

مفاهيم يجب أن تصحح

Notions That Must Be Corrected

Shaykh Muḥammad b. ʿAlawī al-Mālikī al-Ḥasanī رضي الله عنه